THE HISTORY OF THE GLOUCESTERSHIRE CONSTABULARY 1839 TO 1985

Frontispiece: Anthony T. Lefroy, Esq. Chief Constable 1839–1865

THE HISTORY OF THE GLOUCESTERSHIRE CONSTABULARY 1839–1985

HARRY THOMAS, Q.P.M.

Published by the Gloucestershire Constabulary 1987

ISBN 0 9512913 0 0

Produced for the Constabulary by
Alan Sutton Publishing, 30 Brunswick Road, Gloucester
Printed in Great Britain

CONTENTS

PREFACE

Disappointment expressed by others and felt by myself that a history of the Gloucestershire Constabulary should never have appeared in print, and an impression that a considerable amount of interesting information relative to it might be brought together, combined I may add with the fact that there seemed no probability of such a work being otherwise undertaken until old usages and traditions had passed away, have induced me to attempt compilation. I here venture to publish the fruit of my labours, in the hope that the reader may derive some portion of that pleasure which the prosecution of the work has afforded me.

I have endeavoured to make it as complete as possible by supplying every known circumstance, mostly in the words of the original reports of the various Chief Constables and Committees, and yet trying so to harmonise the whole as to engage the attention of the general reader, but more particularly of the past and present members of the Gloucestershire Constabulary, by acquainting them with the past and present state of one of the most interesting and remarkable County Police Forces in the country.

Harry Thomas,
Q.P.M.

April, 1986

CHAPTER 1

How it all began

> The origin and growth of the Police Service is a striking illustration of the ability of the English Nation to adapt itself to the circumstances and to make the best of its old institutions.
>
> C.C.H. Moriarty.

This opening comment by Dr. Moriarty in his standard Police reference book indicating the way in which the Police system of this country has developed applies as aptly to the County of Gloucestershire as to the rest of England.

The years of unrest during and after the French Revolution were ones of anxiety for the British Government. Gloucestershire experienced riots over bread prices and the introduction of power looms in the cloth mills of the Stroud area where there was strong support for the Chartists. The County also had troubles from farm laboureres who were taking part in the 'Swing Riots' protesting against the introduction of threshing machines. The movement spread from Hampshire, most of their activities in Gloucestershire being concentrated around Beverstone and Fairford. The Government feared riots for without a Police Force there was no adequate means of dealing with them except by calling out the militia or regular troops.

Over the course of years this country has been policed under three main systems:-

(a) the Anglo-Saxon Tythingman system
(b) the Parish Constable and the Watch system, and
(c) the whole time paid Police Service.

The unpaid Parish Constable or Tythingman was usually appointed by the Manor Court, but with the decline of Courts Leet, during the seventeenth and eighteenth centuries, it became necessary for Constables to be appointed by the Parish Vestry or by Justices of the Peace, though there seems to be no legislation authorising this.[1]

During the eighteenth century we saw the formation of the notorious Bow Street Runners and Patrols together with the Bow Street Horse Patrols, that was 1748.

In 1792 The Middlesex Justices Act came into operation and allowed the appointment of 21 Stipendiary Justices and 42 paid constables in London.

Six years later – 1798 – fifty paid constables were appointed to deal with crime on the River Thames and operated from Wapping Steps.

It was during 1786 that we saw the passing of the Dublin Police Act and this was the first instance of the use of the word 'Police' in relation to a body of constables. The origin of the word, so I have been informed, is the Greek word 'Polis' meaning a City or 'Polituo' meaning to govern a city.

Moving to the nineteenth century we find that in London, in addition to the Watchmen there were five classes of Police Officers, Parish Constables, Proxies or Deputies, Bow Street Runners and Patrols, the 42 paid constables appointed under the Middlesex Justices' Act and 50 constables of the Marine Force stationed at Wapping.

In the provinces policing was still solely in the hands of the Parish Constable and the Watchman.

Parliamentary Committees were appointed in 1812;1818;1882 and 1828 to report on the then existing police systems. All, except the last, reported that it was impossible to establish any effective system of policing which would not interfere unduly with the liberty of the subject. The 1828 Committee made recommendations which enabled Sir Robert Peel to place before Parliament the Metropolitan Police Improvement Bill of 1829.

On the 19th. June, 1829 the first 'Peelers' appeared on the streets of London and the first Commissioners of the Metropolitan Police Force, that now is, were Colonel Rowan and Sir Richard Mayne. There was considerable opposition to this new Police Force. Not from the criminal classes, who were contemptuous of it, but from law abiding citizens who felt that their liberty was in danger.

In 1833 the Lighting and Watching Act was passed and that was the first real attempt to provide a whole-time Police Service outside London.

The Municipal Corporations Act of 1835 made provisions for efficient Police Forces in Cities and Boroughs and established Watch Committees. As a result of this Act we find that Cheltenham; Gloucester; Worcester; Bath and Bristol set up their own Police Forces.

In 1839 Peel's County Police Act was passed. This later became known as the 'Permissive Act' as it empowered Justices in Quarter

Sessions to appoint paid Police Forces for the protection of Counties, if they thought fit.

Some Counties did not set up a paid Police Force until it was made compulsory by the County and Borough Police Act of 1856.

It is the County Police Act of 1839 with which we are concerned.

At a General Quarter Sessions for the County, held at the Shire Hall, Gloucester on Monday, 4th. November, 1839, a discussion took place regarding the formation of a County Constabulary and the appointment of a Chief Constable.[2]

The Chairman of Quarter Sessions that day was Charles Bathurst, Esq., supported by, The Lord Lieutenant of the County, Lord Segrave; Lord Ellenborough; Lord Morton; The Hon. G. Berkeley, M.P.; The Hon. Craven Berkeley, M.P.; Sir Matthew Wood M.P.; M.P.C. Greenway, Esq., M.P. and others.

It is recorded that Lord Ellenborough said that the Magistrates should apply to Colonel MacGregor – Inspectorate of Constabulary in Ireland – to see if he had anyone serving under him who would be suitable to be recommended for the post of Chief Constable so that there was no chance of its being supposed that the office of Chief Constable was given by acquaintances, by connection with the County, by private intimacy on the part of the Magistrates or otherwise than by the appointment of the very best man.

The Lord Lieutenant concurred but suggested that a letter should go to the Secretary of State – The Marquis of Normanby – requesting him to communicate with the heads of London and Irish Police.

The Quarter Sessions were adjourned until Monday, 18th November, 1839.

In the meantime the Clerk of the Peace for the County wrote to the Secretary of State asking him to communicate with the heads of the London and Irish Police.

The Secretary of State replied that Colonel Rowan of the London Police was not likely to be able to propose a person fit to be placed at the head of a County Constabulary, as the Force at his disposal, although containing men whom he wished to promote, was not of a description to undertake so high an office. The Irish Commissioner was differently situated and a letter had been sent to Colonel MacGregor asking him if he was prepared to recommend an officer.

At the Adjourned General Quarter Sessions held at Gloucester Shire Hall, Monday, 18th. November, 1839 a Minute was approved and recorded agreeing to the establishment and appointment of County and District Constables.

A letter dated 11th. November, 1839 from the Marquis of Normanby – Secretary of State – re Anthony Thomas Lefroy of the Irish Constabulary was then discussed together with a Testimonial from Colonel MacGregor of the Irish Inspectorate.

The Testimonial from Colonel MacGregor stated that Lefroy was 36 or 37 years of age – not a military gentleman. That he was an extremely gentlemanly man. An Englishman believed from Cumberland and had served in the Irish Police Force for several years to the entire satisfaction of Colonel MacGregor.

There must have been other applicants for the post as it is recorded that Charles Bathurst, Esq., Chairman of Quarter Sessions, proposed Lefroy for the post of Chief Constable and that Lord Segrave seconded the proposal. Captain St. Clair proposed a Captain Tinling and this was seconded by W. Guise, Esq.; a Lieutenant Colonel Ellis was proposed by Captain Jones but, after voting had taken place, Anthony Thomas Lefroy was elected the first Chief Constable of Gloucestershire.[3]

A letter dated 9th. December, 1839, from the Secretary of State, confirmed the appointment of Mr. Lefroy as Chief Constable and thus the Gloucestershire Constabulary was recognised and given the Government's blessing.

It had taken approximately one month from the conception of the scheme and the signing of the original requisition to the formal Governmental recognition of the Force.

Prior to the General Quarter Sessions held at Gloucester on the 4th. November, 1839 a letter from Whitehall dated 18th. October, 1839 requested the Clerk of the Peace to make sure that the strength of the Gloucestershire Constabulary should not exceed the number of constables as laid down according to the population of the County i.e. 250. It must be remembered that, at this time, Gloucester City and the Boroughs of Cheltenham and Tewkesbury had their own Police Forces.

In preparation for the formation of the Constabulary the Clerk of the Peace for the County of Gloucestershire received the following qualifications, necessary for Superintendents and Constables, from the Secretary of State.[4]

> To be under 40 years of age
> To stand 5 feet 7 inches, without shoes
> To read and write and keep accounts
> To be free from any bodily complaint; of strong constitution and generally intelligent
> No person appointed a Superintendent or Constable who shall be a Gamekeeper, Wood Ranger, Bailiff, Sheriff's Bailiff or Parish Clerk or who

shall be a hired servant in the employment of any person or who shall keep or have any interest in any house for the sale of beer, wine or spirituous liquors by retail and if any person who should be appointed a Superintendent or Constable, should at any time after such appointment became a Gamekeeper, Wood Ranger, Bailiff, Sheriff's Bailiff or Parish Clerk or shall act in any capacity or shall sell or have any interest in the sale of any beer, wine or spirituous liquor, such person shall thereupon become and be incapable of acting as such Superintendent or Constable and shall forfeit his appointment of Superintendent or Constable and also all salary payable to him as Superintendent or Constable.

Rates of pay were laid down as follows:–

Chief Constables ... Not less than £250 or more than £500 per year
Superintendents ... Not less than £75 or more than £150 per year
Constables .... Not less than 15/–d. or more than £1.1.0d. a week

A scale for issue of uniform clothing was laid down as under.

1st Year	*2nd year*
One Greatcoat	One coat (Badge to ditto)
Cape to ditto	One pair of trousers
Badge to ditto	One pair of boots
Coat (Badge to ditto)	One pair of shoes
Two pairs of trousers	Hat
One pair of shoes	
Hat	
Stock	

Supply for the Third Year will be the same as for the 2nd. year and so on for successive periods.

Accoutrements to be supplied
A constables staff is to be supplied to each constable and a small Cutlass may be supplied to any constable who is so situated that, in the opinion of two Justices of the Peace of the County, it is necessary for his personal protection in the performance of his duty. The Cutlass to be worn at night only or at times when rioting or serious public disturbance has actually taken place, or upon orders by the Chief Constable who shall, on each occasion of giving such order, report the same and the reason for such order, to any two Justices of the Peace for the County, as soon afterwards as is practicable, who shall immediately transmit the said report to the Secretary of State.

On the face of what I have written it would appear that there was no difficulty in forming the Constabulary for the County but this was far from the truth as there was considerable and apparently well organised local opposition.

For instance the following Petition, although not dated, was submitted in 1841 from the Parish of Compton Greenfield, near Bristol and is typical of many received from rural parishes, which objected to having to pay rates for a paid police force, described as 'unnecessary and useless'.

TO THE CHAIRMAN AND MAGISTRATES OF THE COUNTY OF GLOUCESTER IN QUARTER SESSIONS ASSEMBLED.

THE PETITION OF THE UNDERSIGNED INHABITANTS OF THE PARISH OF COMPTON GREENFIELD IN THE COUNTY OF GLOUCESTER HUMBLY SHEWETH.

That your Petitioners first heard with surprise of the establishment of a County Police; a measure which they consider not only as exceedingly expensive but absolutely unnecessary and useless.

That the peaceful habits of our Population require no such watch upon their actions nor any such check upon their innocent amusements; and when any mistrust or disturbance has arisen amongst them a single admonition from their Masters and Employers has always been found a sufficient corrective without the aid of a constable.

That if the small and large towns of the County should require a Police Force for the maintenance of order in their respective localities your petitioners are decidedly of opinion that they ought to pay for their own advantages, and not to draw from the pockets of the Agriculturists and Agricultural Poor the money to pay a Force from which they derive no advantage.

That the tax for keeping up such a Force bears most unproportionally upon the Farmers, the Mechanics and the Poor, in as much as the Tradesman with a large stock of valuable goods and the Gentleman with an expensive Establishment and costy furniture to be protected being rated only in proportion to the value of the premises they occupy, pay considerably less (even supposing the Police Force effective) than those who have little or nothing to guard or those who have hundreds of acres of land to be rambled over.

That such a Force can never possibly be of the slightest service to the Farmer, nor prevent nocturnal depredations amongst his sheep, lambs, fowls or potatoe heaps, because as many of our rural Parishes consist of from 2,000 to 6,000 acres with a population less than perhaps of 1,000 inhabitants not one, two, nor even ten policemen can possibly keep watch over such an extent.[5]

Admiral Henry Christian, M.V.O. Chief Constable 1865–1910

Lt. Colonel R.C. Chester-Master, D.S.O. Chief Constable 1910–1917

Major Frederick L. Stanley-Clarke, OBE. Chief Constable 1918–1937

Colonel William F. Henn, M.V.O., C.B.E., Q.P.M. Chief Constable 1937–1959

John S.H. Gaskain, Esq., O.B.E., Q.P.M. Chief Constable 1959–1962

E.P.B. White, Esq., O.B.E., Q.P.M. Chief Constable 1962–1975

B. Weigh, Esq. Q.P.M. Chief Constable 1975–1979

L.A.G. Soper Esq. Q.P.M., Chief Constable 1979–

Map giving proposed scheme for new arrangements of Districts and Stations.

Members of the Gloucestershire Constabulary photographed at NORTH-LEACH about 1860.

TETBURY Police Station 1880–1970.

CHAPTER 2

Anthony Thomas Lefroy
18.11.1839 – 1.7.1865

The new Chief Constable, his appointment confirmed, lost no time in travelling to England and touring the County, both to get to know the area and to recruit men for the Force. Only three weeks after his appointment the following advertisement was issued giving details of the Chief Constable's 'Circuit' to interview candidates. It was issued under the signature of the Clerk of the Peace and dated the 18th December, 1839.[1]

> 'Notice is hereby given that it is the intention of the Chief Constable appointed for the County under the Act of the 2nd and 3rd Vict: Cap. 93 to attend the Magistrates of the different Divisions who are requested to assemble in their several Petty Sessions at the places and on the days and times following to consult on the mode of carrying the Constabulary Act into execution that is to say:–
>
> For the Division of Gloucester at the Shire Hall in Gloucester on Saturday, the 14th inst. at the same hour. (i.e. 12 o'clock)
>
> For the Division of Cheltenham at the Public Office in Cheltenham on Monday, the 16th inst. at the same hour.
>
> Candidates for employment as Superintendents or Constables must attend with their testimonials and recommendations at such places of meeting above mentioned as may be most convenient to them and where they are best known'.

There appears to have been little difficulty in finding the necessary recruits from the County. For instance, below is a copy of a letter from Henry Waterson of Moreton-in-Marsh – one of the old unpaid Parish Constables or Tythingmen – to Edward Bloxsome, Esq., Deputy Clerk of the Peace, Dursley, Glos., applying for a post in the New Constabulary Force about to be established in Gloucestershire. The letter dated 19th November, 1839, must have been one of the first applications to be received and can be seen in the County Records Office, Gloucester.

Moreton-in-Marsh,
19th November, 1839

Sir,
Being now on the Police establishment for the County of Gloucester and feeling a great desire to join the New Constabulary Force about to be established in the County I should feel much obliged by your sending me the proper introductions as to the principal on which I am to apply for an appointment and also if there are any forms to be filled in will thank you to send one of them with also the resolutions come to by the Magistrates on Monday last and if it is finally decided to appoint the Sergeants from the Metropolitan Force or if I, by proper recommendation could obtain an appointment to that rank, as my memorial for conduct is very numerously and respectably signed as for instance by the Right Honourable Lord Redesdale and the Rev. Dr. Warneford and the whole of the gentlemen forming the Police Committee and most of the inhabitants of the town of Moreton-in-Marsh and neighbourhood. Waiting your reply.

Henry Waterson,
Police Officer.[2]

Mr Lefroy did not, however, start completely from scratch. When he came over from Ireland he brought with him 13 constables from the Royal Irish Constabulary to serve as a trained nucleus around which he could build his new Force. One of these 13, Charles Reilly, was soon to become the first Deputy Chief Constable of the County.

Soon after the introduction of the New Force, in November, 1839, the Chief Constable was faced with the problem of what came to be called 'The Cheltenham Case'. Briefly, the facts were as follow:–

In the winter of 1831 Cheltenham had instituted its own Police Force set up on the Metropolitan pattern. It consisted of an Inspector and 25 men. For this service the inhabitants of Cheltenham were paying £1470 per annum. With the inception of the County Force, Cheltenham sought to remain independent, as was the City of Gloucester, under the Municipal Coporations Act of 1835, and the case was submitted to the Law Officers of the Crown for opinion.

The Law Officers judged for the County giving the Chief Constable the services of several more experienced police officers.

In view of this the Headquarters of the Force was established in Cheltenham, at No. 1, Crescent Terrace. It was here that the administrative machinery of the Force was based, while the 45 men allotted to Cheltenham went to the Central Police Station just across the road in Crescent Place, now used by the Countryside Commission.

Before Mr Lefroy unleashed his new Force into the County, they were issued with uniform and given a brief period of training by the trained Irish Constables.

Police officers were enrolled and posted to the various towns and villages in accordance with the original strength and distribution, as detailed by the Clerk of the Peace. A hand written report, in the County Records Office, Gloucester gives the distribution of the new constabulary as under:–

Kingswood, Winterbourne, Westbury-on-Trym	30	Nailsworth	5
		Minchinhampton	5
		Tetbury	5
Berkeley	6	Stroud	20
Dursley	8	Whitminster	5
Wotton-under-Edge	10	Cirencester	10
Thornbury	5	Fairford	5
Moreton-in-Marsh	5	Northleach	5
Stow-on-the-Wold	5	Cheltenham	45
Great Barrington	3	Winchcombe	5
Chipping Campden	7	Tewkesbury	10
Lydney	3	Coleford	5
Mitcheldean	5	Newnham-on-Severn	5
Newent	5	Gloucester	10
Marshfield	5	Chipping Sodbury	7
		Total	244

It will be noted that men were detailed for Gloucester and Tewkesbury but they would only be responsible for the County area adjacent to these places and would do no duty within the city or Borough Boundary.

In his original deployment of his force the Chief Constable saw to it that no man was stationed on his own.

Now that most of the external worries of the force had been settled the Chief Constable and his men could turn to their first duty, that of policing the County. With such a young and inexperienced Force as Mr Lefroy's was, it was understandable that many things happened which prompted the Chief Constable to issue Orders for the guidance of his men. The first of these Circular Orders issued on the 8th April, 1840 concerns the over-zealous performance of duty.

> The Superintendents in charge of Districts will direct the constables under their command not to interfere with drunk persons unless they are incapable of taking care of themselves or in case they should be creating a riot or breach of the peace, but on no account should they detain any drunken person when proceeding quietly to his home![3]

In his guidance of his new Force, the Chief Constable must have had in his mind the criticisms which were being levelled at the 'New Police' by many people. Many considered the introduction of a police force totally unnecessary for crime prevention and an expensive charge on the County rates. People also feared they would be Government Agents similar to the Paris Police. The new Force, therefore, was watched carefully and any deviation reported to the Chief Constable. However, complaints often helped to make the force more efficient. For several years petitions against the formation of the police were still being sent to Quarter Sessions but by the 1850's most people had come to accept their usefulness.

It was because of the complaints the Chief Constable had to be most efficient in the rectification of any over-zealous behaviour on the part of his men. It was, and, indeed still is an offence to be drunk in a public place, but it has been long understood to be standard practice that no one who is only drunk will be arrested; only if the offender is incapable or disorderly is any action taken.

Since the question of duties weighed heavily on the Chief Constable, it is perhaps hardly surprising that the next Circular Order was in much the same vein.

> *20th April, 1840*
>
> It having come to my knowledge that unnecessary and severe treatment was used by the constable at Dursley on the 17th inst., while conveying a prisoner to the Station House. The Superintendents will instruct their men that when a prisoner or prisoners are taken into custody particularly when drunk, the Constables are on no account to use unnecessary force. It appears to me that in this case three men could have taken the prisoner to the Station House without using the force complained of. I am perfectly aware there may be cases in which force is necessary but it must be used with great discretion on the part of the constables.[4]

It is interesting that in this order the name of the station appears although not of the men. The order also sets out one of the principles on which the police of this country still operate – no unnecessary force.

The Chief Constable's early difficulties did not all come from over-zealous conduct of his men, and the failings of human beings play just as much part in the complaints levelled at the 'New Police' as do other considerations. A further order dated 28th April, 1840 touched on a subject which was at that time still a national disgrace – drink; and as the severity of the threatened punishment shows, the Chief Constable was not allowing any latitude in this field.

> Several reports have reached this office stating that constables have been in the habit of going into Public Houses under the pretence of getting

refreshments, the Superintendents and Constables in Charge of Stations will inform the men under their command that if any Constable shall be seen in any Public House when not necessarily there on duty he will be instantly dismissed.[5]

The prevalence of drinking and drunkenness amongst the men of the 'New Police' may be judged from the figures for dismissals from the Force for the first half of the year 1840. Twenty-nine men were dismissed during this period, of which number 14 cases were for being drunk. The following is a list of Constables dismissed from the Constabulary from 1st December, 1839 to the 30th June, 1840[6]:–

Thomas Bloomfield	22.12.1839	Previously convicted on a charge of Felony
John Lewis	22.12.1839	–do.– –do.–
George Clarke	25.12.1839	For drunkenness
Charles Bennett	29.12.1839	For fighting in the street with Constable Waterson
Henry Waterson	29.12.1839	For fighting in the street with Constable Bennett
John O'Brien	4.1.1840	For drunkenness
Edwin Winterson	12.2.1840	For refusing to stay in quarters and insolence to his Superintendent
Thomas Davis	1.3.1840	For drunkenness
Walter Jones	1.3.1840	For drunkenness
James Jones	1.3.1840	For drunkenness
John Petty	1.3.1849	For drunkenness
Joseph Smith	4.3.1840	Previously convicted on a charge of Felony
John Hopgood	1.4.1840	Absent without leave for four days
Joseph Jennings	1.4.1840	Allowing prisoner to escape at Stow
George Lardner	1.4.1840	For breaking out of the Station House at Gloucester
John Rafferty	1.4.1840	Having been previously dismissed from the Bristol force
Nathanil Russell	4.4.1840	For drunkenness
John Dovey	6.4.1840	For making use of insolent language to Mr. Lefroy
Samuel Jacques	11.4.1840	Allowing prisoner to escape at Westbury
Thomas Cole	13.4.1840	For drunkenness
William Hopkins	17.4.1840	Disobedience of orders in refusing to go to an Out-Station
William Merrett	25.4.1840	For drunkenness
William Ridler	29.4.1840	For drunkenness
George Caudle	9.5.1840	For getting married without leave
Charles Clapton	12.5.1840	For drunkenness
Thomas Staite	13.5.1840	For drunkenness
William Bailey	17.5.1840	For assaulting Constable Samuel Ford
Edward Banks	1.6.1840	For drunkenness
James Phipps	10.6.1840	For drunkenness

The Henry Waterson referred to in this list appears to be the Parish Constable who applied to the Deputy Clerk of the Peace for the post of Sergeant in the new Constabulary Force.

On the 30th June, 1840 Mr Lefroy submitted the first of his Quarterly Reports. It was hand written and can still be seen in the County Records office at Gloucester.

Addressed to the Chairman and Bench of Magistrates assembled at the Quarter Sessions of Gloucestershire, it reads:–

> I beg leave to lay the following papers before the Bench for their information.
>
> A return showing the strength of the County Constabulary Force at the present time. The Station and number of men at each, together with the annual rent.
>
> One showing the names of men who have been dismissed during the Quarter ending 30th June, 1840 and also a return of Constables fined, with the amount imposed on each individual, since the formation of the Force the total amount of which is in my hands.
>
> One showing the crimes that have been committed and the number of prisoners that have been arrested in the County during the Quarter.
>
> The district of Tetbury, which for some time has been in a disturbed state, is now become perfectly tranquil.
>
> The sub districts of Berkeley and Mitcheldean are now also in a tranquil state. When the force first went down to those Stations they met with some opposition from the labouring classes.
>
> In consequence of a report received at this office from the Superintendent of the Newnham district, that serious disturbances and rioting was expected to take place at the fair at Coleford on the 20th instant, I ordered an additional force of one Superintendent and nineteen Constables to attend there and I have much satisfaction in stating that everything passed off peaceably and that there was not the slightest disposition to disturb the public peace.
>
> I have inspected all the Stations in the County during the present Quarter, several of them frequently, and find that the men are going on as well as I could possibly expect them, from the time they have been in the Force, and that the various duties appear to be correctly and efficiently performed.
>
> Constable Thomas Gordon has been promoted from the Stroud District to that of Superintendent of the Sodbury one, for his great exertions and general good conduct – promotion taking place on the 1st May.
>
> Signed. Anthony Thos. Lefroy
> Chief Constable of Gloucestershire
>
> Cheltenham
> 30th June, 1840.

Apparantly Mr Lefroy was not satisfied with the distribution of the Force, as set out by the Clerk of the Peace, and with his report to Quarter

Sessions on the 30th June, 1840 he submitted details of the strength and distribution as it was at that particular time and date i.e.

STATION	Superintendents	Constables	
Cheltenham	2	47	
Frogmill		4	
Northleach		4	
Dursley	1	7	
Wotton-under-Edge		8	
Berkeley		6	
Hanham	1	11	
Hambrook		9	
Westbury		8	
Thornbury	1	5	
Newnham-on-Severn	1	5	
Mitcheldean		5	
Coleford		7	
Gloucester	1	8	
Newent		4	
Cirencester	1	9	
Fairford		4	
Campden	1	6	
Moreton-in-Marsh		5	
Stow-on-the-Wold		4	
Quinton–(Quenington)?		3	
Nailsworth	1	5	
Minchinhampton		4	
Whitminster	1	4	
Tetbury	1	8	
Tewkesbury	1	6	
Winchcombe	1	4	
Chipping Sodbury	1	6	
Marchfield–(Marshfield)		5	
Stroud	1	10	
Painswick		5	
Great Barrington		3	
	16	229	Total 245

As was to be expected the Force could not run without money and it was at this Quarter Sessions the Mr Lefroy submitted 'An estimate for pay amounts of bills delivered together with the probable expenses required for the quarter ending 30th September, 1840.'[7]

DETAILS OF ESTIMATE

PAY

	£	s.	d.
1 Chief Constable for one Quarter @ £300 p.a.	75	0	0
4 1st Class Supts. for one Quarter @ £120 p.a. each	120	0	0
11 2nd Class Supts. for one Quarter @ £100 p.a. each	275	0	0
4 3rd Class Supts. for one Quarter @ £80 each	80	0	0
230 Constables for one Quarter @ £49.10.8½d. each p.a.	2847	13	9
	£3397	13	9
John Hennesy – Barrack furniture & repairs to Cheltenham Police Station	11	16	9
Stationery – Edward Power	6	17	9
4 Iron bedsteads – Messrs. Montague & Church @ 26/–d. each	5	4	0
Stationery acc. – Mr Harper	3	6	9
Coals and Candles for Stations	100	0	0
Extra pay to Supts. and Constables and incidental expenses for the Chief Constable	150	0	0
	£3674	19	1

In the case of the 230 constables @ £49.10.8½d. per annum the total given is not correct and it appears that cash has been deducted from some of the constables, no doubt to cover the fines referred to by Mr Lefroy in his Report or perhaps an arithmetical error was made.

Gloucestershire was not one of the Counties which paid the minimum rate to their men. The Chief Constable received £300 per annum which was £50 above the minimum rate, whilst an ordinary constable was to receive £49.10s.8½d., again above the stated rate.

It was at this meeting of the Magistrates that the appointment of a Deputy Chief Constable was approved. The man appointed was Charles Reilly, one of the original Irish Constabulary contingent which had come over with Mr Lefroy.

The Force was beginning to work as a coherent unit and the public distrust of the 'New Police' was beginning to abate a little as it was generally realised that they were not moving into a Police State.

The problem which faced the men of the New Police was that once a fugitive slipped into an unpoliced county the only method of pursuit lay either with the constable alone or with the aid of the local Parish Constable – if he could be found and was willing to assist. No matter how efficient the police in one county were it was still possible for a wily criminal to get away by crossing the county boundary at some convenient point and evading pursuit.

It is fairly certain that Mr Lefroy was well aware that whilst the public were prepared to tolerate a certain amount of human indiscretion in many things they would most certainly and properly make an issue out of impartiality and its abuse by the police. Such an event as is here commented on would have given those persons who were opposed to the police just the chance they wanted to smear the Force's good name. The Chief Constable must have been particularly displeased when he had again to refer to this kind of failure:–

> With reference to the Circular Order of the 29th October, 1841, relative to evidence given by Constables in Courts of Justice, I have again to call the attention of the Superintendents to this important part of their duty, as it appears that at the present Assizes one of the Judges felt it necessary to reprimand Superintendent King and Constable Powell for asking a prisoner questions, which lead to a confession of guilt, and I wish it to be clearly understood by every member of the Constabulary Force that they have no right to ask a prisoner any question or to hold out any threat or promise that may induce them to say anything prejudicial to themselves, but should merely hear any voluntary statement which the prisoner might wish to make, and of which the Constables whould be most particular to take down in writing.
>
> 15th August, 1842[8]

After this warning there can have been little doubt in the Force as to the fate awaiting anyone who tampered with the rules of evidence. The Chief Constable had made this abundantly clear.

Not all the actions taken by the Chief Constable involved threatening and warning his men with discipline; indeed his concern for them and for their welfare can be seen from the fact that in October, 1840 the Chief Constable requested that a Superannuation Fund be provided, that deductions be made from pay and that fines and moities of fines alluded to in Section 10 of the Act be added to the Fund. It was in 1840 too that the Force recruited its first sergeants and a number of additional superintendents. On the 7th November, 1840 the Home Office approved the appointment of 28 sergeants at 22/–d. per week, and the payment of £100 per annum to 9 superintendents. At the same time the initial pay of the constables on joining was reduced to 16/-d. per week subject to a further promotion. As an after-thought Whitehall added that a further £40 should be paid annually to each superintendent to cover the expenses of finding and keeping a horse and travelling expenses.

The vexed question of arming the police arose in 1842 and although the original Home Office Rules had provided for cutlasses to be available for issue, the Chief Constable was very clear on the question of his men carrying firearms:–

> The Superintendents will inform the Sergeants and Constables of their districts that on no account or under any pretence whatever will they be allowed to carry pistols or other firearms with them when on duty and the first man reported for so doing will be instantly dismissed.
>
> 24th September, 1842[9]

By this time the Force was beginning to settle down and was more readily accepted by the population who were beginning to lose their previous suspicion of the 'New Police'.

The disciplining of the Force involved Mr Lefroy in many hours of chiding, complaining and making orders. These Orders were issued in the form of a Circular – hand written – and sent from one Station to another. The Circular being copied into the Station Book, kept for that purpose, before being passed on to the next Station. The Chief Constable seems to have managed to deal with each trouble as it arose. It was not until 1847 that he had occasion to comment unfavourably on the turn-out of the Force, presumably before which date everything was in order.

In 1849 the Constabulary finished its first ten years of service, a period during which many problems had been met and overcome. By this time the majority of the population recognised the usefulness of the police and accepted them as part of the social order. In 1854 the Borough of Tewkesbury decided to amalgamate and the City of Gloucester followed suit in 1859. By these amalgamations the strength of the Constabulary was increased by 24, making a Force total of 274.

The following is a copy of the Agreement between the County of Gloucestershire and the City and Borough of Gloucester to consolidate the Police Establishments of the County and City.[10]

> The agreement made the Seventh day of March in the year of our Lord one Thousand Eight Hundred and Fifty Nine, between Purnell Bransby Purnell., Esq., and John Curtis Hayward, Esq., two of her Majesty's Justices of the Peace of and for the County of Gloucester of the one part and the Mayor, Aldermen and Citizens of the City of Gloucester in the County of the City of Gloucester being the Town Council of the said City of Gloucester and County of the same City of the other part.
>
> Whereas the Justices of the Peace of and for the County Gloucester in Quarter Sessions assembled and the Mayor, Alderman and Citizens aforesaid in Council assembled have mutually agreed to consolidate the Police

Establishments of the said County and City of Gloucester and the provisions of the several Acts of Parliament relating thereto upon the terms and conditions hereinafter contained. Now these presents witness and the said Purnell Bransby Purnell and John Curtis Hayward on behalf of themselves and other Justices of the Peace of and for the said County and the Town Council of the said City of Gloucester do hereby agree to consolidate the Police Establishments of the said County and hereby agree to consolidate the Police Establishments of the said County and City of Gloucester and that such consolidation shall commence on the First day of May next, and the said Purnell Bransby Purnell and John Curtis Hayward do hereby agree with the Town Council of the said City of Gloucester that upon such consolidation there shall be stationed in the said City of Gloucester a combined Force for the said City of Gloucester and County consisting of thirty two Constables and that one Superintendent, two Sergeants and seventeen Constables of such Combined Force shall be deemed the Contingent furnished by the said County. The whole of the said Force to be applicable under the orders of the Chief Constable of the said County and the said Superintendent for the preservation of the Peace and the security of property within the said City of Gloucester and the suburbs thereof including such portion of the County as hath hitherto been watched and patrolled by the County Force stationed at Wotton near the said City. And also that four members of the said Force shall be appointed to perform, in addition to their police duties, the duties of Mayor's Officers and that the Superintendent of the time being of the said Consolidated Police Establishment shall himself attend or depute some other member of such Force in his stead to attend the Magistrates in Petty Quarter Sessions assembled and shall provide for the attendance of a Constable on the Town Council in their Municipal capacity and as a Burial Board and Board of Health at their several Council Meetings. And also provide for the attendance of not less than four Constables at the Quarter Sessions of the said City, and the said Council of the said City of Gloucester doth hereby agree with the said Purnell Bransby Purnell and John Curtis Hayward and other Justices of the Peace of the said County of Gloucester to pay for each of the twenty of the said Combined Force of the thirty two Constables so to be kept and employed in the said City and Districts of Gloucester, for his pay and clothing such sum per annum as the average cost of the whole Police Establishment of the said County for these items shall amount to the payment at the present time being computed at fifty-nine pounds, sixteen shillings per Constable. And also such further sum for each Constable per annum for the rent of Police Stations, interest of money expended on Police Stations (exclusive of Petty Sessional Courts) and other payments as those items collectively taken shall on an average amount to the present payment being computed at eight pounds sixteen shillings and one penny. And shall and will quarterly upon receiving an amount of such costs, pay to the Treasurer of the Police Funds of the said county of Gloucestershire the amount so due. And it is hereby agreed by and between the said Purnell Bransby Purnell and John Curtis Hayward and other Justices of the Peace for the said County and the said County of the said City of Gloucester that the sum herein before stated as the average payments in respect of the several items before mentioned shall be considered as fixed for five years from the day of the date hereof and from the expiration of that period shall be regulated according to the basis above prescribed for a further term of five years subject to the powers of variation given to Her Majesty in Council under and by virtue of the fifth Section of the Act nineteenth and twentieth Victoria Chapter sixty-nine and it is hereby further agreed by and between the said parties hereto that the appointing and dismissal of all constables constituting the said Consolidated Force shall be made by the Chief Constable of the said County. And here unto we the said Purnell Bransby Purnell and John Curtis Hayward do on behalf of the said justices of the Peace of the said County of Gloucester subscribe and set our hands and Seals and the said Council of the said City have affixed their Common Seal the day and year first above written.'

Signed. Purnell B.Purnell. Curtis J.Hayward
Countersigned. George Riddiford
Dy. Clerk of the Peace

In 1856 the Government made a further move in the problem of Policing Britain and one which was to be of inestimable benefit to the Gloucestershire Constabulary. This was the passing, not without great opposition, of the County and Borough Police Act which forced the local authorities to form paid Police Forces. This meant that the policed counties now had neighbours with some form of police with whom they could work. To the criminal population who had seen the red light in 1839 and promptly moved to unpoliced areas this Act was the beginning of the end.

The provisions of the Act meant that it was now possible for the effective standards to be maintained throughout the country by virtue of the provision of a number of Inspectors of Constabulary whose duty it was to visit each force and present reports on its efficiency. For instance, in 1860 Her Majesty's Inspector of Constabulary, a Captain Willis, reported that he had inspected the Force and considered it to be 'In an effective state.' It is interesting to note that, after all these years, H.M. Inspector of Constabulary still carries out an Annual Inspection of this and every Force in the country.

These inspections meant that there was a closer liaison between Government and Police Forces which enabled problems to be examined both at national and local level. However, as Gloucestershire was already possessed of an efficient Force it merely meant that they could now rely on better co-operation from neighbouring counties, in particular Monmouth and Somerset.

In connection with the welfare of his men, the Chief Constable was able to make a concession to the Force, which, compared with today, high-lights the arduous conditions under which the early policemen worked. It was as follows:–

> The Superintendents of the Gloucestershire Constabulary will so arrange the duty at the different stations in their Districts that each man will have one whole night's rest in the week except anything extraordinary should occur.[11]
>
> Dated. 8th July, 1856

The Forest of Dean has always had the reputation of being a rough and ready sort of area, and the early days of the Police Force were no exception. It was during Mr Lefroy's term of office that we have recorded the first murder of a Gloucestershire Police Officer whilst on duty.[12]

In 1861 Samual Beard was a Police Sergeant stationed at Littledean. He was described as an active and energetic man and when, in August of that year, he received a complaint from Mr Guest, a farmer at Flaxley, that sheep were being stolen from the Speech House area in the Forest of Dean, he immediately made enquiries and on the night of the 16th August went to Speech House with Mr Guest's son to keep observation for the culprits.

At about 11.00 p.m. they saw four suspicious persons near a field and the Sergeant decided that they should split up. When Sergeant Beard challenged the men he was immediately attacked by them and beaten with clubs and cudgels, and although he called for assistance, Mr Guest later insisted that he did not hear him. He did say he heard the beating going on but thought the men were beating a donkey.

Sergeant Beard was left in a state of semi-consciousness in a ditch beside the field, and was not found until 4 o'clock in the morning. He was taken to Speech House where it was found that he had suffered appalling injuries, including a fractured skull and that every tooth in his upper jaw was broken.

At the place where the assault took place, Police Superintendent Taylor found cord-wood and an iron bar which had been used in the attack. The following day four local men were arrested and taken to Speech House where Sergeant Beard was able to make a definite identification and also a deposition in the presence of a Justice of the Peace. He died from his injuries a few days later at the age of 37 years.

Thomas Cooper 29 years, George Cooper 23 years, Richard Roberts 34 years and Thomas Gwilliam 34 years, were at Gloucester Winter Assizes, each sentenced to 15 years Penal Servitude for the murder.

Over 500 people attended the funeral of the Sergeant who was buried at Littledean Church. On his gravestone is the inscription –

> Overwhelmed with pain, sunk within this cell, and bid the anxious cares of life farewell. Farewell fond wife and young children dear, in whom was centred all my earthly care.

Mr Lefroy retired as first Chief Constable of Gloucestershire, on the 1st July, 1865 with 25 years and 7 months service. He left behind him a Force which had passed its infancy and become an efficient and well run law enforcement agency of 288 officers and men.

On the day of Mr Lefroy's retirement, 60 members of the County Constabulary assembled in the library at the Cheltenham Police Station for the purpose of presenting him with a token of their esteem, upon his retirement from the office of Chief Constable after 25 years service.

The present consisted of a large and handsome Silver Salver, supplied by Messrs Martin, and bore the following inscription, beneath the Family Crest.

> Presented to A.T. Lefroy, Esq., by the members of the Gloucestershire Constabulary as a token of their esteem, on his retirement, after a period of 25 years service to the county as their Chief Constable, July 1st, 1865.

The presentation was made by Mr J. Nicholls, the Deputy Chief Constable, on behalf of members of the Force.

The Salver, which was highly embossed, weighed 100 ounces and was valued at 50 guineas.

Captain Christian, who succeeded Mr Lefroy as Chief Constable, was at the presentation.[13]

Mr Lefroy lived to enjoy a Police Retirement Pension of £333 per annum for nearly 25 years. His death taking place at 2, Segrave Place, Pittville, Cheltenham, on the 23rd March, 1890, at the age of 88 years.

CHAPTER 3

Admiral Henry Christian, M.V.O., K.P.M.
1.7.1865 – 2.5.1910

Captain Henry Christian, later to become Admiral Christian, Royal Navy, took over as Chief Constable of Gloucestershire on the 1st July, 1865.

Captain Christian's background was varied and interesting. The son of Samuel, a merchant in Malta, he was directly related to Fletcher Christian of 'Mutiny on the Bounty' fame and like his illustrious, or infamous, distant cousin, went to sea in 1840 at the age of 12.

In 1860 Captain Christian became second-in-command of the Royal Yacht *Victoria and Albert.*

In 1863 he bacame Captain and had the distinction of taking Princess Alexandra and a posse of foreign aristocrats to London for the wedding to Prince Edward. Soon after this trip, Captain Christian retired from the Navy, took a holiday in London, went racing and found himself a wife, Emily Margaret, daughter of James Moore of Liverpool.[1]

His next appointment was as Chief Constable of the Gloucestershire County Police and in 1865 he moved to Cheltenham, near the County Police Headquarters, at No.1, Crescent Terrace, just across the road from the Cheltenham Central Police Station and now occupied by the Countryside Commission.

Christian was a man of imposing demeanour and photographs of him in latter life, when on the Retired List he had been promoted to Admiral, show him as rather a formidable Chief Constable.

The Gloucestershire Constabulary was a well established Force of 288 men when Captain Christian took over, distributed by rank as follows:–

1	Chief Constable
1	Deputy Chief Constable
5	1st Class Superintendents
6	2nd Class Superintendents
43	Sergeants
138	1st Class Constables

88	2nd Class Constables
6	Vacancies

The efficiency of the Force as an agency of the law enforcement at this time was as with any Police Force rather difficult to estimate but an indication of the type of crime current and of the measures of success achieved in its detection can be gathered from the undermentioned crime returns for the years 1862–63.[2]

	Number of Offences	Arrests
Assault with intent to murder	6	6
Assault on police	62	68
Common assault	87	90
Burglary	13	6
Robbery	67	71
Larceny	69	67
Horse stealing	9	7
Sheep stealing	16	4
Riot	4	4
Rescuing prisoners	4	4
Injury to property	15	11
Crimes against owners of Beer Houses	68	68
Threatening notices	1	1
Vagrancy	88	88
Uttering false coin	2	2
Intoxication	89	88
Illegal pawning	1	1
Trespass	6	3
Concealed on premised	1	1
Stifling (Infants?)	2	2
Selling without licence	1	1
Deserting family	5	5
Cruelty to animals	1	1
Embezzlement	3	
Forgery	1	1
Picking pockets	1	1
Cutting wood	2	2
Robbery from the person	2	1
Cock fighting	2	1
Shoplifting	1	1
Receiving stolen property	1	1
Obtaining money under false pretences	3	3
Breach of the peace	9	9

Creating a disturbance	5	5
Attempted suicide	1	1
Importuning	1	1
Detaining property	1	1
Sleeping in open air and in outhouses	7	7

It is curious to note the number of offences which now appear strange to us, and the high state of crime detection in the county at the time. It is more than probable that these figures in fact cover only a quarter as the incidence of crime seems particularly low for a whole year.

Troubles with the Fenians (a brotherhood of American/Irishmen) touched the County of Gloucester and on 27th December, 1867 the Home Secretary informed the Chief Constable that he had reason to believe that a Danish Brigantine was likely to land shortly on the shores of the Bristol Channel about 30 persons who had embarked in her from America. He said he was unable to give any description of these persons. They were likely to choose some unfrequented spot for their landing. The instructions were to have them arrested on a charge of Treason Felony.

The persons referred to were undoubtedly recruited by the Fenians from the more unruly elements of the Union and Confederate Armies recently discharged at the end of the American Civil War. The faith of the Home Department in the ability of the Police to deal with them was touching. The Chief Constable could never have spared a sufficient number of men to patrol the Severn and Channel Coast, and even had he been able to do so it is fairly safe to assume that they would have fared badly at the hands of armed men who had seen service in such a recent and savage war. It is fortunate that the Danish Brigantine referred to did not appear in the Bristol Channel.

During his period as Chief Constable Admiral Christian introduced a check ticket system in an attempt to ensure that each beat was properly worked. Each constable was issued with a number of tickets and a list of addresses (usually of local notables) where he was to leave them. It remained with the Force right up until the Second World War.

The life of the ordinary constable was a hard one and there was a constant vigil of the public on his activities. They could not, even whilst off duty, take a drink in a public house in their own districts and nor could they keep pets, particulary dogs. Even the make of the matches which they used was the concern of the Chief Constable who ordered that only Bryant and May's safety matches were to be brought into police Stations. On the 15th June, 1881 the first Warrant Cards were issued. They were then annual and had to be handed in on the 28th December of each year for renewal. Smoking was also frowned upon and several men were cautioned for doing so whilst off duty. It was also ordered by Admiral Christian that men were to 'wash and clean themselves as soon as they got up'. In 1887 a constable was dismissed for leaving his beat and being found eating and drinking in a gentleman's house with the servants who, it was said, were robbing their master – 'as the food was not theirs to give'. Officers were forbidden to accept food or drink from anyone. The Chief Constable also noted that certain constables had females visit them in Police Station, this was also forbidden.[3]

There were one or two interesting landmarks during Admiral Christian's command.

During 1894 a Sergeant J. Williams instructed a Prudence Villis to attend as a witness at Newent Police Court. The Magistrates refused to pay her expenses. Not to be outdone Prudence sued the Sergeant in County Court, for her expenses, on the 12th July, 1894. It has not been possible to find out what happened at the hearing but it is recorded that the Standing Joint Committee allowed the Sergeant the sum of £1.18.0d. towards the cost of defending the action.[4]

On the 23rd June, 1895 a Police Sergeant Theyers was found dead in his room at Gloucester Central Police Station, having bled to death from a burst vein in his leg. He was 46 years of age, a bachelor, and had served for 26 years and 7 months. Death was certified by Doctor William Washbourne who continued his work in Gloucester, as Police Surgeon, right up until the Second World War.

The second murder of a Gloucestershire Police Officer occurred on the 10th November, 1895. Sergeant William Morris and Police Constable Cornelius Harding were on duty at Viney Hill in the Forest of Dean when they came upon a party of Foresters from the Whitecroft and Pillowell district.

These men had been to Blakeney and on their way back home had stopped at various public houses with the result that they were under the influence of drink.

It appears that the Sergeant and Constable remonstrated with them whereupon a scuffle ensued during which both officers were struck down by stones, the men making good their escape. P.C. Harding recovered consciousness but Sergeant Morris was found to be dead, having received a fractured skull and broken neck. Three young colliers from Whitecroft and Pillowell, James Morgan, 24 years; George Morgan, 19 years and George Hill, 18 years, were arrested and charged with the murder of Sergeant Morris and the attempted murder of P.C. Harding and were later convicted of manslaughter.

Sergeant Morris was 32 years old at the time of his death and had served for over 10 years in the Force. He left a widow and three small children. A great deal of public sympathy followed and as a result a subscription fund was set up and after expenses the sum of £1,084 was realised – no small sum in those days. When this was invested the widow found that she was in receipt of £55 a year to keep herself and three children, made up as follows[5] :–

From investment	£32.10.0d.
Police pension during widow-hood	£15. 0.0d.
£2.10.0d. for each child until 15 years of age	£7.10.0d.
	£55.0.0d.

Sergeant Morris was buried at Lydney Churchyard and his gravestone bears the insription,

> In the midst of life we are in death. Of whom may we seek for succour but Thee O Lord.

Also in Lydney Churchyard and next to the grave of Sergeant Morris is a grave bearing the inscription,

> In loving remembrance of Charles Albert Clark late Sergeant of Police, Lydney, Gloucestershire, who died August 21st, 1881, aged 29 years. This stone was erected in his memory by his comrades and friends, by whom he was respected.

As there is no official record of this Sergeant's death it can only be presumed that he died of 'Natural Causes'.

It was during Admiral Christian's tour of duty as Chief Constable that bicycles were first introduced to the Force and on the 7th April, 1896, the Standing Joint Committee for the County approved the purchase of 12 bicycles at a cost of £12.13.0d. each. The machines to be selected by M.W. Colchester-Wemys and J.E. Griffiths from R.E. and C.Marshall of Cheltenham.

The Bristol Corporation Act came before Parliament and was passed in 1897. As a result Bristol City took over the following Police Stations from the Gloucestershire Constabulary, Fishponds; St. George; Two Mile Hill; Lawrence Hill; Horfield; Church Road, Horfield; Eastville; Stapleton and South Street, Kingswood. With the Stations there was a transfer of 10 Sergeants and 45 Constables.

Second Class constables in the County Police Force who served in Gloucester City were paid 24/11d. (about £1.25p.) a week in 1907 and a 4/4d. (22p.) a week rent allowance for those not living in Police Stations.

In an effort to increase their pay they had a petition printed and circulated to the Standing Joint Committee of the County Council complete with a statement of their cost of living. This is reproduced below and the Board of Trade figures for Gloucester City added so that, where possible some comparisons can be made.

It is clear that the money for weekly necessities exceeded the pay of the constables. These family men were living near to subsistence level – at a time when summer wage rates for City bricklayers were 37/8d. (£1.87p.) for a 56½ hour week and engineering fitters had 32/–d. (£1.60p.). Besides, 4th and 5th class constables were paid several shillings less a week which put them into an even worse position.

The Cost of living for Constables, 1907 and the cost of some necessities, Board of Trade Enquiry Gloucester City, 1905

Second Class Constables' list of Weekly Necessities, 1907	£	s	d	Board of Trade Figures for Gloucester City, 1905 pub. 1908		£	s	d
Rent per week		5	6	Rent 5 room tenement			5	0
					or		6	0
Coal at 1/1d. per cwt.		2	2	Coal per cwt.			1	0
Wood			3	N.A.				
Light, oil or gas		1	0	N.A.				
Bread		3	0	Bread per 4 lbs				4½
Flour			9	Flour per 7 lbs				9
Meat Beef @ 8d. per lb				Meat(mutton per lb)				9–10
Mutton @ 10d. per lb.		4	0	Meat(Beef per lb)				8–9
Fish @ 4d. per lb		1	0	N.A.				
Bacon @ 8d. per lb			8	Bacon per lb				6½–7
Cheese @ 8d. per lb			8	Cheese per lb				6½–7
Butter @ 1/1d. per lb		1	1	Butter – colonial per lb			1	1
Jam			4	N.A.				
Tea @ 2/–d. per lb		1	0	Tea per lb			1	0
					or		1	6
Sugar @ 2½d. per lb			10	Sugar per lb				2½
Milk @ 1½d. per pint		1	0	N.A.				
Eggs @ 1d. each			7	Eggs per dozen			1	0
Rice for puddings		1	0	N.A.				
Lard @ 8d. per lb			4	N.A.				

Soda, soap, blacking, etc.	1 0	N.A.
	£1. 6. 0	
Second Class Constable's pay	£1. 6. 0	

Whilst on the question of pay it is interesting to note that at the Standing Joint Committee Meeting at Gloucester on the 20th October, 1891, the Chief Constable submitted a Memorial from the Deputy Chief Constable, Superintendents and other members of the Force, pointing out the inadequacy of the pay as compared with that of other Counties and Boroughs.

In presenting the Memorial Admiral Christian stated, 'I beg to report that the pay of this Force has been the same for the last seventeen years.'

The Constabulary Superannuation Fund for 1890/1891 was presented to the meeting and one item of interest was, 'Lucretia Bird widow of Inspector Bird late of the Fishponds Police District, who died on the 4th July, 1890, was paid a gratuity of £91.5.0d'. It is very rare, these days, that a police widow is paid a gratuity. More often than not the police widow today receives a Police Widows Pension, on the death of her husband, based on his salary and length of service and, providing she married him before he had retired from the Force. This pension is forfeited should the widow re-marry. However should that second husband die the present day Regulations allows the Chief Constable to apply to his Police Committee for a re-grant of the Police Widows Pension.

Like the pay in those days pensions were not high and it was recorded in the Standing Joint Committee Report dated 7th April, 1871 that the Chief Constable recommended a Pension of 2/8d. per day be granted to Sergeant Edwin Shipton of Stow-on-the-Wold. Sergeant Shipton was 64 years of age, had served 31 years and 127 days in the Police Force of the County, and who, according to a certificate of the Chief Constable, 'is quite worn out and unable to perform the duties of his office efficiently.'

It was about this time when approval was given, by the Standing Joint Committee, for a new police station to be built at Avonmouth, which was then in the County of Gloucestershire, for the sum of £1,887. James Greenslade of Bowbridge Wharf, Stroud, Glos., was granted the contract.

We cannot leave the reign of Admiral Christian without mentioning Ex. Superintendent Frank Hallett of Brockworth who, when being interviewed by the local press[6] in 1970 on his 90th birthday, recalled his time as a young constable at Tewkesbury in 1900. Mr Hallett said that Admiral Christian was a man of humanity and humour behind an awe-inspiring countenance and went on to describe how he had to show

Admiral Christian the cells at Tewkesbury Police Station and accidently locked himself in the cell, with the Chief Constable. By the knocking on the ceiling of the cell with Admiral Christian's walking stick they were able to attract the attention of the Sergeant who lived in quarters over the cells. What the Sergeant said, after the Chief Constable had left, has never been recorded. Mr Hallett died in the Knoll Nursing Home, Tuffley, Gloucester on the 3rd May, 1972 in his 93rd year.

Other landmarks during Admiral Christian's service as Chief Constable include the Lloyd Police Home, Cheltenham. At the standing Joint Committee Meeting held at Gloucester on the 15th October, 1895, the Chairman stated that the Deed of Trust, vesting the Lloyd Police Home, Cheltenham, in certain Trustees, had now been executed by all parties concerned and the buildings itself completed and that a Superannuated member of the Police Force was about to reside there.

On the motion of the Chairman it was Resolved that the Clerk of the Peace be instructed to convey to the Rev. J.E. Walker, the thanks of the Standing Joint Committee, for his generous gift of the Lloyd Police Home, Cheltenham.

From 1895 the Lloyd Police Home, Cheltenham was let to Gloucestershire Police Pensioners at a nominal rent and was occupied, over the years, by various Police Pensioners. The last Police Pensioner to occupy the Lloyd Police Home was Ex. P.C. James E. Bartlett who died on the 26th December, 1962 aged 85 years. Owing to lack of Funds the Trustees decided to sell the property. This they did and invested the proceeds, the interest therefrom being paid, at intervals, to the Gloucestershire Constabulary Benevolent Fund which at various times throughout the year makes grants to the Police Widows of Gloucestershire.

In 1897 the Chief Constable was authorised to have the telephone connection between Gloucester and Cheltenham Police Stations converted from the Single Line to the Metallic Circuit system. The same year Superintendent Harrison applied for Dursley Police Station to be connected to the telephone system. It was not until 1898 that permission was given, by the Standing Joint Committee, for the Police Stations at Coleford, Lydney and Cinderford to be connected to the National Telephone Company.

It is interesting to note how clothing prices have changed over the years. On the 5th April, 1898 the following Tenders were approved.[7]

Messrs J & B Pearse & Co.,London
327 Tunics for Sergeants & Constables @ 18/8d. each
654 Pairs of Trousers for Sergeants & Constables @ 11/4d. per pair

Messrs Plant & Co., Cheltenham
12 caps for Superintendents @ 16/–d. each
6 caps for Inspectors @ 9/6d. each
327 helmets for Sergeants & Constables @ 5/6d. each

Messrs Dicks & Sons Ltd., Cheltenham
11 Patrol Jackets for Superintendents @ 44/–d. each
22 Pairs of Trousers for Superintendents @ 17/9d. per pair
6 Patrol Jackets for Inspectors @ 29/–d. each
12 pairs of Trousers for Inspectors @ 12/6d. per pair

Messrs D.Lane & Son, Gloucester
690 Pairs of Boots @ 15/–d. per pair
344 Pairs of Leggings @ 4/6 d. per pair

During 1899 Admiral Christian was able to report that 230 members of the Police Force were holders of the St. John Ambulance certificate.

With the outbreak of the South African War the Standing Joint Committee met at Gloucester Shire Hall on the 2nd January, 1900, when it was agreed that, acting under suggestions contained in a letter from the Home Secretary, the Chief Constable should be authorised to allow half-pay to the wives and families of all Gloucestershire Police Officers, belonging to the Army Reserve, who had been called up for Active Service in South Africa.

The following details show the distribution of the Senior Officers within the County Constabulary, during the year 1902, together with operational Police Stations.[8]

Chief Constable	Admiral Henry Christian Tele. No. 38
Deputy Chief Constable	Nehemiah Philpott Gloucester
Superintendent and Chief Clerk	Young Sainsbury
Assistant Clerk	Sergeant Henry Woodward
Cheltenham District	Superintendent Arthur W.Hopkins Inspector John Henry Parker
Stations	Charlton Kings*; Cheltenham; Prestbury
Tewkesbury District	Inspector Edward Selwood
Stations	Beckford; Bishops Cleeve; Coombe Hill; Kemerton; Tewkesbury; Twyning; Winchcombe*.

Gloucester District	Deputy Chief Constable Nehemiah Philpott Inspector Daniel John Elliott
Stations	Cheltenham Road; Churcham; Churchdown; Corse; Dymock; Fretherne; Gloucester; Hardwicke; Hartpury; Newent*; Tuffley; Upton St. Leonards; Whitminster*.
Bristol District	Superintendent Edward Cooke – Staple Hill Inspector Harry Ricketts – Kingswood Hill
Stations	Filton; Frampton-Cottrell; Hallen Hanham*; Horfield; Kingswood Hill; Lawfords Gate*; Mangotsfield; Marshfield; Oldland Common*; Pucklechurch; Shirehampton; Southmead; Staple Hill; Stoke Bishop; Stoke Gifford Westbury-on-Trym*; Wick; Winterbourne*.
Forest District	Superintendent Grantley Ford – Coleford Inspector Thomas Griffen – Lydney
Stations	Blakeney*; Cinderford*; Drybrook; Littledean*; Longhope; Lydbrook; Lydney; Mitchel-dean; Newnham-on-Severn*; Parkend; Ruspidge; St.Briavels; Tidenham; Westbury-on-Severn; Woolaston; Yorkley.
Stroud District	Superintendent William Harrison – Stroud
Stations	Avening; Birdlip; Bisley; Brimscombe; Cainscross; Chalford; Horsley; Minchinhampton; Nailsworth*; Painswick; Stonehouse*; Stroud; Whiteshill.
Dursley District	Superintendent James B.Briggs – Dursley
Stations	Berkeley*; Cambridge; Charfield; Dursley;

	Kingscote; Newport; North Nibley; Sharpness; Tetbury*; Uley; Wotton-under-Edge*.
Chipping Sodbury District	Superintendent Frederick S.Phelps – Chipping Sodbury
Stations	Acton Turville; Almondsbury; Chipping Sodbury; Didmarton; Falfield; Hawkesbury Upton; Iron Acton; Old Sodbury; Alveston; Redwick; Thornbury*; Wickwar.
Cirencester District	Superintendent Frank Webb – Cirencester
Stations	Bibury; Cirencester; Fairford*; Kemble; Lechlade; Sapperton; South Cerney.
Chipping Campden District	Superintendent Frederick Jones – Chipping Campden
Stations	Chipping Campden; Long Marston*; Moreton-in-Marsh*; Stanton.
Stow-on-the-Wold District	Superintendent George Everiss – Northleach
Stations	Andoversford*; Bourton-on-the-Water*; Chedworth; Guiting; Northleach; Stow-on-the-Wold*; Windrush; Withington.

* Denotes Sergeant Stations

ACREAGE – POPULATION – FORCE STRENGTH

GLOUCESTERSHIRE	ACRES	POPULATION	STRENGTH
Cheltenham	15,229	51,854	65
Tewkesbury	70,060	19,209	17
Gloucester	96,066	65,805	76
Bristol	52,937	42,719	52
Forest of Dean	82,940	45,445	41
Stroud	72,987	46,831	32
Dursley	61,153	22,816	19
Chipping Sodbury	84,686	20,841	25
Cirencester	92,468	22,079	18
Chipping Campden	57,326	11,474	10
Stow-on-the-Wold	109,415	16,697	17
Totals	795,267	365,770	372

Deputy Chief Constable Nehemiah Philpott served for 45 years, 8 months and 13 days in the Police Force of the County and retired on the 31st January, 1902, aged 63 years and 6 months. His annual pay was £220 and he was paid a Police Pension of £146.13.4d. per annum.

Superintendent William Harrison of Stroud was appointed Deputy Chief Constable on the 1st February, 1902 and was posted to Gloucester.

In the days of Admiral Christian any act of bravery was reported to the Standing Joint Committee and it is recorded that Police Constable Edward Aston was awarded a gratuity of £5 for stopping a pair of runaway horses in Cheltenham 'At great personal risk'.

Seven officers, all Army Reservists, returned safely from the War in South Africa and resumed their duties with the Constabulary. They were William Fowler, Charles C. Jackson, John W.Greengrass, George S.Hodgkin, Alfred H.Hayward, William J.White and James Stanley. Donald Dow returned safely to Great Britain but died on the 30th August, 1901, at Piershill Barracks, Edinburgh, from Double Pneumonia and Heart Failure, before he could be discharged back to his Constabulary duties. He joined the Gloucestershire Constabulary on the 17th March, 1897, was 29 years of age when he died and had served as a Constable for 2 years and 6 months.

Admiral Christian remained in office for 44 years and 6 months, retiring on the 2nd May, 1910, aged 81 years. A truly remarkable man and a strict disciplinarian. His salary when he retired was £570 per annum and he received a Police Pension of £380 per annum.

At the Standing Joint Committee meeting held at the Shire Hall, Gloucester on the 28th June, 1910, the Chairman and Vice Chairman presented Admiral Henry Christian with an Illuminated Address, subscribed for and signed by members of the Committee and of the County Council and County Magistrates, recording the appreciation of his long and valued service as Chief Constable of Gloucestershire.

Admiral Henry Christian died on the 10th June, 1916. He was the holder of the M.V.O. and the King's Police Medal.

Sergeant W. Morris (on left) murdered in the Forest of Dean on 10th November 1895. Photograph kindly loaned by his granddaughter.

Presentation photograph to Inspector Chas. HAWKINS on his retirement October 1897.

Retirement of Supt. MORGAN, Cirencester 1902.

Tewkesbury Police 1906.

Superintendents Gloucestershire Constabulary 5th October 1910.

Winners of 'Shewell' Shield Cheltenham Ambulance Brigade, 1910.

Glos. Police – Tonypandy Miner's Strike 1910–11.

First 10 Police Women for Glos'shire.

Cheltenham Police – Picnic on the Avon, 9th July 1913.

New Court, 1919. First Class of Recruits to be taken in after the 1914–18 War.

Headquarters staff 1920.

Holland House, Police H.Q.
1921–1965

Gloucestershire Constabulary Football Team 1922–23.

Glos'shire Con. Mounted Police – Miners Strike, Forest of Dean 1926.

Women Police on a Course at Police H.Q., Cheltenham 1928.

Glos'shire Con. Motor Cycles – Forest of Dean, Miners Strike and General Strike.

P.C. C.A. SMITH, Lydney 1931–32.

CHAPTER 4

Lieut. Col. Richard Chester Chester-Master, D.S.O.
3.5.1910 – 30.8.1917

When Admiral Christian announced his retirement the Standing Joint Committee formed a Selection Committee under the Chairmanship of F.A. Hyett, Esq. with a view to the appointment of a new Chief Constable. After advertising the post in various newspapers including The Times, Morning Post, Army and Navy Gazette and Gloucester Journal, 115 applications were received. The Committee sifted through these and selected a short list of six. Four candidates were finally selected to appear before the Standing Joint Committee at the Shire Hall, Gloucester on the 5th April, 1910. They were Captain C.L. Armitage, Major R.C. Chester-Master, Captain Sir Henry E.Hill, Bart. and Major J.H.Thresher. At the conclusion of the interviews a vote was taken of the 81 members present with the result that Major Chester-Master received 54 votes, Captain Armitage 21 votes, Captain Sir Henry Hill 4 votes and Major Thresher 2 votes, so Major Richard Chester Chester-Master was appointed Chief Constable of Gloucestershire, to succeed Admiral Christian, subject to the approval of the Secretary of State. The approval was forthcoming and Major Chester-Master was able to take up his appointment on the 3rd May, 1910.

Major Chester-Master's tour of duty as Chief Constable was cut short on the 5th January, 1915 when he was recalled to the Colours, following the outbreak of the First World War in 1914. Never-the-less his five years with the Gloucestershire Constabulary was full of interest.

One of the first things the Chief Constable did was to call the Chief Constable's Circular Orders – General Orders. General Orders began the present practice of including not only details of new legislation and Force instructions but also news, good and bad, from within the Force itself. In the very first we find that a 3rd Class Constable was permitted to resign and another was discharged for theft from a comrade. Today, Force Weekly Orders Nos. 1,2,3 and 4 have replaced the old General Orders.

Even the organisation of the Force received a drastic overhaul and the first Divisions were formed: In this initial plan there were eleven in all, lettered as follows[1]:–

A. Campden — B. Bristol
C. Cirencester — D. Dursley
E. Tewkesbury — F. Forest of Dean
G. Gloucester — H. Chipping Sodbury
J. Stroud — K. Stow-on-the-Wold
L. Cheltenham

On the 18th October, 1910, the Chief Constable submitted a scheme for providing a force of Mounted Police for the County. This was due to H.M. Inspector of Constabulary reporting back to the Secretary of State that, 'No provision was made in the County of Gloucestershire for the maintenance of Mounted Police as suggested by the Secretary of State in letter dated 15.4.1909'.

The scheme comprised the purchasing of saddlery and equipment for use with horses hired, whenever necessary, and ridden by police officers with riding experience mainly through serving in a cavalry regiment of H.M. Forces. This system was maintained until just after the Second World War.

Complaints against the Police are not new. It was reported on the 4th April, 1911, that a Committee had carefully considered letters which had been received from the Rev. J. Priestley Foster complaining as to the action of the Police with regard to an Alehouse at Duntisbourne and in licensing matters generally and had passed the following Resolution – 'That having considered the charges made by the Rev. Priestley Foster against the police, the Committee do not think they are called upon to take any action in this matter'.[2]

During the same year, 1911, we find that a 'Tramp Census' was taken on the night of the 4th April and it transpired that there was a total of 221 persons sleeping in Casual Wards, in Gloucestershire, that night. The average for the previous 10 years was 204.

Although out of date sequence it is appropriate to mention here The Police (Weekly) Rest Day Act of 1910. Under this Act the Standing Joint Committee were obliged to make arrangements so that every constable – not above the rank of Inspector – was allowed at least 52 days of a year off duty, save when required on occasions of emergency. These Rest Days had to be distributed throughout the year so as to secure to every constable, so far as practicable, one day's rest in every seven.

On the 27th June, 1911, the Secretary of State agreed to the strength of the Force being increased by an additional 12 constables to enable the Chief Constable to implement the Police (Weekly) Rest Day Act.

Only a month after his appointment the Chief Constable was looking around for a physical training instructor and approval was granted to him to obtain the services of a Mr J. Donovan – known as Ajax – at a cost, not exceeding £20 to give a course of lectures and instruction in physical exercises and Ju Jitsu to members of the Force.

A typewriter was a luxury in those days, never-the-less Major Chester-Master applied for and obtained permission to purchase two machines for use at Police Headquarters, Cheltenham and at the Central Police Station, Gloucester.

During the miners strike in South Wales in 1911, rioting broke out at Tonypandy. The Chief Constable of Glamorgan was not slow in asking for assistance and on the 7th February a contingent of 2 Sergeants and 23 Constables left Gloucestershire under the command of Inspector Dennis. It was not until the 20th April, after order had been restored, that the party returned home.

On the 15th September, 1911 the Home Office issued Circular No. 212556 in which the Secretary of State strongly urged, 'All Police Authorities should now take immediate steps to build up adequate Police Reserves which will enable them to cope with further trouble without having recourse to Military Aid'. It was further stated that, when called out for duty, the Reserve Constable should not be paid less than 5/–d. per day. (25p. today).

By April 1912 Gloucestershire Constabulary had enrolled 218 Reserve Constables, 26 of these being ex-police officers.

Reserve Constables remained as part of the County Police right up until after the Second World War, when they were abolished.

On two occasions during 1911 the Chief Constable was able to send officers and men to the aid of Cardiff City Police, during disturbances caused through labour disputes.

At the Standing Joint Committee meeting, held on the 17th October, 1911, the Chief Constable was granted permission to pay all detective constables an allowance of £8 per annum in lieu of uniform clothing.

Up to now Superintendents and Inspectors had been issued with boots by the Police Authority. At this meeting it was agreed that, in future, both ranks would be granted an allowance, at the rate of one penny a day, in lieu of boots. Boot Allowance has now been abolished.

It was during April 1912 that Gloucester City Corporation applied for the service of six constables as members of the Gloucester City Fire Brigade. Subject to conditions laid down by the Chief Constable the application was approved. For some reason or other this service was discontinued in April 1913.[3]

We now have the first instance of a motor vehicle being used within the Force. Superintendents who wished to do so used a horse and carriage for travelling about their Divisions. The Superintendent at Northleach wished to keep up with the times and applied for permission to use a motor car instead of his horse and carriage. The Chief Constable submitted his application to the Standing Joint Committee on the 15th October, 1912, with a recommendation that it be approved. Needless to say the application was approved together with the cost of the licence, £6.6.0d., in lieu of the licence duty paid for the carriage.

On the occasion of Royal visits to Cardiff and Bristol the County Police were asked to help with men for crowd control duty. On the 26th June, 100 officers and men went to Cardiff and on the 28th June, 1912, 130 officers and men were sent to Bristol.

Major Chester-Master was not satisfied with the 'Conditions of Service' for men joining the Gloucestershire Constabulary. On the 15th October, 1912 he submitted his own 'Conditions of Service' to the Standing Joint Committee – see below – and without hesitation they were accepted and approved.

Conditions of Service of Gloucestershire Constabulary

1. Each member of the Force shall serve and reside wherever he is appointed.
2. He shall devote his whole time to the Police Service and shall not directly or indirectly carry on any trade or calling, nor shall his wife be allowed to keep a shop.
3. He shall remain single until his appointment to the First Class and has received the permission of the Chief Constable to get married.
4. He shall provide himself with a respectable suit of plain clothes, and shall keep himself clean and neat in his personal dress. He shall always appear in uniform when on duty unless otherwise directed.
5. He shall promptly obey all lawful orders which may be received from those placed in authority over him, and conform to all regulations which may be made from time to time concerning the Service.
6. He shall not, directly or indirectly, be interested in any public house or beer house. He is prohibited from borrowing

money from publicans, beer house keepers and other tradesmen or being in any way indebted to them. He shall not reside in a house licensed for the sale of intoxicating liquor.

7. He shall not retain any money or other thing given to him by way of fee, reward or presentation, without permission of the Chief Constable.

8. He shall pay all debts owing by him as the Chief Constable directs.

9. He shall be vaccinated to the satisfaction of the Police Surgeon on joining.

10. He shall carefully abstain from the expressing of any political or religious opinion calculated to give offence.

11. He shall not resign his office or withdraw himself from the duties thereof unless he has given one month's notice of his intention in writing, or has received the written sanction of the Chief Constable.

12. He is liable to instant dismissal for unfitness, negligence, or misconduct, in addition to any punishment to which by law he will be subject. The Chief Constable may also remove him from the service without assigning any reason.

13. On ceasing to hold office he shall forthwith deliver up all the clothing, accoutrements, appointments, and other necessaries which have been supplied to him.
If any of these have, in the opinion of the Chief Constable, been improperly damaged, a deduction from the pay then due to him shall be made, sufficient to make good the damage or supply a new article.

14. He shall not receive a Certificate of Good Conduct in the Police Force under the following circumstances:

(a) If he shall have been Dismissed from the Service.
(b) If he shall have been frequently guilty of misconduct, although of light nature.
(c) If he shall have quitted the Service without having given due notice of his intention to do so.
(d) If he shall have served a less period that one year.

15. He shall be required to obtain a Certificate from the St John Ambulance Association before he is promoted to the First Class.

16. He shall not be promoted to a higher rank until he shall have passed an Examination in such subjects as the Chief Constable may direct.

17. No period during which he is suspended from duty for misconduct or is absent from his Station without leave shall be counted for the purpose of pay or pension.

18. He shall receive pay from the date of enrolment according to the authorised scale in which the minimum rate shall not be less than 21/–d. per week.

19. He will be entitled to a pension in accordance with the provisions of the Police Act, 1890, subject to any regulations made thereunder from time to time by the Standing Joint Committee.

20. A deduction of 2½% will be made from each Constable's pay as a contribution towards the Pension Fund, two thirds of which will be refunded if he leaves the Force after completing three or more years' service without a pension, gratuity or allowance.

21. Members of the Force are excepted from the provisions of the National Insurance Act, 1911, and any constable who leaves the Force and enters insurance will be granted half of the Capital Sum required to enable him to qualify for full benefits under the Act.

22. He will receive his ordinary pay during absence from duty certified by a qualified Medical Practitioner to be due to sickness or injury, and he will not be discharged from the Force upon a Medical Certificate until he has been absent on Sick Leave on Full Pay for at least thirteen weeks.

23. If he is Discharged on a Medical Certificate without a pension, he will be entitled to receive an allowance of 5/–d. a week during disablement, or a gratuity of one month's pay for each years' service, at his option. Provided that if the disablement allowance is paid, and he dies before the weekly payments have reached the amount of the above mentioned gratuity, the balance of such gratuity shall be paid to his representative.

24. He is entitled to such allowances and subject to such deductions as may, from time to time, be approved.

Coronation Medals were presented to 20 officers of the Gloucestershire Constabulary on the 17th August, 1912. Included in the twenty were Superintendent and Deputy Chief Constable William Harrison, Superintendent Young Sainsbury, Superintendent Edward Cooke, Superintendent Thomas Griffin, Superintendent Arther W. Hopkins and Superintendent Edward Selwood.

During October, 1913, the Chief Constable was authorised to obtain four Oilskin coats for constables engaged on Point Duty during wet weather. No doubt the Point Duty referred to was being performed at Gloucester Cross. For many years Gloucester Cross was known as 'The Cross Roads of England'.

The Annual Return of Crime, for 1913, submitted to the members of the Standing Joint Committee made better reading than the average for the previous five years. The figures were:–

	YEAR 1913	PREVIOUS 5 YEAR AVERAGE
Indictable offences known to police	640	682
Persons proceeded against for non-indictable offences	4,793	5,584
Persons proceeded against for drunkenness	561	649

During 1914 the country began to prepare for war. On the 30th June, 1914, the Standing Joint committee agreed that the application, by the Military Manoeuvres Commission, for the service of certain members of the County Police Force, in connection with the forthcoming Army Manoeuvres, be accepted. It was also agreed that members of the Force, so engaged, be permitted to receive the allowances offered by the Military Authorities. These were, Sergeants at 4/–d. a day and Constables at 3/–d. a day, less a deduction of 1/–d. each day to be contributed to the Police Pension Fund. Two Sergeants and twelve Constables were detailed for this duty, the Constables to take bicycles with them.

On the outbreak of the 1914–18 Great War, 22 Police Officers, Army Reservists – were recalled to their Regiments and one Constable was recalled to the navy. To replace the men called up for service, 21 members of the Gloucestershire Constabulary Reserve were called up for temporary duty and added to the Force.

Up to the end of September 1914, between 400 and 500 persons had registered themselves as Special Constables, should the need arise, and further names were being received. Many were prepared to serve in any part of the County and to provide their own means of transport.

Four Constables were selected for secondment, as Drill Instructors, and sent on the 8th September,1914, to the Depot of the Gloucestershire regiment at Horfield Barracks, Bristol. Pay and allowances being recovered from the Military Authorities.

An armed Police Guard was provided at Gloucester docks as a precautionary means to support the Customs and Aliens officers in execution of their duties in connection with foreign shipping. Sharpness Docks and the Severn Railway Bridge were also given Police protection. The Railway Bridge was badly damaged in a tragic accident during 1960 and demolished in 1967.

Twenty-two persons were detained in the County by Police, immediately after War was declared, and handed over to the Military Authorities as Prisoners of War.

At the same time some 2,000 persons applied for permits to keep Homing and Carrier Pigeons in the County.

The standard of education in the Force at this time was not good and on the 20th October, 1914, the Chief Constable was authorised to pay one half of the amount of the fees charged in respect of the attendance of Constables at Educational Courses, arranged by the local Educational Authorities.[4]

Superintendent and Deputy Chief Constable William Harrison entered his 50th year of Police Service with the Gloucestershire Constabulary in September 1914. The following year, on the recommendation of the Secretary of State, he was awarded the King's Police Medal for Distinguished Police Service.

The Standing Joint Committee, meeting at Gloucester Shire Hall on the 5th January, 1915, granted Leave of Absence to the Chief Constable – Major Chester-Master – so as to enable him to offer his services to the Army Council, during the period of the War.

At the same meeting, the Chairman, M.W. Colchester-Wemyss, Esq., offered to carry out, with the Deputy Chief Constable, the administration of the Police force during the Chief Constable's absence. The offer was accepted and it was agreed that the Acting Chief Constable should be reimbursed any expenses falling upon him whilst performing this service. Mr Colchester-Wemyss was to hold this unpaid position for three years, although during this period the Force was effectively run by the Deputy Chief Constable, William Harrison.

On the 24th April, 1915, the Finance Sub-committee of the Standing Joint Committee held a special meeting to consider an application by the Police Force for a War Bonus. After careful deliberation the Sub-committee unanimously decided to recommend the Standing Joint Committee to grant to the Sergeants and Constables a War Bonus of 2/–d. per week, as from the 1st April, 1915, until the day on which Peace was declared or until further orders. The Report was accepted by the Standing Joint Committee.

The first casualty of the Great War, as far as the Gloucestershire constabulary was concerned, was P.C. George W. Howley who joined the Force on the 2nd July, 1914, and being an Army Reservist was recalled to the Colours on the 5th August, 1914. In consequence of a wound received at Ypres, Howley's right leg was amputated. He was discharged from the Army and granted a pension of 25/–d. per week for a year, when his case would be reconsidered. As P.C. Howley was no longer considered to be fit for further Police duty he was also discharged from the Force.[5]

By June, 1915, 98 members of the Force had enlisted into H.M Forces, in addition to the 22 Army Reservists and 1 Naval Reservist, bringing the total number who had gone on service to 121. At a Standing Joint Committee meeting on the 29th June, 1915, the Chairman reported that the new Police recruits, before their departure to the Army had been entertained to lunch at the cost of the members of the Standing Joint Committee, a compliment which appeared to have been much appreciated by the men.

On the recommendation of the Secretary of State the King's Police Medal was awarded to Superintendent Young Sainsbury, Chief Clerk, who entered his fiftieth year of Police Service in April, 1916.

The death, on the 10th June, 1916, of the Ex. Chief Constable Admiral Henry Christian, M.V.O., was reported to the Standing Joint Committee on the 26th June, 1916. The Chairman placed on record great appreciation of the untiring energy, ability and perseverance which Admiral Christian, had devoted to his duties during the 45 years in which he acted as Chief Constable. Admiral Christian left a widow, Mrs Emily Margaret Christian who was granted a Police Widow's Pension by the Police Authoriy.

It was during 1916 that the Chief Constable, Lt. Col. Chester-Master was Mentioned in Despatches for distinguished and gallant conduct on the Field of Battle. Early in 1917, Col. Chester-Master was again Mentioned in Despatched and awarded the D.S.O. for services rendered abroad during the War.[6]

The year 1916 saw Parliament confer upon the Police Authorities, throughout the country, powers to deal with Street Collections. As a result the Finance Sub-Committee prepared certain Regulations and submitted them for preliminary approval of the Secretary of State. With one or two slight alterations the Regulations were approved, by the Secretary of State, placed before the Standing Joint Committee on the 17th October, 1916, and accepted.

On the 17th October, 1916 it was agreed that, for the period of the War, such members of the Police Force as were engaged at the Chief Constable's Office and Superintendent's Offices, as clerks, be granted an increased allowance of 1d. per day as recommended by the Deputy Chief Constable.

Although bicycles were issued to Constables as far back as 1896 it was not until the 8th November, 1916 that the first serious accident was reported and then the Deputy Chief Constable had to announce that P.C. Ernest Albert Cooper had died, at Bradley Court, Mitcheldean, as the result of injuries received in a bicycle accident, whilst on duty. P.C. Cooper was aged 40 years with 17 years service.

April 1916 saw the Standing Joint Committee approve a subsistence of 5d. per meal for prisoners, the meal usually being provided by the wife of the Officer in Charge of the Police Station where the prisoner was held. Due to the very large increase in the cost of food during the war years the Deputy Chief Constable reported that he had received numerous applications for the amount allowed to be increased. On the 8th November, 1916 the Standing Joint Committee resolved that, in future, the subsistence allowance for each meal, provided to prisoners, would be 6d.

Early in 1917 the Home Office called for a further number of men from the Police Forces of the Country, to join the Army. The proportional number asked for from Gloucestershire was 8. There were then 138 officers, of military age, still in the Force; of these only 80 were classed 'A' men. Volunteers for the 8 places were asked for, 41 officers responded and those selected were[7]:–

P.C.Samuel Morgan	Campden District
P.C.Christopher Beddis	Bristol
P.C. Walter C. Saunders	Dursley
P.C. Frederick Bedford	Tewkesbury
P.C. Charles G. Batts	Forest
P.C. Charlie Hamblin	Gloucester
R.C. Jesse R. Sollars	Stroud
P.C. Henry C.S. Mawstone	Cheltenham

All eight officers joined the Army.

By this time three Military Medals had been awarded to Gloucestershire Police Officers serving with H.M. Forces. They were, P.C. Frank Smith, P.C. Frederick Wearing and P.C. Charles Chamberlain.

A special meeting of the Standing Joint Committee was called and met on Saturday 22nd September, 1917, when the Chairman reported with very great and deep regret the death, in action, on the 30th August, 1917, of Colonel R.C. Chester-Master, D.S.O., the Chief Constable of the County. The following tribute was issued to the Police Force, by the Chairman and Acting Chief Constable,

> In him the Country has lost a brave and experienced soldier; the County of Gloucester has lost a valued and high minded official; the Police Force has lost a head who had devoted the best energies of his life, since he became Chief Constable, to their official and private welfare; and a great many people have lost a friend whom they had learnt to honour and love. He has Passed away in the midst of what promised to be a brilliant military career, leaving behind him a memory which will never be forgotten of a great gentleman in the best and noblest sense of the words.

Various Newspapers were used to advertise the post of Chief Constable for Gloucestershire. The advertisement stating –

> The person will be required to reside in the County (wherever the Committee

> may determine), to commence his duties on the 1st January, 1918, or as soon after as possible and to promote the whole of his time to the duties of the office.

– Applications to be received by the 29th October, 1917.

When the Standing Joint Committee met on the 24th November, 1917 it was reported that 37 applications had been received for the post of Chief Constable. Six of these had been invited to attend for interview but a Major Percy Laurie withdrew. He did not wish to leave the Services. From the remaining five candidates two gentlemen had been selected to attend before the Committee, that day, and from whom the recommended one should be selected for the position. The two candidates were, Major J. Becke and Major F.L. Stanley-Clarke.

After discussion the two candidates appeared before the Committee. After their withdrawal voting papers were distributed amongst the 61 members present. The result of the voting was 50 to 11 in favour of Major Stanley-Clarke.

The Chairman thereupon declared Major F.L. Stanley-Clarke to be elected and moved that,

> Subject to the approval of the Secretary of State, Frederick Laurence Stanley-Clarke, late Deputy Chief Constable of Kent, be appointed Chief Constable of the County of Gloucester, upon the terms and conditions stated in the advertisement for candidates, as modified at the last meeting of the Committee.

It was then agreed that Major Stanley-Clarke's appointment should take effect at once but that he be given Leave of Absence until the 1st January, 1918. Thereupon Major Stanley-Clarke, under Section 7 of the County Police Act 1839, appointed Mr William Harrison to continue his duties as Deputy Chief Constable, during his absence. This latter appointment was approved by the Committee.

Thanks were also expressed, at this Meeting, to Mr M.W. Colchester-Wemyss for the valuable service which he had rendered in the performance of the duties of Acting Chief Constable during the last three years.

During 1917 the Deputy Chief Constable reported, to the Standing Joint Committee –

> I have on two or three occasions received letters from Societies interested in the subject to request the Standing Joint Committee to ask the Home Office to sanction the addition to the Force of Women Police. From the experience derived from the service of women patrols who have been from time to time sent to Cheltenham and Gloucester, and from other information I have

obtained, I do not think sufficient necessity exists for making this addition to the Force.

Although precise details cannot be determined there is evidence in records to show that from time to time, prior to 1917, women patrols were sent to Cheltenham and Gloucester, both of which places were at the time receiving a great number of soldier patients in the hospitals. Perhaps, it could be that as and when circumstances required, requests were made to the Auxiliary Police Service which had been formed in London and Bristol under the respective commands of Miss Damer Dawson and Miss Peto, for the services of Women Police to patrol the streets.

The Acting Chief Constable received many requests, during 1917, from various women's organisations and societies advocating for Women Police to be attached to the County Force, as a result of which application was made to the Home Office for permission to appoint a certain number of women as Special Constables. After much consideration, the Home Office decided that women should not do duty as Special Constables.

N.B.

Colonel R.C. Chester-Master, a Gloucestershire man, was born at Stratton, Cirencester on the 29th August, 1870, and served with distinction, in the Armed Forces during the South African Campaign. He married Geraldine Arkwright of Hampton Court, Herefordshire and there were two sons of the marriage.

CHAPTER 5

Major F.L. Stanley-Clarke, O.B.E.
1.1.1918 – 30.4.1937

With previous Constabulary experience behind him Major Stanley-Clarke soon settled down as Chief Constable of Gloucestershire. One of the first things he had to deal with was to look into the question of appointing and employing Women Police and to report back to the Standing Joint Committee. After much correspondence and many meetings approval was given for Women to be enrolled as Police Constables. To give a more detailed account of what transpired, over the following years, a Chapter dealing specifically with Women Police in Gloucestershire will be outlined later.

Despite three years of War, The County Crime figures were relatively good. The figures given to the Press for 1917 were:–

	YEAR 1917	PREVIOUS 5 YEAR AVERAGE
Indictable offences known to Police	562	558
Persons proceeded against for non-idictable offences	3,973	4,461
Persons proceeded against for drunkenness	113	439

On the 9th April, 1918 P.C. Archibald A. Willis, previously stationed at Cheltenham, was congratulated by the Standing Joint Committee on his award of the Distinguished Conduct Medal whilst serving with H.M. Forces.

Constable Robert C. Hayward who joined the Force on 11th May, 1914 and enlisted on the 5th May, 1915, was reported as having been severely wounded. As a result both feet were amputated and he was discharged from the Army on a pension of 27/6d. per week. During 1918 the Chief Constable was able to find suitable work for Hayward at Cheltenham

Central Police Station Enquiry Office; a post he held until his retirement from the Force.

In the days we are writing about the general public were always prepared to come to the assistance of Police – not always with good results. A Mr Daniel Lapper of Cheltenham was kicked on the knee when assisting police to arrest a violent drunk. He was incapacitated for many weeks and in June 1918 received an ex-gratia payment of £75 as compensation.[1]

At about this time it was reported that Military Medals had been awarded to P.C. Albert H. Davis and P.C. Charles S. Gowing, members of the Force fighting with H.M. Forces. Prior to enlistment P.C. Davies was stationed at Stroud and P.C. Gowing at Long Marston.

The Great War was still dragging on and the Home Office called for the release of a further number of men, fit for General Service, from the Police Forces of the Country. Gloucestershire Constabulary provided eleven Officers and the following enlisted on the 20th April, 1918:–

P.C. Charles F. Large	Headquarters	P.C. William Reeves	Dursley
P.C. Wilfred J. Miles	Campden	P.C. Frederick Smith	Tewkesbury
P.C. Oliver Mince	Bristol	P.C. Albert Barnfield	Gloucester
P.C. Albert A. Oakley	Bristol	P.C. Frederick W. Mustoe	Gloucester
P.C. John Attwood	Cirencester	P.C. George H. Wickham	Sodbury
P.C. Alfred W. Perry	Stow-on-the-Wold		

These particular men were selected after due consideration as to physical fitness, age and the smallest number of dependants.

Prior to 1918 the Chief Constable had received approval for many Constables to use their own bicycles on duty and they were paid an allowance of ½d. a mile. This was increased to 1d. a mile by the Standing Joint Committee on the 2nd July, 1918. Later in the year it was agreed that, for the duration of the War, the allowance would be £3 per annum.

H.C. Burder, Esq., J.P. was appointed Chief Special Constable for the County in July 1918 for the purpose of organising and co-ordinating, under the Chief Constable's direction, a Force of Special Constables throughout Gloucestershire. The number of Special Constables enrolled by the end of that year was over 800.

The Standing Joint Committee approved, during 1918, that any

Superintendent, on appointment, who wished to purchase a motor car or other vehicle, for the purpose of his duties, be made an advance (if he so desired) of 75% of the cost, to be repaid without interest in three years.

With the signing of the Armistice, 11th November, 1918 a number of the older serving Police Officers applied to be pensioned. The Chief Constable controlled the retirements so as to maintain the force strength to a reasonable figure. On the 13th April, 1919 the Force lost two of its longest serving officers. Superintendent William Harrison, who had acted as Deputy Chief Constable for nearly seventeen years, and Superintendent Young Sainsbury, who had occupied the post of Chief Clerk for 43½ years. The two officers had completed 53 and 52 years approved service respectively and their periods of serving were longer than those of any of the 4,093 men who had joined the Constabulary since its foundation in 1839. Both officers held the King's Coronation Medal. The Deputy Chief Constable received a pension of £248.13.4d. per annum. Superintendent Sainsbury was granted a pension of £213.6.8d. per annum.

It is not possible to give a date when Gloucestershire Police Officers were first used on what has always been termed 'Requisition Duty' i.e. to keep order at Race Meetings, Fetes, Athletic Meetings, etc. It is recorded that to hire a Police Officer for such a duty a charge was made of 1/–d. per hour or 6/–d. a day. When the charges were fixed the cost of a Constable, to the County, was only about half of what it was in 1918 therefore it was agreed by the Standing Joint Committee, on the 31st December 1918 – 'That the charges for the services of the Police, within the County, be fixed at 2/–d. an hour or 12/–d. per day'.

The charges for Police Officers on Requistion Duty today – March 1985 – now stand at:–

	Hourly Rate	*Daily Rate*
Chief Inspectors	£24.48	£195.85
Inspectors	£21.86	£174.89
Sergeants	£19.35	£154.76
Constables	£15.81	£126.51

With the end of hostilities the Special Constabulary were 'Stood Down' but not before a copy of the following Resolution, passed by the Standing Joint Committee on the 8th April, 1919, was sent to each Special Constable –

That the best thanks of the Standing Joint Committee be accorded to the Special Constables of Gloucestershire for the valuable assistance, during the War, in undertaking the duties of the Regular Police whenever required and thus enabling the policing of the County to be efficiently carried out during the absence, with the Colours, of a large number of Constables.

With the end of hostilities it was time to assess the loss, to the County of those Police Officers who had been called up for service with the Armed Forces. Altogether 15 Police Officers, of the Gloucestershire Constabulary, gave their lives duing the 1914/1918 Great War. They were[2]:–

P.C. William H. Drake, who joined on the 10th march 1910, was recalled to the Colours on the 5th August, 1914 and was reported Missing presumed Killed on the 7th November, 1914. He was 31 years of age and left a widow and one child.

P.C. William T. Kilby, joined 6th April, 1910, was recalled to the Colours on the 5th August, 1914 and was reported Missing presumed Killed on the 17th December, 1914. P.C. Kilby was a single man aged 28 years.

P.C. Arthur B. Carter, joined 25th October, 1906, recalled to the Colours on the 5th August, 1914. P.C. Carter was Killed in Action 12th October, 1915. He was 29 years of age and left a widow and one child.

P.C. Francis T. Nash, joined 1st August, 1912, was recalled to the Colours on the 5th August, 1914. Reported Killed in Action on the 17th October, 1915. P.C Nash was a single man aged 23 years.

P.C. William S. Shute, joined 1st January, 1909, voluntarily enlisted 5th May, 1915 and was reported Killed in Action, in Egypt, on the 23rd April, 1916. P.C. Shute was aged 31 years and left a widow with two children.

P.C. Dick Townsend, joined 1st October, 1914, voluntarily enlisted 5th May, 1915 and was reported Killed in Action, in Egypt, on the 23rd April, 1916. Townsend was a single man aged 22 years.

P.C. George Ingram, joined 1st May, 1912, voluntarily enlisted 7th September, 1914. P.C. Ingram died in Southmead Hospital, Bristol on the 14th October 1916 as a result of wounds received. He was 25 years of age and left a widow.

P.C. George Boulton, joined 23rd July, 1908, voluntarily enlisted on the 5th May, 1915 and died in the Military Hospital, Frensham Hill on the 21st February, 1917. Aged 32 years he left a widow and two children.

P.C. Henry James Surrett, joined 4th December, 1912 and voluntarily enlisted on the 5th May, 1915. A single man aged 26 years, he was reported Killed in Action, in France, on the 5th July, 1917.

P.C. Leonard C.J. Reubinson, joined 19th August, 1914, voluntarily enlisted on the 5th May, 1915 and was Killed in Action, in France, on the 31st July, 1917. P.C. Reubinson, aged 23 years, was a single man.

P.C. Walter C. Saunders, joined 1st May, 1913, enlisted 4th June, 1917, as an Able Seaman of the Royal Naval Division and died of wounds on the 1st January, 1918, aged 27 years. He was a single man.

P.C. Charles G. Batts, joined 1st January, 1913 and enlisted on the 4th June, 1917. Reported Killed in Action on the 21st April, 1918, Batts was 30 years of age and left a widow.

P.C. William A. Curry, joined 16th June, 1902 and voluntarily enlisted on the 17th July, 1915. (P.C. Curry also served in the South African War). On the 9th October, 1918 he died at a Casualty Station in France. He was a single man aged 39 years.

P.C. Charles A. Chamberlain, joined 23rd February, 1909, recalled to the Colours on the 5th August, 1914 and was Killed in Action on the 4th November, 1918. At the time of his death P.C. Chamberlain held the rank of Battery Sergeant Major and had previously been awarded the Military Medal with Bar. He was aged 30 years and left a widow and one child.

Although Deputy Chief Constable William Harrison retired on the 13th April, 1919, the Chief Constable was in no hurry to appoint his replacement. It was not until the 14th October, 1919 that the Chief Constable, Major Stanley-Clarke, reported that he had appointed Superintendent Arther William Hopkins to act as Deputy Chief Constable, in accordance with Section 7 of the County Police Act 1839.

The County Constabulary Headquarters, up to this time had been at No. 1 Crescent Terrace, Cheltenham but with the end of the 1914/18 Great War and with a large intake of recruits expected for training, it was agreed by the Standing Joint Committee to hire, for two years, premises in Lansdown Road, Cheltenham known as 'New Court', at a rental of £320 per annum. The lease expired on the 25th March, 1921 by which time 'Holland House', another large building in Lansdown Road, had been purchased for £300 and after structural alterations, was taken over by Police on the 28th June, 1921. The structural alterations having cost the County £4536. Police Headquarters, to this day, is still at Holland House but the original building suffered severe damage as a result of a high explosive air raid attack in 1940, after which part of the building was evacuated and for some considerable time afterwards the North end was propped and shored up to prevent collapse. In 1965 the original Holland House was demolished to make way for the present building. No. 1 Crescent Terrace, Cheltenham, formerly the Chief Constable's office, was sold on the 18th October, 1921.

It was during this period that the Police Service nationally had been going through difficult times. Police strikes had occurred in some parts of the Country but fortunately they did not effect Gloucestershire.

However, a Committee was formed under Lord Desborough to report upon conditions within the Police Service. The Report was published towards the end of 1919 and gave an increase in Pay and Pensions to those Officers who were serving on the 1st April, 1919. The Report came to be known as the Desborough Report and affected one Constable in Gloucestershire in particular.

P.C. Albert Henry Green was serving in the Gloucestershire Constabulary and asked to be retired on pension on the 31st March, 1919. On that day, for some reason best known to his Sergeant, P.C. Green was put on a 'split' duty and his last tour of duty was from 10.00 p.m. on the 31st March, to 3.00 a.m the next day, 1st April, 1919. In addition to this he was told to hand in his uniform that day, 1st April, after completing duty. Naturally, when the Desborough Report was published, Ex. P.C. Green tried to establish that he was a serving officer on the 1st April, 1919, the date to which the Desborough Award had been made retrospective. The Standing Joint Committee would not agree but Ex. P.C. Green put his case into the hands of a Solicitor and Counsel who took it to the High Court. Judgement of the High Court, on the case stated, determined that Ex. P.C. Green was employed as a Constable on the 1st April, 1919 and was therefore entitled to a Pension on the higher scale amounting to £165.4.8d. a year. His initial Pension being £86.19.3d., quite a substantial increase.[3]

The Desborough Report also recommended that Sergeants and Constables should be allowed to take 12 days Annual Leave – each year – exlusive of 2 Rest Days; Inspectors to be allowed 18 days, exclusive of 2 Rest Days and Superintendents not less that 36 days. The Chief Constable was given authority, by the Standing Joint Committee, to grant Annual Leave in accordance with the Desborough Committee's recommendation.

A fatal accident, involving Police, was reported when P.C. Walter H. Hayward died in the Royal Infirmary, Gloucester, on the 26th July, 1920, as the result of injuries received in an accident when cycling along the Oxenhall road, two miles from Newent, soon after midday on the 24th July. P.C. Hayward was 29 years of age and left a widow. The irony was that he had served throughout the Great War from May 1915.

The Chief Constable was concerned that many acts of gallantry, by members of the Force, were going unrewarded. He ensured that deeds were properly recognised monetarily and, as an outward sign, introduced 'The Chief Constable's Silver Braid', a silver braid medal ribband which was to be worn on the right breast. The Standing Joint Committee insisted that the Committee's consent should be asked for in each case, as it arose. On the 5th April, 1921 P.C. George Stevens was awarded £2 for gallant conduct in stopping a runaway horse. He was the first Officer to be awarded the Silver Braid.

Up to 1920 oil lamps were used by officers on patrol. On the 19th October, 1920, the Chief Constable was authorised to purchase 24 electric pocket lamps, at a cost of 10/–d. each and also extra batteries, when required, so that they could be tested by officers in Cheltenham and Gloucester and, if satisfactory, extend their use. They were satisfactory and a further 300 were purchased in June 1921. Extra batteries were 1/3d. each and bulbs 8d. each.

Button sticks and button brushes were issued to officers during 1921. These were finally discarded after the Second World War.

An interesting recommendation came from the Finance Sub-Committee on the 28th June, 1921, concerning Police Officers in Charge of Police Stations. It was –

> An officer in charge of a Police Station, at which during a portion of the day no member of the Force is required to be on duty, shall be paid 2/6d. per week for providing that some suitable person shall be in attendance to answer telephone and other calls.

The Report and recommendation was adopted by the Standing Joint Committee. Usually the 'Suitable person' was the wife of the Officer in Charge and it was only on rare occasions that husband and wife could go out together. The Second World War was to alter all this.

During the 1921 Strikes five motor cycles, property of the Disposals Board, were borrowed for urgent police business and sending dispatches when no other means were available. These had to be returned but at the the Standing Joint Committee meeting on the 28th June, 1921, it was agreed that the Chief Constable should hire not more than four motor cycles - one with a side-car – at any one time for use of the Police in an emergency. Such hiring to be subject, on all occasions, to the approval of the Chairman of the Committee.

It was also agreed at this meeting that those Inspectors and Sergeants who used their own motor cycles, for the purpose of certain of their duties, should be paid a mileage allowance.

Although having his own troubles with Strikes Major Stanley-Clarke was able, on the 7th May, 1921, to send 1 Inspector, 3 Sergeants and 46 Constables to Glamorgan where assistance was needed. The men returned on the 7th and 9th July that year and cost the Glamorgan Police Authority £3,250.

Today the emphasis is on cutting down expenditure but with a growing population and an expanding Force it is a very difficult task for those persons responsible for the running of the Force, or what is technically known as the, 'Administration Department'.

1921 saw the start of the depression after the First World War and on the 18th October, 1921, the Standing Joint Committee met and discussed a report, submitted by the Finance Sub-Committee, wherein, at the request of the Secretary of State, recommendations were made to effect economies in the administration of the Police Service.

The recommendations were as follows:–

1. That the employment of Women Police be discontinued except that women in the City of Gloucester and Borough of Cheltenham be retained, if the Corporations of those Boroughs so desire and are prepared to pay the whole of the cost which is not borne by the State. (The Corporations agreed to the proposal.)
2. That the strength of each of the Ten Police Divisions be reduced by one man.
3. That the Headquarters Staff be reduced by one man.
4. That the Training staff be reduced by one man.
5. That members of the First Police Reserve, instead of Regular Officers, be employed as Superintendents' chauffeurs and Station Officer at Police Headquarters. These men, in later years, were referred to as Superintendents' Orderlies and were finally dispensed with when Mr J.S.H. Gaskain became Chief Constable in 1959.
6. That a boy be employed as telephone operater at Headquarters and that the present boy become staff shorthand typist.
7. That the numbers of Drills be reduced from two to one per month.
8. That the Annual Refresher Courses of training be discontinued.
9. That Officers who have to leave their Stations on duty for a short period only, be requested to take refreshments with them instead of receiving subsistence allowance.

It was estimated that these economies, when in full operation, would produce a saving of between £9,000 and £10,000. Needless to say it was resolved that the Report be received and adopted.

The Chief Constable reported in April 1922, that he had formed an 'Old Comrades Association' for officers of the Gloucestershire Constabulary. At the commencement there were eight serving officers and 83 Police Pensioners enrolled. All were prepared to pay a small subscription of 6d. per month, the intention being to hold a meeting and luncheon annually.

The Association ran for many years generally meeting the same day as the Annual Police Sports, held at Gloucester and Cheltenham in alternate years . With the termination of the Police Annual Sports, the last was held in July 1965 and the formation of the Gloucestershire Branch of the National Association of Retired Police Officers, the Old

Comrades Association was disbanded. However, the luncheon was continued, and is still held each year, in conjunction with the Annual General Meeting of the National Association of Retired Police Officers – Gloucestershire Branch.

When called to accidents or serious assaults Officers had no means of rendering First Aid, despite being qualified to do so. All this was changed on the 2nd January, 1923, when the Chief Constable, Major Stanley-Clarke, was authorised to purchase 500 Ambulance packages for use of Police, cost not to exceed £47.18.4d. In later years the packages were replaced by small tins which fitted into the hip pocket of the uniform trousers.

Early in 1923 the Chief Constable was authorised to make arrangements for holding Police Promotion Examinations, from time to time, to be conducted by R.R. Dobson, Esq., Headmaster, Cheltenham Grammar School, and that a fee of 4/–d. per head be paid to Mr Dobson for his services.

The first examination was held at the Cheltenham Grammar School on the 11th, 12th and 13th July, 1923. Altogether 15 Sergeants took the examination for promotion to the rank of Inspector and 66 Constables sat the examination for promotion to Sergeant. Of this number, 12 Sergeants and 38 Constables made the grade for a 'Pass'.[4]

On the 10th April, 1923 the Chief Constable reported to the Standing Joint Committee that in view of an outbreak of Small Pox in Cheltenham and the fact that a large number of Police, from all parts of the County, had come to Cheltenham to do duty at the Races on the 6th, 7th and 8th March, he had consulted the Police Surgeon as to the necessity of having Police Officers vaccinated without delay. This resulted in an Order being sent out for all ranks of the Force to be vaccinated unless they had been during the past seven years. The cost was £10.18.6d. and the Chief Constable's action was endorsed by the Standing Joint Committee.

It was after a conference between representatives of Chief Police Officers in Great Britain and consultation with the Automobile Association that, on the 3rd July, 1923, the Chief Constable was able to report that an illustrated pamphlet had been prepared and issued, by the Home Office, giving particulars of Traffic Signals, recommended by the Secretary of State and Secretary of Scotland, for adoption throughout the country. A copy of the pamphlet was issued to every Police Station and Police Officers told to make themselves conversant with it. The Chief Constable was later authorised to purchase 500 copies of the pamphlet, at a cost of £1.11.3d., and issue one to every member of the Force. One could say that this was the original 'Highway Code', as a further 1,000 copies were ordered and put on sale to the public at 1d. each.

Although Major Stanley-Clarke had formed a Mounted Section within the Force he was finding it expensive to hire Saddlery from the Somerset Police, in addition to hiring horses. To save this recurring expense he was given instructions to purchase 19 sets of Saddlery for use of the mounted police and one set of Officers Saddlery.

Superintendent John Evans retired on Pension, from Dursley where he was Divisional Commander, on the 30th November, 1923. His age on that date was 54 years and 355 days and his length of approved service, 30 years and 91 days with 3 years and 214 days as Superintendent. His pension, on retirement, was £283.6.8d. per annum. Superintendent Evans lived to see his 101st Birthday. He died at Shurdington, at the home of his daughter, on the 27th January, 1970, having been able to enjoy his Police Pension for 47 years. Mr Evans had two sons who also completed their approved service for pension in the Gloucestershire Constabulary. William E. Evans (Ted), who was Coroner's Officer in the City of Gloucester for many years and Edmund H. Evans (Hector) who was, in later years, Officer in Charge at Minsterworth and Cheltenham Road, Gloucester. Hector was the only Police Officer, ever, to patrol to the Minsterworth Beat Boundary. It was during the winter of 1940 when the River Servern was frozen over and Hector, with his bicycle, was photographed, on the ice in the centre of the river, i.e. the boundary of his beat.[5]

Police Sergeant John Hobday, stationed at Coleford, was awarded the Silver Braid for Gallantry in rescuing a black and tan sheep dog from an old mine shaft in Oaken Wood Enclosure, Parkend in the Forest of Dean, at 8.30 p.m. on the 28th August, 1923. Sergeant Hobday was also presented with a Medal and Certificate by the Royal Society for the Prevention of Cruelty to Animals. At the scene of the rescue he was assisted by P.C. Joe Ireland of Parkend Police Station and the R.S.P.C.A. Inspector, for the Forest of Dean, Sam Parry of Ruspidge, who was, at that time, licensee of the White Hart Inn, Ruspidge, near Cinderford.

To give an idea of how prices have changed over the years, the following prices refer to Uniform Clothing ordered in January 1924.

	Caps	Helmets	Jackets	Trousers	Knicker-bockers	Riding Breeches
Supts.	17/–d.		48/5d.	23/6d.	25/7d.	26/7d.
Insptrs.	15/6d.		44/10d.	23/6d.	25/7d.	
Sergts.& P.C.'s		12/6d.	39/9d.	22/10d.	25/11d.	

Greatcoats for men 36/5d. each. Sergts. & P.C.'s Black Gloves 2/1d. a pair. White Gloves 1/4½d. a pair.
Hats for Women Police cost 16/–d. Tunic & Skirt 68/2d. light weight Macks. 43/8d.

On the 8th April, 1924 a Sub-Committee of the Standing Joint Committee was formed to look into and consider the question of Motor Trials and Highways. The members selected were:–

Lt. Col. Russell J. Kerr	Mr William Constance
Major F.W.B. Cripps, D.S.O.	Mr Stamford Hutton, M.B.E.
Mr W.A. Rixon	

The Standing Joint Committee did not appear to be too happy with the results of the recent Examinations for Promotion and, on 1st July, 1924, they requested the Chief Constable to issue an order, to members of the Police Force, directing them that they should not enter an Examination for Promotion unless they felt confident of passing such examination

October 1924 saw the Chief Constable purchasing 50 new Army Stretchers, at 5/–d. each, for issue to the most important Police Stations in the County.

Refresher Courses were now becoming fashionable with Police Forces throughout the country and Major Stanley-Clarke, between April 1924 and April 1925, arranged six such courses. 60 officers attended with most satisfactory results. Careful instruction was given in certain special subjects and the chief constable reported that the men had shown considerable interest in the course of instruction and the result justified the expense.

Another act of gallantry came to light early in 1925 and P.C. James G.Gay was awarded £5 for his great efforts in endeavouring to rescue a boy aged 5 years who had fallen down a well at Sheepscombe, Nr. Painswick. P.C. Gay was obliged to make a second descent into the well to recover the body.

It was during the year 1925 that the Chief Constable, Major Stanley-Clarke, was granted permission, by the local police Authority, to apply for the post of Commissioner of Police for the City of London. He was not successful.

On the 30th June, 1925, the Chief Constable revised the 'Conditions of Service for the Gloucestershire Constabulary'. They were very much on the lines of those drawn up by the previous Chief Constable Lt. Col. Chester-Master, except that the latest 'Conditions' gave details of 'Terms of Appointment as Regards Pay and Pensions'. These were as follows:–

> Under the present Regulations the pay for Constables is 70/–d. weekly on appointment rising, in 19 years, to 90/–d. weekly, with further advances of 2/6d. weekly after 17 and 22 years service, subject to continued efficiency and good conduct.

The scale for Sergeants is 100/–d. weekly rising in 5 years to 112/6d. weekly.

Everyone has an opportunity to gain, by good conduct, intelligence and activity, promotion to higher ranks carrying higher rates of pay.

The pay of all ranks is subject to a deduction of 5% under the Police Pensions Act, 1921, and a Regulation by the Secretary of State.

A pension is granted on retirement at any time after completing 25 years approved srvice, the rate of pension ranging from half the rate of pay the man was receiving on his retirement up to the maximum pension at the rate of ⅔ of the pay on retirement, after 30 years service or more.

Chief Superintendent and Deputy Chief Constable Arthur W. Hopkins entered his 47th year of approved service in April 1925. He was recommended, by the Secretary of State, for the King's Police Medal for Distinguished Service and this honour was conferred upon him by His Majesty King George V, in 1926. He received the congratulations of the Standing Joint Committee on his award.

The 'General Strike' of 1926 affected everyone. It commenced at Midnight on the 3rd May – a Monday – and ended on Wednesday May 12th. During that period the Chief Constable found it necessary to employ 152 of the First Police Reserve and 130 Foot Special Constables. The Police owed a great deal of gratitude to these officers.

Although the 'General Strike' came to an end on the 12th May, 1926 the Miners decided to stay out on strike and the Chief Constable found it necessary to move additional Police Officers into the Forest of Dean where 75% of the working population were on strike. The extra men, of all ranks, who were sent to the Forest amounted to 175 including mounted men and motor cyclists. These men, and those already stationed in that Division, carried out their duties most commendably.

There was very little trouble there and when the Miners Strike did eventually fold up the Chief Constable, Major Stanley-Clarke, upon the recommendation of the Secretary of State, was awarded the O.B.E. Superintendent John Shellswell, who was in charge of the Forest Division during that time, received the M.B.E. and Inspector Alan Bent, the Inspector in charge at Coleford the B.E.M.

At this time, road traffic and the resultant spate of accidents that came with it, was beginning to rear its ugly head and the Chief Constable was allowed to purchase 20 First Aid Haversacks at a cost of £45. These were sent to each Divisional Headquarters and to Main Road Stations for use in Road Accidents.

The First Aid Haversacks were a real necessity in those days. It was not until after the Second World War that we saw the build up of the County Ambulance Service as we see it today. For instance up to 1938, when a serious road accident occurred in the Stow-on-the-Wold district, the nearest ambulance was at Chipping Norton, in Oxfordshire, 8 miles away, and this was manned by a volunteer crew.

Large measuring tapes were also issued to each Police Station to enable accurate measurements to be taken at all serious accidents.

During the early days of traffic control Police Officers on Point Duty were supplied with White Waterproof Coats for wet weather and white linen coats during the summer months. No doubt with an eye on the purse strings someone thought up the idea of using 'White Sleeves'. Thus we find that, during October 1927, the Chief Constable was authorised to purchase a sufficient number of 'White Sleeves' for officers engaged on Point Duty. Sleeves were used in the City of Gloucester right up until the Second World War, when they appeared to disappear; no doubt due to shortages of material plus economy cuts.

Serious flooding was reported, from time to time, at Bream Police Station in the Forest of Dean and in 1927 it was agreed to spend £45 on drainage work around the Station with a view to stopping the flooding and, if possible, eliminate dampness from the living quarters and kitchen.

Having been appointed to a Special Confidential Home Officc Committee, Major Stanley-Clarke found that, every other two to three weeks, he had to travel to London. With this in mind he applied to the Standing Joint Committee for an increase in his Travelling Allowance. The application was approved and he was granted an allowance of £3 for each visit to London. However, he had to make a Quarterly Return, to the Committee, for such visits and they, in turn, asked the Home Office to defray the whole of the expenses incurred. After many months, and much correspondence, the Home Office agreed to pay all expenses so it was not necessary for the Chief Constable to claim against the County.

The Chief Constable's Report to the Standing Joint Committee for the first Quarter of 1928 gave details, for the very first time, of Coroner's Inquests within the County. The Report covered the year 1927 when 447 deaths were notified to H.M. Coroner. In 289 cases Inquests were held with the following result:–

Accidental Death 95; Death from Natural Causes 108; Suicide 44; Murder 1; and other verdicts 41.

Police Officers authorised to use their motor cars on duty found their Allowances changed again in 1928. As from the 1st August, that year, when using a motor car they were paid 4d. per mile for the first 5,000 miles and for every mile over 5,000 it was 3d. per mile. For all vehicles, except motor cars and ordinary cycles, they were paid 2d. per mile. For ordinary cycles it was 1d. per mile.

The 1st May, 1928, saw the death of Inspector Arthur Fluck, at

Cheltenham Central Police Station, after only a few days illness. Inspector Fluck was in his 53rd year and had completed 29 years service. He left a widow and one son.

Police Constable Francis G. Newman who was involved in an accident when riding his motor cycle, off duty, sustained such serious injury to his right leg that it had to be amputated. He was certified unfit for further Police Service and was discharged with a gratuity of £67.12.0d., being 1/12th of his annual pay for each years' service. He was 25 years of age, at the time, with 4 years service in the Force.

The Chairman of the Standing Joint Committee reported, on the 16th October, 1928, that the Grand Priory in the British Realm of the Venerable Order of St. John of Jerusalem had selected Mr A.W. Hopkins, the Deputy Chief Constable of Gloucestershire, for admission as an Officer of the Order in recognition of the continued interest he had taken in Ambulance work for nearly 40 years. The appropriate award and decoration was presented to the Deputy Chief Constable, by the Chairman, that day.

Although the West Gloucestershire Power Station became operational, at Lydney, in 1923 it took a long time for electricity to reach the Coleford area. It was not until the latter part of 1928 that permission was given for electric lighting to be installed at Coleford Police Station, at a cost of £45.

By 1928 traffic on the roads was on the increase with the result that more accidents were being reported to Police. When persons, who were involved or interested in road traffic accidents, desired to obtain an 'Abstract of the Police Report' they were supplied with details at a charge of 2/6d. To the Gloucestershire Police this meant an income of approximately £100 per annum being received from this source. Home Office said that the charge was inadequate and instructed that, in future, a charge of 5/–d. should be made. This charge, over the years, has been gradually increased and an 'Abstract of the Police Report' today is now supplied at a cost of £24 for a full report or £9 for an abridged version.

Ex. Superintendent Young Sainsbury who retired on pension on the 13th April, 1919, after 52 years approved service, died at Prestbury on the 3rd November, 1928. He left a widow who was granted a Police Widow's pension of £50 a year from the 1st December, 1928. Ex. Superintendent Sainsbury is buried in Cheltenham Cemetery, close to the Chapel, and brief details of his service in the Gloucestershire Constabulary can be seen on his gravestone.

Gloucestershire, like other police areas, has had its share of major incidents, one of which happened in the early hours of the 13th October, 1928, when a railway accident occurred on the old L.M. & S. Railway line at Charfield, between Bristol and Berkeley.

Constable Frederick J.Nash, the Officer in Charge of Charfield Police Station, was in bed when he was awakened at 5.40 a.m. on the 13th October, 1928 and informed that there had been a terrible railway accident and he at once went down stairs and found several injured men and women at the front door of the Police Station. He assisted them in, telephoned Wotton-under-Edge for two doctors and then told the Superintendent of his Division and the Sergeant of his Section and also to Chipping Sodbury. He then rushed to the scene of the disaster and found that the flames, from the burning wreckage, were about 20 feet above the side of the Charfield Railway Bridge and he had to cover his face with his tunic to enable him to get across. He arrived at the scene of the accident at 6.10 a.m. and saw several men cutting through the bottom of a railway truck which was lying on its side. He enquired if there was anyone in the wreckage and was told that there was a woman trapped. He at once crawled on his hands and knees for 5 or 6 yards, through the wreckage, and then for 6 or 7 yards more on his stomach but, on reaching the woman, found she was dead. Having no assistance at hand it was impossible for him to get the body out as the heat was unbearable and the fire was spreading so quickly and owing to explosions taking place, at intervals, the wreckage was moving. He finally had to scramble over the top of a goods truck to get clear himself.[6]

Subsequent investigation into the accident left a query which remains unanswered to this day; when the fatal casualties were accounted for the Police remained in possession of a spare pair of shoes and speculation remains that there was an additional unidentified fatality.

The Chief Constable received letters from the Postmaster General, the General Superintendent of the L.M.& S. Railway, the Coroner and two civilians, calling his attention to the valuable assistance rendered by the Police and two of the letters particularly directed to the gallantry shown by P.C. Nash.

At the Standing Joint Committee Meeting held at Gloucester Shire Hall, on the 9th April, 1929, P.C. Nash was awarded the Silver Braid and a reward of £5, from the Police Authority. In addition he received awards from the Order of St. John of Jerusalem and the Society for the Protection of Life and Fire. The Chairman stating that P.C. Nash 'Was credit to himself and to the Police Force to which he belonged'. When he retired from the Force Fred Nash went to live at Sneedhams Green, Upton St. Leonards, near Gloucester and was Steward at the Birchall Memorial Institute for many years. He died on the 20th August 1967, aged 80 years and left a widow and grown up daughter.

On the 1st January, 1929 there was a re-arrangement of Divisions within the County and the Chipping Sodbury Division was merged

with the Dursley and Staple Hill Divisions. At that time the authorised establishment was:–
Chief Constable 1, Chief Superintendents 2, Superintendents 8, Inspectors 12, Sergeants 58, Constables 353. Total 434.

The Roneo duplicator at Cheltenham Central Police Station was getting the worse for wear and in the early part of 1929 the Chief Constable was authorised to replace the old machine with a new one at a cost not exceeding £25.10.0d. The actual cost of the new machine was £35.10.0d but Roneo, out for business, offered an allowance of £10 on the worn out machine.

On the 2nd July 1929, the Chief Constable was able to report that the existing water pump in the yard at Coleford Police Station, which had been badly damaged by frost, had been replaced by a new one and this had been fixed near the Single Mens' Quarters.

A Promotion Examination was held at Cheltenham Grammar School on the 16th and 17th May, 1927, when 5 Sergeants sat for examination and 2 for re-examination. Two of the former and both of the latter passed. 27 constables sat for examination and 38 for re-examination. Of the former 9 and of the latter 14 were successful. The fee charged by Mr Dobson, Headmaster of the Grammar School, was again 4/-d. per man, examination and re-examination. In submitting his account Mr Dobson remarked,

> The candidates seem to have prepared for the examination with much care. There is very great improvement since the first examination five years ago. On the whole the candidates made a very favourable impression.

There was also a 'definite improvement' in the replies to the questions on the Police Subjects.

Police Sergeant Edwin C. Gasside of Northleach Police Station, was killed in a motoring accident on the 21st December, 1929, as a result of his motor car running into a bank and turning over – no other vehicle was involved. He was 51 years of age, with 29 years service, 7 years as a Sergeant. He left a widow and grown up daughter.

On the 31st December, 1929 the Chief Constable asked the Police Authority for a Police Motor Van to be provided in some districts of the County, notably Cheltenham, Gloucester and Staple Hill, for the conveyance and escort of prisoners and for the rapid concentration of Police and other purposes. His request was turned down. At the same meeting he asked that Police Telephone Boxes be provided in and on the outskirts of Gloucester and Cheltenham and possibly other Urban areas to maintain rapid communication with Divisional Headquarters, at an estimated cost for Gloucester and Cheltenham of £134 and £230 respectively. This request too was turned down.

Nevertheless the Chief Constable was authorised to purchase Stop Watches, for the use of for Police Motor Cycle Patrol Officers, at a cost not exceeding 35/–d. each.

Road traffic by this time was becoming a problem, not only to the County, but to the country as a whole. The car had arrived thus, in accordance with a Home Office memorandum, the Finance Sub-Committee reported and recommended, to the Standing Joint Committee, on the 14th April, 1931, that the following motor vehicles should be purchased with a view to setting up a Motor Patrol Department.

Five Ford Saloon Cars at £180 each ..	£900	
Six B.S.A. Motor-Cycle Combinations at £92 each	£552	
Equipment	£48	Total: £1,500

The Home Office Memorandum stated that a grant would be made from the Road Fund, in respect of depreciation and running costs, at the rate of £150 per annum for each motor car and £80 per annum for each motor cycle combination.

On the 30th June, 1931, the Sub-Committee reported back to the Standing Joint Committee that they had inspected certain cars and had decided to purchase the following viz:-

1 Morris Oxford Tourer at a cost of ....£210.0.0.d.

1 Morris Oxford saloon, with sliding roof ....£239.8.0d.

2 Ford Tourers at a cost of £179 each.......................£358.0.0d.

1 Ford Tudor Saloon at a cost of ....£174.0.0d.

Plus the six B.S.A. motor cycle combinations.

The Chief Constable to report in twelve months time as to the running of the cars and motor cycles.

Ambulance work has always been taken seriously within the Force and during 1930 an Ambulance Team, representing Gloucestershire Constabulary, was successful in defeating Plymouth City Police in the No. 7 District Eliminating Contest and therefore took part in the St. John Ambulance Competition, in London, later that year. Nine teams from all over England and Wales competed and Gloucestershire was placed sixth, the two teams immediately above only obtaining 1 mark and ½ mark respectively, more than Gloucestershire.

The Standing Joint Committee were in a generous mood during 1931 as on the 30th June that year they authorised the Chief Constable to purchase a motor mower for use on the lawns at Police Headquarters, at an approximate cost of £40. He was also given instructions to purchase further Ambulance Haversacks for use of the several Motor Police Patrols, and Stop Watches for each additional Motor Police Patrol.

With regret, the Chief Constable had to report to the Police Authority on the 30th June, 1931, that Chief Superintendent and Deputy Chief Constable Arthur W. Hopkins, who had been his Deputy at Gloucester for the past 12 years, had applied for permission to retire on pension on the 15th August, 1931. On that date his age would be 72 years and 51 days, length of approved service 52 years and 130 days with length of service, as a Superintendent, 39 years and 288 days. Mr Hopkins held the rank of Superintendent for a longer period than any other member of the Gloucestershire Constabulary and had been awarded the Kings Police and Coronation Medals. His pension, which commenced on the 16th August, 1931, amounted to £353.6.8d. per annum.

Chief Superintendent Robert Hy. Hopkins was appointed to act as Deputy Chief Constable, in place of Chief Superintendent Arthur W. Hopkins, as from the 16th August, 1931. These two officers were not related.

Superintendent Percy Jones, Commander of the Dursley Division for 7½ years also applied for permission to retire on pension on the 30th June, 1931. He met with an accident in February, 1931, when he was knocked down by a motor cyclist and received such serious injuries to his leg that he was not able to perform his police duties efficiently. He retired on a pension of £293.6.8d. per annum.

On the 30th June, 1931, the Chief Constable reported the appointment of Doctor Arther Barrett Cardew, M.C., M.B., of Cheltenham, as Police Surgeon in place of Doctor Ronald B. Macfie, F.R.C.S. The Chief Constable placed on record his appreciation of all that Dr. Macfie had done for the Police and their Ambulance work and expressed his regret that he had been compelled, by ill-health, to retire from practice in Cheltenham.

As the result of a report submitted by W.P.C. Rosa Rouse, who complained about Women Police having to search dirty and verminous female prisoners, the Chief Constable applied to the Police Authority, on the 28th June, 1932, for permission to purchase Rubber Gloves. He was authorised to buy three dozen pairs of Rubber Gloves at a cost not exceeding 4/–d. per pair and also to replace them from time to time. The gloves were eventually issued with instructions to be used when searching prisoners who were in a very dirty or diseased condition or when handling dead bodies.

It was thought necessary, at about this time, to improve the Criminal Investigation Department at Police Headquarters to a standard befitting of the Force and this was done by the introduction of a Photographic Department, but even in these times economy was a byword and to complete his plans the Chief Constable had to cancel lectures on Scientific Criminal Intelligence Investigation, which would have cost considerably more. However, at their meeting on the 28th June, 1932, the Police Authority approved expenditure, by the Chief Constable, of sums not exceeding £75 and £7.10.0d., in the purchase of Photographic Material and books respectively, for use of Police at Headquarters engaged in Criminal Investigation. At a later meeting the Chief Constable was given approval to purchase a Cooke Avine Lens and a Kodak Special Finger Print Camera, in addition to the other items, at a cost of a further £36.12.0d.

The Chief Constable was also allowed to purchase a second hand car at a cost of approximately £40 for use of the CI.D. at Staple Hill.

Approval was also given for the Chief Constable to purchase a B.S.A. motor three wheeler for Police Motor Patrol duties, to replace one of the first batch of motor cyle combinations which was now in an exceedingly bad condition and not worth repairing.

The Police Housing situation in Gloucestershire, in the early thirties, was far from good and the 2nd January, 1934, it was agreed to set up a sub-committee to consider the whole question of the housing of police.

The sub-committee, comprising members of the Standing Joint Committee were:-

Major Sir Frederick W.B. Cripps, D.S.O.
Lt. Col. Russell J. Kerr
Brig. General R.C.A. McCalmont, D.S.O.
Stamford Hutton, Esq., O.B.E
W.S. Rudge, Esq.,

together with representatives of each of the Boroughs of Gloucester and Cheltenham.

When females were arrested and Women Police were not available it was usual for the female prisoner to be searched by a 'Matron' who could have been the wife of a serving police officer or, as was the case in Gloucester for many years, a lady cleaner 'called out' for the occasion. Due to a direction from H.M. Inspector of Constabulary, concerning the charges for the searching of female prisoners, the following fees were recommended by a sub-committee and adopted by the Standing Joint Committee, in January 1934:-

(i) For search made between the hours of 8.00 a.m. and 10.00 p.m. .... 1/–d.
(ii) For search made between the hours of 10.00 p.m. and 8.00 a.m ..... 2/–d.
Searches to be made at Divisional Headquarters only, whither females arrested shall be taken forthwith.

On the 2nd January, 1932, the Chief Constable asked for authority to install electric light at the following police stations, viz:-

(a) Hopewell Street, Gloucester, in lieu of gas – estimated cost £11
(b) Parkend (Forest Div.), in lieu of oil lamps – estimated cost £7

Needless to say, the Chief Constable's request was approved.

The number of deaths reported to H.M. Coroners, in Gloucestershire, for the year 1933 was 513 and in 277 cases inquests were held, with the following results:-

Accidental death	134
Death from Natural Causes	86
Suicide	42
Manslaughter	1
Other verdict	14

P.C. Edwin T.Handley, Painswick was awarded the Silver Braid and highly Commeded by the Chief Constable, during 1934, for bravery. He was also rewarded with the sum of £5 from the Police Authority. At 8.00 a.m. on the 22nd January, 1934, two men started to clean out an old well at Sheepscombe. When working at the bottom of the well part of the stone lining of the wall collapsed on Frank Wallace, partly burying him and killing him instantly. His workmate, Richard Cox, went down the well but could not release Wallace. P.C. Handley arrived on the scene at about 10.50 a.m. and immediately went down the well. After working for an hour and a quarter the body was recovered and, with the aid of other police officers, brought to the surface. Whilst at the bottom of the well P.C. Handley ran a great risk of being killed or injured by a further fall of the stone lining. The well, about 100 years old, was 65 feet deep and 3 feet in diameter. The Royal Humane Society awarded the Bronze Medal to Richard Cox for the part he played in trying to release Wallace and P.C. Handley received a Testimonial on Vellum.[7]

By October, 1933, there were 125 police officers in receipt of a cycle allowance for using their own bicycles on duty. As a result the Chief Constable was authorised to purchase 25 additional bicycles, each year, until enough machines had been provided to do away entirely with the annual allowance of £3.

By July, 1934, the total number of county bicycles had risen to 105 and the Chief Constable hoped to increase the total to 171.

Although the Police Federation had been in existence for a number of years it was not until 1934 that we find the Joint Branch Board of the Gloucestershire Branch of the Police Federation speaking up on behalf of its members. On the 3rd July, 1934, the Board asked the Chief Constable for a general review of the Fuel and Light Allowances at County Police Stations. The Chief Constable promised to look carefully into the matter and bring foward his recommendations to the Standing Joint Committee, at their October meeting.

Dr. Arthur Barrett Cardew, M.C., M.B., due to pressure of work, had to resign his duties as Police Surgeon in 1934 and the Chief Constable arranged for Dr. John Howell, Jun., M.D., to take over and to undertake such work as was necessary from time to time.

At their meeting on the 9th October, 1934, the Standing Joint Committee instructed the Chief Constable to allow members of the Force to affix 'Notices' at authorised Public Notice boards, when requested by the County Council, for matters connected with the Police mainly dealing with Elections and Diseases of Animals. It was agreed that the officers concerned would be paid the following allowance, to include the cost of paste:-

For each bill posted within one mile of a Police Station, one penny, beyond that distance two pence. Paste tin and brushes to be supplied by the Police Authority. Throughout the Force this was eventually referred to as (Bill Posting).

On the 9th April, 1935, the Standing Joint Committee considered a report by the Chief Constable in which he reported that an inspection had been made of Police Stations in which single-men were quartered and in which he recommended that the following articles of furniture be provided for the use of single-men:-

1 Chest of Drawers, 1 Wardrobe, 1 Improved Bedstead (3 feet wide), 1 Mattress, 2 Pillow Cases, 1 Chair, and in Stations where there were no convenient washing facilities, a Washstand, jug, basin and bowl or pail.

The Chief Constable obtained quotations for supplying the above articles, to meet requirements, and these amounted to £469.13.10d. A sub-committee recommended that the quotation be accepted. Prior to this single-men, in quarters at Police Stations, lived under very sparse conditions. In addition they had to find their own food with very few facilities for preparation and cooking.

Rent Allowance, for serving officers, came under discussion during 1935 and it was agreed that, as from the 6th April that year, every member of the Police Force who was not provided with a house or quarters be granted a 'Maximum Limit Allowance' (non-pensionable), equal to the actual amount paid by him in rent, rates and taxes, subject to a maximum limit of 16/d. per week in every case. This meant an increase, to the Police Authority, in Rent Allowance of £432.8.0d. per annum.

Telephones had been in use throughout the Force for a number of years but the Chief Constable found that many of these instruments were attached to the wall in the Police Station Office or Guardroom. These were both inconvenient and unsatisfactory when it came to writing down the many informations which were then being circulated. On the 9th April, 1935, Major Stanley Clarke asked for 33 wall telephones to be removed and table instruments substituted at a cost of 7/6d. each. His request was approved by the Standing Joint Committee.

On the 2nd July, 1935 approval was given for electric light to be installed in the Training Hut, cubicles and Sergeants cottage at Holland House (Police H.Q.) with a recommendation that the County Architect be authorised to obtain tenders, and accept the lowest, for carrying out the work at a cost not exceeding £40.

At Gloucester Assizes, 1935 P.C. Percy J. Wilkes was sentenced to 12 months imprisonment for shop-breaking and stealing various wireless accessories. He was dismissed the Force. His wife had just given birth to her first child and on the recommendation of the Chief Constable, the Standing Joint Committee on the 2nd July, 1935 resolved that the sum of £35.1.5d., being the rateable deductions made from the pay of Ex. P.C. Percy J. Wilkes, during his service with the Force, be paid to his wife at the rate of £3 a month.

On the 31st May, 1935, Lt. Col. Sir Russell James Kerr, Chairman of the Standing Joint Committee, presented Silver Jubilee Medals to 28 members of the Force and 2 Special Constables, at a parade held at Police Headquarters, Lansdown Road, Cheltenham.

When the celebrations for the King and Queen's Silver Jubilee came along the Chief Constable was compelled to borrow a Union Jack from Gloucester City Authorities, to enable the Force to show its loyalty. It was not possible to borrow a flag pole so he purchased one at a cost 3/–d. As a result Major Stanley-Clarke asked the Standing Joint Committee for permission to buy a Union Jack for use at Police Headquarters on future occasions. "The cost of the flag would be 32/–d. and it would last for many years". Approval to purchase the flag was given on the 2nd July, 1935.

As part of the Silver Jubilee celebrations H.M. King George V held a parade and inspection of contingents from all the Police Forces in Great Britain, in London (Hyde Park) on the 20th July, 1935. Gloucestershire Police were represented and on the 15th October, 1935, the Chairman of the Standing Joint Committee read a letter from the Secretary of State conveying the congratulations of H.M. the King upon the smartness and bearing of the Police inspected at Hyde Park, and expressing His Majesty's appreciation of the manner in which the Police had carried out their responsibilities during the Silver Jubilee celebrations.

At the Police Authority meeting held at Gloucester on the 15th October, 1935, the Chairman reported, 'with great regret', that Chief Superintendent and Deputy Chief Constable Robert Hy. Hopkins, who had been in command of the Gloucester Division for the past four years, had applied for permission to retire on pension on the 30th November, 1935. At that time his age would be 62 years and 312 days. Length of approved service was 44 years and 112 days and his pension, starting on the 1st December, 1935, would be £353.6.8d. per annum.

The Chief Constable also reported that on the retirement of Chief Superintendent and Deputy Chief Constable Robert Hy. Hopkins, he proposed to appoint Chief Superintendent Joseph William Parry Goulder to act as Deputy Chief Constable, under Section 7 of the County Police Act 1839.

Up to this period, Police Subjects for Promotion Examinations were set and checked by the Chief Constable and some of his senior officers. Owing to the fact that he and his men had not the necessary amount of time at their disposal to do this work, it was agreed by the Police Authority, on the 15th October, 1935, for the Chief Constable to arrange for these papers to be set and marked by the Birmingham Police Instructor, for a fee of 3/–d. per man or 1/–d. per paper if the number exceeded 3.

Ex. Deputy Chief Constable William Harrison, who was pensioned on the 13th April, 1919 after 53 years service, died at 40, Conduit Street, Gloucester on the 3rd February, 1936, aged 90 years. He left three grown up daughters. After his retirement from the Force he served for many years on Gloucester City Council.[8]

By 1936 the threat of the Second World War was looming and the Police were becoming increasingly involved in preparation. However, the authorities seemed to be preoccupied with ideas of Gas Attacks and on the 7th April, 1936, Major Stanley-Clarke reported that an Anti-Gas School had been established, within the county, at

Eastwood Park, Falfield, for the purpose of giving instruction, to members of public bodies, in the steps to be taken in the event of gas attacks should war break out. He further reported that, on the 15th April, 1936, the first of the Police Classes for training Police Instructors would commence and last for about 14 days. Police Sergeant Midwinter of Tetbury was selected to attend the class which commenced on the 14th May, 1936 and was awarded a First Class Instructors Certificate. As a result P.S. Midwinter was seconded from ordinary duty and temporarily attached to Police Headquarters so that he could instruct all members of the Force accordingly. Protective clothing had been received and gas masks were expected and the necessary arrangements for training members of the Force were put in hand.

The Home Secretary's influence on Police Forces was very apparent and on the 30th June 1936, the Chairman laid before the Standing Joint Committee a letter from the Secretary of State stating that, having given full consideration to all the representations made to him on the subject, he adhered to the view that in the interest of efficient administration the Deputy Chief Constable should, for the future, be stationed at Headquarters, Cheltenham and that the officer put in charge of the Gloucester Division should, in future, hold the rank of Chief Superintendent.

On the 5th January, 1937 the Chairman of the Standing Joint Committee read a letter from Major F.L. Stanley-Clarke, O.B.E., asking, on medical grounds, to be allowed to retire from the post of Chief Constable at the end of April 1937, or as soon thereafter as his successor could take over the duties.

The Chairman stated that the Chief Constable's resignation had been considered by the Finance Sub-Committee who had drafted an advertisement for his successor. The advertisement stated that the post was subject to the apporoval of the Secretary of State and unless the applicant had previous experience he must possess some exceptional qualifications or experience specially fitting him for the post. Salary was £850 per annum rising by increments of £25 to £1,100 per annum to cover use of a motor car and travelling and subsistence expenses either within or without the County, in addition an Annual Allowance for Rent and Rates would be allowed. A chauffeur would be provided. The advertisement was placed in the Army and Navy Gazette; The Times, The Morning Post; The Muicipal Journal; Justice of the Peace; and the Local Government Chronicle.

As a result of the advertisements being published a Special Meeting of the Standing Joint Committee was called for the 5th March, 1937, when the Sub-Committee reported that 98 applications had been received for the appointment of a successor to Major F.L. Stanley-Clarke, O.B.E. The applications had been considered and the Committee invited seven candidates to appear befor them. After interviewing such candidates the Sub-Committee asked the following to appear before the Standing Joint Committee that day, namely:-

Col, W.F. Henn, Commandant of the Alexandria City Police.
Capt P.C. Perfect, Det. Constable, C.I.D., Edinburgh City Police
Mr A.E. Senior, Assistant Commissioner, Metropolitan Police College, Hendon.

After the interviews had been carried out it was resolved that, subject to the approval of the Secretary of State, Colonel W.F. Henn be appointed.

In accordance with a letter from the Home Office, it was agreed by the Police Authority, 'That one day's leave with pay, in addition to the ordinary leave and weekly Rest Days, be granted to members of the County Police Force in connection with the Coronation of their Majesties The King and Queen.'

At this same meeting, on the 6th April, 1937, Major F.L. Stanley-Clarke asked for permission to retire on the 6th April, 1937 and allow his pension of £403.6.8d. per annum to commence on the 7th April, 1937. In the event, Colonel W.F. Henn was unable to take up his post as Chief Constable until 1st May, 1937 and Major F.L. Stanley Clarke continued serving, as Chief Constable, until the 30th April, 1937.

The Chairman of the Standing Joint Committee referred to the approaching retirement of major F.L. Stanley-Clarke, O.B.E., from the office of Chief Constable, and spoke with appreciation of the valuable services which he had rendered to the County during his long service in that post.

An Air Raid Precautions Organisation Scheme was adopted by the Standing Joint Committee at this meeting, whereby the County, for the purposes of the scheme, was divided into seven areas. It was also agreed that each Area Authority would, as soon as may be and from time to time thereafter, transmit to the Central Authority, for submission to the Home Office, a list of persons willing to undertake training as Instructors for any service in their area, specifying the type of training to be undertaken.

Motor Patrol outside Holland House, Cheltenham H.Q. 1932.

Supt. SHELLSWELL with Inspectors & Sergeants, Forest of Dean Division.

Recruits Class 1935.

Chipping Campden Police. 1937

Headquarters staff. 1932–33

H.M.I. Inspection, Cheltenham 1938.

'B' Division 1942.

Motor Patrol 1946–47.

Federation members with Colonal HENN, Chief Constable.

CHAPTER 6

Colonel W.F. Henn. C.B.E., M.V.O., K.P.M.
1.5.1937 – 8.4.1959

Colonel Henn took up post on the 1st May, 1937. At a meeting of the Police Authority on the 29th June, 1937, he submitted his first Report. At this meeting Police Constable Walter J. Lafford was awarded his Silver Braid and an honorarium of £5 in recognition of his gallantry in saving Mrs Fitzgerald, the District Nurse, whose house was on fire at Wickwar on the 31st October, 1936.

On the 20th May, 1937, the Chairman of the Police Authority presented Coronation Medals to 22 members of the Force at a Parade held at Police Headquarters, Lansdown Road, Cheltenham.[1]

Another step forward was made on the 19th October, 1937 when approval was given for electric lighting to be installed at the following Police Stations, namely:– Bibury, Charlton Kings, Gloucester (Bristol Road), Newent and Ruardean.

The new Chief Constable was soon making changes within the Force and during 1937 the Cirencester Division was enlarged by adding to it the whole of the Chipping Campden Sub-Division, the Birdlip and Bisley Stations from Stroud Division and Tetbury Station from Dursley Division. The enlarged Cirencester Division being under the command of Superintendent John H. Jotcham.

On the 1st September, 1937, Dursley Division ceased to exist and its Stations were transferred to the Stroud and Bristol (Staple Hill) Divisions, as shown below:–

To Bristol Division – Alveston, Charfield, Didmarton, Falfield, Hawkesbury, North Nibley, Olveston, Thornbury, Wickwar and Wotton-under-Edge.

To Stroud Division – Berkeley, Cam, Cambridge, Dursley, Kingscote, Newport, Uley and Sharpness.

Superintendent William E. Wakefield was in charge of the enlarged

Bristol (Staple Hill) Division and Superintendent Frederick J. Williams was transferred from Dursley to take command of the enlarged Stroud Division.

Superintendent John Shellswell, M.B.E., retired on pension on the 20th December, 1937. His age was 64 years and 362 days; length of approved service 45 years and 353 days; he held the rank of Superintendent for 16 years and 295 days during the whole of which period he had been in command of the Forest of Dean Division.

On the 27th August, 1938, Ex. Chief Superintendent and Deputy Chief Constable Arthur Wm. Hopkins died, at Gloucester Royal Infirmary, after an operation. He had retired on the 15th August, 1931, after 52 years service. Mr Hopkins was living at Hucclecote, Gloucester, at the time of his death and was buried in Hucclecote Churchyard after a Service conducted by the Rev. David Evans.[2]

The Chief Constable, Col. Henn, thought it desirable for each of the large Police Patrol Cars to be fitted with a sign, at the back, bearing the word 'Police' which could be illuminated when necessary. This to be used when stopping vehicles at night. On the 3rd January, 1939, he was authorised to purchase 9 of these signs at a cost of 35/–d. each, including fitting. When the cars to which they were fitted were disposed of, the signs were to be transferred to the new cars. The Committee also agreed to the purchase of a number of portable signs for use in case of accident. The cost of each set of two per car not to exceed 32/–d. and the total cost not to exceed £25.

On the 4th April, 1939, plans were approved for improvements at Lydney Police Station by providing a recreation room, accommodation for 5 single men and a garage. The work to be carried out at a cost of £862.0.1d. Later that year the Police Authority – 'in light of the International situation' – deferred this work. The 'International Situation' was the declaration of war by this country against Germany on the 3rd September, 1939.

Seven Reserve Constables, who acted as chauffeurs and orderlies applied to the Chief Constable for rent allowance. They were all married men living in their own accommodation. Police Regulations did not apply to them and the Chief Constable referred their request to the Standing Joint Committee on the 4th April, 1939. The Committee agreed to pay these men 10/–d. per week and that a similar allowance be made to future Reserve Constables, in this category, after the completion of 15 years service.

To enable him to carry out the wishes of the Home Office, in connection with air Raid Precautions, the Chief Constable asked for the establishment of the Force to be increased by 1 Inspector and 3 Constables. These men would form the staff of the Air Raid Precautions Department which it would be necessary to add, to his Headquarters. One of the Constables, when not otherwise engaged, would act as a relief driver of the Home Office Gas Van.

The Standing Joint Committee agreed, at their meeting held at Gloucester on the 4th April, 1939, to supply the Constabulary with seven copies of Stone's Justice Manual for the year 1939. The manuals to be issued to Divisional offices. A request for a supply of Patersons Licensing Laws was turned down.

At the beginning of April 1939 there were 71 men in the First Police Reserve of the Gloucestershire Constabulary. The Special Constabulary was being re-organised and it was hoped to reach a probable strength of 1,200 or more. The Secretary of State had written and suggested a strength of Police War Reserves to equal that of the Regular Force. In time of war these men would give whole time service and be paid at the rate of £3 a week. The Home Office Circular dealing with this matter laid down that uniform should be provided for them, in advance. The Chief Constable recommended to the Police Authority that up to 250 be enrolled as a beginning and asked for authority to provide uniform, for them, at a cost of approximately £5.10.0d. per man, or a total of £1,400. This would allow each man to be issued with a Cap; Great-coat; Mackintosh; jacket and two pairs of Trousers, similar in quality to the uniform worn by the Metropolitan Special Constabulary. These men would not be entitled to pay except if called upon in time of war.

A promotion examination was held at the Grammar School, Cheltenham, on the 14th and 15th April, 1939, when 20 Sergeants sat for examination and 7 for re-examination; 5 of the former and 3 of the latter passed. 51 Constables sat for examination and 24 for re-examination; of the former 19 and of the latter 10 were successful.

On the 27th June, 1939, the Standing Joint Committee agreed that the salary of the Chief Constable be fixed at £900 as from 1st January, 1939, rising by biennial increments of £75 to a maximum of £1,200.

It was also agreed at this meeting to adapt the basement of the Shire Hall, underneath the County Treasurer's Department, as a County Control, Report Centre in an emergency, such as the outbreak of war.

As the build-up to war continued so the requirement for 'Back-up' resources became more important and plans were made to increase the strength of the Special Constabulary. In view of this the Chief Constable appointed Colonel J.S. Sleeman, C.B., C.M.G., C.B.E.,

M.V.O., who had been Commandant of the Herefordshire Special Constabulary since 1926, as Commandant of the Gloucestershire Special Constabulary, assisted by Captain C.C. Naumman as his Deputy, as from the 22nd August, 1939. The County being divided into eleven districts, each under a Special Superintendent, with the necessary establishment of Inspectors, Sergeants and Head Constables. By this time the approximate strength of the Special Constabulary, in Gloucestershire, was 3,400 and a Training Programme was arranged to commence straight away. The Chief Constable made it clear that the Special Constabulary was a voluntary and unpaid body. There were no paid Special Constables in Gloucestershire.[3]

War was declared on the 3rd September, 1939 and on the 10th October that year the Chief Constable, Colonel Henn, reported to the Police Authority that he had ordered 140 stirrup hand pumps, for the protection of police buildings, at a cost of £91. His action was endorsed by the Committee.

Up to October 1939 three members of the Force, who were members of the Army Reserve and classed as 'key men', had been called up for service with their Units. It was anticipated that a further 25 Reservists would, in all probability, be re-called to their Units in due course.

Circulars had been received from the Home Office giving particulars of the terms of employment of women in the Womens Auxiliary Police Corps. The Chief Constable asked the Police Authority for permission to enroll up to 50 women with the Corps, 25 to be used as drivers for the Special Constabulary and engaged in part-time unpaid service. The remainder to be employed in clerical duties, about a dozen to be employed full time and paid at the rate of £2 per week, as laid down by the Home Office.

At the Standing Joint Committee meeting held at Gloucester on the 10th October, 1939, the Chief Constable paid tribute to the manner in which the Regular Force, the First Police Reserve and the Special Constabulary had undertaken the various duties assigned to them since the emergency and the valuable assistance which had been rendered by the wives of many police officers. The Chairman – on behalf of the Committee – associated himself with the remarks of the Chief Constable and congratulated him on the efficiency of his organisation.

At the outbreak of war the Home Office notified Chief Officers of Police that Government Notices would be broadcast and stated that receiving sets should be provided at Police Headquarters to receive them. The Chief Constable reported to the Police Authority on the 2nd January, 1940, that he had purchased a satisfactory set at a cost of £6.6.0d. and asked the Committee to approve of the expenditure.

The Police and Firemans (War Service) Act, 1939 was passed by Parliament and this, under Section 1, empowered the Police Authority to make an allowance to a Police Officer who joined the Army, Navy or Air Force, or to his wife or dependents. Twenty six members of the Force, who were Reservists, had joined H.M. Forces and it was recommended that these men should be paid the allowance, which brought their service pay into line with their Police pay. Section 10 suspended, during the emergency, the right of a Police Officer to retire on pension without Medical Certificate, except with the authority of the Chief Constable.

Under Police Regulation 64, the Secretary of State approved the payment of a non-pensionable allowance, equal to 12½% of his pay, to any officer who applied for it and who, but for the Police and Firemans (War Service) Act, would be entitled to retire, without a Medical Certificate, on a pension equal to ⅔ of his pay. An additional allowance equal to 5% of his pay (being equivalent to his rateable deductions) would also be paid if he was in receipt of the maximum pay of his rank. Although it was only 1940 many items were in short supply and when it was found necessary to provide new floors in the guardroom and living room at Pilning Police Station, the Police Authority recommended that concrete floors be laid in view of the difficulty in getting timber. The cost of the work was £15.7.0d.

The Committee also agreed to tenders for the erection of surface air raid shelters at Kingswood and Staple Hill Police Stations. At this meeting 2.4.1940 it was reported that the sand-bags, which had been provided at Police Stations, were in a dilapidated condition and would have to be replaced. The Committee authorised the County Architect to use hollow concrete blocks, built dry and filled with sand, and to use this method, as it became necessary, to replace existing sand-bags.

It was 1940 when the Home Office decided to set up certain Police Services on a Regional basis. Home Office Circular No. 819/479/6 dated 7/2/40, was received by the Police Authority of Gloucestershire in which it explained that, to meet half the cost of Forensic Science Laboratories, a Regional police Wireless system, Clearing House for Criminal Records and the Training and Experimental Centre for Police Dogs, which had been established by the Home Office, a deduction was to be made from the Government Grant towards the cost of the Police equal to 2/7d. per head of the authorised establishment of the Force.

A further letter from the Home Office dated 22-2-40, asked all Police Authorities to give early consideration to the question of economies in the issue of clothing and equipment to regular members of the Force and to Police Auxiliaries. Attention was drawn to the importance of making every possible economy in expenditure and the use of materials. The Chief Constable informed the Standing Joint Committee on the 2nd April, 1940, that he would go into the matter carefully and report fully, in October next, when he would make his proposals and his suggestions for saving approximately £1,000 on the clothing required for 1941.

On the 2nd July, 1940 the Chief Constable reported that, with the approval of the Chairman, a War Bonus of 4% of their pay to those who were unmarried with no dependants, and 6% to others, had been paid as from the 1st April, 1940, to the shorthand typists and Junior Clerks employed in Police Offices. A War Bonus at the rate of 1/6d. per week had been paid to cleaners as from the same date.

To deal with the ever increasing problems of subversives and sympathisers, the Home Office directed the Chief Constable to arrange for the formation of a 'Special Branch', within the Gloucestershire Constabulary. The Chief Constable reported to the Police Authority that this had been done mainly by the transfer, to the Special Branch, of members of the Criminal Investigation Department and he asked for their approval of his action. Seven Special Branch Offices were opened throughout the County and to assist their mobility the Chief Constable was given permission to purchase four second hand cars, whilst a gentleman from Gloucester kindly gave the Unit his 1929 13 h.p. Austin Saloon, which was 'in good condition and running order'. The officers concerned in the remaining Units were allowed to use their own cars and claim mileage allowance on the scale approved for the Police.

At a meeting with the Standing Joint Committee on the 15th October, 1940, the Chief Constable reported that Home Office Circular No. 826/855/3, dated 26.8.40, had been received in which it stated that it had been decided to adjust the pay of the lower ranks of the Police Service by granting the following allowances with effect from 1st July, 1940:–

Supplementary Allowance This to be granted in consideration of the increased cost of living and to be payable at the rate of 5/–d. per week to Constables and 4/–d. per week to Women Police Constables.

War Duty Allowance This was granted in consideration of the conditions of service then prevailing and the suspension of certain rights in

> connection with hours of duty, rest days, etc. It was payable at the rate of 4/–d. per week to Sergeants, 3/–d. per week to Constables and 2/6d. per week to Women Police Constables.

The Secretary of State considered it desirable that these allowances be paid immediately so, with the Chairman's approval, the Chief Constable reported that he had arranged for these amounts, due from the 1st July, 1940, to be included on the Pay Sheets for September.

The pay of the Police War Reserves and Womens Auxiliary Police Corps was increased from Friday 28th June, 1940. This meant that Police War Reserve's pay was increased from 60/–d. to 65/–d. per week, proficiency pay to be 5/–d. instead of 6/–d. per week. The Womens Auxiliary Police Corps pay was increased from 40/–d. to 43/6d. per week.

The Chief Constable had to report to the Police Authority on the 31st December, 1940 that,

> During the recent air raid on Cheltenham considerable damage was done to the foundations of the north end of the single storey annexe of the main building at Police Headquarter (Holland House), and numerous cracks caused in the fabric. The more seriously affected portion of the building had been propped up and shored in order to prevent a collapse.

Fortunately there were no casualties from this incident. After inspecting the premises the County Architect considered that part of the building should be evacuated and alternative accommodation found. The Chief Constable was able to rent two large furnished rooms on the ground floor of a house almost immediately opposite Police Headquarters, and a large store in the basement, at a rental of £2 per week including the provision of fires. His action was approved by the Standing Joint Committee.

Motor Mileage Allowances to Police in Gloucestershire came up for discussion by the Police Authority on the 31st December, 1940, when the following rates – including the cost of petrol – were recommended and be paid from 11th January, 1941.

Motor cycle, combinations and three wheelers	2d. per mile
Cars up to 8 h.p.	2¾d. per mile
Cars of 9 or 10 h.p.	3¼d. per mile
Cars over 10 h.p.	4d. per mile

With petrol at 2/–d. per gallon, the suggested rates allowed 32 miles per gallon in the case of cars of 10 h.p. or less and 24 miles per gallon in the case of larger cars which, according to the Chief Constable, seemed to be a fair average.

At the same meeting Sir Francis Colchester-Wemyss gave instances in which Army vehicles had been driven at excessive speed. As a result it was Resolved,

> That the Committee do draw the attention of the Secretary of State for War to the excessive speed at which Army vehicles are driven in the County and do express the hope that instructions will be issued that the speed limits should be observed except in cases of emergency.

Chief Superintendent Albert J. Wayman applied for permission to retire on pension on the 3rd January, 1941. On that day his age was 60 years and 172 days. Length of approved service, 41 years and 38 days. His pension, which commenced on the 4th January, 1941, was £346-13-4d. per annum.

Towards the end of 1940 the Police Station at Filton was considerably damaged as a result of air raids and first-aid repairs to roofs and windows was immediately carried out and other work was undertaken in order that the premises could be used as hitherto. The cost of the emergency repairs was estimated at £60.

The Chief Constable had to call attention to the unsatisfactory condition of the sanitation at Whiteshill Police Station and he asked that the old fashioned Hopper type water closet be replaced by a washdown pedestal, connected to the water supply, and that a new septic tank be provided on adjoining land belonging to the County Council. Tenders were obtained and on the 8th April, 1941, the Police Authority approved the tender of £60.

During the year 1940, Police in Gloucestershire reported 768 deaths to Coroners and in 470 cases inquests were held. Particulars of the verdicts were:–

Accidental death	272
Death from Natural Causes	90
Suicide	45
Murder	2
Other verdicts	61

On the 10th March, 1941, at Gloucester City Petty Sessions, Ex. P.C. Richard A. Stephens, who pleaded guilty to a charge of stealing a £1 note, from one of his comrades (P.C. Charles Hammond), was bound over and ordered to pay 15/–d. costs.

In compliance with a Home Office Circular drawing attention to, 'the urgent necessity for providing loud-speaker equipment in Police vehicles', the Chief Constable had 12 patrol cars fitted with loud-speaker equipment at a cost of £28.5.0d. per car, plus £12.8.6d. for fitting to the 12 cars.

It was agreed by the Standing Joint Committee, on the 8th April, 1941, that a small wooden building be supplied for the use of the Special Constabulary working from the Cheltenham Road Police Station, in the Gloucester Division. With the Chairman's approval a telephone extension was fitted to it so that Special Constables could deal with calls during the absence of the Constable in Charge, on duty.

The Chief Constable reported that the telephone operator, at Police Headquarters, was frequently engaged in dealing with trunk and local calls and was unable to deal promptly with internal calls. In these circumstances he asked the Police Authority to agree to a private automatic telephone system to be installed, with eight instruments, at a cost of £6.3.0d. per quarter, so as to make immediate connection between the various offices possible.

At the Standing Joint Committee meeting, held at Gloucester on the 8th April, 1941, the Chief Constable, Colonel Henn, reported as follows:–

> Referring to my Report in October, 1939, altogether 26 members of this Force, who were Reservist, were re-called for War Service. 24 of them, including one who is a prisoner of war, are still serving. The undermentioned Constables were returned to the Force, from the Army, on the dates shown
>
> P.C. Philip I.Brett, left to re-join the Army on the 9th September, 1939. Returned to Police Force, 15th February, 1941.
>
> P.C. Arthur Temple, left to re-join the Army on the 13th September, 1939. Returned to Police Force, 1st March, 1941.

Special Constable Ronald Walter Clement Smith, of Drybrook, did a guard duty at a place near Lydney from 6.00 p.m. to 10.00 p.m. on the 19th August, 1940. When returning to his Station in his car, accompanied by another Special Constable, he was shot and fatally injured by a member of the Home Guard soon after 10.00 p.m. and died within a few minutes. At the inquest held on the 19th September, 1940, a verdict of 'Justifiable Homicide' was returned. At the Standing Joint Committee meeting held 8.4.1941, it was agreed that Special Constable Smith's fatal injury should be classified as a 'War Injury' and therefore that Mrs Ivy Marion Smith, his widow, be granted a special pension of £60.13.4d. per annum, commencing on the 20th August, 1940.

On the 1st February, 1941, the pay of Police War Reserves was increased from 65/–d. to 70/–d. per week. Proficiency pay to remain at 5/–d. per week. The Womens Auxiliary Police Corps pay was increased from 43/6d. to 47/d. per week.

At their meeting held 8.4.1941, the Chairman of the Standing Joint Committee presented a letter from the Home Office suggesting the exchange, for short periods, of members of Police Forces in heavily bombed, and quieter areas. It was Resolved,

> That in view of enemy action in the Bristol area, the Chief Constable do confer with the Chief Constable of Bristol, with a view to providing relief, for short periods, for members of the Bristol Police Force, by the transfer of members of the Gloucestershire Force.

During 1941 an air raid shelter was erected at the Central Police Station, Cheltenham, at a cost of £371.11.0d.

Up until 1941 the Police Authority were paying 1/–d. a day for the haulage of water to the Saul Police Station. A public supply was brought to the locality and the County Architect was asked to consider the most economic way of connecting the property to the public supply. This was done at a cost of £81.

It was agreed by the Police Authority that, as from the 1st July, 1941, the allowance for providing meals for Prisoners be fixed at 1/–d. per meal. Previous to this it was 9d. per meal.

As from the 1st March, 1941, the Supplementary Allowance to Constables was increased from 5/–d. to 10/–d. per week and for Women Police Constable from 4/–d. to 7/6d. per week. An allowance of 5/–d. per week was granted to Sergeants.

The War Duty Allowance for Sergeants, Constables and Police Women remained unchanged at 4/–d.; 3/–d. and 2/6d. per week respectively, but an allowance of 5/–d. per week was granted to Inspectors.

Owing to the lack of pressure of gas supply at the Chalford, Stonehouse and Bisley Police Stations, the Police Authority agreed, on the 14th October, 1941, that electric light be installed in certain rooms. Chalford Police Station, service rooms only, at a cost of £12; Sergeants quarters, additional £15. Stonehouse Police Station, service rooms only and Sergeants' quarters £20; Bisley Police Station £15.

An interesting item appeared in the Chief Constable's Report to the Standing Joint Committee on the 6th January, 1942. It was headed, 'Light Refreshments for Police on Night Duty' and the Chief Constable reported that, acting upon instructions received from the Home Office, and with the Chairman's approval, arrangements had been made to provide light refeshments, consisting of a cup of tea with sugar, and a biscuit, for Regular Members of the Force and Special Constables on duty at night. If the period of duty exceeded 4 hours, a second cup of tea with sugar, and a biscuit, could be provided. Permits enabling the Chief Constable to obtain the necessary supplies had been issued by the Ministry of Food, on the basis on 1lb of tea; 1¼lbs of sugar and 4lbs of biscuits for every 200 'subsidiary meals'.

Referring to the Chief Constable's Report of July, 1923, when the Standing Joint Committee agreed to the purchase of 20 sets of new, store-soiled saddlery, for the use of the 'mounted police', at a cost of approximately £4.10.0d. per set, Colonel Henn reported that this number was far in excess of his requirements. As it was difficult to provide suitable storage room and labour to keep it properly cleaned and in good condition, he recommended that 10 sets be sold and the remaining 10 sets retained. An offer of 30/–d. per set had been made and as the saddlery had been in use for 18 years, the Chief Constable suggested that the offer be accepted.

On the 1st February, 1942, the Chief Constable had to relinquish the temporary accommodation taken in the house opposite, after Police Headquarters was damaged by enemy action, the propery having been sold. New accommodation was found in Wilton House – next door to Police Headquarters – where four furnished rooms were rented.

Trouble with the Police Account and Gloucester Corporation arose in June, 1942, when the Gloucester Corporation objected to the inclusion of certain items in the Police Account submitted to them for the year 1940/41. This had occurred previously when the account for the year 1939/40 had been submitted. In order to avoid uncertainty and delay, each year, the Standing Joint Committee provisionally agreed with the Corporation that, for the year 1940/41 and any subsequent years during the war, the Corporation would pay on the basis of the ratio of the authorised strength of the City Force, to the authorised strength of the whole of the County force, applied to the total nett expenditure charged to the Police Account, provided that the Corporation were safeguarded against the Standing Joint Committee carrying out any extensive capital work and charging its cost to Revenue Account during and while the arrangement was in operation.[4]

During 1942 the Police Station at Hucclecote, Gloucester, sustained damage as a result enemy action. Repairs were carried out at a cost of £93 and a claim was registered with the War Damage Commission.

On the 23rd May, 1942, Inspector Fitzroy F. Taylor died suddenly whilst on duty at Dursley Police Station. He was 41 years of age and had nearly completed 22 years service. He left a widow and three young children, aged 15 years, 11 years and 8 years. The widow was granted a pension of £40 a year for herself, commencing on the 24th May, 1942, and an allowance of £12 per annum in respect of each of her three children, commencing on the same date, and payable until the children attained the age of 16 years.

Home Office Circular No. 864,040/37, dated 28.4.42, stated that all Police officers who were under 25 years of age at the time they registered for National Service, and all members of the Police War reserve who were under 30 years of age on the 1st May, 1942, would be de-reserved on the 1st July, 1942. This Circular applied to 72 Regular Constables but all the members of the Police War Reserve were above the age limit.

To make it possible to fill a certain number of these vacancies, when necessary and when suitable applicants could be found, the Chief Constable asked the Home Office to increase the authorised establishment of the Police War Reserve from 200 to 210, and of the Womens Auxiliary Police Crops from 32 to 40. In addition, he asked for an establishment of 15 for the Police Auxiliary Messenger Service.

It was during June, 1942, that the Board of Trade sent a letter to the Standing Joint Committee, regarding the issue of uniform to the Police and other employees of Local Authorities. It laid down that periodical issues should be suspended and that garments should be replaced only as they wore out.

The Home Office, in a letter dated 6.6.1942, informed the Chief Constable that a Home Office Wireless Station would be erected at Shapwick, near Bridgwater, and that Police Forces in that area should provide the necessary wireless apparatus for use at Headquarters, Divisional Headquarters and on Police Patrol Cars. Colonel Henn sent a letter to the Clerk of the Standing Joint Committee giving details of the apparatus required. The cost, based on Home Office figures would be £812.10.0d. plus cost of installation and asked for authority to place an order accordingly. Up to this period, the Metropolitan Police and the Lancashire Constabulary were the only Police Forces, in England and Wales, using wireless.

The Finance Sub-Committee of the Standing Joint Committee had been considering the pay of Superintendent and Inspectors and recommended that, subject to the approval of the Home Secretary, the scales of salaries for Superintendents and Inspectors, from the 1st October, 1942, would be as follows:

Superintendents –	£460 per annum rising by annual increments of £20 to £540 per annum.
Inspectors –	£325 rising by annual increments of £10 to £375 per annum.

The Sub-Committee also recommended that, subject to the approval of the Home Secretary, the allowance to the Chief Superintendent, who acts as Deputy Chief Constable, be increased as from 1st October, 1942, from £50 to £75 per annum.

Up to the end of September 1942, 42 of the 72 men who were under 25 at the date of Registration had joined H.M. Forces. One had been rejected on medical grounds and the remaining 29 were waiting to be called. To counteract these men being called-up the Home Office fixed the following establishments for full time paid Police Auxilaries in Gloucestershire viz:– First Police Reserves 10; Police War Reserves 210; Womens Auxiliary Police Corps 40; Police Auxiliary Messenger Service 15. The Government to pay 50% of the cost of the First Police Reserve and the whole of the pay of the other three branches of the Police Service.

Prior to 1922, members of the Force were not required to hand in their old uniform when they received a new issue. At their meeting on the 27th June, 1922, in consequence of Police Regulation 84, the Standing Joint Committee agreed to the recommendation of the then Chief Constable that members of the Force be allowed to retain their old uniform trousers, if they so desired, on payment of 2/–d. a pair. The price which could then be obtained for these garments, from the contractors, was 4/–d. At the Standing joint Committee meeting held on the 5th January, 1943, the Chief Constable reported that trousers could be sold for 11/9d. a pair and, in Home Office Circular No. 863,971/30, dated 13th November, 1942, it was suggested that the price charged to members of the Force should be increased so as to represent 75% and 80% of that which could be obtained from contractors. To comply with this suggestion Colonel Henn recommended that, until further notice, the price be raised from 2/–d. to 9/–d. a pair, on the understanding that he would recommed a reduction when the price, at which old uniform trousers could be sold, fell appreciably below the then abnormally high level.

The Home Office directed that from the 2nd November, 1942, the following increase of pay should be granted to Police Auxiliaries:–

Police War Reserve, from 74/–d. to 78/6d. a week. Proficiency pay after 6 months' service, to remain at 5/–d. a week, in addition.

Womens Auxiliary Police Corps, from 52/–d. to 55/–d. if 20 years of age or over. From 47/–d. to 49/–d. if between 19 and 20 years. From 47/–d. to 48/6d. if between 18 and 19 years.

Police Auxiliary Messenger Service, no change, 70/–d. if 20 years of age or over. From 60/–d. to 63/–d. if between 19 and 20 years. From 50/–d. to 52/–d. if between 18 and 19 years. No change, 29/6d. if between 17 and 18 years. No change, 24/–d. if under 17 years of age.

On the 6th April, 1943, the Chief Constable reported to the Police Authority that during the year 1942, 110 persons were killed, 693 seriously and 1,800 slightly injured, in road accidents in the County. Of these 34 were killed, 231 seriously and 535 slightly injured, during the hours of darkness. 48 persons were killed, 270 seriously and 841 slightly injured, on roads subject to a speed limit.

The number of persons killed in 1941, was 167 and, in 1940, 143.

The Chief Constable was able to report that, as from the 1st November, 1942, the Home Office had agreed to increase the strength of the Police War Reserve from 210 to 236. This was due to the fact that 1 regular Sergeant and 26 Police War Reserves, the cost of whose emloyment had been refunded by the Ministry of Supply, would form part of the authorised establishment of the Force, as from that date.

The Police (Appeals) Act, 1927, gave members of the Force the right to appeal to the Secretary of State if they were dismissed, or ordered to resign as an alternative to dismissal. The passing of the Police (Appeals) Act, 1943, extended this right to cases in which members of the Force were punished by reduction in rate of pay, but *not* to cases in which fines were inflicted.

By March 1943, the re-building of the damaged portion of Police Headquarters, (Holland House), had been completed and the new rooms occupied. The rooms at Wilton House, which had been rented since the 1st February, 1942, were given up on the 27th March, 1943.

On the 29th June, 1943, the Chief Constable reported to the Standing Joint Committee that the Home Office had sent him a Circular stating that the establishment of the Force had been fixed at 570, for normal police duties, as from the 1st January, 1944. The figures to apply to whole time personnel, including both men and women. It did not include 87 men employed on Special duties nor the Police Auxiliary Messenger Service, the establishment of which had been increased from 15 to 20, by a Home Office letter dated 27.5.43. The establishment of the Police War Reserve and Women's Auxiliary Police Corps, as previously fixed at 236 and 40 respectively, no longer applied, but all were included in the figure of 570 and 87, given above. All this was due to Home Office Circular, 868,040/165, dated 18.2.43, in which it stated that the Government had decided that the Police Service would have to make a further contribution to the Armed Forces and to industry, and that whole-time strength of the

Force, including both men and women, would have to be reduced to a certain total by the end of 1943.

The Buildings Minor Committee of the Gloucestershire County Council, meeting on the 13th September, 1943, had their attention brought to the undesirability of the County Council renting properties, sometimes 'council houses', from the local authorities for occupation as Police residences. The Committee recommended that, 'the Standing Joint Committee purchase 5 houses belonging to the Gloucester Corporatation, occupied by Police in the City of Gloucester'. The properties were, 17 & 19, Dean's Way, 14, Bowly Road and 37, The Oval (Police Residences), and Bristol Road Police Station.

The Supplementary Allowance, payable to members of the Force was altered again on the 1st June, 1943, viz:– Superintendents – first grant of £25 per annum; Inspectors and Sergeants – increased by 6/6d. a week to 14/–d. a week; Constables and First Police Reserve – increased by 3/6d. a week to 17/–d. a week; Women Police Constables – increased by 3/6d. a week to 13/6d. a week.

The Chief Constable was again notified by the Home Office, on the 16th August, 1943, that it had been decided to reduce the establishment of the Force to 541, for normal police duties. This compared with 570 fixed by the Home Office in April, 1943. The establishment of 87 for special duties remained unaltered. The new figures to take effect from 1st January, 1944. No more Regular members of the Force were to be withdrawn but the establishment would be reached by calling up 21 members of the Police War Reserve, who were under 35 years of age, for the Fighting Services or Mining, and 20 who were over military age, for industry.

At the Standing Joint Committee meeting, held at Gloucester, on the 5th October, 1943, a motion was moved by The Right Hon. Viscount Bledisloe, seconded by Mr L.G. Heath, and it was Resolved – 'That the Committee do record their high appreciation of the Service rendered by members of the Force during the present emergency.'

The same meeting Resolved that a reward of £5 be made to P.C. John Buckle, on the recommendation of the Chief Constable. He was also awarded the Silver Braid for Gallantry and 'Very Highly Commended' by the Chief Constable. The Royal Humane Society awarded the Bronze Medal and Certificate to P.C. Buckle and the Society's Testimonial on Parchment to Thomas Cripps, the man who assisted him. On the 4th July, 1943, a boy was standing in the lobby of his father's house when the floor suddenly collapsed and he fell into a concealed well. P.C. Buckle was informed by telephone, at Minchinhampton Police Station, and drove to the scene immediately with ropes. The well was 102 feet deep and 6 feet in diameter at the top. With the help of some members of the National Fire Service P.C. Buckle was lowered into the well where he found the boy, seriously hurt. The boy was hauled to the surface, followed by the Constable who was in the well for just over two hours. The boy's life was undoubtedly saved by P.C. Buckle and later recovered from his injuries and the effects of the accident. Mr E.S. Tarlton, father of the boy rescued, expressed his gratitude to the officer's prompt and courageous actions.

During the year 1943, 1669 pedal cycles were reported stolen. Of these 295 were recovered and no offences recorded, 168 were recovered and offenders detected, 12 were not recovered but offenders were detected, 2 were recovered but offenders were not detected, 1,192 remained undetermined.

During the same year, 1943, 45 motor vehicles were reported stolen. Of this number 42 cases were recorded as 'taking without owner's consent' and 3 cases recorded as 'Larceny'. Proceedings were taken against persons in 24 cases of 'taking without owner's consent', 18 cases remained undetermined. Proceedings were taken against persons in 3 cases of 'Larceny'. 45 vehicles were recovered.

Complaints were received from local residents of the nuisance caused by stray dogs detained at the Central Police Station, Stroud. The Chief Constable reported to the Standing Joint Committee, on the 21st March, 1944, that the complaints were not without justification. With the approval of the Chairman and with the kind co-operation of the Stroud Urban District Council, the dogs were allowed to be detained on the site of the ash destructor. A double pen had been constructed at a cost of £12 and the dog kennels had been moved there. The foreman at the ash destructor, agreed to look after the dogs for 5/–d. a week.

As from the 1st February, 1944, Boot Allowance to all Regular members of the Force and full time paid auxiliaries was increased from 1/6d. to 2/–d. a week.

On the 27th June, 1944, the Chief Constable reported to the Police Authority that on the recommendation of the Secretary of State, His Majesty had been pleased to confer the King's Police and Fire Service Medal upon Chief Superintendent Joseph William Parry Goulder, Deputy Chief Constable, who entered his 47th year of Police service in May, 1944. The Chief Constable was asked to convey the Committee's congratulations to Chief Superintendent J.W.P. Goulder, Deputy Chief Constable.

It was agreed, on the 26th September, 1944, that Inspectors would, in future, wear open neck jackets instead of the closed neck pattern and thus bring them in line with the Superintendents.

Home Office Circular No. 181/44, dated 23.6.44, stated that the Secretary of State considered that the Status of a Superintendent, justified the grant of First Class rail travel and that it was important that there should be uniformity of practice, in this matter. With the Chairman's approval, Colonel Henn issued instructions to his Superintendents to travel First Class, by rail, when on duty.

The Pensions (Increase) Act, 1944, increased from the 1st January, 1944, pensions which did not exceed £300 in the case of married men and single men with dependants, and £225 in the case of single men without dependants. Pensions up to one-third of the above amounts were raised by 30%, those up to two-thirds of these amounts by 25% and larger pensions by 20%. To qualify, a Police Officer had to be either – (a) At least 60 years of age or (b) permanently incapacitated. A widow had to be either – (a) At least 40 years of age, (b) permanently incapacitated or (c) have at least one dependant. The increase not to raise the total income above £300 or £225, but the first £52 a year of any increase, other than the pension, was not to be taken into account.

A Home Office Circular No. 229/44F, dated 28.8.44, notified certain alterations made in the Police Regulations and Police (Women) Regulations. The effect of this was that on the 31st August, 1944, the payment of Supplementary Allowance would cease. From 1st September, 1944, a similar amount, known as War Supplement, would be added to the pensionable pay, and rateable deductions made from it. This arrangement increased the full pension for a man by 12/8d. and for a woman by 10/4d. a week, which would be deducted from any increase payable under the terms of the Pension (Increase) Act, 1944. The amount of the War Supplement could be varied from time to time, as in the case of the Supplementary Allowance, which it replaced, but a pension once granted would not be varied. First Police Reserves were to be treated similarly to members of the Regular Force.

It was during 1944 that, following the Roche Report, the Standing Joint Committee recommended the use of the title 'Magistrates Court' instead of 'Police Court' or 'Courts of Petty Sessions'.

At the Standing Joint Committee meeting held at Gloucester, on the 19th December, 1944, the Chief Constable submitted a Report in which he estimated that the heaviest Capital Expenditure required by the

Police, immediately after the War, would be for the provision of Police Stations and Police Officers' residences. A very detailed report, setting out likely requirements, followed this statement and it was Resolved that the Chief Constable's Report be received and adopted.

Early in 1945 the Chief Constable, with the approval of the Chairman of the Police Authority, placed an order for a portable electric-sander, a mobilectric engine workshop, an acetylene welder, and a set of expanding reamers, for use in the Police Garage, at a total cost of approximately £133.4.0d. The tools would enable the mechanics to do a great deal of work which they could not do in the past and would save both expense and delays. The Chief Constable thought that the money saved would be sufficient to pay for the tools, within a comparatively short period.

Police Sergeant Victor G. Davies of Tewkesbury Police Station was injured by a vehicle belonging to the United States Army Authorities, while riding a bicycle on the 1st January, 1944, and in consequence of his injuries was totally incapacitated for duty, from the 1st January to the 5th September, 1944. Although he recovered from his injuries he was not able to undertake the full duties attaching to his position as a Sergeant.

A claim was submitted to the United States Army Claims Commission which amounted to £673.17.9d. The Claims Conmmission were unable to recognise the claim as the Foreign Claims Act of Congress, under which all payments to injured parties were made, did not authorise payment of compensation for loss of services to the employer of the party injured.

On the 5th May, 1945, the 'Cease Fire' was sounded in Europe and, at their meeting on the 3rd July, 1945, the Chairman of the Standing Joint Committee reported, with regret, that the following Police Officers had been killed on War Service between the outbreak of hostilities and the 31st May, 1945.

(1) P.C. Robert E. Mason, No. 1339125 Pilot Officer, Royal Air Force. Killed in England on the 16th December, 1943, when his bomber crashed after returning from a raid on Berlin. P.C. Mason was born on the 4th March, 1922, was employed as a Junior Clerk at Police Headquarters from 1st March, 1939, until he joined the Force on the 6th October, 1941. He was unmarried.

(2) P.A.M. Frank Woodward, No. 114330, Royal Marine. Fell overboard and drowned on the 16th June, 1944, during operations for the invasion of Normandy. P.A.M. Woodward was born on the 5th November, 1924 and was employed at Police Headquarters, first as a Junior Clerk and then as a member of the Police Auxiliary Messenger Service, from the 13th August, 1941, until he left to join the Royal Marines on the 12th April, 1943. He was unmarried.

(3) P.C. Clifford J. Dibden, No. 1338174, Flying Officer, Royal Air Force, killed in Italy on the 22nd January, 1945, when on operations. P.C. Dibden was born on the 23rd February, 1917, and joined the Gloucestershire Constabulary on the 6th March, 1939. He left to join the Royal Air Force on the 8th September, 1941. He left a widow, Mrs Pearl F.D. Dibden, who was informed by the Police Authority that, as the pension she would receive from the Royal Air Force was in excess of the maximum pension payable to a Police Constable's widow, no payment, by way of pension could be made from Police Funds. However, with the passing of the Police and Firemens (War Service) Act, 1944, the Chief Constable was able to report that Mrs Dibden qualified for a Police Widow's pension which, in her case, would be £30 a year. A Police Widow's Pension of £30 a year was granted to Mrs Dibden, commencing on the 23rd July, 1944, and payable during widowhood.

(4) P.C. Herbert A.Hall, No. 1575839, Warrant Officer, Royal Air Force, reported missing on the 24th February, 1945, when returning from a raid on the Continent. P.C. Hall was born on the 16th February, 1920. He joined the Gloucestershire Constabulary on the 6th March, 1939, and left to join the Royal Air Force on the 6th October, 1941. He was unmarried.

With the cessation of hostilities in Europe, things began to move within the Police Force and on the 3rd July, 1945, the Chief Constable submitted a Memorandum, on Police Housing, setting out a definite programme of building for the consideration of the Standing Joint Committee.

The Chief Constable also informed the Committee that the last Examination for Promotion was held on the 14th and 15th April, 1939. It was not obligatory to hold examinations during the War years but he was now making arrangements to hold one in September 1945 and he thought it would be necessary to hold another in the early part of 1946 to enable men returning from H.M. Forces to sit within a few weeks of their demobilization. As on previous occasions the examination would be held at Cheltenham Grammar School. Educational subjects being set by the Headmaster and papers on Criminal Law, Evidence and Procedure, General Statutes, etc., would be set and marked by the Instructor of the Birmingham City Police.

At the request of the Branch Board of the Police Federation the Chief Constable recommended, to the Standing Joint Committee, that the allowance paid for cleaning Magistrates Courts should be increased as follows:–

(1) The allowance for cleaning Courts be at the rate of 5/–d. for each regular Court, not exceeding one a week. This would increase the cost from £96.8.0d. per annum to £142 per annum.

(2) The allowance of 2/6d. per day, paid when the Court was used as a County Court, or for any other authorised purpose, be increased to 4/–d.

The Committee approved the alterations, as recommended by the Chief Constable, and agreed that the new rates should operate from the 1st July, 1945.

Colonel Henn, Chief Constable, was asked by the Sudan Government to allow 3 selected Sudan Police Officers to be attached to the Gloucestershire Constabulary for a period of three months, from October, 1945, for the purpose of studying Police organisation in the area. The Home Office had supported the request. Should the Standing Joint Committee agree, Colonel Henn was quite prepared to do this. All expenses would be met by the Sudan Government. Approval was given for the attachment.

Home Office Circular No. 157/45F, dated 14.6.45, informed Chief Constables that the Secretary of State had decided to disband the Police Auxiliary Messenger Service. They would be given a month's notice of dicharge, but those who were required as Cadet Clerks could be engaged in that capacity. There were 20 members of the Police Auxiliary Messenger Services employed in various Police Offices in the County and as it was almost impossible to dispense with their services, the Chief Constable asked for authority to employ the 20 youths, until the end of the year.

Home Office Circular No. 160/1945, dated 19th June, gave permission to part-time members of the Special Constabulary, the (Volunteer) Womens Auxiliary Police Corps and the Police Auxiliary Messenger Service, to retire if they so wished, on and after the 1st July, 1945. Colonel Henn immediately took steps to implement the Circular and this resulted in the gradual reduction of the Special Constabulary to a peace time establishment.

In order to put the Special Constabulary on a similar footing to other part-time defence organisations, such as the Home Guard and Warden's Service, the Chief Constable asked if the Standing Joint Committee would agree to those members who retired be permitted to retain a pair of uniform trousers and either a mackintosh or a greatcoat, for civilian wear, if they so desired.

Ex. Chief Superintendent James B. Biggs, died at Stroud on the 2nd July, 1945, aged 83 years. He retired in 1925 and was a widower.

A serving officer, Police Sergeant Joseph W.A. Ireland, died suddenly at Blakeney Police Station, after only a few hours illness, on the 3rd September, 1945. He was 53 years of age and had served for 31 years which included his service in H.M. Forces during the First World War. He left a widow and two grown up daughters. Mrs Ireland was granted a pension of £46.12.8d. per annum, payable during widowhood.

At the Standing Joint Committee meeting on the 25th September, 1945, the Chief Constable reported upon the then condition of the Force and the steps to be taken to fill vacancies when recruitment was opened again. He also gave the Committee details of the new scheme for training Police recruits and for refresher courses, for senior officers, which would be carried out at a Regional Training School. Up to this time all Gloucestershire Police recruits had been trained at Police Headquarters, Cheltenham, under Force Instructors.

The Committee, at this meeting, gave the Chief Constable authority to purchase one air-compressor, for use at the Police Garage, Cheltenham, at an approximate cost of £95.

A significant change was about to take place in the Force establishment when the Chief Constable reported to the Finance Sub-Committee, on the 3rd December, 1945, that Chief Superintendent and Deputy Chief Constable J.W.P. Goulder, in charge of the Criminal Investigation Branch, had signified his desire to retire on pension, on the 31st December, 1945. As a result of his resignation the Chief Constable proposed that, with effect from the 1st January, 1946, the post of Deputy Chief Constable be abolished and a new post – that of Assistant Chief Constable – be created, subject to the approval of the Home Secretary.

The difference between the post of Deputy Chief Constable and Assistant Chief Constable was explained by Colonel Henn, as follows:–

(a) A Deputy Chief Constable was appointed by the Chief Constable, with approval of the Police Authority, under the County Police Act of 1839 and would act for the Chief Constable whenever the latter was absent from the County for any reason, including sickness. When the Chief Constable was present, the Deputy Chief Constable attended to his own work, which may be in charge of a Division or, as in this case, of the criminal Investigation Department. He was in no sense 'a second-in-Command'. In the Gloucestershire Force the Deputy Chief Constable drew the pay of his rank as Superintendent, plus £50 per annum, as Chief Superintendent, and for his duties as Deputy.

(b) An Assistant Chief Constable was appointed by the Police Authority, on a scale of pay between that of a Chief Superintendent and a Chief Constable, as approved in each case by the Home Office. The appointment could be made, with the Home Secretary's approval, from either inside or outside the Force. An Assistant Chief Constable so appointed was exactly what the title implied – he was 'Assistant' to the Chief Constable in every branch of the work and at all times. During the absence of the Chief Constable he carried out the Chief Constable's duties. His position was the same as the 'Second-in-Command of any disciplined formation.[6]

In making his suggestion to the Police Authority the Chief Constable explained that the work of the Force was still increasing. Quite apart from the primary duties of prevention and detection of crime, the work of administration had grown enormously. The post-war Force would be in need of most careful training, in the many scientific branches which had recently developed and the administration – housing and so on, would occupy a great deal of time and though, Colonel Henn stated that he was prepared to continue to the best of his ability, if the Police Authority so wished, nevertheless he felt that the services of an Assistant would benefit the Force.

The Chief Constable pointed out that, should his proposal be acceptable to the Police Authority, it would be necessary to obtain the Home Secretary's sanction. This, he thought, would be readily forthcoming. He also recommended that the appointment of the Assistant Chief Constable be made from within the Force.

The Committee were also informed that, assuming that an Assistant Chief Constable was appointed, the direction of the Criminal Investigation Department would have to be re-organised. At that time the Criminal Investigation Department was commanded by a Chief Superintendent (Mr Goulder), assisted by an Inspector and a temporary Inspector at Headquarters. In the event of the Assistant Chief Constable being appointed, Colonel Henn thought the Criminal Investigation Department should be in charge of a Superintendent and an Inspector. If this was approved, the post would require Home Office sanction.

The Standing Joint Sub-Committee Report was received and adopted. The Chairman reported that the Secretary of State had indicated his preparedness to approve the establishment of the rank of Assistant Chief Constable, the holder to act as Deputy Chief Constable, and had suggested that the appropriate scale of pay for the rank would be £600 a year, rising by annual increments of £50 to a maximum of £750. The Secretary of State was also prepared to agree to the substitution of the rank of Superintendent for Chief Superintendent for the officer in charge of the Criminal Investigation Department and to authorise the variations of establishment required for that purpose.

The Committee then considered the method by which an appointment to the post of Assistant Chief Constable should be made. It was resolved:–

(1) That, subject to the approval of the Secretary of State, an appointment be made from within the County Police Force.

(2) That Superintendent Albert Harry Carter be appointed Assistant Chief Constable from the 1st January, 1946.

It was further resolved:–

That formal application be made to the Secretary of State for his approval to the appointment of an Assistant Chief Constable, at a scale of pay of £600 a year, rising by annual increments of £50, to a maximum of £750, to the appointment to the post of Superintendent Albert Harry Carter, a member of the Gloucestershire Police Force, and to the substitution of the rank of Superintendent for Chief Superintendent, for the officer in charge of the Criminal Investigation Department.

Police pay came in for discussion at the Police Authority Meeting on the 18th December, 1945, when the Chief Constable gave details of the new scales of pay for Superintendents and Inspectors, which took effect from the 1st April last. The rates applicable to officers of the Gloucestershire Constabulary were as follows:–

Superintendents	£565 on appointment, rising by £20 per annum to £645 with £50 extra for the Chief Superintendent who was Deputy Chief Constable and £20 for the Chief Superintendent at Gloucester
Inspectors	£415 on appointment, rising by £10 per annum to £465.

These amounts were £45 per annum, in the case of Superintendents, and £30 in the case of Inspectors, more than the old scale of pay, plus the War Supplement of £60 per annum which ceased to be payable from the 1st April, 1945. With the Chairman's approval, arrangements had been made to pay these officers on the new scale for November, together with arrears from the date on which it became effective.

In view of Home Office Circular No. 278/45F1, dated 6.10.45, the Chief Constable thought it advisable to discuss, with the Standing Joint Committee, the question of the amount to be charged for Police on Requisition. the rates in operation were 2/–d. an hour, or 12/–d. a day, plus travelling expenses and allowances payable to men in respect of the duty performed. In the case of men attending Cheltenham Races, 2/–d. a day extra was being charged, plus a small amount for insurance, in view of the extra risk involved. Colonel Henn said that he would be glad to know whether the Committee wished to make any alterations, in the amounts to be charged. He was of the opinion that they were reasonable.

The results of the Examination for Promotion, held at Cheltenham on the 10th and 11th September, 1945, were given to the Police

Authority on the 18th December, 1945. 25 Sergeants sat for examination, of whom 9 passed and 8 sat for re-examination of whom 5 passed. 43 Constables sat for examination and 23 for re-examination; 24 of the former and 14 of the latter were successful. The fee charged by the Headmaster of Cheltenham Grammar School was 4/–d. a head for those examined or re-examined in Educational Subjects, which amounted to £17.4.0d. for the 86 men in question. In addition a payment of £1 was made to the caretaker of the Grammar School for the cleaning and other extra work caused by the examination. The fee charged by the Instructor of the Birmingham City Police for each person examined or re-examined in three Police Subjects was 3/–d., and 1/–d. a paper for those examined in less than three Subjects. The total for 84 candidates was £12, making a total expenditure of £30.4.0d. for the 99 members of the Force who attended the examinations.

The Chief Constable informed the Police Authority on the 18th December, 1945, that, within a few weeks, he proposed to be able to submit to the Chairman a carefully considered report on the Post-War establishment of the Force. To enable the necessary duties to be efficiently performed it was clear that, in the County, as in others, it would be necessary to make a substantial addition to the strength of the Force as soon as the men could be recruited and trained. He suggested a Sub-Committee be appointed to consider his Report, as soon as it was ready, so that their recommendations could be laid before the Standing Joint Committee at their next Quarterly Meeting. The Sub-Committee appointed to consider the Chief Constable's Report, on the Post-War establishment of the Force, consisted of:–

Major Sir Frederick William Beresford Cripps, D.S.O.
Captain Foyle Fawcett
Captain R.A. Bennett
Lieut. Colonel J. Godman
T. Hannam Clark, Esq.
C. de Courcy Parry, Esq., C.B.E. and
Captain J.H. Trye, C.B.E., R.N.

Chief Superintendent Joseph W. Goulder, K.P.M., Deputy Chief Constable, retired on the 31st December, 1945, aged 69 years and 129 days. Length of approved service, 47 years and 245 days. Length of service as a Superintendent, 24 years and 46 days.

On the 1st January, 1946, Albert H. Carter was appointed the first Assistant Chief Constable of Gloucestershire.

Following the revision of the Scales of pay of Superintendents and Inspectors, the Secretary of State had under consideration recommendations made to him by the County Councils Association and the Association of Municipal Corporations for revising and consolidating the scales of pay of Chief Constables. The Secretary of State accepted these recommendations, which involved the adoption of the revised scales with effect from the 1st April, 1945, and their maintenance for a period of 3 years from that date, unless there was a radical change in general economic conditions. The salary scale for the Chief Constable of Gloucestershire was recommended to commence at £1,050 a year, rising by biennial increments of £75 to a maximum of £1,350 a year. At the meeting on the 11th March, 1946, the Finance Sub-Committee recommended that the scale of pay be adopted and applied as suggested by the Secretary of State.

The same meeting recommended:–

(1) That financial assistance be given to members of the Force who are required to provide motor cars for use on duty.

(2) That application be made to the County Council to extend to members of the Force the loan facilities granted to the Council's officers.

P.C. Wilfred K. Clarke died suddenly at Hucclecote, Gloucester, on the 28th January, 1946. He was 46 years of age and had served for just over 25 years. Before joining the Constabulary P.C. Clarke served for over two years in H.M. Forces during the 1914–18 war. He left a widow and three sons aged 22, 18 and 9 years respectively. Mrs Clarke was granted a pension of £31.19.7d. per annum for herself, commencing on the 29th January, 1946, and an allowance of £10 a year for the younger child. The allowance to end on the 10th April, 1952. Arising out of consideration of this item, the Police Authority passed the following Resolution, 'That representation be made to the County Councils Association as to the inadequacy, under present conditions, of the pensions payable to widows of Police Officers under the Police Pension Act of 1921'.

It was agreed by the Standing Joint Committee, at their meeting on the 26th March, 1946, that as the newly appointed Assistant Chief Constable would be travelling much longer distances, in covering the six Police Divisions in the County, he would be granted a Travelling and Subsistence Allowance of £180 per annum. He was also allowed to claim for travelling and subsistence when outside the County, in addition.

At a meeting of the Police Authority on the 2nd July, 1946, it was resolved,

> That the Committee do approve a scale of pay for the Assistant Chief Constable commencing at £720 a year and rising by biennial increments of £50 to a maximum of £870 a year, with effect as from the date of his appointment, and that such scale be submitted for the approval of the Secretary of State.

Major F.L. Stanley Clarke, O.B.E., who was Chief Constable of Gloucestershire from 1918, until he retired on account of ill health in 1937, died suddenly at his residence in Cheltenham on the 6th April, 1946, aged 70 years. He left a widow and a grown up daughter. His widow, Mrs Muriel Stanley Clarke, was granted a pension of £50 a year commencing on the 1st May, 1946.

Superintendent Frederick J. Williams, Stroud, retired on pension on the 31st July, 1946. He was 60 years of age and had served for 34 years. His pension, commencing on the 1st August, 1946, was £430 per annum.

At their meeting on the 2nd July, 1946, the Police Authority considered a Report by the Chief Constable in respect of the Police Motor Patrol. Colonel Henn stated that the question of replacing the existing fleet of Patrol cars now had to be faced. The fleet consisted of 17, 30 h.p. Ford V.8s, 7 of which were purchased new between February and June, 1939, and 10 were purchased second hand between January 1940 and November 1941. The total mileage run by the fleet to the 31st March, 1946, was, 1,650,000 miles. The average mileage of all cars was 97,000. The cars were only kept on the road by the ceaseless efforts of the garage staff and drivers. He therefore asked the Committee to approve the principle of replacing the existing fleet of Ford V.8.s by ten 12 h.p. and six 16 h.p. Riley cars, the proceeds of the existing fleet to be set against the purchase cost.

In accordance with the post-war Training Scheme, laid down by the Home Office, each recruit had to undergo a thirteen weeks' course of instruction at one of the Regional Training Centres, before he commenced patrol duty. The Training Centre for Gloucestershire was situated at Eastwood Park, Falfield, within the county. Between the 1st January, and the 30th June, 1946, 26 recruits had joined the Force. Ten of these passed through the Training Centre at Eastwood Park and were posted to Divisions. A further ten were completing their Course at that Centre and six were undergoing instruction at No. 8, Training Centre at Bridgend, Glamorgan, due to the accommodation at Eastwood Park being limited.

On the 24th September, 1946, the Standing Joint Committee approved the proposed establishment of a Police Motor Driving School at Devizes, Wiltshire, and agreed to contribute to the cost, on the basis proposed by the Wiltshire Standing Joint Committee, including the suggested initial advance payment of £1 per head of authorised strength.

Seven tenders were received for erecting a new Police Station at Birdlip and on the 24th September, 1946, it was agreed to accept the lowest tender, by Mr. M.J. Partridge, of Birdlip, for the following amounts, namely:–

Police house, office and garage	£1,985.3.0d.
Site Works	225.6.7d.
	Total £2,210.9.7d.

Ex. Superintendent Alfred Cooke died at Downend on the 23rd July, 1946, aged 78 years. He was pensioned in 1928 and left a widow, Mrs Fanny Cooke, aged 79 years, who was granted a pension of £50 a year, from the 1st August, 1946, and payable during widowhood.

Between the 1st July and 24th September, 1946, thirteen recruits had joined the Force, making a total number enrolled since the 1st January, 1946, thirty-eight. Nineteen recruits had passed through Training Centres and posted to Divisions.

On the 17th December, 1946, it was agreed by the Police Authority, to accept the tender of Mr C.H. Hunt, of Drybrook, amounting in total to £2,158.3.0d., for the erection of a new Police Station at Drybrook in the Forest of Dean.

The Home Office issued particulars of new scales of pay for Inspectors, Sergeants, Constables, Police Women, First Police Reserve, Police War Reserve and Womens Auxiliary Police Corps (Class A.), which came into effect on the 6th November, 1946:–

Inspector – New scale started at £475 rising to £515 per annum
Sergeants – New scale started at 150/–d. rising to 165/–d. per week
Constables – New scale all started at 105/–d. rising to 140/–d. per week
Women Police Constables – New scale commenced at 94/–d. rising to 125/–d. a week

First Police Reserves and Police War Reserves together with the Womens Auxiliary Police Corps, were paid on the old scale applicable to Constables and Police Women, and became entitled to the new scales mentioned above.

During 1947, the Chief Constable was granted permission to spend a sum, not exceeding £250, in replacing old apparatus and purchasing new for the Photographic Section of the Criminal Investigation Department at Police Headquarters. The Section was doing valuable work at the scenes of crime, accidents, etc.

The Chief Constable pointed out to the Police Authority the inadequacy of the allowance for Prisoners' Meals, as laid down on the 1st July, 1941, viz:– 1/–d. per meal. He recommended that the allowance be increased to one meal at 2/–d. and two at 1/6d. each, per day, thus raising the cost of maintenance from 3/–d. to 5/–d, per 24 hours. The Report was received and adopted.

When Colonel Henn was appointed Chief Constable in 1937, he was granted an allowance of £250 per annum which was expressed to cover the use of a motor car and travelling and subsistence expenses, either within or without the County. As circumstances had changed, it was agreed, on the 25th March, 1947, that the following should apply, as from the 1st January, 1947:–

(1) The Chief Constable's existing allowance of £250 per annum to continue, such allowance to cover the provision of a motor car (including mileage of all journeys undertaken by car inside and outside the County) and all lodging and susistence within the County, when absent from home.

(2) The Chief Constable to be allowed First Class Railway fare when travelling outside the County by rail.

(3) The Chief Constable to be allowed a subsistence and lodging allowance, when outside the County, at the following rates:–

Day between 4 and 8 hours	6/6d.
Day over 8 hours and not including night	21/–d
Day and night	36/–d.

(4) The Chief Constable to be granted an Annual Uniform Allowance of £22.10.0d. in consideration of which he would continue to provide his own uniform.

Superintendent Arthur W. Hopkins retired on the 30th April, 1947. He was 62 years of age. His approved service, which included service in H.M. Forces from 5.5.15 to 6.1.19, was 43 years and 159 days. His pension, which commenced on the 1st May, 1947, was £463.6.8d.

On the 19th December, 1946, the Home Office issued particulars of new scales of pay for officers above the rank of Inspector, to take effect from the 6th November, 1946. They were as follows:–

Chief Constable	On appointment £1,100, rising by annual increments of £60 to a maximum of £1,400 per annum.
Assistant Chief Constable	On appointment £770, rising by annual increments of £30 to a maximum of £920 per annum.
Superintendent	On appointment £615, rising by annual increments of £20 to a maximum of £695 per annum.
Chief Superintendent	£20 per annum in addition to the Superintendents' scale.

During the year 1946, 68 persons were killed, 597 seriously injured an 1,931 slightly injured in road accidents in the County.

Of these, 27 were killed, 181 seriously injured and 462 slightly injured during the hours of darkness. 33 persons were killed, 235 seriously injured and 925 slightly injured on roads which were subject to a speed limit.

As from the 1st July, 1947, the Police Authority agreed to pay the Gloucester and Forest of Dean Branch of the Royal Society for the Prevention of Cruelty to Animals, a sum of 7/–d. in respect of each dog, found straying by Police, and sent to the Society's Dogs' Home.

Proceedings were instituted by a Mr R.O.H. Law against a Cheltenham Police Officer for unlawful arrest. The case was heard at Gloucester Assizes on the 5th June, 1947, when judgment was given for Mr Law and the Constable was ordered to pay £25 damages and the Plaintiff's taxed costs. The Finance Sub-Committee were satisfied that the Constable had made a bona fide mistake of identity and they recommended that the damages, and the Plaintiff's taxed costs and the cost of the defence be paid by the Police Authority.

During June 1947 it was agreed that electric lighting should be installed in Hanham and Bishops Cleeve Police Stations. Later in the year approval was also given for Chedworth Police Station to have electric lighting installed.

At their meeting on the 24th June, 1947, the Standing Joint Committee discussed the post-war establishment of the force. The Chief Constable fully explained his proposals, which had been discussed informally, and agreed, with officers of the Home Office. It was agreed by the Committee that the recommendations be adopted, thereby increasing the strength of the Force from 519 to 652, as set out in the following statement:–

	C.C.	*A.C.C.*	*Chief Supts.*	*Supts*	*Chief Insp.*	*Insp.*	*P.S.'s*	*P.C.'s*	*WPS.*	*WPC.*	*Total*
Present Strength	1	1	2	6	–	20	64	418	–	7	519
Proposed	1	1	2	6	3	26	82	523	1	7	652
Increase	–	–	–	–	3	6*	18	105	1	–	133

*Included three Detective Inspectors

With the cost of living rising quite rapidly, the Home Office decided to increase the grants for transfer expenses to serving Police Officers. The expenses were paid to officers when they were transferred, for duty, from one area to another. The amounts were as follows and came into operation on the 1st April, 1947.

Sergeants and Constables	£15. 0.0d.
Superintendents & Inspectors	£22.10.0d.
Assistant Chief Constables & Ch. Supts.	£30. 0.0d.
Chief Constable	£40. 0.0d.

The old rates were, Constable £6.10.0d., Sergeants £8.0.0.d., Inspectors £11.10.0d. Superintendents and higher ranks £16.0.0d. to £21.0.0d.

Between the 1st March and the 31st May, 1947, fifteen recruits joined the Force, making a total of seventy-six enrolled since February, 1946, Sixty-one recruits had passed through Training Centres and posted to Divisions.

As the suspension of periodical issues of uniform clothing had worked satisfactorily for the past five years, with quite a substantial economy, which was important while material and labour remained in short supply, the Chief Constable recommended that the arrangements be continued for another year. The Police Authority, on the 24th June, 1947, agreed to the Chief Constable's recommendations.

By 1947 motor vehicles began to give work to Police. For instance, the total motoring offences during the three months ending 31st May, 1947, were 863, and 526 persons were proceeded against. viz:–

	Offences	*Persons proceeded against*
Taking a m/car without the consent of the owner	53	17
Driving or in charge of a m/vehicle when under the influence of drink or drugs	4	4
Driving dangerously	12	6
Driving carelessly	49	41
Other offences	745	458

The Police Authority agreed to establish a Police Station on the Lynworth Estate at Prestbury, Cheltenham, to Police that estate and the Whaddon Estate which, more or less, adjoined it. The Chief Constable had accepted the offer of the Cheltenham Town Council to rent one of the semi-permanent houses on the Lynworth Estate, and also 73 Humber Road, Cheltenham, which was suitable for use as a Police Station, until a permanent one could be provided. On the 23rd September, 1947, the Committee confirmed the action of the Chief Constable.

Ex. Superintendent Edward Selwood died at Gloucester on the 22nd October, 1947, aged 87 years. He retired on pension on the 16th April, 1922, and was a widower.

P.C. Robert B. Robbins, married with one child, joined the Force on the

7th February, 1938. He had previously served with the Welsh Guards and was recalled to the Army on the 1st December, 1939. He served in Africa, Italy, etc., until the 30th August, 1945, when he resumed his Police Duties. At the latter end of 1947, P.C. Robbins was certified, by the Police Surgeon, to be unfit for further Police service owing to the fact that he was suffering from Phthisis. The officer appealed against the decision and, in accordance with procedure, the matter was referred to the Home Office, who appointed a Medical Referee. The Medical Referee allowed the appeal against the Police Surgeon's Certificate and P.C. Robbins was allowed to remain in the Force on full pay. At their meeting on the 16th March, 1948, the Chief Constable reported to the Standing Joint Committee that, up to then, Robbins had not been able to resume duty and that the Medical Referee thought he might be incapacitated for about six months, from the date of his examination which took place on the 5th December, 1947; he actually resumed duty on the 15th May, 1948. P.C. Robbins eventually completed his service, with the Force, and retired on pension. After another severe illness he died on the 28th January, 1983.

At the urgent request of the Home Office, the Finance Sub-Committee considered a revision of the maximum weekly rent allowance, payable to married Police Officers and of the allowances to single men and Police women. As a result the following revised rent allowances were submitted for the Home Secretary's approval, namely:–

Maximum weekly rent allowance for married men:-
Constable ....30/–d.
Sergeant ....32/–d.
Inspector ....35/–d.
Flat rate allowance for single men and Police Women:–
Constable ....15/–d.
Sergeant ....16/–d.
Inspector ....17/6d.

At their meeting on the 16th March 1948, the Police Authority were informed that the Home Secretary had approved the proposed allowances and had also re-affirmed the rent allowance of £125 per annum, payable to the Chief Constable.

Boot allowance was also increased from 2/–d. to 2/6d. per week from the 1st January, 1948. Plain Clothes Allowance was increased at the same time, viz:–

Superintendent increased from £22.10.0d, to £35 per annum
Inspectors increased from £20.0.0d. to £32 per annum

Sergeants increased from 7/6d. to 11/0d. per week
Constables increased from 7/6d. to 10/0d. per week

Gloucestershire Constabulary provided their first Instructor for the new Police Training Centre, at Falfield, on the 1st March, 1948, when Police Sergeant Walter G. Horton was appointed to fill a vacancy at the Centre. It was anticipated that his services would be required for about eight months. While so employed, his pay, etc., was a charge to the Home Office and not on County Funds. P.S. Horton resumed his normal duties, with the Force, on the 6th December, 1948, as the Training Centre was closed down owing to the building being required for other purposes.

During the year 1947, 63 persons were killed, 642 seriously injured and 1,918 slightly injured, in road accidents in the county.

Of these, 17 were killed, 162 seriously injured and 1,918 slightly injured on roads subject to a speed limit.

In the Birthday Honours for 1948, the Chief Constable, Colonel Henn, was awarded the King's Police and Fire Service Medal and was duly congratulated by the Chairman, on behalf of the Standing Joint Committee, at their meeting on the 22nd June, 1948.

A Refresher Course for Police Inspectors of No 7 Police District was being held at Cowley Manor, near Cheltenham, from the 21st to the 26th June, 1948, and an invitation was extended to members of the Standing Joint Committee to attend any of the lectures taking place.

Tenders were received for the erection of a Police Station at Hartpury, Nr Gloucester and the lowest, namely that of Messrs Turner & Co. (Gloucester) Ltd., amounting to £2,289.0.0d. was submitted to the Home Office for approval. On the 21st September, 1948, the Police Authority were informed that Home Office approval had been given.

It was during 1948 that a tragic accident struck the Lydney Police Station, in the Forest of Dean. A large hut had been purchased by the members of the Forest Division, for use as a Police Social Club, and off duty Police Officers were voluntarily demolishing it and loading the sections on to a lorry, when a brick wall, which divided the hut into two rooms, collapsed killing P.C. Alway immediately and injuring P.C. Park so seriously that he died on the following morning. In addition, Police War Reserve Edward E. Trotman was seriously injured.

The accident occurred at Naas Camp, Lydney on the 22nd April 1948. At an adjourned inquest, held at Lydney on the 6th May, 1948, a verdict of 'Accidental Death' was returned in both cases. Below are given details of the deceased Constables:–

> P.C. Bruce Alway. Aged 49 years and 187 days. Length of approved service 27 years and 14 days.

> P.C. Clifford Fowler Park. Aged 41 years and 202 days. Total length of service 22 years exactly. Length of approved service 21 years and 202 days.

Both officers left widows. P.C. Alway's only child, a daughter, was married. P.C. Park had no family.

Mrs Amy Alway was granted a pension of £36.8.0d. per annum, from the 23rd April, 1948. Mrs Kathleen Ann Park was granted a pension of £30 per annum from the 24th April, 1948.[7]

Between the 1st March and 31st May, 1948, 25 recruits joined the Force making a total of 160 enrolled since the 1st January, 1946. 132 recruits had passed through Training Centres and posted to Divisions.

It was during 1948 that the Home Office, in Circular No. 56/1948.F.2, stated that it had been represented to the Secretary of State that hardship was sometimes caused to retiring Police Officers, or to the widows of Police Officers, by delays in awarding their pensions and children's allowances, and in payment of the first instalment, especially where the Police Authority only met Quarterly, and suggested that alternative arrangements be considered. The Chief Constable informed the Standing Joint Committee that it was a fact that if a retirement, or a death, took place immediately after a meeting of the Standing Joint Committee, about three months could elapse before the first payment could be made, so he recommended that authority be given for pensions, etc., to be paid as soon as possible after the retirement, or death takes place. In each case he would notify the Clerk of the Standing Joint Committee and the County Treasurer.

Various amendments were made to Police Regulations during 1948. Regulation 39A – an additional Regulation – entitled all members of the Force to leave of absence on the six public holidays or on six other days in lieu, or if this could not be arranged, to payment instead.

Regulation 73(3) – paragraph 3 of the Regulation contained a list of duties which the Police should not be required to perform, and to this was added:–

> (iv) the regular duty of cleaning, or any part of the cleaning, of a particular Police Station which the Secretary of State has directed is NOT duty which the Police may be requested to perform.

Regulation 69 – was cancelled and a new one substituted, under which, as from the 10th May, 1948, the allowances to Detective Officers who were normally engaged on outside duty were increased to 25/–d. per week, for Superintendent and Inspectors and 20/–d. per week for Sergeant and Constables.

In the case of officers normally engaged on duty, other than outside duty, the allowances were fixed at 15/–d. per week for Superintendents and Inspectors and 12/6d. for Sergeants and Constables.

The Police (Women) Regulations were amended in 1948 so as to entitle each Police Woman to a free issue of 12 pairs of stockings per annum, as part of her uniform. There appears to have been a diversity of opinion, amongst Women Police Constables as to the most suitable kind of stockings so Colonel Henn suggested a cash allowance of 1/3d. per week be granted instead, which was approximately equal to the cost of 12 pairs of stockings per annum. The Standing Joint Committee agreed to this arrangement and the allowance was paid, as from the 10th May, 1948. However, this allowance ceased on the 31st August, 1948, as the Home Office objected to the payment of the cash allowance to Police Women, in lieu of stockings.

By the end of 1948, Wireless Services for the Police was beginning to take shape, especially in Gloucestershire and, by the 14th December, 1948, the Standing Joint Committee were informed that a wireless mast had been erected at Police Headquarters and the work at the Cleeve Common Wireless Station was well in hand. There had been some difficulty with regard to the site for the Edgehills Wireless Station, in the Forest of Dean, but it was hoped that this would soon be overcome.

The introduction of wireless made it necessary for motor patrol cars to be equipped with specially large and powerful generators, batteries, etc. These could not be fitted to the existing cars without alterations, which would have been expensive and unsatisfactory. In consultation with the Home Office, the makers of the Riley cars produced a 2½ litre model, specially adapted for Police Wireless purposes. In view of this the Chief Constable asked the Police Authority for permission to dispose of the existing fleet of Patrol Cars and order 16 of the new cars. Approval to the Chief Constable's request was quickly forthcoming.

Owing to the very considerable housing development which was taking place at Lower Tuffley, Gloucester, the Chief Constable suggested to the Police Authority that a Twin-station be provided. The Police Authority agreed and approved an enquiry being made of the Gloucester Corporation as to whether they would agree to allocate a suitable site for this purpose.

By September, 1948, tenders had been received for the erection of a new Police Station at Longhope and, subject to the approval of the Home Office, the lowest tender, namely that of Mr P. Bowkett of Longhope, amounting to £2,424.4.7d. was accepted.

In accordance with Home Office Circular No. 185/1948, dated 20th August, 1948, the Chief Constable decided to discontinue the employment of Police War Reserve Constables on the 31st December, 1948. The number of men affected was 14.

After the Second World War the Home Office set up a Committee of the Police Council on Uniform Clothing for the Police. Among the most important recommendations was one, which received the Secretary of State's approval, to the effect that Sergeants and Constables be provided with open neck jackets, shirts, collars and ties, and that, if obtainable in time, they be taken into use by the Summer of 1949. Apart from one jacket per man, the first issue would be as fixed by the Home Office, at two shirts; six collars and two ties. With the Chairman's approval Colonel Henn arranged with his Uniform Contractors to take the necessary steps to obtain the material needed for 1,800 shirts and 5,400 collars, without delay. Arrangements for procuring the ties were to be made later. As regards the new pattern jackets, 452 were ordered.[8]

On the 14th December, 1948, the Police Authority dealt with tenders for the erection of a new Police Station at Whaddon, Cheltenham, and it was agreed that the tender of Messrs R. Eldridge & Sons of Chelenham, amounting to £4,651.3.0d., which was the lowest, be accepted.

Superintendent Frederick Wearing of Staple Hill died in a Bristol Nursing Home on the 19th October, 1948, after an illness extending to just over six weeks. He was 58 years of age. Length of pensionable service 35 years and 202 days which included service in H.M. Forces from the 5th May, 1915, to 1st February, 1919, when he was awarded the Military Medal. He left a widow and a grown up daughter. Mrs L.R. Wearing was granted a pension of £81.17.6d. per annum.

The Buildings Minor Committee met on the 28th February, 1948, and considered a request, from the Chief Constable, for the provision of an office and garage at the Coney Hill (Gloucester) Police Station. It would be necessary for the work to be done in brickwork which, it was estimated, would cost £250. The Committee recommended that the work be carried out.

P.C. John H.R. Attwood, Police Headquarters, died on the 6th January, 1949, a few minutes after his admission to the Radcliffe

Memorial Hospital, Oxford. He had been ill for only a few hours. P.C. Attwood was 33 years of age. Length of pensionable service 11 years and 123 days which included service in H.M. Forces from 3.9.42 to 7.1.43, when he was discharged as 'Permanently unfit for any form of Military Service.' He was married twice and left one daughter by his first wife. His second wife was a widow when he married her and she had two children by her first husband. Mrs Attwood was entitled to a pension of 11/6d. per week which could be increased to 36/-d. a week for 13 weeks and to 26/-d. per week afterwards. In addition some allowances would be payable in respect of P.C. Attwood's child and his two step children, but this could not be dealt with until after hearing from the Ministry of National Insurance.

The Chief Constable was allowed to purchase a petrol pump for installation on the premises at Stow-on-the-Wold Police Station. The cost of the pump and petrol tank, which had a capacity of 250 gallons, was £55.15.0d. The cost of installation was £15.14.0d.

During the year 1948 – 122 males and 6 females were proceeded against for drunkenness, resulting in 119 of the former and 5 of the latter being convicted. This was an increase of 18 cases and 22 convictions, compared with the figures for 1947.

At the Standing Joint Committee Meeting on the 15th March, 1949, The Right Honourable Viscount Bledislow, P.C., G.C.M.G., K.B.E., referred to the Chief Constable's statement on Juvenile Crime and on his Propostion, seconded by Mr R.R. Dobson, it was resolved:–

(1) That the Gloucestershire Standing Joint Committee are strongly of the opinion that the provision of further facilities for recreation would go far to decrease the amount of Juvenile Crime prevalent in the County.
(2) That the Resolution be forwarded to the National Playing Fields Association and any other Association concerned with the provision of Playing Fields.

The Gloucester Division Recreation Club, through the Chief Constable, asked the Police Authority whether a hut could be erected at the rear of the Central Police Station, Gloucester, for skittles, miniature range, etc. In considering the matter the Committee bore in mind the policy of the Home Office advocating the provision of recreational facilities when new Divisional Police Stations were erected and, as it would be some time before a new Central Police Station could be provided at Gloucester, they were of the opinion that the request was a reasonable one. It was recommended on the 21st June, 1949, that a recreational hut be provided at the Central Police Station, Gloucester, at an estimated cost of £2,000 and that the Chairman of the Standing Joint Committee be authorised to agree a rent payable by the Police Recreational Club.

An application for the provision of a recreation room at Lydney Police Station at an estimated cost of £360, was also approved. The building to be erected by Mr F.N. Wright of Lydney, at a cost of £328.17.6d. Electric light to be installed at an approximate cost of £50.

On the 21st June, 1949, the Chief Constable reported to the Police Authority that P.C. John B. Sinclair, had been certified to be physically unfit for further Police Service. On the 2nd July, 1949, his age was 37 years and 185 days. Length of pensionable service 15 years and 22 days. By that date he would have been on the Sick List, on full pay, for upwards of 13 weeks. He was granted an ordinary ill-health pension of £86.1.6d. While in hospital his right leg was amputated. P.C. Sinclair was kicked on this leg in the execution of his duty in January, 1949, and he appealed against the grant of an ordinary pension, as he attributed the loss of his leg to this injury.

The Home Office appointed a Medical Referee to deal with the matter and he allowed the appeal. As a result P.C. Sinclair was found to be entitled to a supplemental pension, the amount of which depended on his degree of disability. P.C. Sinclair was examined by the Police Surgeon who reported that his degree of disability was 100% and that it would remain so until three weeks after he had been fitted, satisfactorily, with an artificial leg, when it would be 50%. This officer was later employed as a civilian clerk in the Gloucester Divisional Office and remained there over 25 years, until his retirement.

By the 31st May, 1949 193 Gloucestershire recruits had passed through Training Centres and had been posted to Divisions.

As the Chief Constable could no longer retain the Petrol Pump at Stroud, which Police had been renting for some years, he was obliged to purchase one at a cost of £75.15.0d. which figure included the cost of installation.

With the Government accepting the recommendations as to pay, etc., contained in the Report of the Oaksey Committee, it was agreed that the new scales of pay would take effect from the 1st July, 1949. One change brought about, affecting Sergeants and Constables, was, instead of being paid on a weekly basis they were to be paid, in future, like the higher ranks on an annual basis. The new scales of pay were as follow:–

		OLD SCALE	OAKSEY SCALE
POLICE WOMEN			
Constables	On appointment	£245.1.5d.p.a.	£290
	Maximum	£325.17.10d.p.a.	£380

Sergeants	On promotion	£351.19.3d.p.a.		£400
	Maximum	£385.17.2d.p.a.		£440
POLICEMEN				
Constables	On appointment	£273.15.0d.p.a		£330
	Maximum	£365.0.0d.p.a.		£420
Sergeants	On promotion	£391.0.5d.p.a.		£445
	Maximum	£430.3.7d.p.a.		£485
INSPECTORS				
	On promotion	£475.p.a.		£530
	Maximum	£515.p.a.		£575
CHIEF INSPECTORS				
	On promotion	£550.p.a.		£605
	Maximum	£590.p.a.		£645
SUPERINTENDENTS				
	On promotion	£615.p.a.	Grade 11	£700
			Grade 1	£800
	Maximum	£695.p.a.	Grade 11	£750
			Grade 1	£850
CHIEF SUPERINTENDENT				
	In addition to above	£20		£900 to £950

The Chief Constable thought that the cost of implementing the recommendations of the Oaksey Committee, so far as Gloucestershire was concerned, would probably amount to approximately £28,000 for the three quarters of that Financial Year, and not far short of £40,000 for the full year. A lot depended of course on how rapidly the Force could be brought up to establishment.

In view of the Oaksey Committee Report, the Chief Constable recommended that the charge for Police Officers doing duty on requisition, on or after the 1st July, 1949, be increased from 4/6d. to 5/–d. per hour.

The Police Authority were informed that there were safes at only two of the six Divisional Headquarters. As large sums of money had to be kept there, from time to time, Colonel Henn asked for authority to purchase four additional safes at a cost of approximately £18.17.0d. each.

On the 20th September, 1949, the Minor Committee were pleased to report, to the Standing Joint Committee, that the Wireless Stations at Cleeve Common and Edgehills had been completed and were operational.

With the Police Wireless Stations coming onto the air, the Information Room at Police Headquarters came into operation on the 18th July, 1949. The duties in the Information Room covered the whole of the twenty four hours and employed four Sergeants and four Constables. The Chief

Constable recommended that the Home Office be asked to approve of the augmentation of the Force by the number of officers detailed for duty in the Information Room, making the authorised establishment 652 men and 8 women.

Ex. Superintendent Charles A. Welchman died at Cheltenham on the 22nd July, 1949, aged 75 years. He retired on pension on the 18th November, 1933. He was a widower with a son serving in the Force.

Superintendent John R. Jotcham retired on pension on the 21st November, 1949, on that date he was 60 years of age. Length of pensionable service, which included service in H.M. Forces from 5.8.1914 to 10.1.1919, 38 years and 3 days. He was granted a pension of £500 per annum, commencing on the 22nd November, 1949.

In consequence of the recommendations contained in the Oaksey Committee's Report the Standing Joint Committee discussed various amendments and additions to the Police Regulations. The effect of some of the most important, operating from the 1st July, 1949, were as follow, viz:–

Detective allowance was discontinued from the 1st July, 1949, and those Detective Officers employed on outside duties were entitled to two allowances, viz:–

Detective Duty Allowance which was a consolidated form of overtime, payable at the rate of £42 per annum to Detective Inspectors, £36 per annum to Detective Sergeants and £30 per annum to Detective Constables.

Detective Expenses Allowance of 10/–d. per week, for these three ranks, which was intended to meet small incidental expenses incurred in connection with their duties.

Overtime Allowance which was only payable to Sergeants and Constables who were not employed on detective dutes, was increased by sixpence an hour to 4/9d. for Sergeants and 4/–d. for Constables.

Subsistence Allowance for periods of from 12 to 24 hours was increased by 1/6d. for Superintendents and 1/–d. for lower ranks to 12/–d. for Superintendents, 10/–d. for Inspectors and 9/–d. for Sergeants and Constables.

Lodging Allowance was increased by 7/6d. for Superintendents, 4/6d. for Inspectors and 3/6d. for Sergeants and Constables. The new rates for the ranks mentioned were, 18/–d., 14/–d., and 12/–d. respectively.

On the 20th September, 1949, the Chief Constable was granted permission to purchase a petrol pump for use at Police Headquarters, Cheltenham, the price of which, with the cost of installation, was £91.1.0d.

Prior to the 18th July, 1949, when the Police Information Room was opened at Police Headquarters, Cheltenham, all '999' calls originating in Gloucester and Cheltenham were connected, by the telephone operator, to the Police Stations in the respective towns. With the installation of wireless, the Chief Constable reported that these calls could be more expeditously dealt with if they were terminated in the Information Room. By this means the crew of a patrol car, operating in or near Gloucester or Cheltenham, could be contacted immediately by wireless and proceed direct to the scene of the complaint.

Chief Superintendent Arthur St. Clair Sainsbury, having passed the age limit, applied to retire, 'on account of age', at a date to be fixed later. His application was placed before the Standing Joint Committee on the 13th December, 1949, with a recommendation, by the Chief Constable, that he be allowed to retire, in due course and that he be granted a pension of £633.6.8d. per annum. Chief Superintendent Sainsbury retired on the 31st January, 1950. He had held the post of Chief Clerk, at Police Headquarters, for 30 years and 244 days.

The Buildings Minor Committee met at Gloucester on the 27th February, 1950, and they were informed that the new Police Stations at Birdlip, Drybrook, Ruardean, Longhope, Kings Stanley and Hartpury had been completed.

At the Standing Joint Committee meeting on the 14th March, 1950, the Chief Constable reported that a Special Division dealing with Traffic Matters, (T. Division), was set up at Police Headquarters on the 1st April, 1948, under the command of an Inspector. The establishment of the Division was 55. To bring it in line with Divisions of similar strength, in Gloucestershire and other Forces, it was recommended that it should be put in charge of a Chief Inspector. The proper establishment would then be:– 1, Chief Inspector; 1, Inspector; 8, Sergeants and 46 Constables.

Since the wireless had been installed, a patrol of roads in the County, by Patrol Cars, had been maintained for 24 hours. The number of Patrol Cars were inadequate to cover the County by night and day. On the 14th March, 1950, Colonel Henn asked for authority to increase this number and recommended that four additional cars be purchased and that they be of the new type Wolseley "Six Eighty" model. The cost of the car was £722.8.4d. plus the standard charge of approximately £80 for adapting for use with wireless. It was anticipated that the additional cars would rank for the Home Office Road Fund Grant.

By the 25th February, 1950, 283 Recruits had enrolled since 1st February, 1946. Of these 252 had passed through Training Centres and posted to Divisions.

During 1949, 190 motor vehicles were reported stolen. This was an increase of 13 on the year 1948. Eleven Motor Vehicles reported stolen during the year had not been recovered.

The number of persons killed during the year 1949 was 70. The number of persons killed in 1948 was 61. In 1947 – 63 and in 1946 – 68.

At their meeting on the 5th June, 1950, the Buildings Minor Committee considered a memorandum, by the Chief Constable, on the provision of certain amenities for new Police Stations and houses, in which he suggested that a maximum sum of £20 be allotted to each new Police house for the purpose of providing material to make the surround neat and tidy, including fruit or other trees and also to cover labour in the preliminary digging. The Committee agreed to the request but reduced the figure to be allotted, to £15. Consideration was also given to providing tarmacadam or concrete paths, but the Minor Committee were unable to recommend the carrying out of the work.

During 1950, the Home Office issued a Circular dealing with the employment of civilians on special work connected with Crime, such as the preparation of statistics, etc., which did not call for the exercise of Police powers, as reported in the Oaksey Report. The Chief Constable reported to the Police Authority, on the 20th June, 1950, that six female clerks and one male were employed on such duties, in Gloucestershire. Other duties of this nature, performed by civilians, consisted of one mechanic at the Headquarters Garage and twenty cadet clerks throughout the Divisions. In addition there were fifteen female typists. Under the circumstances, he did not think that very much more could be done in this direction, but he would review the situation and, in due course, would make any further recommendations which might be necessary.

The new open neck pattern jackets for Sergeants and Constables were taken into use, for day duty, on the 1st April, 1950. Now that the lower ranks had been issued with blue shirts and collars the Superintendents and Inspectors made representations that there was not sufficient distinction between the ranks as they too were issued with blue shirts. The Chief Constable recommended that the Superintendents and Inspectors should in future, wear white shirts and collars.

In the Hall at Holland House, Police Headquarters, Cheltenham there was a Tablet recording the names of those officers of the Force who lost their lives, were wounded, or who served in His Majesty's Forces during the 1914–18 War. On the 20th June, 1950, the Chief Constable reported to the Police Authority that three members of the Force and a Cadet Clerk lost their lives while serving with His

Majesty's Forces during the 1939–45 War. He felt sure that the Committee would wish that a Tablet to the memory of these officers should be erected near the existing Tablet. Colonel Henn had obtained a design from Messrs Boulton & Sons., Ltd., of Cheltenham, which was in harmony with the existing Tablet. The design was agreed to and the Chief Constable was authorised to have the Tablet erected at a cost of £55.17.6d., the total cost to include fixing and all lettering.

When the old Holland House was demolished, to make way for the present Headquarters – also named Holland House – the Tablets referred to above were taken down and placed in the basement of the Cheltenham Divisional Headquarters at Talbot House (next door) and were never erected in the new building.

The accommodation for single men at the Gloucester Central Police Station was reported, by the Chief Constable, as being very unsatisfactory. St. Winifred's Denmark Road, Gloucester, came into the market and on inspection was found to be suitable for use as a Hostel for the single men. Authority was given for the purchase of the property for £5,000, which figure the Home Office agreed.

The Wireless Service had been in operation since July 18th, 1949. The following figures were supplied for the year ending at midnight on July 17th, 1950.[9]

Total Transmissions	66,601
of these:–	
On Police Service	58,006
County Fire Brigade Service	5,016
Gloucester City Fire Brigade Service	928
County Ambulance Service	2,651
Interrogations of suspected persons, etc., by the crews of the 16 patrol cars	1,604
Arrests resulting from above	158
Assistance rendered to the public through medium of wireless, occasions	891
'999' calls (since 20.2.50) when the system was instituted	548

After the end of World War 11, difficulty had been experienced with regard to the supply of Medal Ribbon.

As members of the Force in possession of medals were directed to wear them when on duty at ceremonial parades, Assizes, etc., the Chief Constable asked for permission to obtain the required quantity of ribbon for issue to each member of the Force entitled to wear medals, at a cost not exceeding £25, and to obtain quotations, from time to time, for replacements.

When the Assistant Chief Constable was appointed, no scale of allowances was fixed to cover periods of duty he might perform outside the County. It was recommended, by the Chief Constable, and agreed by the Police Authority that, on these occasions he be paid the following allowances:–

(a)	Night and day	£1.16.0d.
(b)	Day exceeding 8 hours but not including a night	£1.1.0d.
(c)	Day not exceeding 8 hours but not less than 4 hours	6.0d.

Home Office Circular No. 223/50, dated 8.12.50, drew the attention of Police Authorities to the recommendation in Part II of the Oaksey Committee Report, paragraph 392, that assistance should be given to foster sports activities in Police Forces, and indicated that the Secretary of State was prepared favourably to consider any suggestions made in this direction.

While the Secretary of State agreed with the opinion expressed by the Oaksey Committee that the members of a Force should make some contribution, he suggested that a Police Authority could properly contribute a sum per head equal to the subscription paid by Police Officers, subject to a maximum sum of 10/–d. per year.

The Chief Constable reported to the Police Authority, on the 13th March, 1951, that in Gloucestershire, athletic activities had expanded greatly since 1945 and were being financed by a subscription of 1/–d. per month per man. Athletics, Rugby and Association Football, Cricket, Bowls, Tennis and Golf were played both between Divisions and against neighbouring Forces and other Clubs. Rifle shooting and swimming were practised and indoor games included darts, billiards, snooker and table tennis. The Force was also represented, whenever possible, in the Police Amateur Athletic Championship, England and Wales, and members had played for the British Police in inter-service Rugby Football matches.

Colonel Henn thought that these activities had an excellent effect on morale. He stated that the monthly subscriptions referred to above did not, of course, cover the cost of these activities and the proceeds of the Annual Sports, about £500, were devoted to the purpose. The cost of the Sports themselves was rising and the profit falling and unless further support was forthcoming, activities would be seriously curtailed. He therefore recommended, in accordance with the Home Office Circular, consideration of the matter by the Police Authority. Other Police Authorities in the South West Area (No. 7 Police District) had already agreed to make contributions. It was agreed, by the Police Authority, that a contribution of 10/–d. per head be made towards the Funds of the Police Sports Club.

As from the 1st April, 1952, it was agreed by the Police Authority that the Leave Year should be determined as beginning on the 1st April. Previously the Leave Year was confined to a Calender Year but the exigencies of duty made it difficult for members of the Force to take the balance of leave outstanding, during the month of December.

At their meeting on the 13th March, 1951, the Standing Joint Committee were told that the Police Hostel, Denmark Road, Gloucester, would soon be ready for occupation. The Chief Constable had advertised for applicants for the joint post of Cook-Housekeeper and Cleaner for the establishment, at a joint salary of £225.0.0d. per annum, plus accommodation, board, fuel and light free of charge. Numerous applications had been received and Mr & Mrs W.J. Nicholls of Hanham, had been appointed. Mr Nicholls had recently retired from the Force with the rank of Sergeant.

On the 19th June, 1951, the Chairman informed the Standing Joint Committee that at midnight on the 31st March, 1951, P.C. Peter Leatherbarrow plunged into the River Severn, near Westgate Bridge, Gloucester, to rescue a man from drowning, at considerable risk to his own life. His Grace the Duke of Beaufort, K.G., P.C., G.C.V.O. (Lord Lieutenant) presented P.C. Leatherbarrow with a parchment Certificate of the Royal Humane Society and congratulated him on his gallant conduct.

It was reported to the Committee, on the 19th June, 1951, that four Police Patrol Cars had recently been sold at prices ranging from £1,030 to £1,160.

At the request of the Chief Constable, the owners of the Police Station at Sapperton were asked to provide a flush lavatory in place of the bucket system and a lavatory basin in the bathroom, etc. After the work had been carried out, on the 19th June, 1951, at a cost of £89.10.11d., the owner of the property increased the rent by £7.2.6d. a year. The Police Authority agreed to pay the increased rent as from Lady Day, that year.

In June 1951, the Chief Constable recommended that four additional civilians be employed, one each in the Detective Office at Gloucester, Cheltenham and Staple Hill and the other in the C.I.D. at Police Headquarters, Cheltenham. At the three places first mentioned, they would replace Constables engaged on clerical duty, who would be available to augment the C.I.D. staff. At Headquarters, extra assistance was required to deal with work in connection with Aliens, Criminal Statistics, etc.

From 1944 an allowance of £1.10.0d. per annum was granted to members of the Force who used their own typewriters for Police purposes. Representation was made that this was insufficient to meet the high cost of maintenance and repairs. It was agreed by the Committee, on the recommendation of the Chief Constable, that the allowance be increased to £2.8.0d. per annum from the 1st July, 1951.

The Buildings Minor Committee, on the 10th September, 1951, considered the question of the provision of 'POLICE' signs at Police Stations which could be illuminated at night. The Chief Constable was asked to carry out a survey of the Police Stations in the County with a view to ascertaining the number of signs which would be required. They approved, as a general matter of principle, that Police Stations in the County should be fitted with a sign which could be illuminated at night and that the type of sign produced be acquired at an approximate cost of £3.17.0d. each. The Chief Constable, after his survey, reported that 115 signs would be required and approval was given for these to be fitted.

The Justice of the Peace Act, 1949, (Commencement No.2 Order, 1951), brought Section 10 and other related Sections of the Act, into force on the 1st October, 1951. As from that date the Borough of Tewkesbury lost its commission and by paragraph 6 (1) of the Second Schedule of the Act the Borough became a Petty Sessional Division of the County and the Clerk of the Borough Justices continued, under paragraph 8 (2) as Clerk to the Justices for that Division. Up to that period Tewkesbury always had their own Quarter Sessions.

During September, 1951, it was reported that two more Police Patrol Cars had recently been sold for £1,150 and £1,130 respectively.

On the 3rd September, 1951, the Minor Committee had to report that no progress had been made with the building of the Twin Police Station at St. Briavels owing to the lack of water. A well had been sunk 30 feet without success and in order to overcome the difficulty, the Committee approved the provision of a storage tank in the roof in order that a supply could be taken from the District Council. In addition to the cost of the tank, the Police Authority would also have to supply the piping.from the main to the house.

The civilian mechanic who was employed at the Police Garage resigned, during 1951, on account of being able to obtain higher wages elsewhere. With the Chairman's approval the Chief Constable increased the rate of pay for the post, from £6.0.0d. to £6.10.0d. per week and the vacancy was filled immediately.

Between the 1st June and 31st August, 1951, five recruits joined the Force, making a total of 341 recruits enrolled since the 1st January, 1946.

325 recruits had passed through Training Centres and been posted to Divisions.

New scales of pay came into force on the 3rd August, 1951, viz:–

RANKS		OLD SCALE	NEW SCALE
Women Police Constables	On appointment	£290 p.a.	£355 p.a.
	Maximum	£380 p.a.	£455 p.a.
Women Police Sergeants	On promotion	£400 p.a.	£485 p.a.
	Maximum	£440 p.a.	£525 p.a.
Police Constables	On appointment	£330 p.a.	£400 p.a.
	Maximum	£420 p.a.	£505 p.a.
Police Sergeants	On promotion	£445 p.a.	£540 p.a.
	Maximum	£485 p.a.	£585 p.a.
Inspectors	On promotion	£530 p.a.	£645 p.a.
	Maximum	£575 p.a.	£690 p.a.
Chief Inspectors	On promotion	£605 p.a.	£735 p.a.
	Maximum	£645 p.a.	£775 p.a.
Superintendents Grade 2	On promotion	£700 p.a.	£830 p.a.
	Maximum	£750 p.a.	£880 p.a
Superintendents Grade 1	On promotion	£800 p.a.	£930 p.a.
	Maximum	£850 p.a.	£980 p.a.
Chief Superintendents	On promotion	£900 p.a.	£1,030 p.a.
	Maximum	£950 p.a.	£1,080 p.a.

The New Scales for the Chief Superintendents and Superintendents were an interim measure and subject to revision. No decision had been made regarding the pay of the Chief Constable and the Assistant Chief Constable.

The additional cost, on account of the New Scales of Pay, was estimated to amount to £31,000 for that Financial Year and to £50,000 for the year 1952/53.

Due to the prompt and efficient action on the part of Mr Reginald Victor Smith, the arrest of a man for housebreaking with intent was effected. In rendering assistance to the Police, Mr Smith's clothes were damaged and the Home Office raised no objection to an ex-gratia payment being made. As Mr Smith was leaving for Canada on the 2nd November, 1951, approval was given to the making of an ex-gratia payment of £10.

His Majesty the King, by Royal Warrant given at the Court of St. James on the 14th June, 1951, authorised the award of a medal, to be styled the Police Long Service and Good Conduct Medal, as a mark of His Majesty's appreciation of long and meritorious service rendered by members of the Police Forces and Constabularies. The qualifying period for the award was 22 years' Police Service. Those eligible for the award had to be full-time serving members of all ranks in Police Forces maintained by local Police Authorities in England, Wales and Scotland.[10]

125 members of the Gloucestershire Constabulary fulfilled the conditions for the award of the Long Service and Good Conduct Medal and upon the recommendation of the Chief Constable, to His Majesty's Secretary of State, the awards had been approved. The medals were to be issued in due course, meanwhile the recipients were authorised to wear the ribbon. Subsequent recommendations were to be made as other members of the Constabulary became eligible for the award. The award of the medal still continues.

The No. 7 District Police Training Centre at Eastwood Park, Falfield, Gloucestershire, closed down in December, 1948. Police recruits from No. 7 District were then sent for Training to the various Centres around the Country, until the 13th August, 1951, when a Training Centre, for Police Recruits in No.7 District, was opened at Chantmarle, Cattistock, Nr. Dorchester.

The various Police Forces in No. 7 District agreed to supply shields, bearing the Coat of Arms of their respective Counties or Cities, for display in the Dining Hall at the Centre. With the Chairman's approval Colonel Henn arranged to supply a shield bearing the Gloucestershire Coat of Arms, at a cost of £22.10.0d.

By arrangements with the Home Office, parties of Greek Gendarmerie and Eritrean Police Inspectors were attached to the Force for the purpose of gaining an insight into the general administration and operation of the British Police Service.

The members of the Greek Gendarmerie, who were all high ranking officers, arrived on the 14th October, 1951, and remained for six days. The Eritrean Police Inspectors stayed for a period of fourteen days from the 19th November, 1951.

After the Second World War, 1939/45, Diseases of Animals still took up much Police time. For instance, in a case of Anthrax the local Police Officer was responsible for reporting to the Ministry and, once it had been confirmed that the animal had died from Anthrax, it was his responsibility to see that the carcase was destroyed, by fire, using wood, coal, etc. The year 1952 saw a change in procedure when the Chief Constable, as Chief Inspector under the Diseases of Animals Act, 1950, was given permission to purchase Twelve high pressure 'Hauck' Flame Guns. The Flame Guns proved to be a huge success and Colonel Henn was allowed to purchase a one hundred and twenty gallon tank for storage of paraffin at a cost of £11.10.0d. The Flame Guns were purchased, during January, 1953, at a cost of £72.0.0d.

By January, 1953, much progress had been made with new buildings on behalf of the Police Authority. For instance, Police

Stations had been completed at Hucclecote and Ruspidge and houses at Minchinhamton, Mangotsfield and Charlton Kings. Other schemes were progressing satisfactorily and the following is a statement of the position, as given to the Standing Joint Committee on the 21st January, 1953.

Police Stations and houses completed 60
Police Stations and house in course of erection 29
Tenders awaiting Home Office approval 6

Ex. Deputy Chief Constable Joseph William Parry Goulder died at Cheltenham on the 28th December, 1951, aged 75 years. He was a widower and retired on pension on the 31st December, 1945.

The Secretary of State made various amendments to the Police Regulations and these came into operation on the 31st December, 1951. These changes mainly affected allowances, details of which are given below:–

Overtime Allowance
Payable only to Sergeants and Constable – increased from 4/9d. to 5/8d. per hour for Sergeants and from 4/–d. to 4/10d. per hour for Constables.
Boot Allowance
Payable to all ranks – increased from 2/6d. to 3/–d. per week.
Detective Duty Allowance
Detective Inspector increased from £42 to £50 per annum
Detective Sergeant increased from £36 to £43 per annum
Detective Constable increased from £30 to £36 per annum

In Home Office Circular No.39/1952, The Secretary of State also approved new Scales of Pay for Chief Superintendents and Superintendents, with effect from the 3rd August, 1951.

	Old Scale	*New Scale*
Chief Superintendent		
On promotion	£1030 p.a.	£1050 p.a
Maximum	£1080 p.a.	£1100 p.a.
Superintendent Grade 1		
On promotion	£930 p.a.	£950 p.a.
Maximum	£980 p.a.	£1000 p.a
Superintendent Grade 2		
On promotion	£830 p.a.	£850 p.a.
Maximum	£880 p.a.	£900 p.a.

During 1952, the system of recording Found Property, which had been in operation for many years, entailed the use of several Forms, with the addition of entries in two separate books was changed. A new method had been devised in which only one book of forms would be used and this simplified the procedure. The cost of printing a supply of Books of Forms, under the new system, was £560.0.0d.

At their meeting on the 16th June, 1952, the Police Authority increased the Chief Constable's travelling allowance of £250 to £375 a year, as from the 1st July, 1952. The Assistant Chief Constable's travelling allowance was increased from £180 to £225 a year, also from the 1st July, 1952.

On the 13th June, 1952, Superintendent A.F. Newman, Chief Clerk at Police Headquarters, Cheltenham, was reported missing and, later in the day, articles of police clothing were found on the river bank near Gloucester. The clothing was identified as belonging to Superintendent Newman, and marks on the bank suggested that he had entered the water. Dragging operations were carried out but were not successful. At 3.30 p.m. on Thursday, 19th June, 1952, his body was recovered from the River Severn at Minsterworth.

On Saturday the 21st June, 1952, an Inquest was held at Minsterworth Memorial Hall by M.F. Carter Esq., H.M. Coroner for the Forest Division of the County. After hearing the evidence, he returned a verdict of 'Death by asphyxia caused by drowning' and that he took his life when of unsound mind.[11]

The late Superintendent Newman joined the Force on the 31st May, 1919. At the time of his death he was 58 years of age and had served for 33 years and 14 days. He left a widow, Mrs Patience Ivy Newman and two daughters, one married and the younger one still at school.

The Secretary of State approved new Scales of Pay for the Chief Constable and the Assistant Chief Constable to take effect from the 3rd August, 1951:–

Chief Constable ....£1,840 x £70 – £2,050 p.a.
Assistant Chief Constable ....£1,250 x £50 – £1,400 p.a.

During September 1952, the Chief Constable was given permission to install a petrol pump at Cirencester Police Station at a total cost of £136.3.11d.

By the 31st August, 1952, 381 recruits had enrolled since 1.1.46, of these, 360 had passed through Training Centres.

Prior to 1952, all Examinations for Promotion had been held at the Grammar School, Cheltenham. April 1952, saw the Examinations being held at the Technical College, Brunswick Road, Gloucester. Of the 12

Sergeants who sat the examination or for re-examination, 8 passed. 56 Constables sat the exmination for promotion to sergeant and 21 passed.

Members of the Force were now allowed to sit for the Educational part of the examination separately and 60 availed themselves of this arrangement. 17 passed the paper for promotion to Inspector and 9 passed the paper for promotion to sergeant.

The Chief Constable reported to the Standing Joint Committee on the 16th December, 1952, that, with the Chairman's approval he had purchased a 5 cwt. van which had been fitted up, in the Police Workshop, for the purpose of transporting the considerable amount of apparatus necessary to the scene of crimes and accidents, and also to serve as a mobile dark-room for the immediate development of the negatives obtained. The cost was £340.0.0d. Colonel Henn arranged for the van to be outside the Shire Hall, Westgate Street, Gloucester, at the end of the meeting in case any members of the Committee wished to examine it.

Home Office Circular No. 273/52.F.1, dated 12th December, 1952, stated that in view of the greatly increased cost of the Police, the Secretary of State considered that it would not be unreasonable to increase the existing charges, in respect of Police Reports, etc., of accidents, by 100% and suggested that the following Scale of Charges should be adopted:–

Abstract of Police Report	20.0d
Search fee (in cases where Police have no information)	5.0d.
Interview with Police Officer	20.0d.
Furnishing copy of witnesses statement to another party	7.6d.

Copy of a photograph of the scene of a road accident would be charged at:–

> Size 12″ x 10″ each copy 5.0d.
> Size 8½″ x 6½″ each copy 2.6d.

All the above charges operated as from the 1st January, 1953.

Early in 1953 the District Auditor raised the question of the agreement with the Gloucester Corporation for the Consolidation of the Police Force, which specified the payments to be made by the Corporation. It was agreed, by the Financial Sub-Committee,

> That notice be given terminating the existing Police Agreement with the Gloucester Corporation as from the 1st April, 1954, or such earlier date as may be agreed, between the two Authorities, and that the County Treasurer be authorised to negotiate the basis of payment by the Corporation and Report.

Chief Superintendent William E. Wakefield died at Gloucester on the

25th January, 1953, after a brief illness. His age was 61 years and 101 days. Length of pensionable service 42 years and 37 days. He left a widow, Mrs Gladys M.M. Wakefield and a grown up son and daughter. The son was serving in the Force at the time of his Father's death. The daughter Mrs E. Smith served in the Womens Auxiliary Police Corps, at Gloucester, throughout World War 2.

With the Accession of Queen Elizabeth II to the Throne and the forthcoming Coronation of Her Majesty The Queen, the Chief Constable recommended that decorations should be provided at 18 of the larger Police Stations, which included Divisional and Petty Sessional Stations, in order that these premises would not look bare among other buildings. An expenditure, not exceeding £20 was approved. In the event, this amount was exceeded by £2.14.7d. and, with the Chairman's approval, this extra expenditure was allowed.

A check of expired motor vehicles licences was held in Gloucestershire during the period 1st – 14th October, 1953. Of 11,476 vehicles stopped by Police, 2,442 were found to be exhibiting licences which had expired on the 30th September, 1953, or earlier. Offences were disclosed in 187 cases which were dealt with as follows:–

Cautions administered in ....58 cases
Mitigated penalties imposed in ....102 cases
Proceedings instituted in ....27 cases

The amount collected in mitigated penalties was £73.17.6d. and fines and costs imposed by the Justices amounted to £81.15.0d., a total of £155.12.6d.

Upon the recommendation of the Secretary of State for the Home Office, H.M. The Queen, in her Coronation Honours List, awarded the M.B.E. to the Assistant Chief Constable, Mr A.H.Carter.

H.M. The Queen also commanded that the Medal issued to commemorate her Coronation should be granted to a certain number of members of every Police Force in the Country, and also to a number of the Special Constables attached to the various Forces. The number of Medals received for distribution among the members of the Goucestershire Constabulary was 38, and 24 were allocated to the Special Constabulary.

At the request of the Commissioner of the Metropolitan Police, a detachment from the Gloucestershire Constabulary, consisting of one Chief Inspector, three Inspectors, five Sergeants, fifty-eight Constables and one Woman Police Constable, were sent to London on the occasion of the Coronation of H.M. The Queen, to assist the Metropolitan Police.

They formed part of the contingent furnished by No. 7 (S.W.) District. In addition one Special Constable attended. The cost of travel was £55 and subsistence approximately £65. When asked, by the Chief Constable, if the Committee wished to claim these amounts from the Metropolitan Police it was Resolved that 'no claim be made'.

The Gloucestershire contingent, with others, were under canvas in Hyde Park, London, for two nights and did duty in Birdcage Walk, Westminster, right outside Wellington Barracks.

During the Second World War the periodical issue of uniform to officers of the Gloucestershire Constabulary was suspended. On the 23rd June, 1953, the Chief Constable reported that the arrangements had worked satisfactorily for the past eleven years and had resulted in a substantial saving of material, labour and expense and recommended that the arrangements be continued for another year.

At the same meeting it was agreed that, in future, Inspectors' uniform would be supplied in 'Manchester Serge', instead of material as used for Sergeants' and Constables' uniform.

After a detailed examination, the Midlands Electricity Board submitted a report on the Wireless masts at the Police Wireless Stations which showed that aeriel clamps and feeder cable brackets had deteriorated from exposure to the weather and certain of the mast stays at Edgehills were rusting and in need of urgent repair. The Chief Constable reported that the Home Office would arrange to replace all defective or rusty cleats and clamps with their associated bolts, nuts, etc., but the renewal or repair of any structural item was the responsibility of the Standing Joint Committee. As the work was urgent the County Architect was authorised, on the 22nd September, 1953 to proceed in respect of those items for which the Committee were responsible.

Prisoner's Meals came under scrutiny again during September 1953, when the following rates were approved. A total allowance of 5/–d. for a person in custody for 24 hours, made up as under:–
One meal at 2/6d., second meal at 1/6d. and a third at 1/–d. The new rates to operated from the 1st October, 1953.

With the passing of the School Crossing Patrols Act, 1953, the County Council delegated their powers under the Act to the County Education Committee. In view of the arrangements to be made for providing training for the persons appointed to be School Crossing Patrols, the Standing Joint Committee were asked to co-operate with the Education Committee in providing the necessary training facilities. At their meeting on the 15th December, 1953, the Standing Joint

Committee agreed to co-operate and assist in every possible way.

The Chief Constable was given authority, at the latter end of 1953, to replace four mechanical Guardroom clocks, which were unreliable and beyond repair, with electric clocks at a cost of £4.18.11d. each. He was making investigation regarding clocks in other Stations and hoped that the Committee would authorise the Chairman to approve of the issue of such clocks as it may be found necessary to acquire. It was, of course, essential that a reliable clock be available at Police Stations where more than one Constable was stationed.

Ex. Superintendent Ezekiel John Perkins died at Stafford on the 3rd June, 1954, aged 85 years. He had been in receipt of a pension since 1st May, 1920. he left a widow Mrs Margaret A. Perkins, who was granted a Police Widow's Pension of 59/4d. per week.

On Wednesday, 14th July, 1954, Her Majesty The Queen held a Review of the Police Forces of the United Kingdom, in Hyde Park, London.

The Review was attended by representatives (including members of the Special Constabulary) of the Metropolitan Police, the County and Borough, Forces of England, Wales and Scotland, also the Royal Ulster Constabulary. A contingent of Police Cadets were included in the Parade.

Gloucestershire Constabulary were allocated the following places in the Parade – 3, Sergeants, 52 Constables, 1, Woman Police Constable, 2, Police Cadets and 5, Special Constables. The Contingent was under the command of Inspector H.D.J. Smith.

The following message was received by the Secretary of State from Her Majesty The Queen, in respect of the Royal Review, with a request that it be forwarded for the information of all Police Authorities[12] –

Buckingham Palace

The Right Honourable Sir David Maxwell Fyffe,
Secretary of State for the Home Department.

I shall be glad if you will convey, to the Police Authorities concerned and to the Commissioner of Police of the Metropolis, the other Chief Officers of Police, and all men and women who took part in this afternoons Review, my congratulations and those of my Husband on the high standard of smartness and discipline shown by everyone on parade.

The Police, in discharging their many varied and responsible duties, maintain the spirit of service towards their fellow citizens which is part of the tradition of the ancient office of Constable. On this depends the friendly co-operation between Police and Public of which this Country is so proud. I know that my Coronation and the Ceremonial events which followed it made heavy demands on the Police, and I am glad to have this opportunity of expressing my warm appreciation of the loyalty, courage and efficiency with which they serve me and my people.

ELIZABETH R

14th July, 1954.

The Secretary of State notified Police Authorities, in Home Office Circulars No's. 22/54, dated 14.1.54 and 45/54, dated 10.2.54, that the Police Council had reached agreement on the increase of pay for Superintendents and Federated ranks. The scales of pay which were increased with effect from 14th January, 1954, were as follows:–

Superintendent (Class 1 & 2)	increased by £55 p.a.
Chief Inspectors & Inspectors	increased by £55 p.a.
Sergeants	increased by £50 p.a.
Constables	increased by £45 p.a.
Women Police Sergeants	increased by £45 p.a.
Women Police Constables	increased by £40 p.a.

The additional cost on account of the new scales of pay was estimated to amount to £6,272 for the current financial year and to £30,109 for the year 1954/55.

Detective Duty Allowance was also increased from the 14th January, 1954. The new rates being:–

Detective Inspector	£54 p.a.
Detective Sergeant	£47 p.a.
Detective Constable	£40 p.a.

When the open-neck type of jacket was taken into use in Gloucestershire, Sergeants and Constables wore the jacket from the 1st April to the 30th September and the closed-neck jacket between the 1st October and the 31st March. At their meeting on the 16th March, 1954, the Chief Constable recommended that no further issue of closed-neck jackets be made and that when those in use were worn out, open-neck jackets would be worn throughout the year. The Standing Joint Committee endorsed the Chief Constable's action.

On the 17th May, 1954, Sergeant W.G. Horton, who was seconded to act as Instructor at the No. 7 District, Police Training Centre, resumed duty with the Force. Constable Henry C.S. Lodge was seconded to the same Training Centre as an Instructor Grade 2.

Superintendent Joseph W. Hallam retired on pension on the 15th June, 1954. His age on that date was 57 years and 277 days. Pensionable service 35 years and 55 days. His pension was £667.9.10d.

Due to the new scales of pay which came into operation in January, 1954, the Chief Constable recommended that the charge for police officers doing duty on Requisition, on and after the 1st July, 1954, be increased from 6/–d. to 6/9d. per hour.

The Chief Constable asked for approval to replace six of the Riley Patrol cars purchased in 1950 and 51. The cars had covered the following mileage – 112, 577; 100, 411; 97, 134; 87, 747; 87, 326; and 85, 962; The normal mileage for patrol cars, as laid down by the Home Office, was 60,000. Riley cars had proved to be most reliable in all respects and the Chief Constable recommended that the six cars referred to above be replaced by six Riley Pathfinders, at a cost of £1,312.5.0d. each.

It was not until June, 1954, that the Chief Constable was given permission to employ a full time female Telephone Switchboard operator in the Headquarters Office at Cheltenham. Up to that time a Cadet Cerk was employed on this duty. The Switchboard, at that time, carried 24 lines.

Mr & Mrs W.J. Nicholls who were appointed to the joint post of Cook – Housekeeper and Cleaner, at the Police Hostel, Gloucester in 1951, resigned their appointment on the 31st March, 1954, owing to the illhealth of Mrs Nicholls. With the Chairman's approval, Mr & Mrs H. Olpin were appointed, by the Chief Constable, to the joint post with effect from 1st April, 1954. Like Mr Nicholls, Mr Olpin was a retired Police Sergeant of the Gloucestershire Constabulary.

In order that the position of the Police Tent could be made known to the members of the public on such occasions as the Three Counties Show, Point-to-Point Races, etc., the Chief Constable purchased a blue pennant with the word "POLICE" theron and a portable sectional flagstaff, at a cost of £15.4.0d. The Three Counties show today is held on a permanent site at Malvern. At the time referred to above the show moved around, every year, between, Gloucestershire, Worcestershire and Herefordshire, in a similar way to which the Three Choirs Festival is held at the present time.

On the 21st September, 1954, the Standing Joint Committee were informed that Home Office approval had been given for the purchase of All Saints Vicarage, Gloucester, for £5,750, to replace the Hopewell Street Police Station.

Inspector George A. Gardner, retired on pension on the 31st August, 1954. He was 55 years of age and had served for 35 years. During the

Second World War Inspector Gardner was seconded to Badminton where he took over duties as personal Detective, and bodyguard, to Queen Mary who had moved to Badminton to avoid the London bombing. He remained with Queen Mary until the end of hostilities and, for services rendered to Her Majesty, he was awarded the Royal Victorian Medal in the Birthday Honours for 1945. For many years after his retirement he lived at Bentham Cottage, Bentham and died at Gloucester on the 19th January, 1979, in his eightieth year. He was a widower with a married daughter, with whom he spent his last days.

After ten years of continual use the flat bed print-dryer in the photography department at Police Headquarters, was worn out. It was replaced by a Rotary Glazing and Drying machine, purchased at a cost of £75.5.0d.

As a point of interest, the Western District Council for Manual Workers recommended an increase in the rate of pay of women cleaners at Police Headquarters, Cheltenham and the Central Police Stations at Cheltenham and Gloucester. The increase became operative on the 16th August, 1954, and was payable at the rate of 2/2,8989 per hour.

The Standing Joint Committee were informed, at their meeting on the 14th December, 1954, that increasing difficulty was being experienced in finding suitable sites in Cheltenham, at a reasonable figure, and as a considerable number of Police Houses were required in Cheltenham it might be necessary, if sufficient sites could not be obtained, to consider the erection of a block of flats to house a number of families which, obviously, would not occupy so much land. Thankfully this did not materialise.

The pay of Chief Constables and Assistant Chief Constables had to be settled by arbitration and the Secretary of State approved the award and stated that the new scales should take effect from the 14th January, 1954. They were:–

Chief Constable	£2,040 x £70 = £2,250
Assistant Chief Constable	£1,350 x £50 = £1,500

At the Standing Joint Committee meeting on the 15th March, 1955, the Chief Constable recommended that Police should no longer serve summonses in respect of the recovery of Rates or Income Tax. The average number of Summonses served by the Police in Gloucestershire was 4,100 a year and as the fee of 1/–d. was charged for Service income amounting to approximately £200 would be lost.

In view of the recommendations of the Committee on Police Extraneous Duties and as there was no legal authority requiring the Police to serve

Summonses of this nature, the Committee agreed with the Chief Constable's recommendation, as the large amount of time spent in serving these Summonses could be more usefully employed on Police duties.

Detective Sergeant Leonard F. Browning died on the 13th January, 1955, after a brief illness. His age was 39 years and 359 days and length of pensionable service 21 years and 55 days. He left a widow, Mrs Betty W. Browning.

During the year 1954, Police in Gloucestershire reported 716 deaths to Coroners and Inquests were held in 267 cases. Verdicts were as under:–

Accidental death	83
Death from Natural Causes	54
Suicide	33
Murder	1
Manslaughter	1
Other verdicts	95

March, 1955, saw the Chief Constable asking for authority to purchase six drag hooks, of an improved design, for use in dragging rivers, ponds, etc., for dead bodies. The drag hooks held at Staple Hill, Lydney, Gloucester and at Tewkesbury, were of a very old pattern, heavy and cumbersome and in need of new rope.

Colonel Henn thought that a drag hook should be available in each Division. The new pattern drag hook was of light weight and easy to transport. The cost of each hook, complete with necessary length of best hemp rope, was £7.16.5d.

During 1954, Police Officers from North Borneo and Peru paid Educational visits to the Force.

Mrs Annie Hannah Sainsbury, widow of the late Ex. Superintendent Young Sainsbury, died at Cheltenham on the 6th July, 1955, aged 90 years. She had been in receipt of a Pension since 1st December, 1928.

The Secretary of State informed Police Authorities in Home Office Circular No. 104/55.F1, dated 27th June, 1955, that the Police Regulations, 1955 (S.I. 1955, No.882), which provided for the reduction of working hours, would come into operation on the 5th September, 1955. The working week of male members of Police Forces, below the rank of Superintendent, would be reduced from 48 to 44 hours, by granting an additional rest-day each fortnight.

As a result of the reduction in working hours the Chief Constable went to the Standing Joint Committee on the 20th September, 1955, and asked for favourable consideration to be given to an increase in the strength of the Force. In addition to the reduction in working hours the changing conditions in the County warranted the proposed augmentation, which was:–

1, Inspector, 9, Sergeants and 60, Constables.

In support of his request the Chief Constable submitted the following Memorandum.

> The 44 hour week is really an 88 hour fortnight as against the present 96 hours. All officers up to and including the rank of Chief Inspector are entitled, as from September 5th., to three rest-days per fortnight, instead of two, as at present. If the interests of the public service render it necessary for an officer to work on that third rest-day, he is entitled to be paid for the eight hours extra duty at time-and-a-half rates. The object of the Regulation is to give the officer another Day's Rest, and not to give him money.
>
> It is impossible to apply this Regulation, and at the same time to give the public proper police coverage on the present Establishment which was calculated for a 96 hour fortnight, and which, as I have indicated, is now inadequate even for that. Whatever the augmentation, finally approved, there must be a time-lag before the extra men can be recruited and trained, and during that period it will be necessary to pay over-time as required. An overwhelming majority of the Force are prepared to work this over-time in view of the necessity of maintaining a public service, though they would prefer the rest day.

The Chief Constable's report was received and adopted.

The Secretary of State notified Police Authorities on the 27th. September, 1955, that agreement had been reached on the new scales of pay for Superintendents. They were:–

Superintendents Class 1 – £1,135 x £30 – £1,195 p.a.
Superintendents Class 2 – £1,015 x £30 – £1,075 p.a.

The new scales of pay were operative from the 8th September, 1955.

Home Office Circular No. 145/55 F2 dated 19th September, 1955, suggested to Police Authorities that the weekly allowances paid to officers attending Courses away from home and living in lodgings, should be increased to the following:

Superintendent	£6. 0.0d.
Inspectors	£5.10.0d.
Constables and Sergeants	£5. 0.0d.

Between the 1st September and 30th November, 1955, six recruits joined the Force, making a total of 497 recruits enrolled since the 1st January, 1946. A total of 486 recruits had passed through Training Centres and posted to Divisions.

On the 13th December, 1955, the Chief Constable reported to the Police Authority that, at that time, none of the Divisional Utility Vans which were used for conveying prisoners, attending scenes of accidents, and emergency calls, etc., were fitted with wireless. It frequently occurred that, when these vans were in one part of the Division Police attendance was necessary in another part and there was no means of getting in touch with the driver. He recommended, therefore, that the six Utility Vans should be fitted with wireless, as and when they were replaced. Installation would be arranged by the Home Office at a cost of £5 per van for wiring plus a rental of £8.10.6d. per quarter.

On the 13th March, 1956, the Chief Constable asked for consideration to be given for the setting up of canteen facilities at Staple Hill Police Station. There were 37 Constables for which, at that time, there was no provision for the supply of meals. The County Architect was asked to produce a modified scheme for consideration by the Committee. The County Architect submitted his Report on the 26th June, 1956, which was estimated to cost £118.10.0d. The Committee recommended that a canteen be provided in accordance with the revised scheme.

The Secretary of State notified Police Authorities that, after going to arbitration, the following scales of pay had been awarded to the Federated Ranks of the Police Force, with effect from the 16th December, 1955.

Chief Inspector	on appointment £910 to £960 per year after 2 years service in the rank
Inspector	on appointment £800 to £860 per year after 3 years service in the rank
Sergeant	on appointment £675 to £735 per year after 4 years service in the rank
Constable	on appointment £475 to £640 per year after 15 years service in the rank
Woman Police Sergeant	on appointment £605 to £660 per year after 4 years service in the rank
Woman Police Constable	on appointment £425 to £575 per year after 15 years service in the rank

The Chief Constable, Colonel W.F. Henn, C.B.E.,M.V.O. attained the retiring age of 65 years on the 4th March, 1957, and the Standing Joint Committee were of the opinion that his retirement should be postponed for a limited period. In accordance with Regulation 51 (2) of the Police Regulations, 1955, the retirement of the Chief Constable was postponed for a period of two years.

Ex. Chief Superintendent and Deputy Chief Constable Robert H. Hopkins, died at Charlton Kings on the 16th April, 1956, aged 83 years. He was a widower and had been in receipt of a pension since 1st December, 1935.

Another Ex. Chief Superintendent passed away the following day, 17th April, 1956. Arthur Sainsbury, who was a bachelor, and had retired from the Force on the 1st February, 1950. He was 69 years of age.

Superintendent Charles F. Large retired on pension, from Cheltenham Central Police Station, on the 17th April, 1956. On that date his age was 63 years and 291 days, and his pensionable service 44 years and 31 days. His pension, on retirement was £770.7.6d. per annum. He was awarded the Queen's Police Medal the same year.

The Police Pensions Regulations, 1956, came into operation on the 1st April, 1956, and introduced a scheme of improved ordinary pensions for widows together with an increased rate of pension contribution, as recommended by the Police Council for Great Britain.

Men joining the Force after the 1st April, 1956, would be required to pay pension contributions at 6¼% of their pay. Policemen serving on that date had the option of (a) continuing paying pension contributions at the rate of 5% or (b) accepting the new conditions and paying the increased pension contribution at the rate of 6¼% with a reduction in their pension on completion of service or (c) paying an additional contribution to the 6¼% if they had less than 20 years service on the 1st April, 1956.

New scales of pay for Chief Constables and Assistant Chief Constables came into operation from the 16th December, 1955, when the increased rates for the Federated ranks came into force. The scales for the occupiers of the posts in Gloucestershire were as under:–

Chief Constable	£2,315 x £75(2) x £85–£2,550 p.a.
Assistant Chief Constable	£1,530 x £55(2) x £60–£1,700 p.a.

On the 26th March, 1956, the Secretary of State informed Local Authorities that he hoped shortly to be in a position to place an order, with the manufacturers, for the supply of wireless equipment for Police Motor Cycles. The Chief Constable said it would be a great advantage if three motor cycles, which were attached to Headquarters and used at Race Meetings, for Traffic Control, etc., were equipped with wireless. The Standing Joint Committee agreed to take advantage of the Home Office order.

An Examination for Promotion was held at the Technical College, Brunswick Road, Gloucester, on the 4th and 5th April, 1956, with the following results:–

Examination Subject	*No. of Candidates*	*No. Qualified*
Police Duties	11 Sergeants	8
Police Duties	45 Constables	20
Educational	6 Sergeants	–
Educational	88 Constables	8

The secondment of P.C. Henry C.S. Lodge as an Instructor, Grade 2, at No. 7 District Police Training Centre, terminated on the 3rd September, 1956 and he returned to duty within the Force.

Gloucestershire Police Officers, ever conscious of their role in Society, were amongst the first to volunteer for the British Police Unit in Cyprus, in response to an appeal from the Colonial Office to assist combat the ravages of Eoka terrorism. P.C. Joseph A. Cook and P.C. Robert J. Watts volunteered and were seconded for duty, with the British Police Unit for an initial period of twelve months, with effect from the 28th August, 1956.

As at Gloucester, accommodation was in short supply for single-men at Cheltenham. On the 18th September, 1956, the Standing Joint Committee were informed, by the Chief Constable, that the adaptation of Malvern Hill House, as a Police Hostel, and the cottage as a residence for the Caretaker, had been completed. The joint post of Cook-housekeeper and Caretaker, for this establishment, at a joint salary of £250 per annum plus accommodation, board, fuel and light free of charge, was advertised and after numerous applications had been received, Mr & Mrs W. Symons of Taunton were appointed. The Hostel was occupied on Monday 12th, November, 1956.

At their meeting on the 18th September, 1956, the Chief Constable informed the Police Authority that the County Police Cricket Team had just won the No. 7 District Knock-out Cricket Competition for the 'Falfield' Cup, for the third time since the competition was inaugurated in 1948.

Police Sergeant William C.R. Wicks, died on the 29th October, 1956, aged 52 years. Length of Pensionable serevice was 29 years and 282 days. He left a widow, Mrs. Elsie E.L. Wicks who was entitled to a Police Widows Pension of £11.18.2d. per month.

The Secretary of State notified the Police Authorities, in Home Office Circular No 152/56 F1, dated the 19th October, 1956, that aggreement had been reached, by Panel 'B' of the Police Council of Great Britain, on the new scales of pay for Superintendents. The new scales of pay, which were related to (a) increase in pay to other ranks of the Police and (b) the introduction of reduced working hours for the Federated ranks, were:–

Superintendent Class 1 – £1,225 x £30 – £1,285 p.a.
Superintendent Class 2 – £1,100 x £30 – £1,160 p.a.

The new rates of pay were back dated to the 16th December, 1955 The duties of Warrant and Coroners Officer at Cheltenham and Gloucester had, up to 1956, been carried out by a Constable. These duties comprised all Police work in connection with Magistrates' Court, keeping of records, execution of Warrants, service of summonses etc., preparation of reports and enquiries regarding Sudden Deaths, and attendance at Inquests.

The Chief Constable was of the opinion that the duties of Warrant Officer were important and exacting and he felt that the time had come when the Department should be staffed by a Sergeant and Constable. He therefore recommended that the strength of the Force be increased by two Sergeants to enable this to be put into effect.

Up until December, 1956, the Stores at Headquarters were controlled by three different departments. The Uniform Stores was dealt with by a Sergeant. Stationery and cleaning materials, by the Accounts department, and cycles and accessories, electric batteries, torches etc., by the Administrative department. The procedure was not satisfactory and with work continually increasing, additional rest-days etc., the service of clerks could not be spared to deal with stores.

The Chief Constable therefore proposed to create a Stores Department which would deal with all stores kept at Headquarters. The minimum staff for the department, he said, would be a Sergeant in Charge and a male civilian, with clerical experience, to keep the necessary records, and a Cadet Clerk. He asked the Committee if they would agree to the strength of the Civilian Staff being increased by a male civilain clerk and a Cadet Clerk. The Report was received and adopted by the Standing Joint Committee on the 11th December, 1956.

In dealing with road accidents at night difficulty was often experienced in giving warning to other road users of the fact that the road was blocked, particularly when there was only one Police Officer present.

The Chief Constable asked the Police Authority for permission to purchase 24 'Flaremaster' lamps. These lamps which were easily transportable, gave an intermittent red light visible for 2/300 yards and were battery operated. At least two lamps would be required for an accident. Two dozen would allow them to be stored in different parts of the

County, with some at Headquarters for use by motor patrol. The cost of a lamp with a suitable container was £2.1.8d. each. On the 19th March, 1957, the Police Authority gave the Chief Constable permission to purchase the 24 lamps.

At the same meeting Colonel Henn referred to the ever-growing number of requests for talks by Police Officers. They came from Clubs, Associations, Guilds and Societies of many kinds. In the two years ending the 31st December, 1956, one hundred and seventy such talks had been given, with the object of explaining the machinery of the Police to the Public and of pointing out how it could be of service to them in particular circumstances.

It was early in 1957 that the County Council decided that, with the object of securing the highest degree of efficiency in their administration, an Organisation and Methods investigation should be carried out. The Police Authority suggested that it would be useful if the investigation could be extended to include the Police clerical administration and they recommended that the County Council be asked to include the Police clerical administration in the Organisation and Methods investigation.

In the Report of the Working Party on Criminal Circulation and Clearing Houses, 1957, it was suggested that consideration should be given to the establishment, in Bristol, of a Regional Criminal Record Office. The office would be used by the Police Authorities in the Region who contributed towards the cost. On the 25th June, 1957, it was agreed that the Chairman of the Police Authority and the Chief Constable should attend a meeting of the Police Authorities for No.7 District and support the setting up of a Regional Criminal Record Office and the payment of a contribution towards the cost.

Home Office Circular No 77/57.F1, dated 17th April, 1957, informed Police Authorities throughout the country, that the Arbitrators appointed by the Prime Minister had awarded the following Scales of pay to the Federated Ranks of the Police Force with effect from the 1st February, 1957.

Constables on appointment £490 to £660 per year after 9 years service
Women Police Constable on appointment £440 to £595 per year after 9 years service
Sergeants on appointment £695 to £755 after 3 years service in the rank
Women Police Sergeants on appointment £625 to £680 per year after 3 years service in the rank
Inspectors on appointment £825 to £885 per year after 2 years service in the rank

Chief Inspectors on appointment £935 to £1,000 per year after 2 years service in the rank.

Detective Duty Allowances were increased at the same time, also with effect from 1st February, 1957. They were:–

Inspectors	£78 a year
Sergeants	£66 a year
Constables	£52 a year

Gloucester City Council were not happy with the way the Park was being patrolled in Gloucester and on the 27th June, 1957, they applied to the Standing Joint Committee, to employ an additional Constable, in the Park, under Section 19 of the County Police Act, 1840. Colonel Henn recommended the application for favourable consideration and should the appointment be approved the person selected would be engaged as a Reserve Constable. The whole cost of such Reserve Constable to be paid for by Gloucester City Council but would not rank for Exchequer Grant.

In June, 1957, the Chief Constable had to report to the Police Authority that, the hand carpet sweeper which was in use at Police Headquarters, Cheltenham, was purchased over 25 years ago and was worn out. With the Chairman's approval he had purchased an electric vacuum cleaner at a nett cost of £27.8.4d.

The number of sheep dipped, in Gloucestershire, during the year 1957, was 220,116, an increase of 14,435 or 7% over 1956. This was one of the extraneous duties that Police had to do in those days. i.e. attend and witness the dipping of sheep to see that the dipping was carried out efficiently and in compliance with the law.

As a result of Home Office Circular No. 121/1957, dated 19th June, 1957, the conditions regarding the position of Police Cadets and National Service were changed. After that date, Police Cadets who reached the age of 19 years before being required to Register for National Service, would be deferred on joining the Regular Force.

In order that the uniform of the Special Inspectors could be of similar pattern to that worn by the Regular Inspectors, Colonel Henn asked for authority to issue them with open-neck jackets. One suit would be required for each Inspector. As regards shirts, collars and ties, he proposed to make an inital issue of one white shirt, three collars and one tie and for any replacement to be provided by the Special Inspectors at their own expense. The issue would be to ten Special Inspectors. The cost of the uniform being £12.1.7d. and the shirt, collars and tie £2.15.0d., making a total of £148.5.10d.

During 1957, P.C. Robert N. Lightfoot volunteered for Police Duty in Cyprus in response to an appeal by the Colonial Office. He was seconded for duty to the British Police Unit in Cyprus for an initial period of 21 months. (P.C. Lightfoot returned to the Force for duty in 1959).

When motor cycles were first brought into use by the Gloucestershire Constabulary they were used mostly on the Trunk Roads throughout the County. There was no provision on these machines for the rider to carry his meal, papers, etc. The Chief Constable, with the Chairman's approval, purchased four pairs of Pannier Bags for use on the motor cycles, at a total cost of £14.10.0d.

With the increase in both Road and other accidents the Chief Constable felt that all Police Stations should be equipped with a First Aid Case. A suitable case containing dressing, bandages, iodine, sal volatile, etc., could be obtained for £1.18.0d. each and he asked for authority to purchase 101 of thise cases to enable all Police Stations to be equipped with a First Aid Case. The total cost would be £191.18.0d. On the 17th September, 1957, the Committee agreed to the purchase of the cases but the Chief Constable was requested to confer with the County Medical Officer of Health as to a substitute for iodine in the First Aid outfits referred to. At this particular time every member of the Force carried a First Aid Packet which contained bandages, in addition there were 35 Ambulance Haversacks distributed, as far as possible, at Police Stations on Main Roads.

At the request of the Chief Constable an inspection of Berkeley Police Station was made with particular reference to the Police Sergeants' accommodation. It was found that the domestic quarters in the main were unsatisfactory particularly the bedroom and kitchen accommodation, as a result, Colonel Henn asked that a site be acquired for the building of a new Station. This was December, 1957.

When the Police No. 2 Regulations, 1957, came into force the Home Office issued a Circular No. 191/57F, asking for Police Authorities to review the maximum limit rent allowances for married officers. When the Gloucestershire Police Authority met on the 10th December, 1957, the Chief Constable recommended that the maximum limit Rent Allowance for married officers, be as follows:–

Superintendent	£140 p.a.
Inspector	47/6d. per week
Sergeants	45/–d. per week
Constable	42/6d. per week

The Chairman added that the Home Office also suggested that where rent allowances were paid to officers above the rank of Superintendent, they should also be reviewed. The Assistant Chief Constable was the only member of the Force affected and his case would be considered at the next meeting of the Finance and Buildings Sub-Committee.

The Chairman added that the revised maximum limit rent allowances were also payable to certain single men and women over 35 years of age and the Chief Constable recommended that these rates would be paid in applicable instances within the Force, which numbered two men and two women. He also recommended that single members of the Force below that age, who were not provided with accommodation should receive a fixed rate of allowance equal to one-half of the amount of the maximum limit allowances, which would be as follows:–

Inspectors	23/9d. per week
Sergeants	22/6d. per week
Constables	21/3d. per week

The Chairman stated that the Regulations also laid down the basis of calculation for an owner/occupier's maximum limit rent allowance which was to be the aggregate of the rates of the house occupied and an amount which, in the opinion of the District Valuer, would be the rent of the house if it were let unfurnished.

The Regulations also provided for an increase in the limits of the allowances payable under Regulation 31 of the Police Regulations, 1952, relating to Removal Allowances. The rates agreed upon by the Police Council and approved by the Secretary of State were as under:–

Superintendent and above	£50
Chief Inspector and Inspector	£40
Sergeant and Constable	£30

It was Resolved by the Standing Joint Committee, 'that the rent and removal allowances referred to above be approved and that provision for the expenditure be included in the Committee's estimate of expenditure.'

The Secretary of State approved new scales of pay for Chief Constables and Assistant Chief Constables, with effect from the 1st February, 1957. They were:–

Chief Constable	£2,385 x £80 (3)	– £2,625
Assistant Chief Constable	£1,575 x £55 x £60 (2)	– £1,750

'Outward Bound' Courses were becoming popular about this time and at their meeting on the 10th December, 1957, the Chief Constable reported, to the Police Authority, that he felt it would be of advantage to the Force to send some selected Cadets to attend these Courses, which were held by the 'Outward Bound' Trust Ltd., at their various establishments. He was of the opinion that the training in leadership and self reliance which was given would be of immense value to the right type of lad.

Each Course lasted about 4 weeks and catered for boys from the ages of 16½ to 19½. Colonel Henn thought that the County Education Committee might be prepared favourably to consider the question of meeting the cost, which was Thirty Guineas for each Course.

He asked for consideration to be given to sending three or four Cadets to attend these Courses per annum and, if this was agreed, that the County Education Committee be approached regarding the question of cost, the system to operate from the beginning of the next Financial Year, 1958/59.

It was during the first half of 1958 that certain repairs were being carried out at the Central Police Station, Gloucester, and after an inspection it was found that dry rot had decayed the main timbers of the structure. Apart from the infestation of rot, the general conditions of the walls, roofs and chimney stack was such that it was undesirable to embark on any further large expenditure in trying to maintain the structure.

In view of the age and condition of the property it was not an economical proposition to carry out extensive repairs which were necessary and the only solution would be to erect a new Police Station on the existing site. To enable this to be done it would be necessary to transfer the Station temporarily to other premises.

The Standing Joint Committee were recommended to approve in principle the erection of a new Station on the existing site and the Estates and General Purpose Committee was asked to consider the Police Authority being granted the use of the College of Domestic Science, which would be vacated by the Autumn of 1958.

In view of the urgency of the matter the County Architect and the Chief Constable were asked to inspect the College of Domestic Science to ascertain what work would be necessary in order to effect the transfer. The College of Domestic Science was then situated in Barrack Square, adjoining the old Barracks, at the rear of the Central Police Station, Bearland, Gloucester.

At their meeting on the 25th March, 1958, the Committee were reminded that the Chief Constable, Colonel W.F. Henn, C.B.E.,

M.V.O. had attained the retiring age of 65 years on the 4th March, 1957 and his retirement had been postponed for a period of two years.

The Committee considered the steps to be taken to appoint a successor who would take office in March, 1959 and recommended:–

(1) That an advertisement for a successor be prepared and issued by the Clerk with the approval of the Chairman after consultation with the Home Office.

(2) That a Sub-Committee be authorised to prepare a short list of candidates for interview by the Standing Joint Committee.

At this same meeting it was resolved, 'That the retirement of Colonel Henn, C.B.E., M.V.O., be postponed until the 8th April, 1959, when he would have completed 22 years service.'

Mr. H.J. Walker, at the Standing Joint Committee meeting held on the 25th March, 1958, referred to the practice of purchasing all Police vehicles from one firm and moved, 'That the purchase of patrol and other vehicles for the Police be distributed throughout the County'. Mr H. Pilkington, M.B.E., seconded the motion.

Major E.E. Mealing moved as an amendement and Mr C.W. Luker seconded, 'That the question of the purchase of Police vehicles be referred to the Finance and Buildings Sub-Committee for consideration and Report'. The amendment was carried. On the 24th June, 1958, the Sub-Committee reported that as purchases in all cases were made from the main county Distributor they could see no useful purpose being served by amending the method and it was resolved, 'That the existing practice be continued'.

Pay for Police Officers was dealt with and Pay Sheets compiled in each Divisional Office. The rises in grade and promotions being recorded in a foolscap book, details of which were sent to the next Divisional Office when an Officer was transferred. A Personal Record Card, for each officer was suggested by a Divisional Clerk at Gloucester and was eventually adopted throughout the County.

During 1958 a more modern Pay Sheet system was introduced and the estimated cost of the new Pay Sheets, slips and Record Cards was approximately £227.10.0d. A reprint of the old Pay Sheets would have cost £100, therefore, the nett cost of introducing the new system was £127.10.0d.[13]

With the inauguration of the South Western Criminal Record Office it was essential that a Teleprinter with Telex System be installed at the Headquarters of all Forces in No. 7 District. On the 25th March, 1958, the Chief Constable was given permission to install a Teleprinter, with the Telex System, at Police Headquarters, Cheltenham. The machine to be rented from the General Post Office at an Annual charge of £160.

During 1957, 39 persons were arrested for driving a motor vehicle whilst under the influence of drink and 22 for being in charge of a motor vehicle whilst under the influence of drink. The 61 cases resulted as follows:–

2 Imprisonment
47 Fined
5 Discharged
7 Committed for Trial

During the year 1957, 214 males and 8 females were proceeded against for drunkenness, all being convicted. This was an increase of 9 compared with the figures for 1956.

Police Authorities were informed, in Home Office Circular No. 45/58/F2, dated 16th April, 1958, that the Police Pensions (No.2) Regulations, 1958, had been approved by both Houses of Parliament, and came into operation on the 14th April, 1958.

The purpose of the Regulations was to enable a regular member of a Police Force to commute voluntarily, part of his pension on retirement –

(i) on completion of thirty or more years' service
(ii) required to retire on grounds of age
(iii) required to retire on grounds of ill-health

The Regulations also substituted new provision for the existing provisions of the Regulations, which enabled a regular member of a Force to allocate a portion of his pension in favour of a dependant.

The Chief Constable informed the Standing Joint Committee, on the 24th June, 1958, of the action taken by members of the Force in effecting the recapture of five prisoners who had recently escaped from H.M. Prison, Gloucester. It was resolved –

> 'That the Clerk be requested to write to the Chief Constable conveying the Committee's appreciation of the efficient conduct of the members of the Force concerned in the recapture of the prisoners and particularly of the promptitude and initiative displayed by the two Constables who first discovered the escaped men.'

P.C. Joseph A. Cook and P.C. Robert J. Watts rejoined the Force during 1958, after completing their tour of duty with the British Police Unit, Cyprus. They were seconded during 1956.

P.C. Clifford Viles was seconded for a period of 21 months with effect from 6th July, 1958. An urgent appeal for further volunteers for Police Duty in Cyprus met with a quick response and the following Officers were seconded for a tour of duty extending to six months, on the dates shown against their names:–

P.C. Sydney W. Parris	6.8.58
P.C. Clive Jefferies	6.8.58
P.C. Gary J. Jones	15.8.58

P.C. Jefferies returned to the Force on 24th August, 1958, on medical grounds.
P.C. Parris rejoined the Force after completing his tour of duty in December, 1958.
P.C. Jones rejoined the Force early in 1959.

The Allowance to members of the Force attending Courses away from home and living in lodgings, was increased in accordance with Home Office Circular No. 99/58 F2, dated 14th August, 1958. The new Weekly Allowances were:–

Superintendent	£6.15.0d.
Inspector	£6.5.0d.
Sergeants and Constables	£5.12.0d.

Under the Police (Promotion) Regulations, 1956, examinations for promotion were conducted by the Police Examinations Board, appointed by the Home Secretary. The first examination to be held by the Board, in Gloucestershire, was on the 6th February, 1958, when the Examination in Educational Subjects was arranged. The Examination in Police Subjects was held on the 27th February, 1958. The number of candidates and the results were as follows:–

EXAMINATION SUBJECT	NUMBER OF CANDIDATES	NUMBER QUALIFIED
Police Duties	14 Sergeants	5
–do– –do–	26 Constables	14
Educational Subjects	7 Sergeants	1
–do– –do–	85 Constables	23

It was of interest to note that –

(a) A Sergeant of the Force gained the highest marks (358/460) in the whole of the Police Forces in England and Wales in the Inspectors' examination in Police Subjects. A Constable of the Force tied for highest marks (372/460) for the Sergeants' examination.

(b) A Constable from Gloucestershire with (308/400) marks was twenty-third out of a total of 8,680 candidates who sat for Educational Subjects.

The percentage of passes in the Gloucestershire Force was 34.44% which gave them 65th position out of 123 Forces who took part.

Approval was given, in September, 1958, for the Chief Constable to purchase the first copying machine to be used by the Force. It was a 'Thermfax Secretary' copying machine which made copies, direct from the original, in 4 seconds and would be particularly useful for quick circulation of photographs of wanted persons. The nett cost of the machine was £130.19.0d.

On the 31st October, 1958, a Special Meeting of the Standing Joint Committee was held at Gloucester when the Chairman presented the following Report of the Finance and Buildings Sub-Committee:–

> The Sub-Committee met this morning when the following were present – Lt. Col. J. Godman, C.B.E., (Chairman), R.R. Dobson, Esq., G.G. Gilmour–White, Esq., O.B.E., C.W. Luker, Esq., Col. G.P. Shakerley, M.C., T.D., and the Right Worshipful the Mayor of Gloucester and W. May, Esq., (Representing Gloucester Corporation)
>
> They dealt with Forty-three applications, received in respect of the advertisement for the appointment of a Chief Constable to succeed Colonel W.F. Henn, C.B.E., M.V.O., who was retiring in April, 1959.
>
> The Sub-Committee interviewed five of the applicants and selected the following to appear before the Standing Joint Committee:–
>
> Mr J.S.H. Gaskain, M.B.E., Chief Constable of Cumberland & Westmorland.
>
> Mr R.B. Greenwood, O.B.E., Chief Constable of Dorset
>
> Mr R.W. Walker, Chief Constable of Eastbourne.

It was resolved – that the Report be received.

The Standing Joint Committee thereupon interviewed the candidates and after they had withdrawn, the Chairman stated that he had been asked by the Sub-Committee to say that they unanimously recommended the appointment of Mr. Gaskain.

It was resolved –

> That subject to the approval of the Secretary of State, Mr John Stuart Hinton Gaskain, M.B.E., Chief Constable of Cumberland & Westmorland, be appointed Chief Constable of Gloucestershire in accordance with the terms of the advertisement.

Police Sergeant William Horton died suddenly at Stonehouse on the 14th November, 1958. His age was 46 years and 203 days. Length of pensionable service 24 years and 360 days. He left a widow, Mrs May Horton and a child. Mrs Horton was granted a Police Widow's pension.

Superintendent Albert Hills retired on pension on the 31st December, 1958. He was 62 years of age and had served for nearly 39 years.

Pay Sheets were still being prepared in Divisional Offices and on the 9th December, 1958, the Chief Constable asked for permission to purchase three Adding and Listing machines, at a cost of £43.4.0d. each, for the cross casting of pay Sheets, etc., and for making the numerous calculations which were necessitated by the Income Tax System, and for other purposes. The machines to be used in the Divisional Offices at Staple Hill, Cheltenham and Gloucester.

It was agreed by the Police Authority, on the 9th December, 1958, that the joint salary of the Caretakers and Cook/Housekeepers at the Cheltenham and Gloucestser Police Hostels, should be increased by £50 to £300 per annum plus accommodation, board, fuel and light free of charge.

The Federated ranks of the Police Force, together with the Superintendents, were awarded a pay increase with effect from the 22nd April, 1958.

Constable on appointment £510 – £695 p.a. after 9 years service
Women Police Constables on appointment £460 – £625 p.a. after 9 years service
Sergeants on appointment £745 – £795 p.a. after 2 years service in the rank
W/P/Sergeants on appointment £670 – £715 p.a. after 2 years srvice in the rank
Inspectors on appointment £865 – £930 p.a. after 2 years service in the rank
C/Inspectors on appointment £980 – £1,050 p.a. after 2 years service in the rank
Superintendent Class 1 – £1,305 x £40 (2) – £1,385
Superintendent Class 2 – £1,170 x £40 (2) – £1,250

As a consequence of the increase in pay the Detective Duty Allowance was increased, with effect from 22nd April, 1958, as follows:–

Inspectors	£82 per annum
Sergeants	£80 per annum
Constables	£55 per annum

The Chief Constable, Colonel W.F. Henn, C.B.E., M.V.O., attended his last meeting of the Standing Joint Committee on the 17th March, 1959. The Chairman, Lt. Col. John Godman, C.B.E., spoke with appreciation of the valuable and efficient service which he had rendered to the County and wished him a long and happy retirement. The Lord Lieutenant (His Grace the Duke of Beaufort, K.G., G.C.V.O.) also paid tribute to the service rendered by Colonel Henn.

Colonel G.P. Shakerly, M.C., T.D., (Chairman of the County Council), the Mayor of Gloucester and Mr W.E. Lane, (Mayor of Tewekesbury), associated themselves with the remarks made.

The Chairman reported that he had received a letter from Mr C.G. Irving, (Mayor of Cheltenham) who was unable to be present at the meeting, who also wished to pay tribute to Colonel Henn's services. Upon the motion of the Chairman it was unanimously resolved –

> That the Standing Joint Committee place on record its appreciation of the valuable and efficient services of Colonel W.F. Henn, C.B.E., M.V.O., as Chief Constable during the past 22 years.

Colonel Henn thanked the Committee for their kind expressions. The last day of service for the Chief Constable was the 8th April, 1959. He retired on a pension of £1,044.16.8d., commencing on the 9th April, 1959. His age was 67 years and 35 days; length of pensionable service 22 years and 2 days.

Home Office Circular No. 27/1959, informed Police Authorities that agreement had been reached on new scales of pay for Chief Constables and Assistant Chief Constables. The new scales were back dated to the 22nd April, 1958, and were as under:–

Chief Constable	£2,485 x £90 (3)	– £2,755
Assistant Chief Constable	£1,640x £65 (3)	– £1,835

During the period 1st December, 1958 and 28th February, 1959, 13 recruits joined the Force, making a total of 654 recruits enrolled since the 1st January, 1946.

At the meeting on the 17th March, 1959, the Chief Constable asked for authority to increase the number of Cadet Clerks to attend 'Outward Bound' Courses from 4 to 6. This was due to the strength of the Cadets being increased from 21 to 34.

CHAPTER 7

John Stuart Hinton Gaskain, C.B.E., M.B.E., Q.P.M.
9.4.1959 – 18.12.1962

The Chief Constable, Mr John S.H. Gaskain attended his first meeting of Gloucestershire Police Authority on the 23rd June, 1959.

One of his first recommendations was that, in order to provide additional office accommodation, the two flats at Police Headquarters, Cheltenham, then occupied by an Inspector and Sergeant, should be converted. The officers occupying the flats could be accommodated in the new houses which had been constructed.

At this meeting it was agreed that, subject to the consent of the Home Office, the rent and travelling allowances payable to the Chief Constable should be:–

Maximum limit Rent Allowance..........£300 p.a.
Travelling Allowance

(1) £375 per annum to cover provision of a motor car (including mileage of all journeys undertaken by car inside the County) and all lodging and subsistence within the County when absent from home.
(2) First Class railway fare when travelling outside the County whether by rail or car.
(3) Scales applicable to Chief Officers of the County Council for subsistence when on duty outside the County.

Up to this period the issue of Certificates under the Firearms Act was dealt with by a Constable. The Chief Constable thought this work could be performed by a Civilian Clerk and he asked for authority to make such appointment.

It was reported, at the meeting on the 23rd June, 1959, that throughout the County there was a total of 104 typewriters, the majority of which were re-built machines on purchase. Many of these were practically worn out and the Chief Constable asked for authority to purchase up to eight machines per annum, as replacements.

The Police Surgeon thought it advisable for all Recruits to undergo a Chest X-Ray examination in addition to the ordinary medical examination and stated that this could be carried out at a cost of two guineas.

Mr Gaskain informed the Standing Joint Committee that it was important that Police should examine the scenes of crime, such as break-in offences and serious assaults, expertly and in detail, in order to give themselves the best possible chance of detection. In 1958 there were more than 1,100 break-ins in the County.

It would be necessary to have six officers specially trained for the work, stationed at three centres in Cheltenham, Gloucester and Staple Hill. Cameras and dark-room equipment would be required at the three centres. These were already available at Headquarters, but new equipment would be required at Gloucester and Staple Hill.
Equipment required:
2 M.P. Cameras. £300 – 2 Kodak Half-plate Cameras. £275
Dark-room equipment – at both places. £100
Extra paper, plates, etc. £200
and he asked for authority to purchase these items.

Referring to Home Office Circular 68/1959, dated 12th May, 1959, the Chief Constable suggested that four dogs and four handlers should be trained during the year 1960/61 and stated that a Force, the size of Gloucestershire, with the amount of crime then being committed should have a dog section as part of its equipment.

In consequence of the alterations at Headquarters the Chief Constable informed the Committee that it would be necessary for the internal telephone system to be extended and modernised. To make inter-communication possible between all the offices, the ten telephones should be increased to 23. He added that The Reliance Telephone Co., Ltd., could provide the system with the latest "Pax-Master" automatic loud speaking instrument fitted in his office for £58.16.0d. per Quarter.

A decision was made, early in 1959, that certain internal work in Police Houses should be carried out by Police personnel. The Finance and Buildings Sub-Committee accepted the views of the County Architect and the Chief Constable, who consulted the County Treasurer, that it would be preferable for materials to be purchased by individual Police Officers rather than they should be purchased in bulk and stored. The Sub-Committee recommended that the following basis be adopted.

Maximum expenditure fixed at	Bedrooms and Living rooms.
	If distempered .... £4 each
	If papered .... £5 each
	Kitchens and Bathrooms
	(including painted walls) ....£4.10.0d. each

These amounts to cover allowance for brushes and inclusive of materials. A proportionate increase to be made for larger rooms.[1]

Efforts had been made to find a suitable site in Cheltenham for the re-building of the Central Police Station. The County Architect informed the Sub-Committee that it would be inadvisable to build a new Station on the old site in the event of the demolition of part of the existing building.

Having received a report from the Chief Constables and the County Architect, the Sub-Committee considered that a new Station and Magistrates Court might be conveniently sited on vacant land, in the ownership of the Standing Joint Committee, adjacent to Holland House in Lansdown Road. The Chief Constable and County Architect also inspected a site opposite the George Hotel in St. Georges Road but were unable to recommend it as it was not large enough.

The new Police Station was eventually built on the site in Lansdown Road, adjacent to Holland House. It was not possible to accommodate the Magistrates Court with the Police Station, on this site, as it was too small. Eventually the Magistrates Court and a Police Enquiry Office was built on the site opposite the George Hotel in St. Georges Road.

H.M. Inspector of Constabulary, F.T.Tarry, Esq., C.B.E., inspected the Force on the 21st and 22nd July, 1959. A number of members of the Standing Joint Committee attended.

At the Standing Joint Committee meeting on the 22nd September, 1959, the Chief Constable asked for authority to engage a Secretary. Such person would not only work for the Chief Constable but also for the Assistant Chief Constable and would also supervise the other female civilian staff at Headquarters.

He also asked for permission to employ a civilian to attend to the Photographic processing work at Headquarters. If approved it would allow one more Police Officer to do outside Police Duties. There was ample photographic work for a full-time civilian engaged on this duty.

When the Standing Joint Committee met on the 23rd September, 1959, the Chief Constable stressed how important it was, in modern policing, that the Force should be mobile, so as to be able to cover large areas more quickly and more effectively and to answer the calls of the public immediately. With this in mind Mr Gaskain made the following proposals:–

(a) 15 Velocettes to be purchased immediately and distributed at various Stations all over the County, as experience showed to be desirable.
(b) As from the beginning of the new financial year, patrol cars during the day time would be manned by the driver only, without an observer unless this officer was training. This would enable the same number of men so employed to use the cars for almost double the amount of time.
(c) All maintenance and washing of cars to be done by garage or civilian staff, so ensuring that drivers were not engaged on these duties instead of being out on the roads. This would mean the employment of a civilian cleaner at Gloucester, Cheltenham and Staple Hill.
(d) The number of vehicles to be increased as follows:–
 4 Morris Oxfords
 10 Morris Minors
 9 Vans
 75 Velocettes in addition to those mentioned above. These to be provided at the rate of 15 additional machines each year.

Wireless to be fitted to all these vehicles and existing vehicles where this was desirable, from an efficiency point of view.

The Chief Constable also suggested that there should be a regular replacement of vehicles each year, so that the number of vehicles replaced would always be about the same. He thought the life of vehicles should be as follows:–

Patrol Cars ....3 years
All other cars, vans and motor cycles .....6 years

The era of the Police Clerk was coming to an end when Mr Gaskain asked that the strength of the Civilian Staff, throughout the County, be increased by 31 in order to ensure that Police Officers did as little inside work as possible, as opposed to outside practical police work.

Despite the considerable building that had taken place within the County since the end of the 1939/45 War the Chief Constable was not satisfied with conditions. He reported to the Standing Joint Committee on the 22nd September, 1959, that the outstanding building requirements were very considerable, they were as follows:–

4 Divisional Headquarters
5 Inspectors' Stations
12 Sergeants' Twin Stations
12 Constables' Twin Stations
11 Constables' Single Stations
189 Dwelling Houses

and also Training Wing, Canteen, Workshop and Clothing Store at Police Headquarters.

176 of the houses were required to house those in rooms or flats and to replace sub-standard houses.

At the same meeting Mr Gaskain suggested that a member of the Standing Joint Committee be selected, in each Division, to visit Stations and Houses with him, by arrangement.

Superintendent Harold J. Price retired on pension on the 18th July, 1959 his age was 59 years and 364 days. Length of pensionable service 36 years and 79 days.

Detective Superintendent Albert V. Hancock applied to retire on pension on the 30th September, 1959, his age then being 62 years and 141 days. Length of pensionable service, 39 years and 146 days.

The new Police Station and Magistrates' Court, Dursley was formally opened by Sir Charles Cunningham, K.B.E., C.B., C.V.O., the Permanent-Under-Secretary of State, Home Office, on the 30th October, 1959.

At their meeting on the 15th December, 1959, the Standing Joint Committee discussed a Report by the County Council in which the Council considered the number of members serving on the Committee was excessive and requested the observations of the Standing Joint Committee and Quarter Sessions as to reducing the number of representatives of the Council and Quarter Sessions to 40 members, 20 to be appointed by the Council and 20 by Quarter Sessions. The Standing Joint Committee at that time consisted of 86 members, 40 being appointed by the County Council and an equal number being appointed by Quarter Sessions together with 6 representatives of the Gloucester City Council appointed in pursuance of Section 13 of the Gloucester Corporation Act, 1945. It was recommended:–

(a) That the County Council be informed that in the opinion of the Standing Joint Committee the Committee should consist of 50 members, 22 to be appointed by the Council and 22 by Quarter Sessions, together with 6 representatives of the Gloucester City Council.

Home Office approval was granted to pay Cadets a lodging allowance of

£1.1.3d. a week, when they were required to go into lodgings at their place of duty.

Pedal cycles found in the County and deposited with Police, which remained unclaimed by the owner or finder, were forwarded to Police Headquarters and eventually sold by public auction. The Chief Constable told the Police Authority on the 15th December, 1959, that it was proposed to do the same with other articles of found property and abolish the system then operating, which was, the articles were forwarded to Police Headquarters and there seperated into various categories and tenders invited from interested persons. The commission charged for selling cycles was 7½%. A commission of 10% was required for selling the other property as there was considerably more work in preparing it for sale.[2]

Crime was rising steadily and new methods being sought to combat it. As far as Gloucestershire was concerned a large amount of crime was being committed by criminals residing in Bristol and in an effort to reduce this the Bristol Crime Squad was formed, on the same lines as the one in London for the Home Counties and in Birmingham for the Midlands. The Crime Squad was to consist of a Detective Sergeant from Somerset, Bath and Gloucestershire with Detective Constables from Bristol City, working under the supervision of the Detective Superintendent at Bristol. The Squad would be centred in Bristol City and would operate from there. The annual cost to Gloucestershire would be in the region of £262.

Two more Superintendents retired this Quarter. On the 16th December, 1959, William Hart retired on pension from Gloucester, where he was Divisional Commander. His age was 60 years and 364 days and pensionable service 40 years and 230 days. Two of his sons were serving with the Force.

Superintendent Harold J. Greenall, who was in charge of 'T' (Traffic) Department, retired on pension on the 31st December, 1959, aged 60 years and 13 days. His pensionable service was 39 years and 33 days.

With a view to relieving Senior Police Officers of the work of conducting Police Prosecutions, it was agreed that where necessary private firms of Solicitors who were on the Panel of Solicitors undertaking Police Prosecutions at County Quarter Sessions should undertake those prosecutions which, owing to pressure of work, could not be conducted by the Assistant Solicitor on the Clerk's staff.

The scheme commenced on the 1st August, 1960, and on the 18th January, 1961, the Standing Joint Committee were told that during

August and September the number of cases exceeded expectations. There had been some criticisms of the scheme and arrangements had been made to ensure that a Solicitor was not instructed where it was known that the defendant intended to plead guilty. The continued operation of the scheme was going to involve the expenditure of a considerable sum of public money and the Committee felt that it would be preferable for additional Assistant Solicitors to be employed by the County Council to conduct Police Prosecutions.

Up until 1960 the Chief Constable, Assistant Chief Constable and Superintendents received an allowance and provided their own uniform. At their meeting on the 15th March, 1960, the Police Authority recommended:– That as from the 1st April 1960, the Chief Constable, Assistant Chief Constable and Superintendents be issued with uniforms and paid an allowance of £25 per annum in respect of their plain clothes.

Home Office Circular No. 1/1960 and copies of the Police (No. 4) Regulations, 1959, were received by the Police Authority on the 6th January, 1960. These Regulations amended:–

(a) Annual Leave for the Federated Ranks so as to increase the leave entitlement as follows:–
Constable with 15 years' service from 17 to 19 days
Sergeant with 7 years' service as a Sergeant from 19 to 21 days
Inspectors with 5 years' service as an Inspector from 22 to 24 days
Chief Inspectors with 5 years' service as a Chief Inspector from 25 to 27 days

The new entitlement applied from the first leave year beginning on or after the 1st January, 1960.

(b) Plain Clothes Allowance so as to provide new rates of Plain Clothes Allowance as follows:–

Superintendents	£43 a year
Inspectors	£40 a year
Sergeants	13/6d. a week
Constables	12/6d. a week

(c) Temporary duty allowance for Superintendents so as to provide that Superintendents, other than Superintendents receiving payment as Deputy Chief Constable, are eligible for temporary duty allowance. In view of the definition of 'Superintendent' in Regulation 155, Chief Superintendents were eligible.

On the 15th March, 1960, the Chief Constable informed the Police Authority that he was setting up a new Communications and Information

Room. When fully operational, he anticipated that nine female civilain staff would be employed in the Department, on shift work, including night duty. To compensate these people for accepting inconvenience of shift work, he recommended that they should be paid 10/–d. per week extra to their weekly pay.

The Department of Scientific and Industrial Research on Traffic was running various Courses at this time and the Chief Constable asked for permission to send Superintendent Robert F. Mayo, the Traffic Superintendent, on a week's Course at Slough the cost of which was £12.12.0d. in addition to the cost of accommodation. Mr Gaskain thought the Course would be of great value to the Superintendent and, in consequence to the Force.

The first two Dog Handlers for Gloucestershire completed their training on the 11th March, 1960, and arrangements were made to send the next pair of Handlers on the 21st March. The Chief Constable asked for authority to continue to build up the Dog Section to a total of eight Handlers and eight Dogs.[3]

The Chief Constable was granted permission by the Police Authority, on the 15th March, 1960, to purchase a Cinematograph Projector complete with stand, spools, covers and screens at a cost of £365. The Projector was to be used in the Training Department at Police Headquarters.

On the 15th March, 1960, Mr Gaskain informed the Standing Joint Committee that the number of Officers at present authorised in the ranks above that of Constable were far short of those recommended by the Post War Committee, which meant that the Force was short of supervising officers and the lower ranks were deprived of their proper chance of promotion. Both these were important matters.

A Schedule of the requirements to bring the Force up to its proper establishment in the ranks of Sergeant and upwards in accordance with the Post War Committee was produced in detail for the information of the Committee. Briefly the figures were:–

	OLD ESTABLISHMENT	SUGGESTED ESTABLISHMENT
Chief Constable	1	1
Assistant Chief Constable	1	1
Chief Superintendents	–	4
Superintendents	9	5
Chief Inspectors	3	12
Inspectors	27	39

Sergeants	97	126
Constables	585	572
Women Police Constables	12	12
	735	772

These figures included three extra Sergeants for supervision of Traffic Patrol, and six additional Sergeants for Training and Road Safety Purposes, and one Inspector at Police Headquarters for Road Safety purposes. Also included was an additional Inspector as Crime Prevention and Public Relations Officer and an additional Sergeant in Charge of the Dog Section.

The Chairman of the Standing Joint Committee, at their meeting on the 21st June, 1960, referred to the impending retirement of Mr A.H. Carter, M.B.E., from the post of Assistant Chief Constable and spoke in appreciation of the valuable and efficient service which he had rendered during his 40 years' service with the Gloucestershire Constabulary and wished him a happy retirement. It was unanimously resolved – 'That the Standing Joint Committee place on record its appreciation of the valuable and efficient service of Mr A.H. Carter during his 40 years' service with the Gloucestershire Constabulary.' Mr Carter thanked the Committee for their kind expression.

Mr A.H. Carter, M.B.E., Assistant Chief Constable retired on pension on the 31st August, 1960, when his age was 65 years and 20 days. Length of pensionable service was 40 years and 240 days. Mr Carter died in Cheltenham on the 12th November, 1973. He left a widow, Doris N. Carter who died at the home of her daughter in Cheltenham on the 21st September, 1983.

1960 saw the change over from manually operated Petrol Pumps to electrically operated Pumps at the various Divisional Headquarters, throughout the County, at a cost of £196.19.8d.

Approval was given to the Chief Constable, on the 21st June, 1960, to purchase six 'Banda' Spirit Copying machines for use at Divisional Headquarters, at a cost of £648, together with three dictating machines, 'Rex Recorders', at £82.19.0d. each; two to be placed at Cheltenham Central Police Station and one at Stroud Police Station. Film Projectors and Screens, for each Division, were also authorised at a cost of £230. These were necessary for Training and Instruction. They would also be used when talks were requested by the various outside bodies and organisations.

Before the Standing Joint Committee met on the 20th September, 1960, His Grace the Duke of Beaufort, K.G., G.C.V.O., presented the Queen's

Police Medal to the Chief Constable, Mr John S.H. Gaskain, M.B.E.

It was stated by the Chairman, after the presentation, that Mr Gaskain joined the Metropolitan Police in 1937 and was appointed Assistant Chief Constable of Norfolk in 1942. From 1946 – 1949 he was seconded as Commandant of No. 5 District Training Centre and in 1952 was appointed Chief Constable of Cumberland and Westmorland. Mr Gaskain was appointed Chief Constable of Gloucestershire in 1959. As Assistant Chief Constble and as Chief Constable he had been responsible for many improvements in the administration and efficiency of three County Forces and the high quality of his leadership and his fine personal and professional qualities had distinguished his career in which he had won the confidence not only of the Officers serving under him but of the Police Authority and the public as well.

Constable Ronald Walter Brookes who was only 33 years of age died suddenly on the 6th July, 1960; he had completed 12 years service and at the time of his death was stationed at Northleach. He left a widow and two children. Mrs Brookes was granted a Police Widow's pension which was supplemented in accordance with the provisions of the National Insurance Act.

On the 14th September, 1960, the Chairman and Vice Chairman of the Standing Joint Committee, together with the Chief Constable, interviewed a short list of candidates for the vacant post of Assistant Chief Constable. The Committee were informed at their meeting on the 20th September, 1960, that Detective Superintendent Robert G. Fenwick, of the Metropolitan Police Force, had been appointed Assistant Chief Constable. At that time he was seconded to the Police College at Ryton–on–Dunsmore as an Instructor and would take up his appointment on the 10th October, 1960.

At this same meeting the Assistant Chief Constable's Travelling Allowance was increased from £225 per annum to £250 per annum, to be paid to the new Assistant Chief Constable on his appointment.

On the 24th June, 1960, a Circular was received from the Home Office calling for volunteers for a British Police Unit for Nyasaland. Volunteers to be of the rank of Inspector or Sergeant. Sergeant Alan A. Moir, stationed at Cheltenham, volunteered and was accepted. He was seconded to the Unit as from the 5th August, 1960, and left for Nyasaland on that day. His period of service was for a minimum of six months. Sergeant Moir recommenced duty with the Force on the 20th February, 1961.

September, 1960 saw the strength of the Police Cadets increased from 34 to 50. This meant that 50% of intake of Recruits to the Force would be ex-cadets. As part of their training the Cadets had weekly drill from an Instructor of the Dean Close School Combined Cadet Force.

When the Ross Spur Motorway (M50) was nearing completion it was decided that Gloucestershire Police would assist in the patrol of the motorway when it was opened. A large amount of special equipment was required to be carried by vehicles for this type of work and the Chief Constable considered that a Land Rover would be an ideal vehicle for this duty. As a result he was given permission to purchase one Land Rover at a cost of £900, providing Home Office approval was obtained.

During the twelve months from 1st April, 1959 to 31st March, 1960, the sum of £659 had been paid for printing. The range of printed Forms in use in the Force at this time was quite extensive and printers' charges heavy. The Chief Constable made enquiries and obtained details of a printing machine on which the same amount of work could have been done for £440, a saving of £219. The machine cost £700 and was capable of printing all the types of forms required. In addition to the cost of the machine however there would be the salary of one extra Clerical Assistant to operate it, at a salary of £250 (18 years). Approval was given to the Chief Constable to purchase the machine.

Mr Gaskain informed the Standing Joint Committee on the 20th September, 1960, that he was going to experiment with the installation of telephones properly enclosed and placed outside the Police Office with suitable instructions, in order to improve facilities for the public at Police Stations on Main Roads when the Officer was away from his Station. If successful, he asked for approval to continue with such installations in suitable cases. Each one would cost approximately £7 and there could be up to thirty of them. This scheme was never really a success and was eventually done away with after a very short period.

At this meeting the Chief Constable gave preliminary details of a scheme for the establishment of a Volunteer Cadet Corps. He enlarged on this at his meeting with the Committee on the 6th December, 1960, when he reported that there were a large number of boys leaving school who were interested in the Police Service as a career but, because there were insufficient vacancies in the Cadets, they went into industry or other employment and by the time they were 19 they had forgotten about the Police Force. This scheme was intended to hold their interest until they were old enough to join the Regular Force and it was hoped that by the time they were 19 some of them would join; even if they did not join they might make very useful Special Constables later on.

This was something quite new that had not been tried out anywhere else and at that moment the ground work of the scheme was being laid. It was his intention to fit each Volunteer Cadet with a cap, gaberdine, tunic and trousers at a cost of approximately £15 per head and the Chief Constable asked for approval to recruit up to a strength of 100. Approval was forthcoming.

Ex. Superintendent John F. Shellswell died at Lydbrook in the Forest of Dean, on the 6th November, 1960, aged 88 years. He had been on pension since the 21st December, 1937.

It was during 1960 that Mr Gaskain gave instructions for a new Filing System to be set up at Police Headquarters, Cheltenham. Roneo Office Equipment gave advice and a visual Filing System was put into operation. When completed the system was adopted in each Divisional Office and, for the first time, there was a universal filing system throughout the Gloucestershire Constabulary.

Standing Orders had been used for many years, within the Force, and consisted of three loose leaf volumes which were amended from time to time. Each serving officer being issued with his own set of Standing Orders. The Chief Constable decided that Standing Orders should be revised and made into one loose leaf album or volume. A small Committee was formed to investigate this matter duting 1960 and eventually the new Standing Orders were produced and issued to the Force.

Home Office Circular No.139/1960, dated 9th September, 1960, had been received by the Chief Constable wherein the Secretary of State brought to the notice of the Police Authoriites, Section 2 of the Road Traffic Act and Roads Improvement Act, 1960, which came into operation on the 1st September and provided for the appointment of Traffic Wardens. Mr Gaskain informed the Committee that he proposed to discuss the question of parking with a number of Local Authorities and would submit a report relating to the appointment of Traffic Wardens, to a future meeting.

Before the Standing Joint Committee meeting on the 14th March, 1961, the chairman referred to the impending retirement of Chief Superintendent C.P. Oakley and spoke in appreciation of the valuable and efficient service which he had rendered during his thirty-eight and a half years service with the Gloucestershire Constabulary and wished him a long and happy retirement. Upon the motion of the Chairman it was unanimously resolved, 'That the Standing Joint Committee place on record its appreciation of the valuable and efficient service of Chief Superintendent C.P. Oakley during his service with the Gloucestershire Constabulary.' Chief Superintendent Oakley thanked the Committee for their good wishes.

Chief Superintendent Oakley was Chief Clerk at Police Headquarters, Cheltenham, when he retired on the 16th April, 1961. His age was 59 years and 362 days while his pensionable service was 38 years and 178 days.

On Mr Oakley's retirement Chief Inspector H. Thomas was pomoted to Superintendent and Chief Clerk in charge of Adminsistration at Police Headquarters, Cheltenham. Superintendent Thomas had been transferred to Headquarters on the 1st January, 1959, on promotion to Inspector and Assistant Chief Clerk.

On the 1st April, 1961, Chief Inspector R.B. Thomas was appointed to the post of Commandant of No. 7 District Police Training Centre, Chantmarle, Cattistock, Nr. Dorchester. The appointment was for two years and was a great credit to Chief Inspector Thomas and the Gloucestershire Constabulary. Chief Inspector R.B. Thomas never returned to the Force and in the course of time he was appointed Chief Constable of the Dyfed–Powis Constabulary in Wales. Commandant R.B. Thomas and Superintendent H. Thomas were not related.

The Chairman informed the Standing Joint Committee at their meeting on the 14th March, 1961, that at Police Dog Trials recently held by the Staffordshire Constabulary, the prize for the best dog was won by Sergeant P.F. Deacon and that P.C. D.P. Keen also received very high marks. He congratulated these officers on their success.

Ex. Superintendent H.J. Price died in hospital at Oxford on the 31st January, 1961, aged 61 years. He had been on pension since 19th July, 1959. He left a widow and daughter. Mrs Margaret Price was awarded a Police Widows' Pension supplemented in accordance with the provisions of the National Insurance Act.

During the year 1960 Police reported 984 deaths to Coroners and Inquests were held in 337 cases, with the following results:–

Accidental death	127
Misadventure	82
Natural causes	40
Suicide	52
Murder	1
Manslaughter	1
Silicosis	11
Other verdicts	23
Pending	5

Superintendent S.D. Smith, Divisional Commander at Stroud, retired on pension on the 7th January, 1961. His age was 60 years and 8 days with pensionable service of 40 years and 245 days.

The Secretary of State informed Police Authorities in Home Office Circular 192/60 that he intended to make Regulations increasing the pay of the Federated Ranks with effect from 1st September, 1960. The new scales of pay were as follows:–

Chief Inspector	Men	£1,355 to £1,445 p.a. after 2 years service in the rank
	Women	£1,220 to £1,300 after 2 years service in the rank
Inspectors	Men	£1,210 to £1,290 after 2 years service in the rank
	Women	£1,090 to £1,160 after 2 years service in the rank
Sergeants	Men	£1,030 to £1,100 after 2 years service
	Women	£925 to £990 after 2 years service in the rank
Constables	Men	£600 to £910 after 9 years service
	Women	£540 to £820 p.a. after 9 years service

In addition there were supplementary payments of £30 per annum to Police Constables at 17 and 22 years service, and of £25 per annum at 17 years and £30 per annum at 22 years service to Women Police Constables.

Detective Duty Allowance was increased at the same time as the pay. The new scales were:–

Chief Inspectors	Men	£127 p.a.
	Women	£115 p.a
Inspectors	Men	£114 p.a
	Women	£102 p.a.
Sergeants	Men	£97 p.a.
	Women	£87 p.a.
Constables	Men	£71 p.a.
	Women	£64 p.a.

The Chief Constable informed the Committee on the 14th March, 1961, that Mr F.T. Tarry, C.B.E., H.M. Inspector of Constabulary had agreed to carry out an Inspection of the Cadets at Police Headquarters, Cheltenham, on a date to be announced. He intended to invite the parents to an 'At home' to see the Parade, have tea and look around Headquarters Departments and hoped that some members of the Standing Joint Committee would also be able to attend. It was later announced that the

Parade would take place on Saturday, 13th May, 1961, and that the Chairman had authorised the provision of tea and a band.

Home Office Circular No. 5/1961, dated 4th January, 1961, increased the allowances for loss of wages to be paid to Special Constables, as from the 1st September, 1960; the new rates were:–

Men – 41/9d. a day Women – 37/7d. a day

Following his report to the Police Authority on the 6th December, 1960, the Chief Constable informed the Committee on the 14th March, 1961, that the employment of Traffic Wardens had been gone into and he considered that they could be used in the County to releive men on the beat for more important duties.

As a start he would like to engage 6 for duty in the City of Gloucester in the areas where 'No waiting' or unilateral parking restrictions applied.

There was no fixed salary for Traffic Wardens but the Chief Constable considered a commencement figure of £500 per annum, rising by two yearly increments of £25 and one of £20 to a maximum of £650 per annum would be suitable. This was similar to the amount paid in Bristol. They would work a 44 hour week with half-days off on a Thursday, which was early closing day, and all day on a Sunday.

The question of employing Traffic Wardens in other parts of the County would depend upon the result of the Gloucester experiment.

In January 1961, the Home Office issued another Circular asking for further volunteers for the British Police Unit, Nyasaland and Sergeant Williams Rowlands of Berkeley volunteered. He was accepted for Service with the Unit and left for Nyasaland on the 21st March, 1961.

On the 20th June, 1950 the Buildings and Minors Committee approved a maximum amenity allowance of £15 to be allocated to each new Police Station and House. This was in respect of the preliminary digging of garden and the provision of material to make surrounds neat and tidy, also for the purchase of shrubs and trees, etc.

Garden paths and line posts were not provided for in the building contract and from 1952 the allowance was intended to cover the cost of clothes posts, trees, grass, etc. £5 of the allowance was allowed to be used for material for garden paths.

The Chief Constable thought it would be far more convenient if the provision of garden paths and clothes posts was allowed for in future contracts for the building of new Police Stations and Houses where considered necessary. The amenity grant of £15 could then be reduced to £10. As a result he asked the Committee on the 14th March, 1961, to authorise the inclusion of laying garden paths and the provision of clothes posts in future contracts and that the amenities grant be reduced to £10.

Consequent upon the opening of the Ross Spur Motor Way (M50) and the decision that the Gloucestershire Police should share in the patrolling of it, the Chief Constable decided that a Mess Room, toilet and Report writing room were necessary for patrol crews performing this duty. A suitable site was considered to be at the Ministry of Transport Maintenance Depot at Bury Court and agreement was reached that the accommodation should be built there.

In addition to the wireless station at Cleeve Hill and Edgehills it was found necessary to site another station to cover the Southern part of the County. In due course this was found, near the Ridge Estate, Dursley, subject of course to the Home Office Engineers' tests being satisfactory.

On the 16th March, 1961 at Down Ampney at about 6.30 p.m. two Constables, P.C. Ronald E. Spencer and P.C. David W. Smeeton, were called to a house where there had been a shooting incident and where they were faced by a Pole named Piechowicz who was holding a revolver. The Chief Constable referred to this incident when he addressed the Standing Joint Committee on the 27th June, 1961 and stated that what followed was well known to Members of the Police Authority so that he did not have to relate the facts, but suffice it was to say that the two Police Officers acted with extreme gallantry. He also wished to bring to the notice of the Police Authority, Mrs Jean May Evans of 6 Broadleaze, Down Ampney who, during the chase when there was a general hue and cry, caught up with the prisoner and was able, by pushing him in the back, to bring him to the ground. It was through this specific action that Piechowicz was arrested.

The following is taken from what was said by Mr Justice Stable, at the Assizes concerning the action of the Police Officers and Mrs Evans–

> Mr Recorder, it would be most inappropriate if the really courageous action of these three persons passed unnoticed. It is really an epic story. Police Constable Spencer goes to the front door and sees two prone bodies. They were both dead. He sees someone – we need not say who – with a revolver in his hand, and yet, to use his own words, he 'decided to go in after him'. He was shot at point blank range and the bullet, according to the Doctors, missed his heart by a hair's breadth. His colleague, Police Constable Smeeton, also of the Gloucestershire Constabulary, having heard the shot and having seen Spencer shot practically at point blank range, followed him into the room and threw himself on this man – whoever it was. After a violent struggle he got the revolver away from him, and set off in pursuit.

> So much for what we might call the 'Armed Forces of the Crown'. But we had not exhausted our National resources. There was Mrs Evans to be reckoned with and what Mrs Evans did, apparently, was to push him in the middle of his back and to trip him, and so, whoever it was, he was arrested before any more damage was done. I think we really can be proud of our Nation and we can be proud of those three individuals.

It was at the meeting of the Standing Joint Committee on the 27th June, 1961 that the Chairman, Lt. Col. John Godman, C.B.E., referred to the Chief Constable's Report relating to the gallant action of the two Police Officers and Mrs J.M. Evans, in apprehending a prisoner at Down Ampney on the 6th March, 1961 and paid tribute to the bravery of Mrs Evans who succeeded in knocking him to the ground and detaining him until Police Officers arrived on the scene.[4]

His Grace the Duke of Beaufort, K.G., G.C.V.O., then presented Mrs Evans with a clock suitably inscribed and congratulated her on behalf of the Committee on her very brave and public spirited action.

Notification was received on the 26th September, 1961 that both Police Constable Ronald E. Spencer and Police Constable David W. Smeeton had been awarded the George Medal for extreme gallantry displayed in connection with the arrest of a Pole armed with a revolver.

These two Constables attended an Investiture at Buckingham Palace on the 14th November, 1961 when they were each presented with the George Medal by Her Majesty Queen Elizabeth the Queen Mother.

On the 1st September, 1960, new rates of pay were introduced for Superintendents and Chief Superintendents with effect from 1st September, 1960. They were:–

Chief Superintendent	£1,925 × £55(2) – £2,035 per annum
Superintendent Class 1	£1,780 × £55(2) – £1,890 per annum
Superintendent Class 2	£1,605 × £55(2) – £1,715 per annum

Back in 1959 the Police Authority agreed that the charges for Police Officers doing duty on Requisition should be 9/6d. per hour. This was a flat rate for all ranks.

In view of the increases in pay and allowances and increase in National Insurance Contributions since 1959 the Chief Constable recommended that the charges be increased from the 1st July, 1961.

The scale of charges recommended are given below. These were the rates charged by the Metropolitan Police and were circulated with Home Office Circular No. 80/1961.

RANK		DAILY RATE	HOURLY RATE	MINIMUM CHARGE
Men – Uniform	Chief Inspector	£9.13.3d.	£1.4.2d.	£3.12.6d.
	Inspector	£8.16.5d.	£1.2.1d.	£3.6.3d.
	Sergeant	£7.9.10d.	18.9d.	£2.16.3d.
	Constable	£5.13.9d.	14.3d.	£2.2.9d.
C.I.D.	Chief Inspector	£10.8.10d.	£1.6.2d.	£3.18.6d.
	Inspector	£9.10.10d.	£1.3.11d.	£3.11.9d.
	Sergeant	£8.13.7d.	£1.1.9d.	£3.5.3d.
	Constable	£6.10.2d.	16.4d.	£2.9.0d.
Women – Uniform	Sergeant	£6.8.2d.	16.1d.	£2.8.3d.
	Constable	£4.11.6d.	11.6d.	£1.14.6d.

On the 27th June, 1961 Mr Gaskain was able to report to the Police Authority that, before the end of the year, every Police Station and every house in the County occupied by a Police Officer would have been visited by himself in company with various members of the Standing Joint Committee. It was hoped to continue the procedure whereby it would be possible for members to see the conditions under which Police Officers and their families were housed and to watch improvements. The Chief Constable expressed the gratitude of the Force for the interest which had been shown in the housing of Police Officers and in particular he would like to thank those Members who had given up so much time in making the visits with him.

The first Cadets 'Open Day' was held at Police Headquarters, Cheltenham, on Saturday 13th May, 1961. The afternoon opened with an Inspection of the Cadets by Mr F.T.Tarry, C.B.E., one of Her Majesty's Inspectors of Constabulary, and the Cadets later gave a display of drill and physical training. During the afternoon the Dog Section gave their first public demonstration, and guests were taken round various Departments of Headquarters.

The 'Open Day' was attended by the Chairman and a number of Members of the Standing Joint Committee and parents and friends of the Cadets; in all about 200 people were present.

The Police Volunteer Cadet Corps commenced training on the 1st March, 1961 at Staple Hill, Cirencester, Stroud, Cheltenham and Gloucester. At the commencement the Chief Constable limited recruiting to twelve Volunteers in each Division and these places were quickly filled at all centres except Cheltenham. However, the Chief Constable permitted recruiting to be increased up to twenty in each Division. The total strength of the Corps at that time was sixty-two.

All Cadets had been equipped with uniform and their training included drill, physical training, first aid, talks on the history of the Police Service, etc., visits to Police Departments and other places of interest and this was superimposed on the Duke of Edinburgh's Award Scheme of which the Gloucestershire Constabulary was an operating authority. From time to time various small items of expenditure arose in connection with the Volunteer Cadets. They were of a miscellaneous nature and the Committee gave approval for the expenditure of £50 per annum on these.

The allowances paid to persons, other than Police Women, for attendance on female prisoners and searching, if necessary, was:–

Between 8.00 a.m. and 10.00p.m. ....1/4d. per hour
Between 10.00 p.m. and 8.00 a.m. ....2/–d. per hour

These rates had been in operation since the 1st July, 1945 and were grossly inadequate. The County Treasurer was asked to suggest a figure more in keeping with the wages at that time. He suggested that they should be paid in accordance with Grade 1 of the Western District Council, at 1/9d. per hour; in addition the persons concerned should receive a 'Calling Out' fee, when called out at night. The Chief constable therefore asked for Committee approval to pay the rate of 1/9d. per hour plus the 'Calling Out' fee of 10/6d. when called out between 10.00p.m. and 7.00a.m. The variation in pay to take effect from the 1st July, 1961.

The Chief Constable reported to the Committee on the 27th June, 1961 that nine new typewriters had been purchased, three for Headquarters and six in Divisions. In addition an electric typewriter had been purchased for use by the Chief Constable's Secretary. The cost of the machines had been allowed for in the current year's Estimates.

H.M. Inspector of Constabulary, F.T. Tarry, Esq., C.B.E., carried out an Inspection of the Force on the 26th, 27th and 28th June, 1961. This Inspection did not take the form of formal Parades, as in former years. H.M. Inspector visited Police Stations on an ad hoc basis, therefore it was not possible to send invitations to Members of the Standing Joint Committee, to attend.

Other than in the Information Room, this Force had never used an efficient and official Message Form. As a result of deliberations by a small

Committee under the Chairmanship of the Assistant Chief Constable, a Message Form was devised and used throughout the Force thereby contributing towards an efficient system of communications. The cost of printing the pads and pad covers was £150 and as this had not been allowed for in the Estimates for the current year, 1961/62, the Chief Constable asked for approval for a Supplementary Estimate to cover the cost.

The small Committee referred to above was formed by Mr Gaskain and consisted of one member from each rank, meeting from time to time, under the Chairmanship of the Assistant Chief Constable or the Superintendent in charge of Adminstration. They dealt with 'Suggestions' sent in by serving officers and, at the same time, carried out an investigation into the many and various Forms being used within the Force, with a view to improving the lay-out and, in some case, dispensing with Forms. All their recommendations being placed before the Chief Constable for his final decision.[5]

A Communications Committee was also operating at this time and they dealt with all matters in connection with Telephones, Wireless, Teleprinter and Telex, etc. One of their recommendations was that in some parts of the County difficulty was experienced, from time to time, in contacting Inspectors, Sergeants and Senior Constables, who were living away from their Stations, and were required urgently but were not connected to the telephone. Although a large number of new telephones had been installed in houses occupied by Inspectors, Sergeants, C.I.D. personnel and Dog Handlers, the Chief Constable reported to the Standing Joint Committee that there had never been a definite policy on the subject and on the 27th June, 1961 the Committee agreed to a policy which the Chief Constable had outlined in his Report and covered:–

(1) Exchange lines and necessary internal extensions, and
(2) Extensions from Police Stations to houses occupied by Section Sergeants or Senior Constables living less than a mile from the Station.

The Chairman informed the Committee, on the 17th June, 1961 that the Secretary of State had approved an increase in pay for Chief Constables and Assistant Chief Constables. The point of entry into the new scale should correspond with the point reached in the old scale but the precise positioning of the scales within the sub-ranges appropriate for the population and establishment was a matter for the discretion of the Police Authority to be exercised in the light of all the relevant factors.

Having been advised that the population of the police district was at present approximately 560,000 and that the authorised establishment of the Force was 722, the Committee considered it appropriate that the Chief Constable and the Assistant Chief Constable should be placed on the maximum scale and it was resolved –

(1) That with effect from the 1st September, 1960 the salary of the Chief Constable be £3,475 rising by two increments of £125 to £3,725 on the 9th April, 1962.
(2) That with effect from 1st September, 1960 the salary of the Assistant Chief Constable be £2,255 rising by three increments of £75 to a maximum of £2,480.

On the 19th September, 1961 it was reported that a Sub-Committee had deferred requests from the Chief Constable for the provision of carpets in the offices of the three Superintendents at Police Headquarters and the Superintendent at the Divisional office at Staple Hill and for the provision of a rug for the Chief Superintendent at Staple Hill. However, expenditure of £129 was approved for the provision of venetian blinds for the Printing Room and the Information Room at Police Headquarters as the Sub-Committee considered these were desirable.

In connection with a previous Report reference the Purchase of Existing Properties for Police Housing, the Chairman informed the Standing Joint Committee that he had discussed with the Chairman of the County Council and the appropriate Officers the question of financial provisions for the purchase of further properties. He stated that the sum of £284,500 had been provided in the Capital Budget and Supplementary Capital Estimates for 1961/62, and it was anticipated that the sum of £325,300 would be spent before the 31st March, 1962. There was, therefore, no financial provision for the purchase of further houses and if the policy was to continue it would be necessary to request the County Council to approve a Supplementary Estimate.

The Committee were of the opinion that their policy of purchasing houses for Police housing was the right one in view of the saving in time and money as compared with building, and of the fact that it relieved the County Architect of a considerable amount of work. Furthermore, they were of the opinion that in the event of the price of houses falling in the next few months in view of the economic situation, the County Valuer might be in a position to take advantage of the market and negotiate further purchases.

It was therefore resolved –

(1) That the County Council be requested to approve a Supplementary Estimate of £100,000, £40,000 to meet the estimated overspending and a further £60,000 to be allocated for the purchase of houses.
(2) That the County Council be recommended to make application to the Ministry of Housing and Local Government for consent to the borrowing of £100,000 in respect of the purchase of property.

An examination for promotion was held on the 1st February, 1961 in Educational Subjects and on the 23rd February, 1961 in Police Subjects. The number of candidates and the results are as follows:–

EXAMINATION SUBJECT	NUMBER OF CANDIDATES	NUMBER QUALIFIED
Police Duties	29 Sergeants	8
Police Duties	47 Constables	15
Education	6 Sergeants	1
Education	57 Constables	24

Of the 24 Constables who passed the Education test, nine passed the standard for promotion to Inspector and 15 for the standard for promotion to Sergeant.

A fee of £4.4.0d. was paid to Gloster Aircraft Co. Ltd., for the hire of Witcombe Residential Club for the use of a hall on the two days. In addition, the sum of £25.7.6d. was paid for meals supplied to candidates on the two days. Those men attending the examinations did not claim Subsistence Allowance.

Referring to his Report of the 14th March, 1961 the Chief Constable asked, on the 19th September, 1961 for the employment of Traffic Wardens in the City of Gloucester to be deffered for an indefinate period. A recent Order prohibiting heavy traffic from travelling through the City and additional restrictions placed on street parking had had a remarkable effect in easing traffic congestion. Heavy goods traffic was barred from the City of Gloucester by the County Borough of Gloucester Prohibition of Through Goods Vehicle Order 1960, and on the 5th December 1961, Mr W.J. Lewis referred to this Order, and on behalf of the Gloucester City Council paid tribute to the Police for the efficient manner in which they were carrying out their duties so as to ensure the smooth working of the Order. It had been most effective in keeping the City clear of heavy traffic and the efforts of the Chief Constable and Chief Superintendent for the Gloucester Division were much appreciated. Mr Lewis also spoke in appreciation of the interest taken by the Chief Constable and the Chief Superintendent in the training of the cyclists and motor-cyclists.

The Royal Institute of Public Administration was holding a Course on Administration for Senior Police Officers at its Headquarters in London, for two weeks commencing Monday 16th October, 1961. The Chief Constable, on the 19th September, 1961 asked the Standing Joint Committee for authority to send Superintendent H. Thomas, of Police Headquarters, the Senior Administration Officer of the Force. As the County Council subscribed to the Institute, the cost would be £12.12.0d. for the two weeks, and, subject to audit, the Home Office had indicated that they would accept expenses incurred in sending Officers on this Course, for grant purposes.

The Chief Constable reported to the Police Authority on 19th September, 1961 that certain posts in the Constabulary were not carrying ranks commensurate with their duties and responsibilities. At Headquarters the following positions carried the rank of Inspector but he considered they should be up graded to Chief Inspector rank:–

Crime Prevention and Public Relations Officer
Training Inspector
C.I.D. Inspector

The volume of work undertaken in the Criminal Investigation Departments at Divisional Headquarters had increased to the stage where it was considered desirable that there should be more supervising officers. In this connection he wished to up grade one Detective Constable in each Divisional C.I.D. to the rank of Detective Sergeant.

The increase in the Establishment of the ranks of Sergeant and above allowed for Chief Inspectors and Inspectors in Charge of Administration at Divisional Headquarters, this being an up grading of the post held by a Clerk Sergeant.

The duties of Warrant Officer at Stroud were performed by a Constable. The Chief Constable considered that this post should be up graded to that of Sergeant to correspond with similar positions held at Staple Hill, Cheltenham and Gloucester.

Mr Gaskain accordingly asked for the approval of the Committee for the proposals as outlined above.

The Chief Constable informed the Police Authority that H.M. Inspector of Constabulary, Mr F.T. Tarry, C.B.E., would be Inspecting the Volunteer Police Cadet Corps at the R.A.F. Station, Innsworth, on Wednesday 20th September, 1961 at 7.30p.m. He would be pleased if any Member of the Committee would like to attend. He further stated that everything was free, thanks to the R.A.F., except refreshments which would be supplied by the N.A.A.F.I., and the Chief Constable asked for authority to pay for these.

The Chairman informed the Standing Joint Committee on 5th December, 1961 that the Advisory Committee to the Board of Governers of the Police College at Bramshill House, Nr. Basingstoke, Hants., had recommended the appointment of Detective Chief Superintendent R.C. Robinson as Director of Studies, subject to the agreement of the Police Authority, with effect from 1st January, 1962.

The normal period of secondment was for two years subject to termination at any time by one month's notice on either side, but by mutual agreement the secondment of the officer might be extended beyond two years. It was Resolved – That no objection be raised to the secondment of Detective Chief Superintendent R.C. Robinson and he be congratulated on his appointment.

At about this time, 1961, some of the civilian staff in Police Offices were members of the National and Local Government Officers' Association (N.A.L.G.O.), and the County Council's Local Joint Staff Committee drew attention to the fact that they did not receive an additional day's leave after a Bank Holiday as the staff of the County Council did, and whilst recognising that they had no standing, so far as the Standing Joint Committee were concerned, the Local Joint Staff Committee asked that sympathetic consideration be given to the matter.

In view of the amount of work arising in Police Offices after Bank Holiday, the Police Authority did not think it would be appropriate for the civilian staff to be on leave. In addition they did not consider that the number of civilians in Police Offices warranted the setting up of a Local Joint Staff Committee, and they were satisfied that any complaint about conditions of service could be satisfactorily dealt with by the Chief Constable in consultation with the Chairman of the Standing Joint Committee. In the event no action was taken.

Mr Gaskain decided that in order to further the training of Cadets, it was desired to arrange for their attachment to industrial firms for periods of either two weeks or one month and asked the Standing Joint Committee for authority to pay the requisite plain clothes, travelling and subsistence allowances to Cadets when they were so attached. The request for authority to pay the allowances was approved by the Committee at their meeting on 5th December, 1961.

Home Office Circular No. 185/1961F2, together with copies of the Police (No.3) Regulations, 1961, were received by the Police Authority on the 5th October, 1961. These Regulations gave effect to a recent agreement of the Police Council of Great Britain for the payment of an allowance of £30 to Police Officers passing the qualifying promotion examinations for Constable to Sergeant, and from Sergeant to Inspector respectively. To obtain the allowance, an officer must have passed such qualifying examinations at the appropriate level in both Educational and Police Subjects, and must have passed one of these examinations since 1st January, 1961.

As a result of the examinations held in February, 1961 twenty-five Officers qualified for the allowance at a total cost of £750. In order that this payment could be made and to meet another, in respect of those men who might be successful in passing the promotion examinations held in November, 1961, the Chief Constable asked for the approval of a Supplementary Estimate of £1,000.

When H.M. Inspector of Constabulary, F.T.Tarry, Esq., C.B.E., carried out his Inspection of the Police Volunteer Cadet Corps at R.A.F. Station, Innsworth on the 20th September, 1961, there were 64 Cadets on Parade with their Instructors and some two hundred parents and guests.

The Chief Constable reported on the 20th March, 1962, that Police Cadets from Gloucestershire attended the Cadet Initial Training Course at the Liverpool Police Training School, Mather Avenue, Liverpool, at a cost of £2.5.0d. per Cadet per week. The charge had now been increased to £5.5.0d., which sum did not include the small charges in respect of Doctor's fees and awards gained. The Chief Constable asked for authority to pay the increased cost of the instruction.

The Police Station at Yorkley in the Forest of Dean was badly in need of replacement but difficulty was being experienced in obtaining a site for the new building. The only site available was one owned by the Forestry Commission who were not prepared to sell the freehold, but were prepared to grant a Ninety-nine year lease. The Chief Constable asked the approval of the Chairman of the Standing Joint Committee to take up the lease, and this was granted after consultation with the Chairman of the County Council. The County Valuer was informed accordingly.

Tenders for the supply of Uniform Clothing were obtained annually, up to 1962, then it was found that due to the delay in obtaining cloth, the manufacturers were finding difficulty in supplying uniform requirements within the stipulated period. Consequently, there was considerable delay between the time the Clothing Tenders were accepted and eventually, delivery of the uniform. To counteract this delay, and to ease work, which was necessary at the Shire Hall and Police Headquarters, when the tender was issued annually, the Chief Constable asked the Committee to agree to the contract period of the next Uniform Clothing tender being extended to cover a period of three years.

In order that he could speak confidentially to the Superintendent in each of the six Divisional Superintendents Stations at, Cheltenham, Gloucester, Staple Hill, Stroud, Cirencester and Lydney, the Chief Constable asked for permission to have a special device fitted on each of the private wire line extensions on the switchboard at Police Headquarterse. Owing to expense the device was never fitted.

After much negotiation with the doctors of the County the Chief Constable was able to agree to a new set of Doctor's fees, or charges, made for their assistance to the Police on various occasions; they were:–

9.00a.m. to 8.00p.m.	under	1 hour £3.13.6d.
	over	1 hour £5.0.0d.
8.00p.m. to 9.00a.m.	under	1 hour £6.10.0d.
	over	1 hour £10.10.0d.

In addition he asked for permission to pay a retaining fee of £50 per annum to one selected Doctor who was prepared to undertake the examination of sexual assaults, etc., which required expert knowledge and experience. Approval was given by the Standing Joint Committee for the new amounts to be paid, on 20th March, 1962.

During 1962 the Chief Constable reported that all Motor Patrol Drivers had attended and passed Standard Driving Courses at Devizes; 32 had passed the Advanced Driving Course, and of them 25 had passed Advanced Refresher Courses.

The policy of one driver in a car in daytime and one driver accompanied by a Beat Officer at night had been continued, and while not an ideal situation, it did enable increased coverage to be maintained throughout the County, making best use of authorised strength of drivers, at that time.

All Patrol Cars had been fitted with the blue flashing roof lamp and two-tone horns. These had proved very efficient in getting cars through congested traffic when answering emergency calls.

The Police Workshop staff consisted of a Sergeant in Charge, four skilled and one semi-skilled mechanics. The sharing of the Highways Workshops and storage facilities at Gloucester had continued satisfactorily, despite cramped conditions which would be overcome when the new

Highways Garage at Gloucester was built. The maintenance of motor cycles and pedal cycles was carried out at Police Headquarters, Cheltenham.

During the year 1961, 418 arrests were made by the crews of mobile vehicles.

The employment of civilian female operators in place of Police Officers in the Information Room had continued to prove satisfactory.

At their meeting on the 20th March, 1961 Mr Gaskain informed the Standing Joint Committee that upon the recommendation of the Secretary of State, Her Majesty the Queen had been pleased to award the Queen's Police Medal to Chief Superintendent Frederick A. Statham, Staple Hill Division. The award appeared in the New Year Honours List on the 1st January, 1962.

In order to gain experience in Police work, two Sudanese Police Officers, Commandants Ibrahim and Sabeel were, at the request of the Home Office, attached to the Gloucestershire Constabulary for two weeks, commencing 12th February, 1962.

During March, 1962, the Chief Constable was authorised to increase the strength of the Police Volunteer Cadet Corps from 100 to 120.

651 motor vehicles were reported stolen during the year 1961. This was an increase of 60 on the year 1960. Of the 651 cases, 610 were recorded as 'taking without consent of the owner' and the offenders were detected in 303 of these cases. The remaining 41 were recorded as 'larceny' and in 33 of these cases the offenders were detected. 14 motor vehicles reported stolen during the year had not been recovered.

During 5th, 6th and 7th March, 1962, the Force was Inspected by H.M. Inspector of Constabulary, F.T.Tarry, Esq., C.B.E.

On the 29th December, 1961, Ex. Superintendent Albert Hills died at Cheltenham. He had been in receipt of a pension since 1st January, 1959. He left a widow Mrs Dorothy A. Hills who was awarded a Police Widow's pension which was supplemented in accordance with the provisions of the National Insurance Act.

The Chief Constable gave details to the Police Authority on the 20th March, 1962, of the proposed upgradings and increase in Establishment whereby there would be, if approved, and overall increase of 122 men and 14 women, making a total of 136.

SUMMARY OF REVISED ESTABLISHMENT

Ranks	*Past Establishment*	*Proposed New Establishment*
Chief Constable	1	1
Assistant Chief Constable	1	1

Chief Superintendents	4	6
Superintendents Grade 1	5	3
Chief Inspectors	14	22
Inspectors	37	35
Sergeants	139	160
Constables	559	654
Women Police Inspectors	–	1
Women Police Sergeants	3	4
Women Police Constables	9	21
Total	772	908

After the Chief Constable's Report had been discussed the Chairman of the Standing Joint Committee moved that, 'The section of the Report on the Establishment of the Force in the City of Gloucester be taken in Committee.'

The Committee were then informed by the Chairman that in accordance with the usual practice and with the terms of the Consolidation Agreement in force with the Gloucester City Council, the Chief Constable had recently attended a meeting of the City Watch Committee to explain his recommendations. The Watch Committee did not agree to the extent to which it was proposed to increase the establishment so far as Gloucester was concerned, and the Chairman read a letter which the Clerk of the Committee had received from the Town Clerk, a copy of which had been sent to the Home Office. The letter stated that the City Watch Committee were not as a whole satisfied with the Chief Constables's explanations and were not prepared to concede that an increase was necessary so shortly after two previous increases.

The Chief Constable submitted a Report on the meeting and gave a detailed explanation of his proposals so far as they affected the City of Gloucester.

Mr I.C. Pritchard stated that the Watch Committee were of the opinion that if any increase was eventually decided upon it should be spread over a period of five years instead of the three years suggested to assist the burden on the rates.

Col. G.P. Shakerley, M.C., T.D., expressed the view that with the continued rise in the population of the County the increase proposed was necessary, but he suggested that the actual trends in population should be taken into account year by year when specific increases were due to be implemented.

After further general discussion, the Chairman moved, Col. F. Seymour-Williams, D.S.O., O.B.E., seconded, and it was resolved –

That this Committee, having considered the letter from the Town Clerk of

> Gloucester and the Chief Constable's memorandum thereon, wish to state with the greatest possible emphasis:–
>
> (1) Their entire disagreement with the suggestion made by certain members of the Gloucester City Watch Committee as to any inefficiency on the part of the Constabulary or the Chief Constable.
>
> (2) Their complete confidence in the Chief Constable and their appreciation of the tact and courtesy which are, and always have been, a marked characteristic of his dealings with the Standing Joint Committee.
>
> (3) That a copy of this resolution be sent to the Secretary of State and to the Town Clerk of Gloucester.

It was further resolved –

> That the recommendations of the Chief Constable for an increase in the establishment be approved in principle on the understanding that the actual trends in population are taken into account year by year when specific increases are due to be implemented and that they be submitted to the Home Office for approval.

On the 19th June, 1962 the Clerk of the Committee submitted a letter from the Home Office stating that in order that recruiting should not be held up, the Secretary of State had approved, as an interim measure, an increase of thirty Constables in the authorised Establishment of the Force. It was further stated that the Police requirements of the County Borough of Gloucester were under consideration and that this interim increase in the Establishment of the Constabulary took no account of the Police requirements of the County Borough, and a further letter dealing with the Policing of Gloucester and of the remainder of the proposals of the Standing Joint Committee would be sent as soon as possible.

Mr H. Layton stated that he understood that a further letter on this subject had been sent to the Clerk of the Committee by the Town Clerk of Gloucester and enquired whether it was to be submitted.

The Chairman gave a resume of the position regarding the Establishment with particular reference to the City of Gloucester and expressed the view that as the matter was now being dealt with by the Secretary of State, it would be preferable to await the outcome of his consideration of the proposals, and in the circumstances he did not propose to submit the letter.

The Chairman informed the Committee on the 19th June, 1962 that subject to the approval of the Home Office, Mr R.G. Fenwick,

Assistant Chief Constable, Gloucestershire had been appointed Chief Constable of Shropshire and would take up his duties on the 1st July, 1962. The Committee expressed their appreciation of Mr Fenwick's valuable service as Assistant Chief Constable since 1960, congratulated him and expressed good wishes for the future.

The two teams of Police Cadets entered from Gloucestershire, for the Tors Competition held on Dartmoor in connection with the Duke of Edinburgh's Award Scheme, did very well. Three hundred teams from all over the country entered the Competition, and in the Senior event, over sixty miles of rugged country, the Gloucestershire team was one of forty-eight and finished a close second to the team from the Royal Naval College, Dartmouth. In the Junior event which took place over fifty miles of similar type of country, five of the six members of the Gloucestershire team completed the course in the fastest times. The Seniors had received medals for their achievement on the 7th July, 1962.

During 1962, 1,100 copies of Force Standing Orders were printed, bound and issued to members of the Force, together with Instructions for Major Incidents. As a result the Chief Constable had to ask the Chairman's approval for a Supplementary Estimate of £2,000 for Printing and Stationery during the 1962/63 financial year.

Two premises were offered, during 1962, for use by Regular and Volunteer Cadets as Adventure Centres. One was two empty cottages at Tormarton, owned by His Grace The Duke of Beaufort, and the other was a boat-house and lake at Tortworth Court owned by the Right Hon. The Earl of Ducie.

In order to make the cottages habitable, a lot of work would be required to be carried out, but the interiors could be done by the Cadets themselves. The roofs of the cottages needed expert attention and it would cost about £30 to effect the necessary repairs. In addition, each place would need equipment such as beds, bedding, cooking utensils, etc., and the Chief Constable asked for authority to expend up to £200.

Cadet Roger A. England, who was stationed at Cheltenham Central Police Station, was accepted by the British Council as one of a party to visit the Soviet Union from 10th July until 3rd August, 1962, under a Youth Exchanges Scheme with the Soviet Union.[6]

At the National Police Dog Trials held at Bedford early in 1962, there were seventy dogs from fifty–five British Forces undergoing six tests, including obedience, tracking and criminal work. Gloucestershire Police Dog Major, handled by P.C. Douglas P. Keene, stationed at Staple Hill, was one of only eight dogs in the country to gain 'Excellent' ratings in all the classes of the Trials.

During the summer of 1962 a garage belonging to the Stroud News and Journal Ltd., at Stroud, was damaged by a cow which had been straying in the centre of Stroud and broke out of the garage after being shut in there by a Policeman on Point Duty. The cost of the necessary repairs was £21. It had not been possible to recover this amount from the owner of the cow so the expenditure was met by the Committee.

Constable Leonard A.W. Hewlett at the age of 36 years died suddenly on the 21st June, 1962. He had completed twelve years service and at the time of this death was stationed at Hardwicke, Nr. Gloucester. He left a widow Mrs Gladys Ellen Hewlett and one child. Mrs Hewlett was granted a Police Widow's Pension supplemented in accordance with the provisions of the National Insurance Act.

Consequent upon the appointment of Mr R.G. Fenwick to Chief Constable of Shropshire, the Chief Constable reported that Chief Superintendent Herbert D.J. Smith, Gloucester, had been appointed Assistant and Deputy Chief Constable of the Gloucestershire Force. He took up his new duties on Monday 30th July, 1962. It was necessary for Mr Smith to move his home from Gloucester to Cheltenham.

Brigadier C.S. Howard, C.B.E., D.S.O., Army Outward Bound School, Towyn, North Wales, carried out an Inspection of the Regular and Volunteer Cadets at Robinswood Barracks, Gloucester, on the 7th July, 1962.

Forty-four Regular Cadets and one hundred Volunteer Cadets were on Parade, with their Instructors, and some four hundred parents and guests were present and watched the Inspection which was most impressive. This was the first occasion on which a combined Inspection of Regular and Volunteer Cadets had been made.

The six Members of the Standing Joint Committee who had accompanied the Chief Constable on visits to all the Police Stations and houses throughout the County during 1959/61, agreed to continue their visits during 1962. During these latest series of visits it was planned to inspect all the new houses that had been built or purchased since previous visits, and also those premises where major alterations had taken place. It was hoped that the Members would also look at the sub-standard houses which remained.

At a meeting of the Chief Constables of Herefordshire, Worcestershire and Gloucestershire, on the 13th July, 1962, it was agreed that, as from 30th July, 1962, Herefordshire and Worcestershire

Police would be wholly responsible for patrolling the Ross Spur Motorway (M50) from its junction with the M5 to Ross-on-wye.

Although this meant Gloucestershire Police would now cease the patrolling of the Motorway, the Chief Constable agreed to assist with incidents requiring Police attention if asked to do so. The Landrover purchased and used for patrolling the Motorway, would, from now on, be utilised for patrolling the Trunk road A38 from Berkeley Road to Twyning.

At the Standing Joint Committee meeting on the 20th September, 1962, the Chief Constable reported the following transport details to the Committee:–

(a) Fifteen motor cycles had been received and distributed throughout the County to Stations policing roads with high traffic density.
(b) Three Ariel motor cycles had been sold and replaced by new machines.
(c) Two Riley Patrol Cars and one Austin A95 had been replaced by Austin 110 motor cars.
(d) Four Bedford Dormobile motor vans had been replaced by four new Morris vans, and the Ford Popular motor car had been replaced by a new B.M.C. Morris van.

On the 4th December, 1962, the Chairman reported to the Standing Joint Committee that Mr J.S.H. Gaskain, M.B.E., Q.P.M., had resigned from the office of Chief Constable, upon his appointment as one of Her Majesty's Inspectors of Constabulary, with effect from the 19th December, 1962. He congratulated Mr Gaskain on his appointment and spoke in appreciation of the valuable and efficient services which he had rendered to the County since his appointment in 1959, and wished him success in his new work. The Lord Lieutenant (His Grace the Duke of Beaufort, K.G., G.C.V.O.), also paid tribute to the services rendered by Mr Gaskain.
It was unanimously resolved –

> That the Standing Joint Committee place on record its appreciation of the valuable and efficient services of Mr J.S.H. Gaskain, M.B.E., Q.P.M., as Chief Constable since 1959.

Mr Gaskain thanked the Committee for their kind expressions.

The Chairman informed the Committee that with the authority of the Finance and Buildings Sub-Committee, the appointment had been advertised on the same terms and the Sub-Committee would meet on the morning of the 10th January, 1963, to interview a short list of candidates with a view to selecting two or three to appear before a Special Meeting of the Standing Joint Committee in the afternoon of the same day.

At this same meeting it was resolved –

> That Mr H.D.J. Smith, the Assistant Chief Constable be appointed Acting Chief Constable for the period 20th December, 1962, until the new Chief Constable takes up his appointment and that the allowance payable to him for the additional responsibility be calculated with reference to the difference between the lowest point of the salary scale of the Chief Constable and Assistant Chief Constable.

Police Sergeant Reginald G. Sandle, stationed at Cirencester, died on the 30th September, 1962, after a long illness. He was 45 years of age and had completed 26 years service. He left a widow Mrs D.D. Sandle, who was awarded a Police Widow's Pension. There were no children.

The Standing Joint Committee meeting held at Gloucester on the 4th December,1962, was the last meeting that Mr. Gaskain attended as Chief Constable of Gloucestershire.

As Chief Constable, Mr Gaskain made his last promotion within the Force when, on the 12th December, 1962, he called Superintendent H. Thomas into his office, thanked him for his help during his office as Chief Clerk at Police Headquarters and told him to appoint himself as Chief Superintendent from that date.

P.S. WATKINS, Littledean.

Presentation of Coronation Medals.

Senior Officers with Colonel HENN, Chief Constable prior to his retirement.

Information Room – P.S. C.J. DAVIS.

Presentation to A.C.C. CARTER, upon retirement 1960.

Ron. SPENCER and David SMEETON – George Medals 26.9.1961.

Motor cycle course 1962.

Senior Officers April 1964 – serving and retired.

New Divisional Headquarters, Cheltenham and old Headquarters, Holland House. Sept. '65

First Panda Patrol outside Divisional Headquarters, Cheltenham. 1968

First Drug Unit June 1967.

Underwater Recovery Section.

H.D.J. SMITH, M.B.E., Q.P.M., Deputy Chief Constable. 1966–1973

CHAPTER 8

Herbert D.J. Smith, M.B.E., Q.P.M.
Acting Chief Constable
19.12.62 – 7.4.1963

Mr Smith, took up his duties as Acting Chief Constable on the 19th December, 1962. He was Gloucestershire born and all his service had been with the Gloucestershire Constabulary, having come up through the ranks. His Father had also served in the Force and retired with the rank of Sergeant, many years previously. Mr Smith's younger brother was also serving with the Force.

At a Special meeting of the Standing Joint Committee held at the Judges' Lodgings, 29 Spa Road, Gloucester, on Thursday 10th January, 1963, at 2.15p.m., the Chairman informed the Committee that 21 applications had been received for the appointment of Chief Constable and that the Finance and Buildings Sub-Committee had interviewed six candidates that morning and had selected the following to appear before the Committee:–

(1) Mr G.R. Glendenning, Chief Constable of Perthshire and Kinross-shire.

(2) Mr E.P.B. White, Chief Constable of East Suffolk.

The Committee thereupon interviewed the two candidates and, it was resolved –

> That subject to the approval of the Secretary of State Mr Edwin Peter Blake White, Chief Constable of East Suffolk, be appointed Chief Constable of Gloucestershire in accordance with the terms of the advertisement.

The Finance and Buildings Sub-Committee was informed on the 19th March, 1963, that Mr E.P.B. White would commence his duties as Chief Constable of Gloucestershire on the 8th April, 1963.

Although the Home Office indicated that they had no objection in principle to the eighteen schemes submitted being commenced in the financial year 1963 – 64, the County Council thought differently and on the

19th March, 1963, the Chairman of the Police Authority informed his Committee that at the request of the County Council, the following twelve projects would not be proceeded with in the financial year 1963 – 64:–

Inspectors Station Tewkesbury
Office at Bourton-on-the-Water
Office at Gloucester Road, Cheltenham
Office at Wotton-under-Edge
Office at Coney Hill, Gloucester
Office at Whiteshill
Office at Pound Road, Kingswood
Office at Rodborough
Office at Mitcheldean
Office at Yorkley
Office at Parkend
Office at Wickwar

It had, however, been made clear to the Chairman of the County Council that if the urgency of a particular project was stressed during the year by H.M. Inspector of Constabulary, the Committee would have to ask the County Council to consider re-instating it in the programme.

Mr W.E. Lane, expressed his disappointment at the deletion of the proposed Inspector's Station at Tewkesbury from the Building Programme for 1963-64 and hoped that H.M. Inspector of Constabulary would stress the urgency of this particular project in view of the unsatisfactory condition of the old Police Station.

When the plans of the proposed Divisional Headquarters at Cheltenham and Cirencester were first prepared a basement was included as a Civil Defence Control and this was done with the concurrence of the Home Office (Civil Defence Department), but owing to operational changes in Civil Defence the Home Office intimated that the basements would not after all be required. The plans were too far advanced for any changes to be made and on a suggestion made by the Acting Chief Constable it was agreed, by the Finance and Buildings Sub-Committee to convert the basements so that they could be used as a Rifle Range/Skittle Alley. The cost, amounting to approximately £14,000 in each project. The Clerk was instructed to write to the Home Office, inform them of what was planned, and request their approval of the additional expenditure, for the purpose of Police Grant.

Home Office Circular No. 210/1962, informed Police Authorities that the Secretary of State intended to make Regulations increasing the pay of the Federated ranks, with effect from 1st February, 1963, they were:–

Chief Inspector	Men	£1,435 to £1,530 p.a. after 2 years' service in the rank
	Women	£1,290 to £1,375 p.a. after 2 years' service in the rank
Inspector	Men	£1,280 to £1,370 p.a. after 2 years' service in the rank
	Women	£1,150 to £1,235 p.a. after 2 years' service in the rank
Sergeant	Men	£1,090 to £1,170 p.a. after 2 years' service in the rank
	Women	£980 to £1,055 p.a. after 2 years' service in the rank
Constable	Men	£635 to £965 p.a. after 9 years service
	Women	£570 to £870 p.a. after 9 years service

In addition there was a Supplementary Payment of £30 p.a. to Police Constables at 17 years service, and a second Supplementary Payment of £35 p.a. on the completion of 22 years service.

Women Police Constables would be paid a Supplementary Payment of £30 p.a. at 17 years service, and a second Supplementary Payment of £30 p.a. after 22 years service.

With the increase in pay it was necessary for the Secretary of State to increase the Detective Duty Allowances with effect from 1st February, 1963. The new rates were:–

	MEN	WOMEN
Chief Inspectors	£135 per annum	£121 per annum
Inspectors	£120 per annum	£108 per annum
Sergeants	£103 per annum	£ 92 per annum
Constables	£ 76 per annum	£ 68 per annum

At the request of the Secretary of State and with the approval of the Chairman P.C. 450 Rowland H. Cox of the Gloucestershire Constabulary was seconded as from the 20th December, 1962, to act as Orderly/Driver to Mr J.S. Gaskain on his appointment as Her Majesty's Inspector of Constabulary.

The Constable's pay and allowances together with travelling and appropriate subsistence expenses, the cost of his uniform and a pension charge of 20% of pay, would be reclaimed each quarter from the Home Office. The amount re-imbursed would be brought to credit in the claim for Police Grant.

By 1st March, 1963, the strength of the Patrol Car Drivers was 11 Sergeants and 70 Constables. All these drivers had passed the Standard Driving Course at Devizes. Thirty had passed the Advanced Driving Course and of these 18 had passed Advanced Refresher Courses.

There were 579 authorised drivers within the Force together with 366 permitted motor cyclists.

During the year 1962, 493 arrests were made by the crews of motor vehicles.

Early in 1963, the Acting Chief Constable was informed by the Secretary of State that arrangements were being made to hold an experimental series of Courses in Crime Prevention at the Constabulary Training School, Staffordshire, for which Officers from all Forces in England and Wales would be eligible, subject to them having the required qualifications.

A request was received from the Home Office to allow Chief Inspector Frederick G. Hudson, the Crime Prevention Officer for Gloucestershire, to be attached to the Staffordshire Constabulary for a period of approximately four months from the 25th March, 1963, to assist in the arrangements for these Courses and to act as a resident Instructor when they commenced. The Chairman gave his approval for the attachment and this was endorsed by the Committee.

It was during 1963 that the Air Ministry required a limited V.H.F. Mobile Radio System for the Royal Air Force Provost Organisation in the United Kingdom, and one of the Headquarters to be provided with a fixed Station was located at Innsworth, near Gloucester. A sitting survey had been carried out and in the absence of a suitable R.A.F. site it was recommended that the Police Wireless Station at Cleeve Hill would be ideal for the purpose.

The Air Ministry requested permission to fix an aerial to one of the existing masts and the Acting Chief Constable raised no objection providing:–

(a) Separate accommodation was supplied for the Air Ministry equipment, and

(b) That there were no objections on technical grounds and no interference was caused to Civil Police Communications.

The Director of Telecommunications, Home Office, had no technical objection to the proposal and a test carried out in the presence of the Home Office Regional Wireless Engineer had confirmed that there was no interference problem.

The Committee recommended that the request be granted.[1]

CHAPTER 9

Edwin Peter Blake White, O.B.E., Q.P.M.
8.4.1963 – 30.6.1975

Mr E.P.B. White, who took up his duties as Chief Constable of Gloucestershire at Police Headquarters, Cheltenham, on the 8th April, 1963, attended his first meeting of the Standing Joint Committee at Gloucester on 10th June, 1963, when the Committee recorded their appreciation of the work carried out by Mr H.D.J. Smith, the Assistant Chief Constable, during the interregnum.

The Chairman, at this meeting, referred to the National Police Dog Trials which were held at South Cerney in the week beginning 27th May, 1963, and stated that he had been asked by Commander W.J.H. Willis, H.M. Inspector of Constabulary, the Chairman of the Advisory Committee on Police Dogs, to thank the Standing Joint Committee, on behalf of the Advisory Committee, for the support and help given in respect of the trials.

In November 1962 the Standing Joint Committee authorised the purchase of fifty illuminated signs for Police Stations at a cost of £445. The signs were not ordered because there was insufficient provision in the Budget but they were now required urgently and more than the original number would now be required. Owing to the lapse of time the cost had risen by 8/–d. per sign. The Committee recommended that 100 signs be purchased at a cost of £900, the cost to be met from the Revenue Budget for 1963/64; the signs to be supplied by Messrs Pearce Signs Ltd., Cardiff.

Home Office Circular 63/1963 provided for increased pay for Chief Constables and Assistant Chief Constables, with effect from 1st September, 1962. The new scales were related entirely to population and having regard to the fact that the population of the Police Authority was approximately 580,000, the Committee were of the opinion that the Chief Constable and the Assistant Chief Constable should be placed on the highest point of the respective ranges as from

8th April, 1963, i.e. the date of the appointment of Mr. E.P.B. White. It was resolved:–

(a) That the salary of the Chief Constable and the Assistant Chief Constable, from the 8th April, 1963, be as follows:–
    Chief Constable £3,750 × £130 (3) £4,140
    Assistant Chief Constable £2,485 × £75 (2) × £80 (1) £2,715
(b) That for the period 1st September, 1962, to 7th April, 1963, the pay of the Assistant Chief Constable be revised by adding to his existing salary a sum equal to 3½%.
(c) That for the period 1st September, to 19th December, 1962, the pay of the previous holder of the post of Chief Constable be similarly adjusted.

The Secretary of State notified the Police Authority in Home Office Circular No. 48/1963, dated 4th March, 1963, that he had approved the agreement reached by Panel 'B' of the Police Council for Great Britain on 5th February, 1963, for increase of pay on behalf of the Superintendents and Chief Superintendents.

The new scales of pay were:–

Chief Superintendents	£2,040 – £2,100 – £2,160
Superintendents Grade 1	£1,885 – £1,945 – £2,005
Superintendents Grade 2	£1,700 – £1,760 – £1,820

At the request of the Secretary of State and with the approval of the Chairman of the Standing Joint Committee, Detective Chief Inspector A.R.J. Carter, was seconded, as from the 16th April, 1963, to act as Staff Officer to Mr J.S.H. Gaskain, one of Her Majesty's Inspectors of Constabulary.

This officer had been promoted to, and served in the rank of Superintendent Grade 1, with an allowance of £100 for which the Secretary of State had given his approval. His pay and allowances, together with a pension contribution assessed at 20% gross pensionable pay was reclaimed each quarter from the Home Office.

A request was received from the Town Clerk, Gloucester, for the appointment of an additional Reserve Constable for patrol duties in the various parks and gardens in the City.

In the past there had been two such Reserve Constables for this duty and the City Council wished to enrol a third so that play-grounds and open spaces in the outlying districts of the City could be adequately patrolled.

This appointment did not involve any additional expenditure by the Police Authority and, if approved, it was proposed to offer the City Council the use of a pedal cycle for the Constable for which a small charge would be made.

Approval was given, by the Standing Joint Committee, for the appointment of a third Reserve Constable, on the 10th June, 1963.

At the request of the Secretary of State and with the Chairman's approval Miss Margaret E. Lightbody, the Chief Constable's Secretary was seconded, as from 2nd May, 1963, to act as personal assistant to Mr J.S.H. Gaskain, one of Her Majesty's Inspectors of Constabulary. The Police Authority would continue to issue Miss Lightbody's pay and would, each quarter, claim reimbursement of this expenditure from the Home Office together with the appropriate Pension contributions.

With the cost of living still rising it was found necessary to look at the allowances in respect of wages lost by Special Constables when on duty. Home Office Circular 94/1963, dated 6th March, 1963, amended these allowances as from 1st February, 1963. They were:–

Men	£2.4.3d. a day
Women	£1.19.8d. a day

The second combined Inspection of the Regular and Volunteer Cadets was held at Badminton House, Badminton on the 4th May, 1963.

His Grace the Duke of Beaufort, K.G., G.C.V.O., carried out the Inspection and forty-three Regular and ninety-seven Volunteer Cadets were on Parade with their Instructors. Some 400 parents and guests were present. The Inspection was followed by the presentation to Cadets of two Gold Awards and seventeen Silver Awards under the Duke of Edinburgh's Award Scheme.

It was in June 1961 when the last increase in charges for Police Officrs doing duty on requisition was agreed. At the same time it was decided that all future rates would be the same as those charged by the Metropolitan Police.

In view of the increase in pay and allowances which came into operation on the 1st February, 1963, the Secretary of State recommended that the charges be increased accordingly. Home Office Circular No. 105/1963, referred.

The Chief Constable therefore recommended that the following revised rates, which were identical to those to be charged by the Metropolitan Police, be adopted, in Gloucestershire, as from 1st July, 1963:–

	RANK	DAILY RATE	HOURLY RATE	MINIMUM CHARGE
Men –	Uniform			
	Chief Inspector	£10.15. 9d.	£1. 7.0d.	£4. 1.0d.
	Inspector	£ 9.17. 4d.	£1. 4.8d.	£3.14.0d.
	Sergeant	£ 8. 8. 8d.	£1. 1.1d.	£3. 3.3d.
	Constable	£ 6.11. 8d.	£ 16.6d.	£2. 9.6d.
C.I.D.				
	Chief Inspector	£11.11. 9d.	£1. 9.0d.	£4. 7.0d.
	Inspector	£10.12. 1d.	£1. 6.6d.	£3.19.6d.
	Sergeant	£ 9.13. 3d.	£1. 4.2d.	£3.12.6d.
	Constable	£ 7. 2. 2d.	17.9d.	£2.13.3d.
Women –	Uniform			
	Inspector	£ 8. 4. 5d.	£1. 0.7d.	£3. 1.9d.
	Sergeant	£ 6.19.10d.	17.6d.	£2.12.6d.
	Constable	£ 1. 7. 9d.	13.6d.	£2. 0.6d.

An Inspection of the Force was carried out on the 23rd, 24th, 25th and 26th September, 1963, by H.M. Inspector of Constabulary, Mr B.N. Bebbington, O.B.E.

The Inspection did not take the form of full formal Parades; H.M. Inspector visited Headquarters and Police Stations and held small Parades at Sub-Divisional level.

Chief Superintendent Raymond C. Robinson, who had been seconded to the Police College at Bramshill, retired on pension on the 15th September, 1963, to take up an appointment at G.C.H.Q., Cheltenham. Chief Superintendent Robinson was 52 years of age and had served for just over 33 years.

Chief Superintendent Frederick A. Statham, Q.P.M., retired on pension on the 28th September, 1963, after 39 years service. His age on retirement was 59 years and 363 days.

The Chief Constable had much pleasure in informing Members of the Standing Joint Committee, at their meeting on the 10th December, 1963, that Superintendent Richard B. Thomas, seconded from the Force as Commandant of No. 7 District Police Training Centre, Chantmarle, had been appointed Chief Constable of the Mid-Wales Constabulary, as from the 11th November, 1963.

For a great number of years an allowance of 4/–d. per month had been made to members of the Force who, with the Chief Constable's consent, used their own typewriters for Police purposes at those Police Stations where there were no County owned machines. In view of the increase in the cost of these machines, the Chief Constable, on the 10th December, 1963, asked that the allowance be increased to 5/–d. per month.

On the 10th December, 1963, the Chief Constable reported to the Police Authority that not all Officers in the Force were housed in Police houses or in official Single Men's Quarters, and it was unlikely that they ever would be. At their meeting held at Gloucester on 10th December, 1957, the Standing Joint Committee had agreed that the following Rent Allowances should be paid to those Ofiicers buying their own houses, renting temporary accommodation or living in lodgings:–

Superintendents	£140 p.a.
Inspectors	47/6d. per week
Sergeants	45/–d. per week
Constables	42/6d. per week

Since that date the cost of accommodation had increased considerably and the Chief Constable felt that by raising the allowance by 10/–d. all round it would ensure that, in the majority of cases, full payment for their accommodation would be met and he asked that consideration be given to raising the Rent Allowance to:–

Superintendents	£166 p.a.
Inspectors	57/6d. per week
Sergeants	55/–d. per week
Constables	52/6d. per week

Those men who were single and living in lodgings normally received a flat rate allowance of half the approved rate for married men of their rank, which would mean:–

Superintendents	£83 p.a.
Inspectors	28/9d. per week
Sergeants	27/6d. per week
Constables	26/3d. per week

The above recommendations were approved by the Standing Joint Committee.

On the 10th December, 1963, the Chief Constable was able to report that the transfer of the Police Motor Patrol Workshops had been completed from Barrack Square to the Police Section of the County Council Depot at Cole Avenue, Gloucester.

Home Office Circular No. 40/1964, dated 6th February, 1964, together with copies of the Police (Amendment) Regulations, 1964, had been received by the Police Authority for Gloucestershire and discussed at their meeting held 17th March, 1964.

These Regulations, of which Parts 1 and 3 came into force on the 10th February, 1964, made a number of amendments to Regulations on conditions of service, including provision for the implementation of the agreement of the Police Council of Great Britain on the 42 hour week.

PART 1

Regulation 4 of the 1952 Regulations specified the licences, the holding of which disqualified a person for membership of a police force.
Regulation 1 of the 1964 Regulations added, to the specified licences, any licence or permit granted under the law relating to betting and gaming.
Regulation 2 permitted, in certain circumstances, leave not taken in one leave year to be taken at the beginning of the next leave year.
Regulation 3 provided that any liability of a member of a police force to pay income tax in respect of his occupation of a police house or quarters shall be discharged by the Police Authority.
Regulation 4 made fresh provisions for allowances in respect of expenditure incidental to a change of home and replaced the then maximum limits by flat rates.

PART 2

The amendments contained in this part took effect on 1st July, 1964.
Regulation 7 provided that, subject to the exigencies of duty, a member of a Police Force below the rank of Superintendent should have seven instead of six rest days in each period of four weeks.

The Chief Constable informed the Standing Joint Committee that he was investigating the implications of the reduction in the working week and would report his findings at the next meeting in June.

Following a review of the current rates of weekly allowances ordinarily paid to officers attending Courses away from home and living in lodgings, the Secretary of State notified Police Authorities (Home Office Circular No. 257/1963, dated 12th December, 1963) that the weekly allowances should be increased to:–

Superintendents	£7.10.0d.
Inspectors or Chief Inspectors	£7.0.0d.
Sergeants and Constables	£6.5.0d.

From September, 1959, members of the Force were permitted to carry out certain re-decorations in the accommodation they occupied and to this end were allowed to expend amounts on the following basis:–

Bedrooms and living rooms –	
If distempered	£4.0.0d. each
If papered	£5.0.0d. each
Kitchens and bathrooms –	
Including painted walls	£4.10.0d. each

In view of the increase in the cost of materials which had taken place since 1959, when the above figures were established, and after consultation with the County Architect, the Chief Constable asked that each of the amounts be increased by 10/–d. as from the 1st April, 1964.

The proportionate increased allowance, up to a maximum of £7, for larger rooms remained the same.

Home Office Circular No. 192/45F of the 17th July, 1945, allowed the payment of a boot allowance of 1/–d. a week to part-time Special Constables who performed four or more hours of duty per week.

In view of the number of Special Constables performing part-time duty in the County, Mr White, Chief Constable asked for permission to introduce this allowance as from 1st April, 1964. If approved, one payment would be made annually.

The Courses in Crime Prevention being run at the Constabulary Training School, Stafford, were well attended and as a result the Home Office requested that Chief Inspector F. Hudson, the Crime Prevention Officer for Gloucestershire, be released for appointment as Director of these Courses, in the temporary rank of Superintendent Grade 2, with effect from 9th March, 1964, until his eventual return to Gloucestershire. With the Chairman's approval the Chief Constable agreed to the attachment. The Home Office was responsible for the payment of this Officer's salary and allowances during his attachment, including the special non-pensionable allowance of £250 per annum.[1]

During the year 1963, 253 males and 11 females were proceeded against for drunkenness, all being convicted. This was an increase of 2 convictions compared with figures for 1962.

The numbers of deaths reported to Coroners, in Gloucestershire, for 1963, were 1,102. Inquests were held in 317 cases and the following verdicts recorded:–

Accidental death	112
Misadventure	74
Natural Causes	21

Suicide	57
Murder	2
Silicosis	23
Other verdicts	24
Results pending	4

At the meeting of the Standing Joint Committee on the 15th June, 1964, the Chairman, Lt. Col. J. Godman, C.B.E., referred, with regret, to the death on the 27th April, 1964, of Colonel W.F. Henn, C.B.E., M.V.O., K.P.M., Chief Constable of Gloucestershire from 1937 to 1959. He paid tribute to his services to the County in that capacity and it was Resolved – 'That a letter of condolence be sent to his widow'. Colonel Henn had been in receipt of a Police pension since 9th April, 1959. He left a widow, Mrs Geraldine Henn who was granted a Police Widow's pension.

The Chairman also informed the Committee, at this meeting, that Her Majesty the Queen had been pleased to award the Queen's Police Medal to the Chief Constable, Mr E.P.B. White and on the Committee's behalf, he expressed their congratulations to Mr White who, in tune, thanked the Committee.

The Police Act 1964, received the Royal Assent on the 10th July, 1964. Under the Act Standing Joint Committees were to be abolished and the Police Authority for a Police Area consisting of a County would be a Committee of the County Council and would consist of such number of persons to be determined by the Council, two thirds being members thereof and one third being Magistrates.

In this, and in most other respects the Act followed closely to recommendations of the Royal Commission on Police and the Home Office were going to issue Circulars, dealing with provisions which were to be brought into force at an early date, would shortly be issued.

Police Constable Morton J. Chappell was fatally injured in a road accident on the 16th April, 1964 at the age of 24 years. He had nearly completed five years service, was a single man and, at the time of his death he was stationed at Stroud.

The third Combined Inspection of Regular and Volunteer Cadets was held at the Royal Air Force Station, South Cerney, on 9th May, 1964. The Right Honourable the Earl Bathurst carried out the Inspection of forty-three Regular Cadets and eighty-six Volunteer Cadets together with their Instructors.

Some 400 parents and guests were present and after the Inspection saw the presentation to Cadets of five Gold Awards and seven Silver Awards under the Duke of Edinburgh's Award Scheme.

At the Standing Joint Committee meeting on the 15th June, 1964, the Chief Constable reported on the reduction of the working week for all ranks below that of Superintendent, from 44 hours to 42 hours with effect from 1st July, 1964. This reduction in hours meant an extra Rest Day every four weeks, which amounted to a 5¼ day week.

The agreement also provided that overtime in respect of the two conceded hours in those Forces in which the new extra Rest Day could not be granted until certain increases in strength had been achieved, should be paid at plain time rates until 31st December, 1964, or until the new extra Rest Days were granted, whichever was the earlier.

As the Force was still substantially below the authorised establishment, the Chief Constable did not consider it practicable to allow the further Rest Day at that time and therefore proposed that until the 15th December, 1964, all officers should be required to work regularly on the fourth Rest Day and to be paid over-time allowances at the prescribed rate in compensation.

In Home Office Circular No. 40/1964 of 6th February, 1964, the Secretary of State asked that every Police Authority should consider what measures would be necessary to provide for the reduction in hours and suggested that an increase in the Establishment would, no doubt, be necessary. Such an increase, the Chief Constable said, would become a necessity in so far as Gloucestershire was concerned, when the Establishment, at that time, was completed on the 31st March, 1965. This increase, together with the suggested increase in Establishment, was being investigated, and would be notified to Members at their September meeting.

By June 1964 it was realised that the existing Police Headquarters building in Lansdown Road, Cheltenham (Holland House), which was purchased by the Police Authority in 1920 and first occupied in 1921, had now become inadequate for use as the Force Headquarters.

The building was some 1,000 square feet short of the scale laid down in the Home Office Memorandum on the Design and Construction of Police Stations, and it did not meet the necessary requirements of the Offices, Shops and Railway Premises Act, 1963, which came into force on the 1st August, 1964.

The existing office accommodation was filled to capacity, in some cases overcrowded, and bearing in mind the proposal to increase the Force Establishment it was imperative that additional modern office accommodation be provided in the near future to cater for the staff needed to administer the Force.

As a result the Chief Constable, Mr E.P.B. White, reported to the Standing Joint Committee on 15th June, 1964, that the new Cheltenham Divisional Headquarters which was in course of construction, alongside the then Police Headquarters building, should be occupied by Headquarters staff when the new building was ready. This would mean that the existing Cheltenham Divisional headquarters would continue to operate. When empty, and with the Committee's approval, Mr White suggested that the old Headquarters Building could be demolished, new premises built on the site and re-occupied.

The County Architect had been approached concerning these proposals and agreed that it was a practical proposition. However, the Committee deferred the Chief Constable's proposition for further discussion between the Chairman and Vice Chairman of the Standing Joint Committee and the Chairman of the County Council, the Chairman of the Council's Estates Committee and the appropriate officers.

The Sub-Committee met and reported back to the Standing Joint Committee on the 22nd September, 1964 that, with the continued expansion of the Force a new Headquarters was a necessity and that Holland House ought to be demolished in the financial year 1965/66 and that rebuilding should take place as soon as reasonably possible.

On the morning of the 26th September, 1963, Constable Stanley G. Armitage stationed at Staple Hill, attended with his Sergeant, at a house in Salisbury Road, Staple Hill, in the garden of which was a sow pig which had escaped from a local slaughter house, ran amok and injured several people.

The animal, at the time, appeared to be quiet, but when the officers turned away momentarily, the sow suddenly charged. P.C. Armitage slipped, fell to the ground and was severely savaged by the pig until it could be driven off. He sustained injuries which necessitated his admission to hospital and the wristlet watch he was wearing at the time was damaged beyond repair. P.C. Armitage was reimbursed the sum of £10, this being the current value of the wristlet watch.

In connection with this incident, Mr. H.G.T. Harris, a member of the Standing Joint Committee, at their meeting on the 15th June, 1964, stated that had it not been for the commendable action of P,C. Armitage, the damage to civilian property would have been considerably worse.[2]

The contract for the cleaning of the Central Police Station, Gloucester which had been in force for twelve months expired on the 30th June,

1964, and tenders were invited for a new contract. The tender of Interior and Structural Cleaners Ltd., was accepted on the authority of the Vice Chairman of the County Council as various other offices in the Shire Hall, under the jurisdiction of the Estates Committee were included and the proportion chargeable to the Standing Joint Committee was £131 per month.

On the 22nd September, 1964, the Police Authority agreed to the Chief Constable accepting the post of Deputy Regional Police Commander No. 7 (South Western) Region comprising, Gloucestershire, Wiltshire, Somerset, Devon and Cornwall, as requested by the Secretary of State.

The Committee also considered a request from the District Organisation Officer, N.A.L.G.O., that consideration be given to the scope of the Local Joint Staff Committee which dealt with employees of the County Council being extended to cover civilian staff employed by the Police Authority.

This was not possible at that time because the civilian employees of the Police Authority were not under the control of the County Council. However, the Standing Joint Committee said the matter could be reviewed again after the 1st June, 1965, when the Police Committee of the County Council had been constituted.

The Selection Committee of the County Council met on the 19th October, 1964, and one of the items on the agenda was the Police Act, 1964, dealing with the information of the Police Committee to replace the Standing Joint Committee which had been operating for so many years.

The Police Committee was to consist of two-thirds County Councillors and one-third magistrates. With regard to representatives from Gloucester Corporation, the Home Office indicated that they were likely to provide for four of their members to be members of the Police Committee in addition to the two City Magistrates.

The Selection Committee considered that the new Police Committee need not be as large as the existing Standing Joint Committee, which consisted of 50 member, (22 members of the County Council, 22 magistrates and 6 representatives of Gloucester Corporation), and they recommended:–[3]

That the Police Committee comprise 36 members to be appointed as follows:–

20 members of the County Council
10 County magistrates
4 members of Gloucester Corporation
2 City magistrates

The Police Act, 1964, contained far too many Sections to be dealt with here other than one or two which actually affected the Force. For instance, Section 8 of Part 1 of the Act reads:–

> In addition to the Chief Constable, the Force shall have a Deputy Chief Constable and the Establishment may include one or more Assistant Chief Constables. These appointments being subject to Regulations made by the Secretary of State and subject to his approval. The Deputy Chief Constable shall have all the powers and duties of the Chief Constable –
> (a) during any absence, incapacity or suspension from duties of the Chief Constable, and
> (b) during any vacancy in the office of Chief Constable.

Section 14 stated that –

> Every Chief Constable shall, as soon as possible after the end of each calender year, submit to the Police Authority a general report in writing on the Policing of the area during the year.

On the 22nd September, 1964, the Committee considered Home Office Circular 131/1964, which provided in two instalments (due on the 1st September, 1964, and the 1st January, 1966) for increased pay for Chief Constables and Assistant Chief Constables.

It was resolved that the salary scales of the Chief Constable and Assistant Chief Constable, from 1st September, 1964, be as follows:–

Chief Constable	£4,040 × 4(£145) – £4,620
Assistant Chief Constable	£2,690 × 2(£80) 2(£90) – £3,030

On the 30th May, 1964, Ex. Superintendent Charles F. Large, died at Bishops Cleeve, Near Cheltenham. His age was 71 years and he had been in receipt of a pension since 1st August, 1956. He left a widow, Mrs Edith Annie Large who received a basic Police Widow's Pension.

The Chief Constable reported to the Police Authority on the 22nd September, 1964, that it was hoped to reach the authorised establishment for the Force by the end of the financial year, 1965. i.e. 31st March.

Due to the reduction of the working week for all ranks below that of Superintendent, from 44 hours to 42 hours, an increase in the establishment was imperative.

In addition, to give full motor patrol coverage to trunk roads, classified through roads and new motorways when completed, a substantial increase was required in the motor patrol strength of the Force.

The Chief Constable, Mr White, suggested an overall increase of 138 men and 12 women making a total of 150, and should approval be given to this, recruitment would be commenced on 1st April, 1965. The Gloucester City Contingent would be increased by 15.

The following is a summary of the Revised Establishment:–

RANK	OLD ESTABLISHMENT	PROPOSED ESTABLISHMENT
Chief Constable	1	1
Assistant Chief Constables	1	2
Chief Superintendents	4	6
Superintendents Grade 1	5	3
Superintendents Grade 2	–	3
Chief Inspectors	22	19
Inspectors	35	41
Sergeants	160	177
Constables	654	768
Women Inspectors	1	1
Women Sergeants	4	4
Women Constables	21	33
	908	1,058

On the 28th, 29th, 30th September and 1st October, 1964, H.M. Inspector of Constabulary, B.N. Bebbington, Esq., O.B.E., carried out an Inspection of the Force, visiting Police Headquarters and Police Stations throughout the County.

The Chief Constable reported to the Standing Joint Committee on the 15th December, 1964 that a letter had been received from the Home Office, referring to the Inspection, stating that the Force was efficient. H.M. Inspector had however drawn attention to the following matters –

(a) That the nine County vehicles available for the C.I.D. and the four vans allocated for the use of Scenes of Crimes Officers were not equipped with wireless and that it was considered that the efficiency of the C.I.D. would be increased if wireless were provided for these vehicles.

(b) That although four car washers were now employed, these numbers were not sufficient and some cleaning was still done by car crews and motor cyclists. It was considered that additional car cleaners should be employed and, further more, that cleaners who were qualified drivers should be authorised to drive Police vehicles so that they could take them to the workshops for servicing and drive them in cases where it was not necessary for a Police Officer to do so.

(c) That the few dictating machines made available to the Force several years ago were used only in the uniform branch and that there was a need for more machines generally and in particular for use by the C.I.D.

The Chief Constable informed the Committee that provision had now been made in the revenue estimates for 1965/66 to implement all these suggestions.

The Chief Constable was informed by the Secretary of State that the Chief Constables' Committee of the No. 7 District Police Training Centre, Chantmarles, had recommended the appointment of Sergeant A.R. Kings, of the Gloucestershire Constabulary, to the Staff of the Centre as Instructor Grade 2 and, subject to the approval of the Committee, the Secretary of State was prepared to approve the appointment, with effect from 1st October, 1964.

Under the Voluntary Service Overseas, young persons volunteered to work in one of the under-developed countries for one year, the Scheme being supported by grants from Industry and bursaries.

The Standing Joint Committee had given authority to send up to two Cadets each year on this Scheme and on the 15th December, 1964 the Chief Constable reported, for the information of the Committee, that Police Cadet Richard V. Chandler left England on the 29th September, 1964 for service as an Auxiliary Instructor at an Outward Bound School in Nigeria, and Police Cadet Michael W. Pennington left on the 14th October, 1964 for service as a Physical Training Instructor at the National Institute of Physical Education, La Paz, Bolivia.

On the 24th November, 1964, Mrs Muriel Stanley-Clarke, widow of the late Chief Constable, Major Frederick L. Stanley-Clarke, O.B.E., died in Cheltenham aged 84 years. She had been in receipt of a Police Widow's pension since 1st May, 1946.

Six Traffic Wardens were approved for duty in the City of Gloucester on the 14th March, 1961 and then deferred owing to the coming into force of the Prohibition of Through Goods Vehicles Order, which had resulted, at that time, in reducing traffic congestion in the City Centre.

However, the number of vehicles using the roads had greatly increased since 1961, and it had become increasingly difficult for Regular Officers to deal with the many traffic problems arising.

In order to relieve men on the beat for more important duties, and after consultation with the Gloucester City Council, the Chief Constable recommended that eight Traffic Wardens be appointed for the City of Gloucester and that they commence their duties on the 1st

April, 1965. There was no fixed salary for Traffic Wardens but a commencement figure of £660 per annum rising to a maximum of £730 per annum after 2 years would be appropriate. They would work a 38 hour week, excluding the daily meal break. Uniform would have to be provided.[4]

Home Office Circular No. 260/1964, informed Police Authorities that the Secretary of State would be making new Regulations giving effect to an agreement providing for new scales of pay for the Federated ranks, with effect from 1st September, 1964.

The agreement also provided the following modification of the Constable's scale:–

(a) the grant of an increment after one year's service, and
(b) with effect from 1st December, 1964 enhancement of the starting rate and first two incremental points for Constable appointed at age 22 and above.

The new normal scales of pay were as given below:–

Chief Inspector	
Men	£1,540 to £1,645 p.a. after 2 years service in the rank
Women	£1,385 to £1,480 p.a. after 2 years service in the rank
Inspector	
Men	£1,375 to £1,470 p.a. after 2 years service in the rank
Women	£1,240 to £1,325 p.a. after 2 years service in the rank
Sergeant	
Men	£1,170 tp £1,255 p.a. after 2 years service in the rank
Women	£1,055 to £1,130 p.a. after 2 years service in the rank
Constables	
Men	£ 700 to £1,040 p.a. after 9 years service
Women	£ 630 to £ 935 p.a. after 9 years service

In addition, there was a supplementary payment of £30 per annum to Police Constables at 17 years service and a second supplementary payment of £35 per annum on the completion of 22 years service. Women Police Constables would get similar supplementary payments of £30 per annum at the completion of 17 years and 22 years respectively.

A special scale was introduced for Constables appointed at age 22 and above and was as follows:–

	Men	*Women*
On appointment	£800	£720
After 1 year	£800	£720
After 2 years	£830	£745
After 3 years	£830	£745
After 4 years	£865	£780
After 5 years	£900	£810

After the completion of 6 years service, these Constables would revert to the normal scale of pay.

Detective Duty Allowance was also increased as from 1st September, 1964. The new rates were:–

	Men	*Women*
Chief Inspector	£152	£136
Inspector	£135	£122
Sergeant	£115	£104
Constable	£ 86	£ 77

With effect from 1st September, 1964, the following new scales of pay came into operation for Superintendents and Chief Superintendents:–

Chief Superintendents	£2,185 – £2,250 – £2,325
Superintendents Grade 1	£2,020 – £2,085 – £2,160
Superintendents Grade 2	£1,820 – £1,885 – £1,960

Seventy officers assisted the Oxfordshire Constabulary on the occasion of the Funeral of the Right Honourable Sir Winston Churchill, at Bladon.

At the Standing Joint Committee meeting held on the 16th March, 1965 the Chief Constable submitted his report on the organisation and work of the Force and upon the crime committed within the County of Gloucester during the year 1964, as required by Section 12 of the Police Act, 1964.

At this same meeting Lt. Col. J. Godman, C.B.E., referred to the fact that on the 1st June, 1965 the Standing Joint Committee would be replaced by the Police Committee of the County Council and he expressed his thanks to the members of the Standing Joint Committee for their support and assistance during his 18 years at Chairman of the Committee.

The allowance to members of the Force attending Courses away from home and living in lodgings was reviewed by the Home Office during 1965 and it was agreed that the weekly allowance paid to

Officers attending Courses away from home and living in lodgings should be increased to:–

Superintendents	£7.15.0d.
Chief Inspectors or Inspectors	£7.5.0d.
Sergeants and Constables	£6.10.0d.

In the past appeals under the National Joint Council's Scheme of Conditions of Service by the civilian staff, employed by the Police Authority, were referred to a Special Committee of the Standing Joint Committee – The Appeals Committee – but with the formation of the new Police Committee, which replaced the Standing Joint Committee, it was felt appropriate for such appeals, in future, to be referred to the Appeals Committee of the County Council and arrangements were made accordingly.

Under Section 109 of the Magistrates Courts Act, 1952, the Police Committee authorised application to the Secretary of State for the certification of the Cells at the new Police Stations at Cirencester, Coleford and Gloucester.

Although it was understood that the power to order detention under Section 109 was not used frequently the Secretary of State considered it desirable that the facilities should be at the disposal of the Magistrates, when suitable accommodation was available.

His Grace the Duke of Beaufort, K.G., G.C.V.O., Lord Lieutenant of the County of Gloucester and Chairman of the Gloucestershire Magistrates' Courts Committee performed the opening ceremony of the New Police Station and Magistrates' Court at Cirencester on Tuesday 28th September, 1965.

During 1965, Superintendent A.R.J. Carter and Constable R.H. Cox returned to the Force after completing their period of secondment as Staff Officer and Orderly/Driver respectively to H.M. Inspector of Constabulary. On the 14th June, 1965, Constable F.J. Gibbs replaced Constable Cox as Orderly/driver.

Detective Sergeant R.G. Watkins was, on the 1st July, 1965, seconded to the South Western Forensic Science Laboratory at Bristol, as Police Liaison Officer.

At a meeting of the Police Council for England and Wales held on the 16th March, 1965, it was agreed that all vacancies in the posts of Chief Constable, Assistant Chief Constable and Deputy Chief Constable in County and Borough Forces and one in three of vacancies in other ranks down to that of Chief Inspector, should be advertised.

In accordance with the above recommendations, which were contained in Home Office Circular No. 78/1966 of 1st April, 1965, three vacancies in the Force, one for the second Assistant Chief Constable and two for the rank of Chief Inspector were subsequently advertised. Fifty-three applications were received for the post of second Assistant Chief Constable and on the 24th November, 1965, a Sub-Committee of the Police Authority selected Superintendent Edward Coppin, of the Essex Constabulary. He commenced his duties in this Force on the 3rd January, 1966.

With regard to the vacancies for Chief Inspector, many applications were received and Inspector P.W. Jenkins, Birmingham City Police was appointed Chief Inspector at Gloucester, commencing duty on the 1st November, 1965, and Inspector G. Buffham, Grimsby Borough Police was also appointed Chief Inspector at Cheltenham, commencing his duties on the 8th November, 1965.

Up to the beginning of 1965 no definite policy had ever been established regarding the grading and promotion within the civilian establishment of the Police Authority. The Chief Constable thought that a structure should be created and thus provide staff with the opportunity to advance through qualification and experience from the lowest to the highest ranks.

In consultation with his Heads of Departments, Divisional Superintendents and the County Council Establishments Officer a review of the civilian structure was carried out and the proposed upgradings and additions were approved by the Police Authority on the 16th March, 1965.[5]

The authorised civilian establishment was then as follows:–

Clerical

Clerical Grade 3	1
Clerical Grade 2	6
Clerical Grade 1	14
Senior Scale 'B'	13
Senior Scale 'A'	2
General Division	25
Qualified Shorthand Typists	39
Telephone Operators	11
Total	111
Technical	13
Miscellaneous Grades	3

Car Washers	5
Handymen	7
Hostel Wardens	4
Canteen Supervisors	2
Canteen Staff	22
Part-time Cleaners	81
Total	248

All were employed in accordance with the Scheme of Conditions of Service approved by the National Joint Council for Local Authorities A.P.T., Clerical and Manual Workers.

Details of the composition of the Special Constabulary, as at 31st December, 1965 were as follows:–

RANK	AUTHORISED ESTABLISHMENT	ACTUAL STRENGTH
Superintendents	6	6
Chief Inspectors	1	1
Inspectors	21	21
Sergeants	66	65
Constables	1,029	695
Total	1,123	788*

* Includes 17 women

The Dog Section in 1965 consisted of eight dogs with one Sergeant and seven Constables stationed at –

Cheltenham	2
Gloucester	2
Stroud	2
Staple Hill	2

Her Majesty the Queen was graciously please to award the Queen's Police Medal for Distinguished Service to the Deputy Chief Constable, H.D.J. Smith, Esq., in Her New Years Honours for 1965.

On the 31st December, 1965 there were 748 married officers serving in the Force.

685 were living in County owned houses
8 were living in County rented houses
33 were living in owner-occupied houses
5 were living in rented houses
17 were living in rented rooms

It was during 1965 that the Chief Constable issued an Order that allowed a person with 20 years service or who was 40 years of age, whichever was the sooner, to be able to apply to purchase his own house in four specified areas, i.e. Cheltenham, Gloucester, Staple Hill and Stroud. By the end of 1966 the permitted maximum total of 50 owner-occupiers had been reached.[6]

On the 31st December, 1965, there were 1,003 registered Aliens resident in the County, a decrease of 80 on the figues for 1964.

H.M. Inspector of Constabulary, N. Galbraith, Esq., carried out the Annual Inspection of the Force on the 28th, 29th and 30th September, 1965 when Headquarters and Stations in the Cirencester and Stroud Divisions were visited.

Sergeant A.R. Kings ended his secondment at No. 7 District Police Training Centre at Chantmarle, having transferred to a County Force upon promotion to Inspector during 1966.

Constable F.J. Gibbs and Clerical Assistant Miss M.E. Lightbody returned to the Force after their secondment as Orderly/Driver and Secretary respectively to H.M. Inspector of Constabulary, consequent upon the H.M. Inspector's Office at Cheltenham closing down on 30th September, 1966. The Secretary of State expressed his warm appreciation of the co-operation of the Police Committee and the Chief Constable, in making the services of these officers available to H.M. Inspector.

Detective Chief Inspector K.F. Clark was, on the 20th June, 1966 appointed Deputy Co-ordinator of the No. 7 District Regional Crime Squad in the temporary rank of Detective Chief Superintendent.

During the year 1966 a Force Under-Water Recovery Section was formed consisting of a Sergeant and three constables.

On the 20th April, 1966 the Police Committee approved the appointment of four more Traffic Wardens for the City of Gloucester. The eight Wardens who had been employed since June, 1965 had proved of great benefit but it had been found that with one or two exceptions the beats they covered were too large to be operated efficiently.

In connection with the Diseases of Animals Act work, Home Office indicated to Police Authorites that H.M. Inspectors of Constabulary were concerned about the amount of Police time being spent on this work and in view of the shortage of Police manpower Local Authorities should appoint civilian Inspectors to relieve the Police of as many extraneous duties as possible.

On the 20th April, 1966 the Chief Constable reported that the duties under the Diseases of Animals Act fell into four categories:–

(a) Marketing Inspectors who were also responsible for issuing Movement Licences.
(b) Regular visits to all farms to examine records.
(c) Visits to stockholders to whom Movement Licences had been issued, and
(d) Posting of notices and general security in times of an outbreak of certain Diseases and the disposal of carcases, etc.

The Committee were of the opinion that the only duties in which Police need not be involved related to the Markets and they considered that Civilian Inspectors could be appointed for this purpose and they referred the matter to the Smallholdings and Agricultural Committee.

During 1966, the Secretary of State gave his approval to an increase in the Authorised Establishment by eleven, plus certain upgradings of ranks. These additions and upgradings would take effect from the 1st April, 1967 then, the new Authorised Establishment of the Force would be:–

1	Chief Constable
1	Deputy Chief Constable
1	Assistant Chief Constable
5	Chief Superintendents
5	Superintendents Grade 1
27	Chief Inspectors
39	Inspectors
179	Sergeants
764	Constables
1	Woman Chief Inspector
4	Women Police Sergeants
33	Women Police Constables
1,060	Total

The new Motor Way Police Station at Almondsbury became operational during August, 1966. It was the first type of its kind to be built in this country and was used solely in connection with the policing of the new River Severn Road Bridge and the Motor Ways within the County. The Control Room was not completely equipped and fully working until 1967. Fifteen houses were built on an adjacent site for occupation by Police Officers operating at, and from the new Motor Way Police Station.

A new Sub-Divisional Headquarters Station at Tewkesbury, which replaced sub-standard property, was officially opened by the Mayor of Tewkesbury on the 2nd September, 1966.

The new Amenities block at Staple Hill Police Station, comprising single men's quarters, canteen and club facilities was officially opened by Colonel F. Seymour-Williams, D.S.O., O.B.E., D.L., on the 13th December, 1966, and replaced inadequate and sub-standard accommodation.

The official opening of the River Severn Road Bridge by Her Majesty the Queen accompanied by His Royal Highness, The Duke of Edinburgh, on the 8th September, 1966, found some 450 members of the Force, including Cadets and Special Constables engaged in this event. Later the same day, Her Majesty and Prince Philip paid an offiicial visit to the Concorde Installation at the Bristol Aircraft Corporation Works, Filton.

During the year 1966, eighty-four persons were arrested and six summoned for driving a motor vehicle whilst under the influence of drink, an increase of 14 persons compared with 1965.

Twenty-nine persons were arrested and one summoned for being in charge of a motor vehicle whilst under the influence of drink. This was an increase of two on the figure for 1965.

The results of the prosecutions in the 120 cases were as follows:–

1 Imprisonment
101 Fined
13 Committed for Trial
5 Acquitted

Of the thirteen persons committed for trial, eight were fined, three were acquitted and two were pending.

1966 saw an increase in drunkenness – 245 males and 2 females were proceeded against – this was an increase of 22 persons compared with 1965.

The Cadets continued to attend Outward Bound Courses during 1966. Attachments were also made to the Steel Company of Wales, Port Talbot and the Cheshire Homes, Cheltenham. Other Cadets joined Community Service Volunteer Organisations for periods of three months. In September, 1966, a Cadet was selected to be attached to Voluntary Services Overseas, and was sent to Tunisia where he helped as a Physical Training Instructor in a small village of under privileged children.

On 31st December, 1966, 4,975 Firearm Certificates relating to 6,231 weapons, were in force in the County and during the year, a total of 362 new Certificates were issued and 1,320 Certificates renewed. Forty-one Firearms Dealers Certificates were also renewed and 5 new ones issued.

Of the 362 new Certificates issued, 42 related to pistols, 22 to revolvers, and 8 to pistols and revolvers, and 38 of these applicants required ammunition. Many Certificates granted contained Conditions restricting the holders in respect of the carriage and use of the weapons.

In connection with the applications for Firearm Certificates and variations of existing Certificates, only two persons were served with refusal notices and only one Certificate was revoked during the year.

During the year, 234 weapons of all descriptions were surrendered to the Police as well as some 9,600 rounds of assorted ammuntion.

During 1966, there were 87 offences committed under the Firemans Act, and proceedings were taken in 63 cases. Juveniles were concerned in five of these cases.

The Annual Inspection of the Force by H.M. Inspector of Constabulary, N. Galbraith, Esq., was held on the 19th, 20th and 21st September, 1966, when Headquarters, and Stations in the Cheltenham, Staple Hill and Lydney Divisions were visited.

Miss J.S. Law, Assistant Inspector of Constabulary, visited the Force on the 28th July, 1966 and Inspected the Police Women.

On the 20th February, 1967 the Police Committee considered Home Office Circular No. 208/1966 in which the Secretary of State asked Authorities responsible for arrangements at Assizes and Quarter Sessions in consultation with Police Authorities and Chief Officers of Police to examine urgently the possibility of replacing by civilians Police Officers employed at these Courts in work which could be done by civilians. After a long discussion the Committee Recommended:–

(a) That a panel of male and female ushers be appointed, sufficient in number to enable a maximum of 12 male and 3 female ushers to be on duty at any one time.
(b) That a senior usher be appointed.
(c) That the Finance Committee be asked to consider making provision for the additional expenditure involved in 1967/68, amounting to £4,500.

An application from the Joint Branch Board of the Police Federation of the Force, asking for the weekly rate of Rent Allowance to be increased, was placed before the Police Committee on 20th February, 1967, and it was agreed that the new weekly rates should be:–

Inspectors	£4.5.6d.
Sergeants	£4.2.0d.
Constables	£4.0.0d.

The Chief Constable received many requests from Local Authorities for the appointment of Traffic Wardens. After consultation with the appropriate Local Authorities and the Clerks to the Justices concerned, the Chief Constable suggested that Traffic Wardens be appointed in the following areas:–

Cirencester	2	Dursley	2	
Filton	6	Cheltenham	8	
Stroud	3	Bristol Road		
		Barton Street	}	Approved by Gloucester City Council

The Committee also approved an alteration in the scale to provide a salary of £681 on appointment, rising to £718 after one year's service to a maximum of £755 after two years service. The Committee approved these suggestions and the necessary provision was made in the estimates for 1967/68.

In May, 1967 the height standard required by Gloucestershire was reduced from 5ft. 9½ins. to 5ft. 8ins., and the eyesight standard reduced to conform with the Home Office recommendations which had been adopted by most Chief Officers.

As a result of these reduced standards, two applicants who were required to wear spectacles and eleven men whose height was between 5ft. 8ins. and 5ft. 9½ins. were recruited.

Inspector D.J. Johnson, on transfer from the Bedfordshire and Luton Constabulary, was appointed to one of the vacancies for Chief Inspector. In addition a vacancy for a Woman Police Inspector was advertised resulting in the appointment of Woman Police Sergeant Mary L. Pincombe, Reading Borough Police, to that rank on the 14th June, 1967.

Chief Superintendent F.W. Hudson continued serving as Director of the Home Office Crime Prevention Course at Stafford and was promoted to his rank of Chief Superintendent on 1st December, 1967. It was during 1967 that Chief Superintendent Hudson was awarded a Winston Churchill Travelling Fellowship to study Police Crime Prevention in Western Europe, for three months.

It was during 1967 that the Chief Constable decided that Girl Cadets should be enrolled as part of the Regular Cadet Force. Initially there was to be a maximum of 4 girls. At the same time, the lower age limit for Regular Cadets was reduced from 17 to 16 years.

Early in 1967, Chief Superintendent H. Thomas, who was then a member of the Superintendents' Association of England and Wales Executive Committee, was nominated by the Home Secretary, to represent the Superintendents' Association on the Board of Governors of the Police College at Bramshill. At the same time he was elected to represent the Superintendents' Association on the Police College Advisory Committee. Chief Superintendent Thomas held these posts until his retirement in January, 1970.

An Inspection of the Combined Regular and Volunteer Cadets was held at the Royal Air Force Station, South Cerney, on the 10th June, 1967, when the Inspecting Officer was Colonel N.A.C. Croft, D.S.O., M.A., the Commandant of the Metropolitan Police Cadet School. The parade was watched by a large number of parents and friends.

After the appointment of civilian Ushers at Courts of Assize and Quarter Sessions representations were made to the Magistrates' Courts Committee for the appointment of civilian Court Ushers at certain of the Magistrates' Courts in the County. This was considered by the Committee on the 13th November, 1967, when they agreed that provision should be made in the Budget for the 1968/69 financial year, for the appointment of one extra Civilian Usher at the Lawford's Gate Court and two each at the Cheltenham and Gloucester Courts. The Committee also made provision for a similar appointment for the Domestic Court at Chipping Sodbury, at the request of the Justices' Clerk.

Thirteen Long Service Medals and Bars were presented to Special Constables during 1967 and Special Superintendent E. Scott Cooper, B.E.M., Cheltenham, resigned on 31st December, 1967, after serving for 41 years in the Special Constabulary.

On the 1st April, 1967 one Sergeant in each territorial Division was appointed as a full-time Divisional Training Sergeant.

The Training Sergeants' duties included Probationer Training, Chairing Directed Study Discussion Groups, recruiting enquiries, supervising entrance exams and Special Constabulary Training.

By now, the various Refresher Courses at Police Headquarters had become a regular feature of the Force. They were essential in as much that they maintained an efficient standard of work within the Force.

The number of Officers attending the Refresher Courses at Headquarters Training Branch, during 1967, were:–

Constables(men)	95
Sergeants(men)	29
Inspectors' Refresher Course	8

During the year 1967, the Gloucestershire Constabulary undertook to organise a Refresher Course for Policewomen of the No. 7 Police District.

Two full residential Courses each of two weeks' duration, were held in April and November, 1967, at the Home Office Civil Defence Training School at Falfield. The total number of students on each Course was 24 and 27 respectively, and six Women Police Constables from Gloucestershire attended each Course.

The Dog Section was beginning to grow in stature and during 1967, handlers and dogs answered 763 calls for assistance in connection with crime and other matters and were responsible for the arrest of 76 prisoners.

Detective Sergeant Brian J. Marshall, Gloucester, was awarded the Queen's Commendation for bravery and the Award was presented to him by His Grace the Duke of Beaufort, acting on behalf of Her Majesty, at Gloucester Central Police Station on the 28th November, 1967.

Her Majesty also awarded Special Superintendent G.C.G. Clifton, of 'C' Division Special Constabulary, the British Empire Medal which was again presented by His Grace the Duke of Beaufort, at Gloucester on the 4th September, 1967.

Sergeant A.A. Moir, of the Staple Hill Division, was made a Serving Brother of the Order of St. John, as from 26th July, 1967.

During the year, a total of 245 letters of appreciation were received from members of the public for services rendered by members of the Force. In addition there were 14 commendations from the Courts.

The new Police Station at Whitminster became operational on the 20th May, 1967. A new Station was opened at St. Marks, Cheltenham, on the 16th November, 1967. This building replaced the sub-standard Gloucester Road Police Station, Cheltenham.

Demolition of Holland House, the old Police Headquarters, was completed during 1967. New Sub-sectional Police Stations were opened at Wickwar, Yorkley and Parkend on the 20th March, 16th August, 1967 and 3rd January, 1968, respectively.

The public having been urged to make use of the '999' Emergency Telephone System, did so in 1967 to the extent of 10,692 such calls being made. Many of these calls either prevented a crime or resulted in the detection of an offender.

Six bright orange waterproof suits were obtained during 1967 for use by Officers engaged on accidents on the Severn Bridge. This type of clothing was found to be essential to protect them when dealing with accidents on the Bridge in conditions of rain and wind. As a further safety measure, white crash helmets were also provided and worn in conjunction with the orange protective clothing. Towards the end of 1967 an Anemometer was set up on the Severn Bridge and connected with the Almondsbury Motorway Police Station, giving Officers on duty there immediate information regarding wind speeds on the Bridge.

There were eight outbreaks of Foot and Mouth Disease in the County during 1967. The first outbreak was at Hayles Farm, Winchcombe, during November. Fortunately, the Disease was contained in the

Northern part of the County and thanks to strict restrictions on the movement of stock the outbreak was soon eliminated.

At the beginning of the year – 1967 – the three Working Party Reports on Police Manpower, Efficiency and Equipment, were received from the Home Office, and immediately a small Committee of all ranks in the Force was set up under the Chairmanship of a Divisional Chief Superintendent to examine the three Reports to see how and if they should be applied to the Force. This Committee met weekly and examined the Reports paragraph by paragraph, applied them to the Force, and also called upon the specialists involved to explain the position when applicable.

The Committee then submitted their recommendations to the Chief Constable who in turn submitted a full report and recommendations to a Sub-Committee of the Police Committee which they considered at their meeting on 15th September, 1967, and which finally came before the full Police Committee on the 13th November, 1967.

A number of the recommendations made in the Working Party Reports were purely domestic which the Chief Constable had already dealt with or was dealing with, and some of the recommendations were already in being in the Force. However, there were two main items which emerged, materially affecting the organisation and running of the Force in the future:–

(a) The introduction of the new system of policing made possible by the use of small cars in conjunction with personal radio sets, known as Unit Beat Policing; and

(b) More widespread employment of civilians in support of the Police.

With regard to (a), the introduction of Unit Beat Policing had been agreed for Cheltenham in the 1967/68 financial year, and it was anticipated for Staple Hill and Gloucester in the 1968/69 financial year. Its introduction at Cirencester and Stroud would follow as soon as finance was available.

As regards (b) the Force was already highly civilianised, far more so than the majority of Forces, but recommendations were made and accepted for further civilianisation of certain posts held by Police Officers. It was hoped that these proposals would have been implemented in the 1968/69 financial year, but for financial reasons the majority of them had to be postponed for twelve months.

The Annual Inspection of the Force was held on the 2nd, 3rd and 4th May, 1967, when Headquarters and Stations in the Cirencester and Gloucester Divisions were inspected by H.M. Inspector of Constabulary, N. Galbraith, Esq.

Miss J.S. Law, H.M. Assistant Inspector of Constabulary, visited the Force on 8th September, 1967, and inspected the Policewomen.

In Home Office Circular No. 119/1967, of 18th July, 1967, the Under Secretary of State notified the Police Authorities that, with the agreement of the Local Authority Associations, arrangements had been made for the inital supply of breath testing devices for use by the Police for the purpose of Part 1 of the Road Safety Act, 1967, to be purchased centrally and distributed to police forces from local Home Office Supply and Transport Stores on a repayment basis. One breath testing device, known as 'Alcotest' had so far been approved by the Secretary of State for the purposes of the Act, and a contract agreed with the Local Authority Associations had been placed for the supply of these devices which were in sets comprising ten devices per set. The cost would be £1.19.6d. per set.

In order that suitable arrangements could be made for the distribution of devices to individual police forces on the basis of possible operational need, a Working Party consisting of representatives of the Local Authority Associations, and of the Association of Chief Police Officers, was set up to consider how the limited number of devices available initially might be allocated. This Working Party had recommended a first allocation of devices to each police force in proportion to the authorised establishment, the number allocated to Gloucestershire on this basis was 500 sets of ten devices which would cost £1,000.

In Home Office Circular No. 51/1967 it was pointed out that Police Authorities should make adequate arrangements for the proper implementation of the provisions of the Road Safety Act, 1967, relating to drinking and driving.

In all Police Areas a 24 hour service of Doctors should be available who were willing to take blood specimens on request at the Police Stations where they dealt with such cases. The Circular suggested that in order that Doctors with the necessary experience and knowledge of the new legislation were readily available, it would be necessary to appoint designated surgeons and the Committee accepted a recommendation by the Chief Constable that nine Police Surgeons be appointed to cover the County.

Retaining fees would be paid, bearing in mind the likely case-load and area of responsibility and the Committee approved the payment of an annual fee to each Doctor totalling £750.

The British Medical Association had suggested a level for retaining fees, which was considerably higher than those previously either in operation or approved by the Association and the County Councils Association advised Police Authorities not to enter into binding agreements based on the terms now suggested by the B.M.A. as they considered that these terms should be negotiated nationally.

The Chief Constable reported to the Police Committee that the Doctors appointed in the County were willing to act as Police Surgeons at retaining fees which had been agreed although they were considerably lower than the figure suggested by the B.M.A. These fees would therefore be regarded as temporary pending the outcome of the Police Committee of the County Councils Association's consideration of the B.M.A.'s letter.

The existing scale of fees had been in operation since 1st October, 1965, and these were revised, by the B.M.A., with effect from 1st October, 1967. As a result the Police Committee recommended:–

> That the Finance Committee be asked to consider making provision for the additional expenditure in 1967/68 namely for £750 in respect of retaining fees to Police Surgeons and for £600 in respect of the revised scale of fees payable to Medical Practitioners and Police Surgeons.

The Police Committee was informed by Home Office Circular 178/1967, that the allowances had been increased for loss of earnings to be paid to Special Constables as from the date shown:–

	With effect from 1st March, 1967
Men	£2.15.10d. a day) Full revised
Women	£2.10.5d. a day) maximum pay

In accordance with the prices and incomes policy, payment at these rates in full and of any arrears should be deferred until the first pay day after 18th November, 1967. Payment at the following interim maximum rates, with maximum rates, with arrears, could however be made from 1st July if in the local circumstances this was thought desirable:–

Men	£2.13.4d. a day
Women	£2. 8.2d. a day

The Secretary of State also reviewed the allowance payable to Special Constables in respect of hours of duty not exceeding five hours and approved an increase in that allowance from 2/9d. to 3/8d.

The Committee adopted these revised allowances.

On the 13th November, 1967, the Police Committee considered a Report by the County Architect following an investigation of the heating and hot-water sysems in all houses occupied by Police Officers with a view to bringing them up to present-day standards. There were 96 properties throughout the County needing these improvements and the approximate cost would be £325 per house.

The Committee considered that some improvement was necessary but that the selection of properties to be improved and the type of equipment to be installed should be examined in detail.

The Committee decided that the work should be carried out over the next six or seven years and that the sum of £5,000 should be included in the Capital Budget for each year until the completion of the work.

The provisions relating to Police Cadets (a) Rates of pay, and (b) Deductions for board and lodgings, became operative from 1st July, 1967.

With regard to (a), the yearly rates of pay for Cadets were as follows:–

Age	£
16 years	375
17 years	410
18 years	450
19 years	485

With regard to (b), it was agreed that the cost of each Cadet's board and lodgings should be defrayed by the Police Authority, including any additional cost incurred while the Cadet was engaged in any form of training by reason of which he was unable to use his normal place of lodging.

Police Cadets in Gloucestershire were accommodated:–

(a) at home; or
(b) in Police Hostels; or
(c) in lodgings

and for the purpose of the new provision concerning deductions for board and lodgings, the Committee approved the payment of:–

For those at (a) £90 per annum (a greater amount if circumstances warranted it)

For those at (b) The weekly rate charged (at present 45/–d. per week)

For those at (c) A minimum of £3.0.0d. per week.

For a large part of the year 1968, the Chief Constable, Mr E.P.B. White, was on secondment to the Home Office as Acting Commandant at the Police College, Bramshill during the illness of Mr J.S.H. Gaskain.

During his absence the Force again, came under the command of Mr. H.D.J. Smith, Deputy Chief Constable. This meant that both Mr Smith and the Assistant Chief Constable, Mr E. Coppin, had to bear a considerable extra burden and Mr White informed the Police Committee that he was greatly indebted to both of them for the efficient manner in which they had carried out their duties, especially at a time when the problems in connection with the complete re-organisation of the physical Divisions of the Force had to be solved.

It was during 1968 that the Home Office told Police Authorities to curtail recruiting. It was this policy which considerably reduced the numbers of Police in Gloucestershire, a County which was growing faster than any other area in Great Britain.

This became more apparent when one gave consideration to the mass of new legislation affecting the Police, introduced during the year.

It had been said that there were 77 new laws and 1,500 changes in the law during 1968 directly affecting the Police, and a number of these laws were seemingly introduced without giving thought to the result which they would produce.

During 1968, arrangements for creating larger territorial Divisions in the Force were completed as recommended in Home Office Circular No. 25/1967, and an adjustment of supervisory ranks made at the same time as recommended in Home Office Circular No. 51/1968. Therefore, on 1st August, 1968, the number of territorial Divisions was reduced from six to four, and with the approval of the Secretary of State, the Authorised Establishment was increased by one Chief Superintendent, three Superintendents (Class I), and one Superintendent (Class II), and decreased by two Chief Inspectors and three Inspectors.

The result of the foregoing variations was that at the end of the year the Authorised Establishment of the Force was 1,060.

The actual strength on the 31st December, 1968, was:–

Headquarters	49
Northern Division	256
Southern Division	222
Eastern Division	200
Western Division	292
Total	1,019*

*This total did not include 17 officers of all ranks seconded for special duties.

One vacancy for the rank of Chief Inspector was advertised during the year 1968. A number of applications were received and a number of candidates interviewed, which resulted in the appointment of Inspector R. Dale, on transfer from the Preston Borough Force.

On the 20th November, 1968, Her Majesty the Queen was graciously pleased to appoint Inspector Sydney T. James a Serving Brother of the Order of St. John of Jerusalem.

Ex. Chief Superintendent Percy Oakley died suddenly on the 2nd February, 1968. He had been on pension since 1961, but was only 66 years of age. He left a widow who was awarded a Police Widow's Pension.

Ex. Superintendent Stanley D. Smith, died at Stroud on the 18th March, 1968, aged 67 years. His widow was awarded a Police Widow's Pension.

On the 5th August, 1968, Superintendent H.C.S. Lodge was promoted to Chief Superintendent and seconded to the Police College, Bramshill, to serve as a member of the Directing Staff.

Sergeant M.H. Sear and Sergeant A.A.D. Philpott were, on 1st July, 1968, and 7th October, 1968, respectively, seconded to the Staff of the Regional Police Training Centre, Chantmarle, as Instructors (Grade II).

Inspector G.W. Jones took up a place at Exeter University, on the 7th October, 1968, to read for an Honours Degree in Law, which would last for three years.

Special Superintendent G.C.G. Clifton, B.E.M., Cirencester, resigned on the 10th October, 1968, after serving for 30 years in the Special Constabulary.

The Under-Water Recovery Section, under the leadership of Sergeant Clive Jefferies, Stroud, was called out for operational purposes on eighteen occasions during the year – 1968 – three times to locate and recover the bodies of drowned persons, ten times to search for stolen property, once to search and recover a large piece of equipment lost in the River Avon at Twyning and also a sunken boat upon which it was loaded, and the remainder were elimination searches to establish whether or not property, and in one case a missing person, were in various stretches of water.[7]

The Divisional Training Sergeants appointed in April, 1967, continued instructional duties during the first half of the year and on the 1st August, 1968, when the territorial Divisions of the Force were re-organised, one full-time Training Inspector was appointed to each of the four Divisions, in addition to the Training Sergeant. It was intended that more training, particularly Refresher Courses, would be given in Divisions in future, and it was because of these additional training duties that the Inspectors were appointed.

The senior Cadets (i.e. over 18 years of age), continued to spend half a day each week on physical activities. During this part of the Cadet's service, the emphasis was upon character training and a number of Courses and attachments were arranged. These included attachments to the Steel Company of Wales, Outward Bound Courses and periods of service at the Cheshire Home, Cheltenham; the Star Centre for Youth at Ullenwood, Nr. Cheltenham; the County Council Home for the Aged at Orchard House, Bishops Cleeve, and other voluntary service attachments in Children's Homes, Approved Schools, Church Army Hostels and Y.M.C.A. Hostels.

In September, 1968, two senior Cadets left the country to carry out Voluntary Service Overseas, both working in Youth Camps in Jamaica.

In September, 1968, Constable P.M. Sharpe from the Force completed the Higher Police Training – sixth Special Course at the Police College and was issued with a Certificate, by the Commandant of the College, stating that he had Passed the Course. He was immediately promoted to the substantive rank of Sergeant.

During 1968, the following new Police Stations were completed and became operational – Rodborough, Tetbury, Wotton-under-Edge, Blockley, Lydbrook and Shurdington. All these new Police Stations replaced sub-standard property.

Work on the new Police Enquiry Office, St. George's Road, Cheltenham, was completed in May, 1968.

The following shows the results of the examination in police subjects held in November, 1967 and January, 1968.

	Sergeant to Inspector	*Constable to Sergeant*
Sergeants/Constables	50 sat with 18 passes	126 sat with 47 passes

On 31st December, 1968, 46 Sergeants and 174 Constables (including one Woman Police Constable) were qualified by examination and eliglible for promotion to the next rank.

Visits to Police Headquarters by organised parties continued to be very popular and 51 such visits were made during 1968. On Saturday, 9th November, 1968, a Day Vocational Conference was held, when 43 young men and women from all parts of the Diocese Of Gloucester spent a day at Police Headquarters, where they were shown various aspects of police work. This Conference was organised in conjunction with the Reverend T. Eric Evans, the Diocesan Youth Chaplain.

Chief Inspector K.W.F. Barker, the Force Public Relations and Crime Prevention Officer, was a member of the Home Office Working Party set up under the Static Sub-Committee of the Home Office Working Party set up on Crime Prevention. This Working Party, under the Chairmanship of Douglas Osmond, Esq., O.B.E., the Chief Constable of Hampshire, had, with other items been considering the security of dwellings, schools and retail shops.

The number of '999' calls made to the Gloucestershire Police in 1968, was 13,108. The figure for 1967 was 10,692.

In June of 1968, automatic signalling apparatus was installed on the River Severn Bridge. This was remotely controlled from the Motorway Police Station at Almondsbury and by the end of the year had been used on 336 occasions . The automatic signals were used for warning motorists of accidents, high winds, breakdowns, road works, ice and fog, and close liaison was maintained with the B.B.C. to keep the motoring public informed of such hazards, both on the Motorway complex, and on a County wide basis.

Unit Beat Policing, made possible by the use of small cars in conjunction with personal radio sets, was introduced in Cheltenham on 25th March, 1968, in Gloucester on 28th October, 1968, and in the Staple Hill, Kingswood and Filton areas on the 1st January, 1969.

In his Annual Report to the Police Committee for the year 1968, the Chief Constable stated –

> It is a little premature at this stage to attempt to evaluate Unit Beat Policing in the County, but it is believed that the new system provides for a rapid response to calls for Police help, promotes good relations with the public, enables information to be systematically collated and swiftly retrieved, and improves morale among the men participating in the scheme.

As regards, 'promoting good relations with the public' Unit Beat Policing proved the exact opposite and just over a decade of this system of policing the general public insisted in wanting the 'Bobby' back on the Beat.

As announced by the Secretary of State on 12th January, 1968, an Amnesty and Appeal for the surrender of firearms and ammunition ran from the 1st February, 1968, until the 30th April, 1968. In so far as the County of Gloucestershire was concerned, a total of 472 firearms of varying description and calibre were surrendered. Some 12,000 rounds of types of ammunition were also surrendered.

Part V of the Criminal Justice Act, 1967, which was subsequently consolidated with the Firearms Act, 1968, dealt with the licensing of shot guns and became operative on 1st May, 1968, when the responsibility for the issue and subsequent renewal of shot gun certificates then rested with the Police.

By 31st December, 1968, 13,229 shot-gun certificates had been issued. There were ten applications which were refused.

During 1968, a total of 1,260 sudden deaths were reported to the Coroner, and in 300 cases inquests were held. A summary of the findings is given below:–

Accidental	111
Misadventure	90
Natural Causes	11
Suicide	54
Murder	–
Industrial Disease	7
Causing death by dangerous driving	12
Open verdict	7
Pending	8

One inquest was held in respect of Treasure Trove found in the Chipping Campden area.

A Senior Civilian Administration Officer was appointed during 1968, and took up his duties at Police Headquarters, Cheltenham.

An Inspection of the combined Regular and Volunteer Cadets was held at the Royal Air Force Station, South Cerney, on 22nd June, 1968, when the Inspecting Officer was Colonel G.P. Shakerley, C.B.E., M.C., T.D., Chairman of the Police Committee.

Officers in Charge of Police Stations at which typewriters were not supplied and who used their own typewriters for reports, etc., were entitled to claim an allowance of £3 per annum.

On the 27th May, 1968, the Police Authority were informed that under Regulation 50 of the Police Regulations 1968, a new rate for typewriter allowance which heretofore had not been specified in Regulations, was to be determined by the Police Authority but should not exceed £4 per year.

The Committee authorised payment of the new maximum allowance.

The Secretary of State notified Police Authorities that the weekly allowance ordinarily paid to officers attending Courses away from home and living in lodgings should be increased with effect from the 2nd January, 1968, to:–

Chief Superintendent or Superintendent	£8.10.0d.
Chief Inspector, Inspector, Sergeant or Constable	£7.17.6d.

Payment of the new rates was authorised by the Police Committee on the 27th May, 1968.

Although Canteen facilities had been made available at Police Headquarters, Cheltenham, great difficulty had been experienced in engaging staff, mainly due to the irregular meal times necessitated by the various tours of duty performed by members of the Force and the need to staff the Canteen for 24 hours a day at weekends and on public holidays.

To overcome these problems the Chief Constable examined the possibility of using Automatic Cooking and Vending Machines. The annual cost in the first year of operation of the service would amount to £8,100, whilst the annual cost of the staff was £8,000.

At their meeting on the 27th May, 1968, the Police Authority agreed to the introduction of the new scheme.

On the 9th September, 1968, the Committee received a Report from the Chief Constable on the work of the Police during the serious flooding in many parts of the County on the 10th July, 1968, and the Committee recorded their appreciation of the work of the Force which had been carried out in the highest tradition of the Police Service.

Home Office Circular No. 239/1968, stated that after consulting the Local Authority Associations and the Police Representative bodies the Secretary of State was satisfied that there would often be a need for a full time deputy to an officer in charge of a sub-division with an adjusted establishment exceeding 100 and that where one was appointed his rank should normally be one below that of the Officer in Charge. Based on these considerations the Secretary of State stated that he would be prepared to approve the rank of Superintendent Class II for the post of Deputy in Sub-divisions with an adjusted establishment of 100 – 150.

The Committee approved the Chief Constable's action in applying to the Secretary of State for approval to up-grade two Chief Inspectors who were deputies to the Officers in Charge of the Cheltenham and Gloucester Sub-divisions, to the rank of Superintendent Class II.

With the reduction of the number of territorial Divisions from six to four the Southern Division Motor Patrol was centralised at the Almondsbury Motorway Police Station and the authorised establishment of officers there was thus raised to 44, with two civilian employees.

In accordance with the scale laid down by the Home Office of supervisory ranks, based on the numbers under command, the rank of the

Officer in Charge of a Sub-division with 25 – 100 personnel under command should be a Chief Inspector.

The Police Committee thereupon authorised the submission of an application to the Secretary of State for approval to the Inspector's post at the Almondsbury Motorway Police Station being up-graded to that of Chief Inspector.

At their meeting on the 17th February, 1969, the Committee confirmed the action of the Chairman in authorising the acceptance of a Tender from Thermionic Products (Electronics) Ltd., of Hythe, for the installation, in the Information Room at the new Force Headquarters, of a 6 channel unit which would record on tape automatically all messages received on the two Radio Channels and from '999' telephone lines, with time injection superimposed. The cost of the equipment was £2,970.10.0d.

Approval was also given on the 17th February, 1969, for the purchase of a 15 – seater Personnel Carrier and Trailer to carry Police Cadets and their equipment in connection with their revised training programme.

On the occasion of the Investiture of His Royal Highness the Prince of Wales at Caernarvon on the 1st July, 1969, the Chief Constable agreed to a request from the Chief Constable of the Gwynedd Police Authority to provide:–

1	Chief Inspector
1	Inspector
4	Sergeants
71	Constables (including 11 Detective Constables)
77	Total

for the period from 28th June to the 2nd July, 1969. A number of other County Forces also sent personnel to assist the Gwynedd Police.

The Chief Constable, Mr. E.P.B. White, Q.P.M., was made an Officer of the Most Excellent Order of the British Empire in the Birthday Honours List for that year – 1969.

The British Empire Medal for Gallantry was also awarded to Constable Albin B. Smith and Constable Brian J.K. Organ, both Motor Patrol Officers attached to Southern Division. The awards arose out of a shooting incident which occurred in that Division on the 23rd February, 1969.

As a result of an incident which occurred at a house in Cheltenham when a mentally deranged man was found standing on a window ledge on the third floor and threatening to jump off, Police Sergeant William H. Abbott and Police Sergeant Charles T. Critchley both received a Commendation for Bravery, after getting the man back into the house despite being attacked with axe and hammer.[8]

Chief Superintendent F.W. Hudson, M.B.E. returned to the Force on the 30th December, 1969, after serving as Director of the Home Office Crime Prevention Courses at Stafford, and retired on ordinary Police pension on the following day after completing 30 years' service.

The new Police Station at Andoversford became operational in 1969, but the completion of the new Force Headquarters, Lansdown Road, Cheltenham, and the installation of essential operational equipment, was unfortunately delayed through water penetrating into the basement.

Gloucestershire Crime Prevention Officers took on the responsibility of inspecting Explosives Stores and Premises Registered under the Explosives Acts, within the confines of the County, during 1969. During that same year H.M. Assistant Inspector of Explosives spent a week in the County and visited a number of Explosive Stores in company with the Crime Prevention Officers.

During the year 1969, 246 males and 7 females were proceeded against for drunkenness, this was an increase of 50 persons compared with 1968.

55,428 photographs were produced by the Headquarters Photographic Department in 1969, as compared with 45,426 in 1968. Nearly 5,000 of these were in connection with murder enquiries and the remainder were related to other criminal offences, accidents, prisoners, documents and television broadcasts.

The Authorised Establishment and Strength of the Force on the 31st December, 1969, was:–

RANK	ESTABLISHMENT	STRENGTH 31.12.69
Chief Constable	1	1
Deputy Chief Constable	1	1
Assistant Chief Constable	1	1
Chief Superintendents (Higher Scale)	2	2
Chief Superintendents (Lower Scale)	5	5
Superintendents Class I	9	9
Superintendents Class II	3	3
Chief Inspectors	21	21
Inspectors	35	36
Sergeants	179	176
Constables	764	730

Woman Police Chief Inspector	1		1
Woman Police Inspector	1		1
Women Police Sergeants	4		4
Women Police Constables	33		22
Total	1,060	Total	1,013*

* Does not include 18 officers of all ranks seconded for special duties.

Details showing the distribution of the Senior Officers within the County Constabulary, during the year 1902, were given earlier. As a comparison, the following details are given for the year 1969:–[9]

Chief Constable	E.P.B. White, O.B.E., Q.P.M.
Deputy Chief Constable	H.D.J. Smith, M.B.E., Q.P.M.
Assistant Chief Constable	E. Coppin
HEADQUARTERS DIVISION	
Administration	Chief Superintendent H. Thomas
Organisation & Planning	Superintendent R. Smith
Accounts Department	Police Sergeant J.W. Owen
Criminal Investigation Department	D/Chief Superintendent R.H. Tilley and D/Superintendent C.W. Trull
Criminal Intelligence Officer	D/Inspector C.E. Avery
Crime Prevention & P.R.O.	Chief Inspector K.W.F. Barker
Traffic Deptartment	Chief Superintendent P.F. Foice Superintendent A.S. Meadows Inspector R.E. Hill
Road Safety	Chief Inspector A.O. Tucker
Information Room	Inspector R.S. Johnson
Training Department	Chief Inspector A.Parker Inspector E.W. Markham
Women Police	W.P.Chief Inspector E.B. Hughes W.P.Inspector M.L. Pincombe
NORTHERN DIVISION	Chief Superintendent W.G. Turner
CHELTENHAM	Superintendent D.G. Baker
Administration Chief Inspector	Chief Inspector D.F. Ryder
Detective Chief Inspector	D/Chief Inspector F.W.J. Coombs
Detective Inspector	D/Inspector A.T. Wadley
Training Inspector	Inspector J.A. Goode
CHELTENHAM SUB-DIVISION	Superintendent G. Buffham Chief Inspector D.J. Johnson Inspector R.J. Davis Inspector J.A. Day Inspector P.A.J. Day Inspector J.G. Jacobsen

	Inspector A.G. McMahon Inspector R.F. Pitman
CHIPPING CAMPDEN SUB-DIVISION	C/Inspector K.W. Golding
TEWKESBURY SUB-DIVISION	C/Inspector D.R. Townsend
SOUTHERN DIVISION – STAPLE HILL	C/Superintendent A.R.J. Carter Superintendent E.D. Jenkins
Administration C/Inspector	C/Inspector D.J. Francis
Criminal Investigation Dept.	Det. C/Inspector D.J. Wise Det./Inspector Vacant
Training Inspector	Inspector P.Legg
Almondsbury Motorway Station	Inspector K.H. Sallis
STAPLE HILL SUB-DIVISION	C/Inspector D.A. Witts Inspector M.H. Causon Inspector W.A. Jelf Inspector K.J.H. Nicholls Inspector R.J. Watkins
FILTON SUB-DIVISION	C/Inspector P.P. Bridgman
KINGSWOOD SUB-DIVISION	C/Inspector C.J. Davis
EASTERN DIVISION – STROUD	C/Superintendent W.J. Howkins Superintendent K. Moss
Administration C/Inspector	C/Inspector J.C. Gray
Criminal Investigation Dept.	Det./Chief Inspector M.H. Cooper Det./Inspector Vacant
Training Inspector	Inspector V.W. Causon
STROUD SUB-DIVISION	C/Inspector T.G. Hart Inspector S.J. Gudge Inspector F. Field Inspector G.W. Lewis
DURSLEY SUB-DIVISION	C/Inspector R. Dale
CIRENCESTER SUB-DIVISION	C/Inspector A.G. Harris Inspector W.J.T. Harris Inspector R.N. Lightfoot
WESTERN DIVISION – GLOUCESTER	C/Superintendent R.F. Mayo Superintendent G. Shellswell
Administration C/Inspector	C/Inspector L.R. Starnes
Criminal Investigation Dept.	Det.C/Inspector J.V. McKnight Det. Inspector W.R. Barnard
Training Inspector	Inspector H.K. Roberts
GLOUCESTER SUB-DIVISION	Superintendent V.J. Bullock C/Inspector A.E. Viner Inspector H.R. Edwards Inspector S.T. James

	Inspector W.H.S. Kingscott Inspector A.J.C. Merrett Inspector L.C. Owen Inspector C.P. Clarke
LYDNEY SUB-DIVISION	Superintendent B.H. Gwilliam C/Inspector J.E. Hemming Inspector E.J. Bradbeer Inspector K.R.S. Parsons

NORTHERN DIVISION – Police Stations

Andoversford
Ashchurch
Birdlip
Bishops Cleeve*
Blockley
Bourton-on-the-Water
Chipping Campden+
Cheltenham+
Coombe Hill
Dymock
Guiting
Hartpury
Moreton-in-Marsh*
Newent*
Northleach*
Stanton
Staunton
Stow-on-the-Wold*
Tewkesbury+
Weston-sub-Edge
Winchcombe*
Windrush

* Sergeants' Stations + Inspectors' Stations

SOUTHERN DIVISION – Police Stations

Acton Turville
Almondsbury
Almondsbury – Motorway+
Alveston
Charfield
Chipping Sodbury*
Cribbs Causeway
Falfield
Filton+
Hawkesbury
Iron Acton
Kingswood+
Marshfield
Olveston
Pilning*
Staple Hill+
Thornbury*
Wickwar
Wotton-under-Edge*
Yate*

* Sergeants' Stations + Inspectors' Stations

EASTERN DIVISION – Police Stations

Berkeley*
Bibury
Bisley
Bisley Old Road
Cam
Chalford
Chedworth
Cirencester+
Dursley+
Fairford*
Frampton-on-Severn
Horsley
Kings Stanley
Lechlade
Minchinhampton*
Nailsworth*
Newport
North Cerney
Painswick*
Poulton
Rodborough*
Sapperton
Sharpness
Slimbridge
South Cerney
Stonehouse*
Stroud+
Tetbury*
Uley
Whiteshill
Whitminster*

* Sergeants' Stations + Inspectors' Stations

WESTERN DIVISION – Police Stations

Blakeney*	Longhope	Ruardean
Bream	Lydbrook	Ruspidge
Cinderford+	Lydney	St. Briavels
Coleford+	Mile End	Tutshill*
Drybrook	Mitcheldean	Westbury-on-Severn
Gloucester	Newnham-on-Severn	Woolaston
Huntley	Parkend	Yorkley
Littledean*		

* Sergeants' Station + Inspectors' Stations

On the recommendation of the Secretary of State, Her Majesty the Queen awarded the Queen's Police Medal, for Distinguished Service, to Chief Superintendent Harry Thomas. The award appeared in the New Years Honours for 1970. Mr Thomas had been closely connected with the Executive Committee of the Superintendents Association of England and Wales and had served on other Committees in the Police Service. He had also taken a close interest in Police Welfare work and maintained contact with former members of the Force, having organised an Annual Luncheon and News Letter for Force Pensioners. The News Letter was commenced in 1962 and was still being published in 1985.

After completing 33 years in the Gloucestershire Constabulary Chief Superintendent Thomas retired on pension on the 31st January, 1970.

During the same month, Chief Superintendent Paul Foice retired on pension. At the time of his retirement, 23rd January, 1970, there was only one other officer in the Force who had served longer than Mr Foice, and that was the Deputy Chief Constable, Mr H.D.J. Smith.

January 27th, 1970, saw the passing of our oldest Police Pensioner, Ex. Superintendent John Evans, who was in his 102nd year. Mr Evans retired on the 30th November, 1923, and had enjoyed a full and healthy life of retirement right up until his death. He passed away at the home of his daughter at Shurdington.

The first few months of 1970, saw recruiting for the Force practically at a standstill, and when it was eventually allowed to recommence in earnest it took some months to regain impetus; however, by the end of the year an average monthly improvement became apparent. In all, some 222 people applied for admission to the Force and of these 62 were accepted. 66% of the rejections were on education grounds.

In July, 1970, Her Majesty the Queen was graciously pleased to award the British Empire Medal for Gallantry to Constable Brian James Doherty. The action which brought about the award took place during the night of 8th January, 1970, when P.C. Doherty in trying to arrest two men for crime was carried on the boot of their car for a considerable distance at very high speeds, and despite all efforts to dislodge him he still managed to broadcast, through his personal radio, and to assist in the arrest of the criminals when they finally stopped.

An experiment involving Gloucestershire and three other Forces took place in 1969/1970. This was controlled by the Home Office Police Research Department and the idea was to establish a formula which would give correct police establishments.

The Department recommended an increase of 498 all ranks which meant raising the Authorised Establishment of the Gloucestershire Force from 1,060 to 1,558. Needless to say the increase was not approved. However, on the 20th October, 1970, the Secretary of State approved an increase of 1 Chief Inspector, 7 Inspectors, 10 Sergeants and 107 Constables, bringing the Authorised Total Establishment up to 1,185.

During 1970, the Chief Constable set up an Incident Room at Police Headquarters to enable major incidents of long duration to be dealt with.

The allowances for the provision of meals for prisoners had been in force since the 1st November, 1959, and by 1970 were quite inadequate. Subject to the approval of the Secretary of State the Police Committee, on the 16th February, 1970, approved the following rates from 1st April, 1970:–

Main meal	7/6d.
One other meal @	4/6d.
A third meal @	3/–d.

Making a total of 15/–d. in any one 24 hour period. The existing daily rate at that time was 9/–d.

The Committee received a Report from the Chief Constable on the measures taken to combat demonstrations organised by Anti-Apartheid and various other groups on the occasion of the Springboks versus Southern Counties Rugby Union match held at Kingsholm, Gloucester, on the 28th January, 1970.

Approximately 700 Police Officers wre deployed, 400 from Gloucestershire Constabulary (some of whom volunteered to do duty on what would have been their normal Rest Day and received payment in lieu thereof) and 300 from six adjoining Forces, under the Mutual Aid Scheme.

The Committee paid tribute to the Chief Constable and members of the Gloucestershire constabulary and other Forces concerned for the excellent arrangement which enabled the match to take place without undue incident.

On the 16th February, 1970, the Police Committee considered an application from the Gloucestershire Joint branch Board of the Police Federation that, with effect from 1st April, 1970, the weekly amounts paid, in respect of Rent Allowance, as allowed under Police Regulations, should be increased to:–

Constable	£5. 5.0d.
Sergeant	£5. 7.6d.
Inspector	£5.10.0d.
Superintendent	£5.15.0d.

The Committee agreed that an application should be made to the Secretary of State for his approval to the amounts requested by the Branch Board.

A vacancy for a Superintendent was advertised, in accordance with Home Office recommendations, and as a result Chief Inspector W.A. Stapleforth of the Cheshire Constabulary was appointed Superintendent and took up his duties with the Gloucestershire Constabulary on the 17th February, 1970.

Chief Superintendent H.C.S. Lodge returned to the Force on the 20th September, 1970, after serving as a member of the Directing Staff at the Police College at Bramshill.

It was anticipated that the Police National Computer building at Hendon would be completed by September, 1971, and that the first shakedown trials would commence in the November of that year.

During 1970 there were 1,488 arrests made by the crews of Police Vehicles in Gloucestershire, compared with 1,337 in 1969.

During 1970 a small number of alterations were made to the Authorised Establishment of civilians which, at the end of the year totalled 300. This total included 73 part-time cleaners.

Recruiting for the Special Constabulary was slow during 1970, only eight being enrolled during the year, The total strength on the 31st December, 1970, was:–

Northern Division	194
Southern Division	149
Eastern Division	170
Western Division	185
	698*

* includes 40 women

The Authorised Establishment of Traffic Wardens was increased by 15 to a total of 58, during 1970, with the following distribution:–

Cheltenham	17
Tewkesbury	2
Staple Hill	3
Filton	5
Thornbury	2
Kingswood	2
Stroud	3
Dursley	2
Cirencester	2
Gloucester	20

The actual strength at the end of the year was 57 – 23 male and 34 female.

Members of the Force continued to take an active part in the organisation of the St. John Ambulance in Gloucestershire. Mr E Coppin, the Assistant Chief Constable, was County Director, Chief Inspector J. Gray, Stroud, was secretary of the Gloucester City Centre, and Sergeant A. Moir, Kingswood, was Secretary of the South Gloucestershire Centre. In addition Inspector R. Pitman was Brigade Superintendent of the Cheltenham Spa Ambulance Division.

On the 31st December, 1970, there were 879 married officers serving and 742 of them were in accommodation provided by the Police Authority and 137 in their own homes.

The new Force Headquarters, Holland House, Lansdown Road, Cheltenham was completed and became operational on the 22nd June, 1970.

The adjacent premises formerly used as Force Headquarters then reverted to their original purpose as Divisional Headquarters for Cheltenham, and were occupied as such on 4th September, 1970, and named Talbot House, Lansdown Road, Cheltenham.

The two buildings were officially opened on the 30th September, 1970, by Sir Phillip Allen, K.C.B., Permanent Under Secretary of State, Home Office.

The new Police Station at Prestbury, which replaced sub-standard property, was completed and the premises occupied during 1970.

During 1970 an experiment was carried out on the M4 Motorway when four raised platforms were constructed to enable Police Patrol vehicles to stop and observe Traffic. If successful the project was to be extended.

During the year 1970, 78 persons were dealt with for offences under the Dangerous Drugs Act, 1965, and the Drugs (Prevention of Misuse) Act 1964. This was an increase of 30 persons compared with 1969.

The information room at the new Police Headquarters, Lansdown Road, Cheltenham, was occupied on the 22nd June, 1970, and consisted of three rooms: teleprinter room, main information room and Inspector's office and Incident room with rest room facilities. The Information Room, entirely self-contained was situated on the second floor of Holland House.

At this particular time a temporary motorway telephone system for the Strensham to Piffs Elm stretch of the M5 terminated on one in the Information room but, eventually all telephones would terminate at Almondsbury Motorway Station when the M5 was completed in 1971.

'999' lines for the County terminated on key and lamp units and were paralleled to all Incident Consoles enabling any operator to accept these calls. In addition to the common group of switchboard extensions, each Console had a key and lamp panel which provided separate communication between each Console.

Direct lines to Fire Service and Ambulance Service Control Rooms were paralleled to Consoles. All telephones with the exception of the temporary emergency motorway telephones, were terminated on key and lamp units.

Arrangements were made for all regular members of the Force to visit the Information Room, followed by further arrangements to cater for members of the Special Constabulary.

There were 91 fatal accidents during 1970 in which 101 persons were killed. Comparable figures of road accidents for 1968, 1969 and 1970 were:–

	1968	**1969**	**1970**
Number of accidents recorded	5,144	4,685	3,946
Persons			
Killed	89	120	101
Seriously injured	1,746	1,668	1,721
Slightly injured	2,508	2,541	2,784
Total	4,343	4,329	4,606

Motor Patrol mileage in 1970 was 1,826,711 compared with 1,817,689 in 1969. The total mileage covered by all vehicles in 1970 was 5,317,694 compared with 5,275,628 in 1969.

The Gloucestershire Male Voice Choir was formed during the year – 1970 – and over the years has gone from strength to strength. The first Conductor of the Choir was Mr Islwyn Jones of Cheltenham.

It was during 1970 that the Chief Constable, Mr E.P.B. White was elected Vice President of the Association of Chief Police Officers.

1971 was a sad year for the Force when five serving officers passed away, all from Natural Causes; three during the month of October. They were:–

Police Sergeant L. Griffiths who died at Cirencester on the 7th March, 1971. He left a widow who was awarded a Police Widow's Pension.

On the 11th June, 1971, Police Constable Royston Burgess passed away in Cheltenham, aged 33 years. He left a widow and young family. A Police Widow's Pension was awarded again in this instance.

Police Sergeant Eric G. Sandells died at Cirencester on the 3rd October, 1971, aged 43 years. His widow was awarded a gratuity.

Superintendent A.E. Viner died in his sleep at Gloucester on the 13th October, 1971, aged 49 years. He left a widow and two children. Mrs Viner was awarded a Police Widow's Pension but has since re-married.

On the 24th October, 1971, Sergeant P.T. Hillier died at Stow-on-the-Wold, aged 44 years. His widow was awarded a Police Widow's Pension.

It was during 1971 that Mr J.S.H. Gaskain, C.B.E., M.B.E., Q.P.M., passed away, after a long illness. He was Chief Constable of Gloucestershire from early 1959 until the end of 1962, when he left to become one of Her Majesty's Inspectors of Constabulary. He was later to become Commandant of the Police College at Bramshill when, due to ill-health, he retired and went to live at Brighton.

Superintendent Gordon Shellswell, Gloucester retired on pension on the 31st March, 1971.

The following are the results of the examination in Police Subjects held in November, 1970, and January, 1971:–

Sergeants – Promotion to Inspector – 25 sat the examination with 14 passes.

Constables – Promotion to Inspector – 61 sat the examination with 27 passes.

On 31st December, 1971, 78 Sergeants and 254 Constables were qualified for promotion to the next higher rank.

The Annual Inspection of the Combined Regular and Volunteer Cadet Corps was held at the Royal Air force Station, Innsworth, on Saturday, 12th June, 1971, when the Inspecting Officer was P.G. Harris, Esq., M.B.E., Sheriff of the City of Gloucester.

The stregth of the Volunteer Cadet Units at 31st December, 1971, was as follows:–

Northern Division	14
Southern Division	11
Eastern Division	23
Western Division	25
(Gloucester 15)	—
(Lydney 10)	73

During the year, two Volunteer Cadets joined the Regular Cadets and two joined the Regular Force as Constables.

The Organisation and Methods team of the County Management Services Department carried out a review of the organisation and clerical procedures affecting the civilian staff and some Regular Officers employed at Force Headquarters and in Divisions.

The team completed its review in December, 1971, and forwarded its recommendations to the Police Authority, and the Chief Constable, for consideration.

The Annual Inspection of the Force by Her Majesty's Inspector of Constabulary, N. Galbraith, Esq., Q.P.M., was made on the 10th, 11th, 15th, 16th and 17th, February, 1971, when Mr Galbraith visited Headquarters and various Police Stations in each of the territorial Divisions.

During 1971 the Underwater Recovery Section discovered, in the River Wye beneath Bigsweir Bridge, two live 3 inch Mortar bombs. These were marked and subsequently exploded by a R.N. Bomb Disposal Unit.

By 1971, officers trained in the use of firearms were distributed fairly evenly throughout the Force, and were from various Departments e.g., C.I.D., Motor Patrol, Sub-Sectional Stations, etc.

1,094 motor vehicles were reported stolen during the year 1971, an increase of 275 of the figure for 1970. Of the 1,094 cases, 656 were recorded as 'taking without authority' and 438 as theft. The offenders were detected in 426 of the 'taking' offences and in 117 of the theft offences. 53 vehicles reported stolen during the year had not been recovered.

On the 31st December, 1971, the final section of the M5 Motorway in the County, from Stroud Water to Almondsbury was opened, including the four level interchange. The Motorway was patrolled by the Almondsbury and Gloucester Traffic Sections, the Almondsbury cars patrolling northwards as far as the Stroud Water Interchange and the Gloucester cars patrolling the remainder as far as the M50 junction at Strensham, the West Mercia cars taking over at this point.

The remainder of the M4 Motorway from Tormarton to Maidenhead was opened to traffic on 22nd December, 1971. This Force patrolled from Newhouse as far as the Tormarton Interchange. The remainder of the M4 Motorway in Gloucestershire being patrolled by the Wiltshire Constabulary.

The problems in the sphere of Welfare were many and varied, and during 1971, Sergeant R.E. Spencer, G.M., the Force Welfare

Officer, or Co-ordinator as he was known then, and the eight Divisional Welfare Officers, maintained a close interest with those people who needed help.

Visits were made to Officers and Pensioners ill in hospital or at home as well as to the widows, over the age of 80 years, who now qualified for State Pensions and assistance was given in the completion of the necessary application forms.

By now – 1971 – Public Relations became very important to the Force and, to demonstrate this, the first 'Open Day' took place in October, 1971. Some 3,000 people were allowed to walk around the various departments at Police Headquarters, viewing all aspects of police work.

1972 saw the appointment of Drug Officers in all Divisions and by 1973 Juvenile Liaison Officers were established.

During 1972, we find the Force had three Officers studying at University. One Inspector at Bristol University, one Inspector at Reading University and one Constable at Manchester University.

The first Woman Police Superintendent to be appointed in Gloucestershire was Woman Chief Inspector E.B. Hughes. In the first instance Miss Hughes came to this Force, from Birkenhead, on promotion to Inspector and was promoted to the rank of Superintendent on the 1st September, 1972.

On the 1st January, 1972, we saw the new Crown Courts come into being at the Shire Hall, Gloucester. The Crown Courts taking the place of the Courts of Assize, the County Quarter Sessions and the Gloucester City Quarter Sessions.

Superintendent T.G. Hart retired on pension on the 31st July, 1972, after seeing service in many parts of the County.

Ex. Superintendent Frank Hallet, who was in his 94th year, passed away in the Knoll Nursing Home, Gloucester, on the 3rd May, 1972. Mr Hallett was always proud of having served in the Gloucestershire Constabulary and loved to reminisce of his service under Admiral Christian, who was Chief Constable during most of Mr Hallett's service.

On the 12th September, 1972, Ex. Superintendent J. Price, passed away at the age of 86 years. He had a brother in the Force who also rose to the rank of Superintendent – Ex. Superintendent H.J. Price – who died in 1959. Both brothers were born at Bream in the Forest of Dean.

Ex. Superintendent J. Greenall, aged 72 years, died at Cheltenham on the 9th October, 1972. Jack Greenall was the first Superintendent to take command of the Motor Patrol Section in the Force.

A comprehensive report, based on the recommendations of the Organisation and Methods Survey carried out by the Organisation and Methods Team of the County Council's Management Services during 1971, was presented to the Police Authority on the 6th June, 1972, and was accepted. In the main, proposals were made both at Force Headquarters and the Divisions on the re-grouping and re-allocation of responsibilities, the proposed re-groupings of work being necessary if realistic staffing levels and a civilian career structure were to be achieved and new equipment used efficiently and economically.

Grading improvements were also made in order that the right rate of pay was given for the level of work undertaken by civilians and in order that a satisfactory range of grades for civilian officers could be introduced.

To assist with Cadet Training, a re-designed course of academic studies was introduced for Junior Cadets at the North Gloucestershire College of Technology. The Course, which embraced a wide range of subjects considered most suitable for potential Police Officers was well received and proved to be very successful. 22 Cadets attended the Course and 20 obtained their 'Certificate in Social Studies'.

In addition to general physical activities, the year also saw the development of a strong life-saving section which took part in competitions throughout the Midlands, South and South Wales with commendable success. A number of Cadets also entered the annual 34 mile Barking to Southend Road Walk and not only finished the guelling course but also obtained awards.

During 1972 a total of 1,459 sudden deaths were reported to the Coroner, and in 310 cases inquests were held. This was seven more than in 1971. A summary of the findings are given below:–

Accidental	168
Misadventure	30
Natural Causes	13
Suicide	46
Murder/Manslaughter	4
Industrial Disease	8
Causing death by dangerous driving	12
Open	24
Pending	5
Total	310

The Criminal Intelligence Department of the C.I.D. continued to provide a very useful service to Investigating Officers, both in this Force and elsewhere.

During the year, there were at least 50 occasions when suggestions as to the identity of an offender were made from the Criminal Intelligence Office, and the success rate was 50%.

These suggestions included 12 to five different Forces, with a success rate of 66%.

1972 saw orders placed for the Pye Mascot equipment at each Divisional Headquarters. This equipment would provide an integrated UHF/VHF control with a landline connection to Headquarters. This would enable every pocket set user to converse with the Visual Display Operator at Headquarters, who would be in a position to interrogate the National Police Computer.

Two new Police Stations were taken into use during 1972, Newnham-on-Severn and Northleach. Both Stations replaced old accommodation. There had been delays all along the line in the construction of the new Divisional Headquarters and Magistrates' Courts at Stroud. By the end of 1972 the work was approximately 46 weeks behind schedule.

Continued encouragement had been given to those officers who wished to occupy their own homes and during the year the total of owner/occupiers had risen to 507, an increase of 182 compared with 1971. The number of officers who were occupying Police Authority houses at the end of the year was 503, compared with 628 on the 31st December, 1971. This of course meant that it had become necessary to dispose of Police houses as they became surplus to requirements and 140 such properties were referred to the County Land Agent and Valuer during 1972, to be transferred to other Departments of the County Council, other Local Authorities, or sale on the open market. Police Officers purchased 74 of them.

At the end of the year under review a total of 34 Police Authority houses were empty and had not been allocated.

The maximum limit Rent Allowances being paid to members of the Force at the end of 1972, was:–

Constables	£7.75 weekly
Sergeants	£7.87 weekly
Inspectors	£8.00 weekly
Superintendents	£8.25 weekly

As a result of the appointment of Drug Officers in Southern and Eastern Divisions in September, 1972, there were now Drug Squads, comprising a Sergeant and a Constable in each Division.

The total number of persons reported for drug offences during 1972, was 144, the corresponding figure for 1971 being 97. The increase was almost entirely in the field of cannabis, for there were some 130 cases involving this drug in 1972, as compared to 78 in 1971.

During 1972 only 9 persons under the age of 18 years were reported for drug offences, whereas in 1971 the figure was 15.

On the 31st December, 1972, 865 registered aliens were resident in the County, an increase of 35 on the figure at 31st December, 1971.

Enquiries were made in respect of a total of 41 applications for naturalisation and a further 10 enquiries were made regarding referees supporting applications for naturalisation.

In the Chief Constable's Report for the year 1972, there was a paragraph which read,

> In January, 1972, an Administration Committee was formed under the Chairmanship of the Force Planning Officer to carry out a detailed examination of the usefulness, design and standardisation of all the forms and books at present in use within the Force. *This is the first time an exercise of this nature has been done,* and was precipatated because of the necessity to change the majority of the printing plates held for the production of forms, due to the adoption of International Organisation of Standardisation paper sizes in this Country.

This statement was not correct. The first time an exercise of this nature was carried out within the Force was just after Mr J.S.H. Gaskain became Chief Constable, when he set up a Working Committee, as previously mentioned, to examine the usefulness and design of all the forms and books then in use throughout the Force. This Committee was formed in 1960 and remained as such until 1962, just prior to Mr Gaskain leaving the Force.

During 1973 the Force said farewell to many senior officers who had served the Force well. Mr H.D.J. Smith, Q.P.M., retired during June after 45 years service. He had come up through the ranks and was Deputy Chief Constable at the time of his retirement. Detective Chief Superintendent R.H. Tilley retired on pension on the 28th February, 1973. On the 30th June, Superintendent B.H. Gwilliam, Superintendent Kenneth Moss and Superintendent Philip Bridgman, all retired on pension and on the 9th September, 1973, Detective Superintendent H.C.W. Trull decided to call it a day and take his pension.

With the retirement of Mr H.D.J. Smith, Mr E. Coppin was appointed Deputy Chief Constable and on the 1st July, 1973, Mr E.W. Whitmore,

Acting Assistant Chief Constable of the Bath and Somerset Constabulary, was appointed Assistant Chief Constable of Gloucestershire.

1973 also saw the passing of three serving Police Officers:–

Superintendent Donald J. Wise, aged 48 years died on the 3rd April, 1973. Police Constable Walter S. Jackson, aged 44 years died on the 16th April, 1973, and Police Constable Albert E. Smith, aged 50 years died on the 8th August, 1973.

On the 7th February, 1973, Ex. Chief Superintendent F.A. Statham, Q.P.M. died at Keynsham, aged 72 years.

Ex. Superintendent A.W. Hopkins died at Cheltenham on the 23rd October, 1973, aged 88 years and thus ended a long family connection with the Gloucestershire Constabulary, his father having been Superintendent and Deputy Chief Constable for many years before him.

Ex. Assistant Chief Constable A.H. Carter, M.B.E., died in Cheltenham, on the 12th November, 1973, aged 78 years.

In connection with the new system of Probationer Training, Tutor Constables' Courses were held at the Training Department, Police Headquarters, Cheltenham, for selected Constables who were to be responsible for the initial training on the Beat of the Recruits. 37 Officers attended these Courses during 1973 and their training was put to practical use with the Recruits who had returned from the Training School during the year.

At the beginning of the year approximately two thirds of the Force, in the rank of Inspector, Sergeant and Constable, received training in Crowd Control based on the Unit Formations recommended and used by the Metropolitan Police.

It was early in 1973 that steps were taken to arrange re-qualification Courses for those members of the Force whose First Aid Awards had lapsed. At this period nine members of the Force were qualified St. John Ambulance Lay Instructors.

The following Driving Courses were attended by motor patrol officers and others during 1973:–

	Standard Courses	*Advanced Courses*	*Advanced Refresher*
Car	85	23	18
Motor Cycle	6	1	–

23,016 '999' calls were received by Police in the year 1973, as opposed to 21,368 in 1972. A very large proportion of these calls were in connection with road traffic accidents and other similar emergency situations and the

Chief Constable appealed to members of the public to make the maximum use of the system by using it to assist police in the fight against crime.

A few more Pocket phones had been obtained for Gloucester and Cheltenham schemes by 1973 but the 3-Channel sets, promised for Gloucester, had not materialised despite funds having been made available for replacement of all the Pocket phones in Gloucester by the new 3-Channel sets, should they have been available.

A new Telex machine was installed in the Information Room at Police Headquarters to cope with the increased traffic mainly generated by the MOTAX system.

Work was also in progress with a view to the transference of all personnel records on to the Local Authority Computer and it was anticipated that the programming would commence in June 1975. The provision of a Terminal at Headquarters Information Room had to be deferred due to financial restrictions.

The maximum rent allowance was revised during 1973, to the following rates:–

Constables Sergeants Inspectors	£10.00p. weekly
Superintendents	£10.50p. weekly

This rate of Rent Allowance was in agreement with the Police Council of the United Kingdom whereby the differentials paid to Sergeants and Constables were discontinued.

With full-time Drug Squads operating throughout the County, for the whole of 1973, it was no surprise to find that the number of offences involving drugs rose from 144 in 1972 to 169 in 1973.

Cannabis was again the main drug involved, featuring in about 90% of the cases. Offenders under 18 years of age totalled 19 in 1973 compared with 9 in 1972.

In order to avoid the necessity of making further adjustments on 1st April, 1974, when the new Avon Authority was due to come into effect the Wotton-under-Edge Police Section, with the exception of the Charfield Sub-section, was transferred from Southern Division to the Dursley Sub-Division of Eastern Division. This affected one Sergeant and three Constables.[10]

To conform more closely with Petty Sessional boundaries, the Newent Police Section was transferred from Northern to Western Division. This involved one Sergeant and six Constables. For the same reason, the

Tetbury Section comprising one Sergeant and four Constables was transferred from the Dursley Sub-Division to the Cirencester Sub-Division.

The old blue/white Warrant Card was replaced during 1973, by a laminated card in plastic which had a photograph of the holder.

A new machine, the 'Keystone' was taken into use at Police Headquarters for testing eyesight of serving officers, especially those on motor patrol. Whenever the machine showed up a defect the officer concerned was sent immediately to a qualified optician.

Following upon representations made by the Chief Constable and resultant discussions with all parties concerned, the County Council decided on the 7th November, 1973, to approve the establishment of a separate Police Prosecutions Department at Police Headquarters, Cheltenham. Details of the proposals were set out in a Joint Report by the Chief Constable and the County Clerk which was considered by the Police Authority on the 10th September, 1973. The original proposals set out in the Report were the subject of a further detailed study with the County Council Personnel Officer and two posts were omitted from the revised establishment. The following establishment was therefore approved for the Department which operated from 1st April, 1974:–

1 Chief Prosecuting Solicitor
1 Senior Assistant Prosecuting Solicitor
2 Assistant Prosecuting Solicitors
1 Managing Clerk
1 Liaison Clerk (for Crown Courts)
1 Assistant Clerk

The objectives of the Department would be to advise the Police on prosecutions and procedure and to take Police prosecutions in Petty Sessional and Crown Courts, although there might well remain some occasions when recourse to Solicitors in private practice would be necessary. Members of the Department would be employed by the Police Authority under the general oversight of the Chief Constable, and under the Clerk of the Police Authority for professional, pay and conditions of service purposes.[11]

A study was to be undertaken towards the end of 1974 of the service provided by the Department and the adequacy of the establishment.

1974 was a year of many changes within the County and the Constabulary. However, the year started well for the Force as Her Majesty the Queen was graciously pleased to appoint Mr H.D.J.

Smith, Q.P.M., lately Deputy Chief Constable, as a Member of the Order of the British Empire in the New Year's Honours List for 1974, an award which was well deserved and brought great pleasure to the Gloucestershire Constabulary.

On the 1st April, 1974, Local Government re-organisation saw a change in the size and establishment of the Force. This affected many Police Forces, with Gloucestershire losing the Southern Division (Bristol suburbs etc.), and some 340 officers to the newly formed Avon and Somerset Constabulary.[12]

It was, therefore, sad to have to say farewell during 1974 to a large part of the Gloucestershire Force who had served the County so well, at the same time it was good to know that the fine reputation built up by the Police in the Southern Division would go with them into their new Force.

On 1st April, 1974 the authorised strength of Regular Cadets was reduced by 10, due to the take over of Southern Division. By the end of the year the actual strength was:–

	Authorised	Actual
Male	50	30
Female	15	17

The Annual Inspection of the Combined Regular and Volunteer Cadet Corps was held at the Royal Air Force Station, Innsworth, on Saturday, 15th June, 1974, when the Inspecting Officer was Wing Commander C.G.H. Pierce, Commanding Officer of R.A.F. Innsworth. Wing Commander Pierce was, for a number of years, actively involved with young people when serving as A.D.C. to the Commandant of the Royal Air Force Technical College, and also as Flight Commander of an Officers' Training Unit.

The strength of the Volunteer Cadet Units at the 31st December, 1974, was as follows:–

Northern Division	14
Eastern Division	14
Western Division	12
Total	40

1974 saw a decrease in the strength of the Special Constabulary by 145 members, of this number 130 were members of Southern Division which became part of the Avon and Somerset Constabulary and accounted for the large reduction in actual strength. However, recruiting figures were encouraging. The Special Constabulary continued to give great assistance to the Regular Force at holiday times and on occasions of Fetes, Football Matches, Carnivals, etc., held during the year.

On Sunday, 31st March, 1974, a Stand-down Parade was held at Gloucester to commemorate the departure of Southern Division Special Constabulary. The Inspection and address was carried out by His Grace the Duke of Beaufort, K.G., P.C., G.C.V.O.

The Annual Inspection of the Force took place on 7th, 25th, 28th and 29th March, 1974, when Her Majesty's Inspector of Constabulary, N. Galbraith, Esq., C.B.E., Q.P.M., D.L., visited Headquarters and Northern, Eastern and Western Divisions.

Two Visual Display Units and a Data-printer were fitted in the Information Room during 1974, giving direct access to the Police National Computer at Hendon. By the end of the year a vehicle index only had been made available but the Force realised the potential of such an index as some 3,000 checks per week were being made via Headquarters terminals with some extremely useful results. Generally, checks were resulting in more arrests for vehicle thefts and general crime and a far quicker return of vehicles to owners who had been so unfortunate as to have had them stolen.

The vehicles owners index had made a slow start, but by the end of the year it was possible to obtain vehicle owners' names and addresses, on a limited scale, within seconds. It was anticipated that all vehicle owners would be recorded in the near future.

The official opening of the new Magistrates' Court and Divisional Police Headquarters at Stroud, was carried out by Sir Geoffrey Shakerley, C.B.E., M.C., T.D., former Chairman of the Gloucestershire Police Committee, on 10th January, 1974. A new Police Office at Newent was completed and taken into use in November of that year, the old Police Station being disposed of.

The means of access for disabled persons to Divisional and Sub-Divisional Headquarters was improved during the year by the provision of ramps.

With effect from 1st April, 1974, the maximum limit rent allowance was for Constables, Sergeants and Inspectors – £13.04 per week. Superintendents and Chief Superintendents – £13.54p. per week.

Despite a busy year in the field of welfare, the Force Welfare Officer, Sergeant R.E. Spencer, G.M., arranged a course of one week's duration in October, for officers contemplating retirement. 14 officers attended and were given the opportunity to discuss with others, and receive expert advice, on the many problems which could arise at this important time in one's life. These courses were very much appreciated by the officers attending.

On the 15th September, 1974, Chief Superintendent R.F. Mayo, Gloucester, retired on pension. He was one of the tallest officers to serve in the Force and was a great sportsman.

As the result of actuarial and legal advice obtained, the Gloucestershire Constabulary Provident Fund was wound up on 1st January, 1974, and the assets were incorporated into the Benevolent Fund. The rules of the latter fund were re-drafted to protect the rights of existing beneficiaries of the Provident Fund, and it was hoped that the wider discretion provided by the new fund would ensure that additional financial assistance would be provided to those who really needed it. By 1985 this assumption proved to be correct.[13]

By the end of 1974, there were 153 widows of ex-members of the Force and 12 children who were receiving benefits.

The Fund mainly derives its income from regular contributions from serving officers and pensioners, but also from donations from members of the public and an annual grant from the National Police Fund.

The Benevolent and Provident Funds were founded in the Gloucestershire Constabulary in 1923 with the proceeds from the Annual Sports Meetings held in Cheltenham and Gloucester. In the early days, the Provident Fund paid 5/–d. per week to widows and 2/6d. per week to fatherless children. Over the years these figures have been greatly increased but, probably, have barely kept up with inflation.

Under Section 220(4) of the Local Government Act, 1972, the County Council were required to consider the division of the new County into Coroners' Districts and appoint new Coroners by 1st April, 1974.

This was done and on the due date two such Districts were established:–

The West Gloucestershire District – H.M. Coroner for the area being R. Jessop, Esq., Gloucester.

The East Gloucestershire District – H.M. Coroner for the area being K.O. Brooks, Esq., Cheltenham.

With effect from 1st April, 1974, the duties and functions of the County Council in respect of the Diseases of Animals Acts and any Orders made thereunder which up to that time had been carried out by the Gloucestershire Constabulary, were transferred to officers of the Environmental Health Unit of the Council. However, in cases of emergency, i.e. confirmed outbreaks of disease in the County, inclusion in Controlled Areas, etc., certain Police Stations could be used by the

Unit for the issuing of movement licences. For this purpose alone, Police Officers in charge of rural Police Stations were authorised to act as Inspectors under the Diseases of Animals Act, subject to the control of the County Environmental Health Officer as Chief Inspector after consultation with the Chief Constable.

None of the foregoing in any way detracted the general powers of the Police to execute and enforce the Act and every Order made thereunder, given in Section 71 of the Diseases of Animals Act, 1950.

Paragraph 19 of Schedule 29 to the Local Government Act, 1972, in conjunction with Sections 179 and 251 of that Act, had the effect of transferring to the new County Councils the local authority functions under the Explosives Acts, 1875 and 1923, with effect from 1st April, 1974. The principal local authority functions under the Acts was to exercise control over the keeping of all explosives, except storages in magazines (which are controlled directly by the Secretary of State), and to enforce the 1875 Act in its application to the conveyance of explosives.

These functions were taken over by the Trading Standards Department of the County Council, and the two main ones to be transferred from Justices of the Peace were:–

the licensing of Explosive Stores, and

the registration of premises for the keeping of explosives.

The Police responsibility of issuing certificates to persons wishing to acquire explosives remained the same and this, in the main, applied to:–

occupiers of licensed Stores;

occupiers of Registered Premises;

Private Use and Immediate Use Certificates; and use of gunpowder and safety fuse under the Control of Explosives Order, 1953.

Full liaison was established and has been maintained between Officers of the Trading Standards Department dealing with explosives and Police Crime Prevention officers in the matter of security of premises.

In a letter dated February, 1974, the Secretary of State approved the Authorised Establishment of the Force, to be effective from 1st April, 1974. Because of Local Government Reorganisation, the whole of the Southern Police Division, comprising an establishment of 340 personnel, was transferred to the new Avon and Somerset Constabulary, resulting in the Authorised Establishment and the actual strength of the Force on 31st December, 1974, being:–

	ESTABLISHMENT		ACTUAL STRENGTH	
	Men	Women	Men	Women
Chief Constable	1		1	
Deputy Chief Constable	1		1	
Assistant Chief Constable	1		1	
Chief Superintendents	6		6	
Superintendents	12	1	12	1
Chief Inspectors	17		17	
Inspectors	50	2	48	1
Sergeants	153	6	152	2
Constables	715	42	679*	36*
Totals	956	51	917	40

* Includes 24 men recruits and 3 women recruits in training.

The actual strength did not include the following officers who were on secondment:–

Regional Crime Squad
1 Chief Superintendent
1 Inspector
4 Sergeants
4 Constables
South West Forensic Science Laboratory, Bristol
1 Chief Inspector
Regional Police Training Centre, Chantmarle
1 Sergeant
Illegal Immigration Intelligence Unit, New Scotland Yard
1 Sergeant
Studying at Reading University
1 Inspector
Studying at Inns of Court, London
1 Sergeant

Details of the Authorised and Actual Establishment of the Special Constabulary at 31st December, 1974, was as follows:–

	Authorised Establishment	*Actual Strength*
Northern Division	300	156

Eastern Division	233	156
Western Division	335	162
Total	868	474*

* Included 24 Women

By 1974 the total Authorised Establishment of Traffic Wardens, after the transfer of Southern Division to the Avon and Somerset Constabulary, was as follows:–

Northern Division	Cheltenham	19
	Tewkesbury	2
Eastern Division	Stroud	3
	Dursley	2
	Cirencester	2
Western Division	Gloucester	22
		50

The actual strength of Traffic Wardens at 31st December, 1974 was 16 men and 34 women.

On 31st December, 1974, 3,778 Firearms Certificates relating to 6,277 weapons were in force in the County. During the year a total of 319 new Certificates were issued, and 949 Certificates renewed. 36 Firearms Dealers' Certificates were also renewed, and 3 new ones were issued. Of the 319 new Certificates issued, 44 related to pistols, 11 to revolvers and 6 to pistols and revolvers and 50 of these applicants required ammunition.

In connection with applications for Firearms Certificates 5 persons were refused. One Firearms' Dealers' Certificate was revoked during the year.

On 1st April, 1974, a total of 776 files relating to Firearms Certificates were transferred to the Avon and Somerset Constabulary.

During the year, 1,309 new Certificates for Shotguns were issued, and 3,803 were renewed. Five Certificates were revoked and a further five refused. By 31st December, 1974, a total of 16,788 Certificates, in respect of Shotguns, were current in the County.

With the transfer of the Southern Division of the Force on 1st April, 1974, the establishment of civilian staff was reduced by 86 personnel. Some minor re-grading took place during the year and at 31st December, 1974, the Establishment was as follows:–

CLERICAL	Senior Officer Grade 1/2	1

	A.P. Grade 4	2	
	A.P. Grade 3	3	
	Clerical Grade 3	2	
	Clerical Grade 2	5	
	Clerical 1 (NRB)	22	
	Clerical 1 (RB)	29	
	Senior Scale 3	11	
	Senior Scale 1	7	
	Typists	25	
			107
TELEPHONISTS			9
TECHNICAL	Technical 3	1	
	Technical 2	2	
	Technical 1 (NB)	2	
	Technical 1 (B)	1	
			6
MISCELLANEOUS	Miscellaneous 5/6	1	
	Miscellaneous 5	1	
	Miscellaneous 4/5	1	
	Miscellaneous 4	18	
	Miscellaneous 3	2	
	Miscellaneous 2/3	1	
	Miscellaneous 1	1	
			25
VEHICLE MAINTENANCE			16
CANTEEN STAFF			21
HOSTEL WARDENS			2
CAR WASHERS			6
DRIVER/HANDYMAN			1
HANDYMEN			7
			200
FULL AND PART-TIME CLEANERS			96
	Total		296

On 31st December, 1974, the actual strength of civilians was 281.

Examination results in Police Subjects

	November, 1974 (To Sergeant)		*January, 1975* (To Inspector)	
	Number Sitting	Number Passed	Number Sitting	Number Passed
Sergeants	–	–	21	4
Constables	157	12	29	5

On 31st December, 1975, 70 Sergeants and 171 Constables were qualified by examination for promotion to the next higher rank. 55 of the 171 Constables had also passed the qualifying examination to the rank of Inspector.

Detective Chief Superintendent Kenneth F. Clark, who was still seconded to the Regional Crime Squad, had to retire on ill-health pension early in 1975. He retired to North Wales where he was able to contine his writing of plays, etc., under the nom de plume of 'Basset'. He died on the 13th September, 1982, after a heart attack.

With effect from 27th June, 1975, the minimum age for joining the Police was lowered to 18½ years.

In order to increase the effectiveness of Police activity in the Gloucester Sub-Division, the unit beat policing system there was substantially modified with effect from 17th February, 1975. That part of the Sub-Division affected was divided into five sections each consisting of several beat areas, and particular Sergeants had responsibility for them.

Each Section was policed throughout the whole 24 hour period each day by a Panda vehicle, and also had its own complement of detective officers and area beat constables. A probationer constable was also attached to each section for short periods as part of the officers' training.

The remainder of uniform patrol personnel were based at the Central Police Station so as to provide additional foot patrol cover in the City Centre and to supplement sectional patrol strength if and when required. This scheme, in the main, followed the pattern of that which had been operating successfully in the Cheltenham Sub-Division for a number of years.

After a little over 12 years as Chief Constable of Gloucestershire, Mr E.P.B. White, O.B.E., Q.P.M., retired on pension on the 30th June, 1975, and went to live at Yarmouth on the Isle of Wight.

During his service with the Gloucestershire Force Mr White rendered valuable support to the County with his wise and efficient management.

First Fraud Squad.

Senior Officers 1976.

Dog Section 1977.

Bamfurlong Motor Patrol Centre. 1978

First Aid Winners 1978–79.

Combined Cadet Inspection June 1979 – Mr. COPPIN, D.C.C.

Presentation to Miss BLAGG by C.C. WEIGH.

Visit of Mayors of Tewkesbury, Cheltenham, and Gloucester to Police Headquarters. 1978

CHAPTER 10

Brian Weigh, Q.P.M.
1.7.1975 – 31.8.1979

Mr Brian Weigh, Deputy Chief Constable of the Avon and Somerset Constabulary, was appointed Chief Constable of Gloucestershire to succeed Mr E.P.B. White, and took up his duties, at Police Headquarters, Cheltenham on 1st July, 1975.

In common with all local government organisations, the Force found 1975 to be a difficult and challenging year, in which it had been necessary to examine closely many of their activities in terms of their efficiency and cost effectiveness.

The Force was still deficient in manpower, but during the year there had been a steady increase in strength. 60 officers had been recruited during the year, 19 of which had been accepted between the age of 18½ and 19 years.

As a result of the Sex Discrimination Act, 1975, the Secretary of State in a letter dated 30th December, 1975, directed that authorised establishments should cease to provide separately for men and women police officers and new establishments would be authorised showing for each rank the total of the male and female posts for that rank in the existing establishment approved by the Secretary of State for the Gloucestershire Constabulary became as follows:–[1]

	1	Chief Constable
	2	Assistant Chief Constable
	6	Chief Superintendents
	13	Superintendents
	17	Chief Inspectors
	54	Inspectors
	174	Sergeants
	834	Constables
Total	1,101	

During 1975, 16 officers were commended for outstanding work and letters of appreciation were received from Chief Constables of other Forces, Courts and members of the public in respect of the actions of 468 officers.

Police Constable William C. Thomas, who had served for 15 years as a Dog handler, retired from the Force on 31st July, 1975. His dog 'King' retired at the same time, and was retained by his master. P.C. Thomas was one of the original Dog Handlers when the Dog Section was formed by Mr Gaskain in 1960.

The Under Water Recovery Section was kept busy during the year and, amongst other duties, carried out eleven elimination searches; mostly involving searches for missing persons who might have drowned, and where there was a possibility that property might be located in the water. This type of work is usually protracted because of the need to ensure that an area is clear. In one instance many hours were spent searching for the driver of a car which had been driven into a canal. The Sergeant of the Section was able to establish that there was no body in the water. The male driver of the car was subsequently traced to another part of the country and charged with an offence.

In another incident a child was believed trapped in a partially flooded under-ground pipe. After all attempts to establish whether or not there was a child in the pipe failed, Constable Sandell volunteered to crawl through the pipe, which only measured approximately ¾ of a metre in diameter. This he succeeded in doing for a length of 18 metres and confirmed that it was clear. On this occasion the officer was commended for his action.

Her Majesty's Inspector of Constabulary, N. Galbraith, Esq., C.B.E., Q.P.M., D.L., carried out his Annual Inspection of the Force on the 25th and 26th November and 2nd and 3rd December, 1975. He visited Headquarters and Stations in each of the three operational Divisions.

Ex. Superintendent Frederick J. Williams died at Stroud on the 20th October, 1975. At the time of his retirement he was Commander of the old Stroud Division.

Detective Sergeant Richings of Cheltenham and Police Constable Farmer of Gloucester retained their positions with the Gloucestershire Branch of the Royal Life Saving Society, namely those of Chairman and Secretary respectively. The Chief Constable, Mr. Weigh, had been Chairman of the Western Region of the Royal Life Saving Society.

During the year a new radio mast was erected on the roof of Police Headquarters, Holland House, Cheltenham, and immediately brought into use. This replaced the original mast which stood on ground adjoining the Dean Close School Playing field and which was later dismantled.

At the end of the year – 1975 – 510 officers were owner/occupiers of their own houses, compared with 447 on 31st December, 1974. As a result a number of Police Authority houses were empty and eight of these were sold during the year; two to Police Officers, five transferred to County Council Departments or District Councils and one on the open market.

On 31st December, 1975, 388 Officers occupied Police houses. This compared with 419 in 1974.

The policy of providing police houses with night storage heaters was continued on a moderate scale.

The Secretary of State, in a letter dated 15th September, 1975, gave approval to a new maximum limit rent allowance with effect from 1st April, 1975, as follows:–

Constables, Sergeants, Inspectors	£13.77p per week
Superintendents, Chief Superintendents	£15.27p per week

The rent allowance actually paid to an individual was, in fact, the value of his/her house in rent, assessed by the District Valuer, plus rates, but subject to the above maxima.

In August, 1975, a scheme was introduced by the Chief Constable whereby any member of the Force, whether Police of civilian, could make constructive suggestions or put forward ideas as to the ways and means in which efficiency could be maintained or improved.

Each suggestion was evaluated by the Organisation and Planning Department at Police Headquarters and then considered by the Chief Constable. The outcome of all items were published from time to time in Force Orders.

During 1975 a total of 121 persons were arrested in the County for drug offences, of these 26 were in Northern Division, 37 in Eastern Division and 58 in Western Division. This was an increase of 13 persons on the figures for 1974.

For the purposes of obtaining drugs, burglaries were committed on 7 chemists' shops, 7 doctors' surgeries and 1 veterinary surgery. There was also one case of drugs being stolen from a doctor's motor car. These figures show an increase compared with 1974 when a total of only 4 offences of a similar nature were committed.

Approximately 68% of all cases involved the use of Cannabis. There were 11 cases involving L.S.D. and 6 cases of cultivating the Cannabis Plant.

During the year, there was a noticeable increase in the abuse of amphetamine sulphate (a powdered substance which is normally mixed with water and injected into the arm). Eight arrests were in respect of this type of drug. It would appear that amphetamine sulphate attracts the same users as those who use Cannabis.

	Head-quarters	*Northern Division*	*Eastern Division*	*Western Division*		
				Gloucester	*Lydney*	*Total*
Chief Superintendents	1	–	–	–	–	1
Superintendents	2	–	–	–	–	2
Chief Inspectors	1	–	–	–	–	1
Inspectors	6	1	1	1	–	9
Sergeants	1	5	5	4	2	17
Constables	11	30	33	48	14	136
						166

The above figures show the Authorised Establishment of the Traffic Department in the County as at 31st December, 1975.

Like every other Police Force in the country, Gloucestershire found that 1976 was a year of economy, when the measures taken by both national and local government to reduce public spending had their effect on every station and department.

The Chief Constable reported that the resultant difficulties had been accepted, 'by all my officers in an excellent spirit and met with a determination to use manpower and equipment as efficiently as possible in order to maintain a high level of public service'.

In his Annual Report to the Police Committee for 1976, the Chief Constable stated, 'Once again, we have enjoyed considerable help from the public in our operations and for this I am grateful'.

A measure of this support was the fact that during the year no less than 779 persons were arrested as a direct result of '999' calls from the public. Many letters of appreciation, expressing gratitude for police help and assistance to members of the public in times of difficulty and trouble, were received, and from this it seems clear that both police and public were playing a full part in the essential matter of co-operation.

There were many changes in personnel during the year and this, together with a steady rate of recruitment, meant that the Force had become progressively younger, particularly at the operational beat level.

1976 saw quite an exodus of Senior Officers and the following retired on pension during the year:–

Chief Superintendent Douglas G. Baker
Chief Superintendent William G. Turner
Chief Superintendent Henry C.S. Lodge
Chief Superintendent Arther S. Meadows

Superintendent Victor J. Bullock
Superintendent Ronald H. Smith
Woman Superintendent Elizabeth B. Hughes.

All the above vacancies were filled by promotions within the Force with the exception of the vacancy caused by the retirement of Woman Superintendent Elizabeth B. Hughes. This vacancy was filled by the transfer of Marion A. Chandler from the Kent Constabulary on the 1st November, 1976.

In a letter dated 18th May, 1976, the Secretary of State approved a reduction of one Sergeant in the authorised establishment of the Force to allow for the appointment of a civilian Force Welfare Officer. Police Sergeant Ronald E. Spencer, G.M., was appointed to this post after his retirement from the Force on pension. Ron. Spencer was the ideal Welfare Officer and over the years became well known throughout the Force and by all Police Pensioners and Police Widows residing within the County.

The Annual Inspection of the Combined Regular and Volunteer Cadet Corps was held at the Royal Air Force Station, Innsworth, on Saturday, 5th June, 1976, when the Inspecting Officer was Her Majesty's Inspector of Constabulary, Mr N. Galbraith, C.B.E., Q.P.M., D.L.

This was the first year that females were allowed to join the Volunteer Cadet Corps and Eastern Division, by the end of the year, had enrolled three on their strength.

In addition to the appointment of a civilian Force Welfare Officer, the Secretary of State approved the appointment of an Assistant Crown Court Liaison Officer in the Prosecutions Department. As a result, the actual strength of civilians on 31st December, 1976 was 279.

During the year 1976 the Dog Section received 668 calls for assistance. This compares with 648 in 1975. 90 arrests were made for crime (46 in 1975), 7 for miscellaneous offences (18 in 1975), 6 absconders (2 in 1975) were apprehended and 8 persons (4 in 1975) missing from home were found and returned to their homes. During the year the Section also assisted in the arrest of 48 other offenders, and recovered stolen property on 26 occasions.

The Underwater Recovery Section was called to two accidental drownings during the year; and in both cases the bodies were located and recovered. 14 other calls were received asking for assistance and property recovered on these occasions varied from safes and electric tills to motor vehicles and jewellery.

By the end of 1976 the underwater section had carried out 265 operations since it was formed in 1966. It is interesting to note that the Officer in Charge of the Section, Police Sergeant Clive Jefferies, had attended no fewer than 257 of these operations.

Her Majesty's Inspector of Constabulary, J.W.D. Crane, Esq., carried out his Annual Inspection of the Force on 21st, 23rd, 28th and 29th September, 1976. He visited Headquarters and stations in each of the three operational Divisions.

209 officers attended a one day course in crowd control techniques which was held at the Army Apprentices Training College, Beachley.

During the year 53 officers took re-qualification courses in First Aid. The Western Division First Aid Team comprising P.C. Williams (Captain), P.C. Christopher, P.C. James, P.C. Manton and P.C. Millin had a successful year winning both the Gloucester Shield First Aid Competition and the Lewis Bowl/Erskine Trophy County Competition. This team also represented the County in the Three Counties Competition held at Gloucester in October and received the Worcestershire Trophy as runners-up to the West Mercia Constabulary team.

The excellent facilities offered by ATV and HTV for Police Five programmes were used extensively during 1976 and 39 items were submitted to ATV and 12 to HTV, a total of 51. The programmes stimulated public interest and awareness and many crimes were cleared up as a result of this valuable means of publicity.

In November, 1976, the first Crime Prevention Panel in Gloucestershire was formed at Cheltenham and its initial task was to consider measures to assist the elderly against criminal exploitation. Crime Prevention officers at Headquarters and in Divisions continued to assist Industry with security training. The Department arranged three Seminars in the Force area, covering bomb incident and terrorist activity and the problems of cash in transit

During 1976 there were 1832 arrests made by the crews of police vehicles, compared with 2078 in 1975.

The Accident Prevention Department was kept busy during the year and the Force Display Caravan was used to great advantage at shows and in town centres, etc. A total of 21 exhibitions were put on to an estimated audience of 150,000 people, a considerable increase over 1975. Many of these were operated in conjunction with the County Surveyor's Road Safety Department and proved most successful.

During the latter part of the year, 2 new Radio masts were erected at the Cleeve Hill site, and taken into use, to replace the then existing masts, erected early in 1977. Progress was well advanced to erect a new replacement mast at Edge Hills, and a further replacement mast at Dursley was planned for the future.

The 3 Force terminals giving access to the Police National Computer (2 Visual Display Units and 1 Data Printer) provided useful aid to efficiency during 1976.

180,330 checks were made on motor vehicles which resulted in the following number of 'traces':–

34,055 owners and
3,171 stolen/suspect vehicles.

During October/November, 1976, the necessary GPO and electrical wiring was installed for a third Visual Display Unit. The Unit to be installed and operational by July, 1977, when it was anticipated that the Criminal Names Index, which was the next step in the Police National Computer Programme, would become available.

During the year the original but now redundant radio mast at Police Headquarters, Cheltenham, was dismantled. This mast was replaced in 1975.

322 males and 24 females were proceeded against for drunkenness during 1976. This was an increase of 28 persons compared with the previous year.

1976 saw a total of 116 persons arrested in the County for drug offences, of these 46 were in Northern Division, 25 in Eastern Division and 45 in Western Division. This was a decrease of 5 persons on the figures for 1975.

For the purpose of obtaining drugs, burglaries were committed on 12 chemists' shops, 3 doctors' surgeries and a hospital pharmacy. Compared with 1975 this was an increase in the burglaries at chemists' shops but a reduction at doctors' surgeries, when a total of 7 chemists' shops and 7 doctors' surgeries were attacked.

Approximately 78% of all cases involved the use of cannabis, compared with 68% for 1975. There were 12 cases involving LSD and 13 cases of cultivating the cannabis plant compared with 11 cases and 6 cases respectively for similar offences the previous year.

During the year 30 search warrants issued in pursuance of the Misuse of Drugs Act, 1971, were executed.

There were two significant seizures of large quantities of drugs in the County during 1976, the drugs being cannabis resin and hash oil. A number of arrests were made which indicated the excellent co-operation between Customs and Excise Officers, Crime Squad and Drug Squad Officers within the Force.

On the 31st December, 1976, 3,747 Firearm Certificates relating to 6,112 weapons were in force in the County. Shotgun Certificates, for the same period, totalled 19,147.

In his Annual Report to the Police Committee the Chief Constable said that he had received details of over 46 members of the Force who were whole-heartedly involved in youth and social work in their own time. Some of these officers were instructors in Cadet Corps, Scouts, Guides, Boy's Brigades and Cubs, Church Clubs and many other organisations.

In addition some 20 officers, in their own time, were driving vehicles for elderly and handicapped persons on evening visits, outings etc. This involvement with the community was, of course, of immense value to public relations.

The fee payable to a member of the public who assisted in identity parades was 25p. As it was becoming increasingly difficult to obtain the services of the public for this purpose, the Chief Constable recommended to the Police Authority on the 14th February, 1977, that the fees be increased. The Association of Chief Police Officers considered this matter back in 1975 and suggested that the fee should be £1 and, in addition, re-imbursement of reasonable expenses. Many Police Forces had already implemented the suggestion and the Chief Constable asked the Committee to approve his recommendation that the fee be increased to £1, with effect from 1st March, 1977.

Amongst the vehicle replacements for 1977/78 were 4 Traffic Motor Cycles and 12 Beat motor cycles but, in his report, the Chief Constable stated that the Traffic Motor Cycle replacements would, of necessity, be B.M.W.'s, since no suitable British machine was available. He was still awaiting specification and prices for a locally produced light-weight machine and, at that time, had not been offered a model for evaluation. Information he had received suggested that the price would be considerably more than that of the light-weight Honda 200 which was proving a satisfactory replacement for the obsolete B.S.A. 250.

On the 21st June and 24th June, 1977, a number of Police Committee Members visited Police Headquarters and Cheltenham Divisional Headquarters, when they were able to meet Divisional Chief Superintendents, members of the staff and visit various Departments.

Superintendent D. Holland, stationed at Police Headquarters, Cheltenham, was awarded a Travel Scholarship of £250 by the International Police Association, to examine the Complaints and Police Disciplinary

Procedures in Sweden. Superintendent Holland was allowed paid leave of absence for 21 days, commencing 20th August, 1977.

Her Majesty the Queen was graciously pleased to award 47 Silver Jubilee Medals to the Force during 1977. The recipients were 40 Regular Officers, 3 Special Constables and 4 members of the Civilian Staff, all of whom had given service in excess of 25 years.

In accordance with Force policy, officers were allowed to carry out certain internal re-decorations of County-owned houses which they occupied. There was an annual review of the allowance and on the 12th September, 1977, the Police Committee agreed that the following figures should apply, as from 1st April, 1978:–

Bedrooms and Living Rooms	£22.50 each
Larger than normal size rooms	£26.25 each
Combined lounge/living rooms	£37.25 each
Kitchen and Bathrooms	£15.00 each

The Annual Inspection of the Combined Regular and Volunteer Cadet Corps was held at the Royal Air Force Station, Innsworth, on Saturday, 4th June, 1977, when the Inspecting Officer was Lieutenant Colonel W.A. McLelland, TD., the Chairman of Gloucestershire County Council.

Various Divisional activities had taken place during the year and the Regular and Volunteer Cadets held a combined expedition to Snowdonia in March.

The strength of the Volunteer Cadet Corps at 31st December, 1977, was as follows:–

	MALE	FEMALE
NORTHERN DIVISION	20	10
EASTERN DIVISION	9	6
WESTERN DIVISION	14	6
	43	22
		Total 65

A combined parade for Special Constables from all three Divisions was held at Gloucester in May, to mark the Queen's Jubilee Year. The Inspecting Officer was Her Majesty's Inspector of Constabulary, Mr J.W.D. Crane, C.B.E.

The Queen's Jubilee Medal was presented to:–

Special Superintendent	R.A. WILLIAMS
Special Chief Inspector	H.G. NELMES
Special Constable	E.V.A. PINCHIN

During January 3 women police constables were given a 1-week basic Firearms Course, and continued training with the Squads.

Various lectures on the safe-handling of firearms continued to be given to recruits and other members of the Force.

On the 29th September, 1977, Inspector J.A. Cratchley, Staff Officer to the Chief Constable, was admitted as a Serving Brother in the Order of St. John of Jerusalem.

The actual strength of the C.I.D, throughout the Force, as at 31st December, 1977, was:–

Detective Chief Superintendent		1
Detective Superintendent		1
Detective Chief Inspectors		3
Detective Inspectors		9
Detective Sergeants		36
Detective Constables		71
Acting Detective Constables		19
	Total	140

Figures include 13 officers on Scenes of Crime duties and 7 for Drugs and Anti-Vice; also 2 Ports Officers.

There was an increase in the number of offenders appearing before courts within the Force area for offences involving the misuse of drugs during 1977. 135 offenders were convicted of a total of 254 offences compared with 116 offenders convicted in 1976. 3 persons were cautioned for drug offences during the year. This compares with 7 in 1976.

Cannabis was the most abused drug as the following tables shows:–

DRUG	OFFENCES
Opiates and Cocaine	23
Cannabis	144
LSD	3
Amphetamines	11
Mandrax	1

The effectiveness of the Drug Squad and an indication of the high level of co-operation with other Departments was illustrated by the successful detection of a number of offences involving large quantities of drugs. For example, in one case during the year, cannabis resin to the value of £250,000 was recovered and the offenders brought to justice.[2]

Stop searches for drugs and warrants executed during 1977, were:–

Number of persons stopped and searched	134
Number of persons stopped and searched and found to be in possession of controlled drugs	40
Number of formal complaints arising from stop checks	NIL
Number of Search Warrants executed	43

Following the sinking of a cabin cruiser in the River Thames at Lechlade, as the result of an explosion and fire, the Underwater Recovery Unit was called to assist in the recovery of valuable property aboard the vessel which included items of gold and cash. The divers, who worked in unpleasant conditions of oil and burnt wreckage were able to recover all the missing property.

During the latter part of 1977 the Fire Service strike made it necessary to have Units of the Task Force readily available to assist in the event of a major fire. Fortunately they were not required to attend a major incident but one Unit was called upon to assist in releasing a badly injured and trapped person at the scene of a road traffic accident.

The Task Force was fully involved during the year and proved to be a valuable asset to the Force.

In September, 1977, a combined '999' event was staged at Staverton Airport which involved co-operation between the Police, Ambulance and the Army Fire Service. As part of this event, the Police tested during the day 52 Ambulance Drivers from a total of 25 Area Health Authorities over a difficult route of 13 miles. At the end of the day the driver of the year was presented with his trophy by the Assistant Chief Constable.

A replacement tower (Radio) was erected during the year at Edge Hills, Cinderford. It was hoped to replace the radio tower at Dursley early in 1979 and this would complete the tower replacement programme.

Between May and December, 1977, 16 Vehicles including dog vans, Task Force transport and outlying Section Sergeants' vehicles were fitted with radio equipment which allowed officers to leave their vehicles but remain in contact with control by means of a personal radio. This equipment proved a great success, assisting in providing permanent contact with the officer and enabling observation duties to be more rewarding.

Additional control systems which enabled officers to have direct contact with the Police National Computer Terminal Operator at Police Headquarters, Cheltenham, were provided at Cheltenham, Stow-on-the-

Wold and Lydney. A UHF system was also provided in the Forest of Dean area which linked Cinderford, Lydney and Coleford by personal radio.

There being a need to replace the Force Teleprinter System, the opportunity was taken, during 1977, to install one of the most sophisticated teleprinter switching systems in the country named ('PATBX') – (Private Automatic Telegraph Branch Exchange).

The PATBX system enabled any operator within the system to type messages at up to 66 words a minute to individual Police Stations throughout the County or to broadcast the same messages to all the Stations in one or every Division simultaneously. By typing special codes every sub-Divisional Police Station in Gloucestershire could switch its teleprinter into the main UK telex network with its 65,000 subscribers, and by dialling the appropriate international telex codes, could switch into direct contact with 109 overseas countries.

One of the attractions of PATBX was its flexibility and the numerous facilities that could be provided to suit different subscribers. In the rare event of a fault the apparatus was even able to diagnose trouble and indicate the faulty component. It was the first production line model to go into service.

Building work commenced on the new Motor Patrol Centre at Bamfurlong, near Cheltenham, in March, 1977, and was expected to be completed by October, 1978.

To comply with the Severn–Trent Water Authority's requirements, car washes at Gloucester and Cheltenham were provided with oil interceptors. The same facilities were provided later at Lydney Police Station.

During the year over 100 police-owned properties were provided with loft insulation. In addition, full central heating systems were provided in four police-owned houses.

Nine houses were disposed of during 1977. One was sold to a Police Officer, four were sold on the open market and four transferred to District Councils.

On 31st December, 1977, 367 officers occupied police houses. This compared with 366 in 1976.

Home Office Circular 193/1977 gave approval for an increase in senior officers' rent allowance and established a differential of 16% between maximum limits of rent allowance with effect from 20th September, 1977.

The current maximum limit rent allowance was thus:–

Constables, Sergeants, Inspectors	£16.84p per week
Superintendents, Chief Superintendents	£19.53p per week

Up to now no mention has been made of the Gloucestershire Constabulary Death Levy Fund. This Fund was inaugurated in December, 1960, when officers of all ranks agreed to have the sum of 50p deducted from their salary. The operation of the Fund was vested in the Joint Branch Board of the Police Federation and the money deposited into a Bank Account. Since 1966 the subscription has been increased to £1.

The Rules of the Fund are that following the death of a serving officer the total sum standing in the Bank Account, which normally amounted to approximately £1,100, is paid to the next of kin. In the case of a widow this means an immediate sum of money available for her use.

The Fund receives 100% support from the Force and many other police forces have set up similar funds.[3]

In the New Year Honours for January, 1978, Her Majesty the Queen awarded the British Empire Medal to Detective Constable Donald E. Deakins, formerly stationed at Police Headquarters, Cheltenham. D.C. Deakins retired from the Force on the 31st December, 1977, after 30 years service. His grandfather, Harry Deakins joined the Gloucestershire Constabulary in 1882. His father Enos Deakins joined the force in 1920, and Don himself, joined in 1947. Don's son Ian joined the Force in 1969 thus making the 4th generation to serve in the Gloucestershire Constabulary.

On the 22nd May, 1978, Ex. D.C. Deakins was presented with his British Empire Medal, at the Shire Hall, Gloucester by His Grace the Duke of Beaufort, K.G., P.C., G.C.V.O.

The Chief Constable reported to the Police Committee on 27th February, 1978, that, during the strike by Firemen it was necessary for Police Officers to assist Royal Naval Personnel in their task of fire-fighting throughout the County. With Units of Green Goddesses (Auxiliary Fire Tenders) based at Innsworth, Stroud and South Cerney, escort vehicles were provided and Police involvement was to maintain radio communication and give guidance to the location of fires to Service Personnel who were not familiar with the area. In addition an Emergency Control Room was set up at Force Headquarters to co-ordinate these Units in conjunction with Senior Fire Officer.

To overcome the unnecessary use of Green Goddesses, Police Officers attended reports of fires to confirm that a fire tender was necessary. Because of the limited number of Fire Units available throughout the County arrangements were made for officers in each of the three Divisions to be available as a support force should a fire-fighting unit not be available.

The Chief Constable received many tributes on the way in which the Police carried out their duties during this difficult period.

Phase one of the Motor Patrol Centre at Bamfurlong became operational on the 9th October, 1978, and was formally opened on 15th November, 1978, by H.M. Lord Lieutenant for Gloucestershire, Colonel M. St. J.V. Gibbs, C.B., D.S.O., T.D.

The Edmund-Davies Committee Report was published on the 17th July, 1978, and its recommendations on pay were fully accepted by the Government subject to their being implemented in two equal stages in September, 1978 and September, 1979. The Official side of the Police Council welcomed the recommendations on pay as being substantially in line with their own pay proposals to the Inquiry.

Following the necessary consultations the Home Secretary made Regulations to give effect to the first instalment of the pay increases. The Regulations came into effect on 1st September, 1978, and the new scales represented the mid point between the then present scales and the final scales recommended by the Edmund-Davies Committee. Under the Regulations the scale for a Constable ranged from £3,189 to £4,809 after 15 years.

Apart from the new pay scales the major recommendations of the Committee could be summarised as follows:–

(1) No right to strike to be introduced.
(2) September to be the review date for all the Service; updating of scales every year by reference to the monthly index of average earnings, and additionally for Chief Officers, changes elsewhere in the community.
(3) National rate of pay, except non pensionable £650 London Allowance (exlusive of existing London Weighting) and £500 R.U.C. allowance. Supplementary pay should be consolidated into the basic pay of the Federated Ranks.
(4) Recruits aged 22 or over to start on the third point of the Constable's scale.
(5) No change to existing rent allowance and overtime arrangements.
(6) Pensions from 1st September, 1978 to be based on Lord Edmund-Davies' full pay recommendations: subject to averaging.
(7) Negotiating machinery. A Whitley type system to continue with Police Authorities representatives fully involved as now. An independent Chairman and independent Secretariat to the body as a whole leaving each side to appoint its own Secretary.

As far as the Gloucestershire Police Committee were concerned, the additional Revenue Expenditure in the current year, 1978/79, pursuant to the Regulations was £443,900 and the full year effect, £761,000, in each case subject to the normal 50% Police Grant.

At their meeting on the 11th September, 1978, the Police Committee recommended 'That the County Council approve a Supplementary Revenue estimate of £443,900 gross, £221,950 net, for the financial year 1978/79.'

At the Police Committee Meeting held at Gloucester on Monday, 20th November, 1978, the Chairman, Lt. Col. W.J. Jones, O.B.E., reported that when Her Majesty's Inspector of Constabulary, Mr J.W.D. Crane, C.B.E. had inspected the Force during September, 1978, he himself, the Vice Chairman Councillor Caldicott and other members of the Committee had attended most of the Inspections. He said that he had been very impressed with the professional approach of all the Officers and the standard of maintainence of Police Property although he had been concerned about the age of some of the equipment in use in Police Stations. These views were endorsed by the Vice Chairman and the other members of the Committee who had joined the Inspection.

Chief Superintendent Geoffrey Buffham who joined this Force from the Grimsby Constabulary on the 8th November, 1965, on promotion to the rank of Chief Inspector, retired on pension during April, 1978.

Following the death of P.C. Caroline Symes in June 1977, as a result of a horse riding accident when off duty, her parents asked that contributions in lieu of flowers be sent to Force Headquarters. Over £200 was donated by friends, colleagues, her family and members of the public, and to commemorate their daughter's memory and her service as a Police Officer , Mr & Mrs Symes decided that the money should be used to purchase a Memorial Bowl.

A silver rose bowl bearing the inscription 'Gloucestershire Constabulary Caroline Symes Memorial Bowl 1977 for Public Service' is thus awarded annually to a member of the Constabulary, whether a Police Officer, civilian employee, traffic warden or Cadet, who has made an outstanding contribution to public service during the year. This would include a single act or service over a period, either by an individual or group.

In 1978 the Bowl was awarded to the Cirencester Sub-Division, the Sub-Division in which Caroline was serving at the time of her death, for the exceptional service given by a number of officers in that Sub-Division. This included assistance to the elderly and disabled, involvement with schools, scouts, guides, youth clubs, fund raising for disabled children and welfare organisations, and the welfare of police pensioners.

Included in the number of commendations for the year 1978, were the following officers who were Highly Commended for the actions as detailed:–

Detective Inspector Herbert W. Thomas
Detective Sergeant Robert J. Dangerfield
Acting Detective Constable Roger S. Turley

On the 4th July, 1978, Detective Inspector Thomas was required to tell a man that his presence was required before the Magistrates in a local Juvenile Court. In the normal course of events this was a routine task to be performed. However, the history of previous encounters by persons in authority with this man had resulted in extreme violence on his part. Thus the officer decided to deliver the message himself, and, as a precaution, he took with him his Detective Sergeant Dangerfield and Acting Detective Constable Turley. In the event, the man savagely attacked the officers with a garden fork, causing all three serious injuries.[4]

On 24th October, 1978, he was convicted at Gloucester Crown Court of wounding the officers and was sentenced to 3 years' imprisonment.

Inspector	Clive Fluck
Police Sergeant	Norman W. Hale
Police Sergeant	Ronald Wasley
Detective Constable	Peter Stoneham
Detective Constable	Brian T. Watkins
Police Constable	Geoffrey W. Evans

On the 11th October, 1978, a man in a disturbed state of mind armed himself with a loaded shotgun and, over a period of 7½ hours kept at bay police officers who were trying to effect his arrest. During this time the man fired several shots in the vicinity of the officers.

Nine other officers were Commended in the same incident for the manner in which they carried out their several duties in a calm, dedicated manner, without regard for their personal safety.

On December 12th, 1978, the man was convicted at Gloucester Crown Court of being in possession of a firearm with intent to endanger life, together with other offences, and was sentenced to a total of 3 years' imprisonment.[5]

The Under Water Recovery Section, now renamed the Sub-Aqua Unit, received a total of 23 call-outs during the year. In one case, following a burgalary in Gloucester, information was received that items of stolen property had been disposed of in the River Severn at Maisemore Bridge. The search was difficult because of the flow of water and lack of visibility and additionally the team had to sift through soft mud on the river bed approximately three inches deep. After two days' work 4 electric typewriters valued at £1,200 were recovered and a successful prosecution followed.

During 1978, Police Seargent Clive Jefferies resigned the leadership of the Unit after 12 years excellent service, and was succeeded by P.S. R. Reynallt, an existing member.

Over the years there had been an increase in the number of offenders appearing before the courts within the Force area for offences involving the misuse of controlled drugs.

In 1978, 172 offenders were convicted of a total of 249 offences compared to 135 offenders convicted in 1977. Eight persons were cautioned for drug offences during the year.

Cannabis was the most abused drug as the following table shows:–

DRUG	OFFENCES
Cannabis	197
Opiates and Cocaine	10
Amphetamines	10
Madrax	1

There were eleven cases involving the cultivation of cannabis plants during the year compared with 18 in 1977 and 13 in 1976.

Two chemists' shops, one doctor's surgery and a hospital on nine occasions were broken and entered during 1978 and controlled drugs stolen. Ten of these offences were detected (one man was responsible for the hospital offences). A further two chemists' shops, one doctor's surgery and a hospital were broken and entered where drugs, although not controlled under the Misuse of Drugs Act 1971, but heavily abused, were stolen. These offences were detected.

The number of persons stopped and searched for drugs during 1978 272
Number of persons stopped and searched and found to be in possession of controlled drugs 76

On the 9th October, 1978 the new Motor Patrol Centre at Bamfurlong became operational. The Traffic Sections amalgamated to become a Traffic Division and personnel and vehicles formerly based at Cheltenham, Stroud, Gloucester and Lydney were removed to the Centre. Headquarters Traffic and Communications Department remained at Force Headquarters, Cheltenham.

Traffic Patrol motor cyclists were formed into a squad with two supervisory Sergeants and used to patrol major routes at peak traffic periods and at special events where a motor cycle patrol was more appropriate than a patrol car.

Vehicle examiners and Accident Prevention Officers, with the exception of the Force Accident Prevention Inspector, were also centralised at Bamfurlong.

At the Police Committee Meeting held at Gloucester on the 14th May, 1979, the Chief Constable reported that recruitment continued at a satisfactory level and that the strength of the Force was only 36 below establishment. This did not take into account 16 new recruits who had been appointed but had not yet joined the Force.

Mr Weigh, Chief Constable, also reported to the Committee on the heavy additional demands placed upon the Force, so far that year, caused by:–

(a) The General Election and the lead up to it.
(b) The Ambulance Drivers' strike
(c) Providing assistance to the Leicestershire and West Midland Forces in connection with demonstrations.

The Chief Constable reported that although it was hoped to recoup some of the costs of these additional duties it meant that, at that stage, more money had been spent on overtime than had been previously envisaged.

Through Industrial Action taken by members of the Ambulance Service during 1979 the Gloucestershire Constabulary were obliged to involve over 60 officers, each day, in assisting with transport of injured or seriously ill persons.

Police involvement commenced with provision of an emergency Control Room, staffed with Police Officers to receive messages from Ambulance Control. These messages were then relayed to Military or Volunteer Ambulances.

It was necessary to provide Police escorts to Military Ambulances and some Voluntary Ambulances for a communication link and quick response to calls for help.

Extra burden was also put upon communications as one of the two Police Radio Channels was being used for the escort vehicles.

In addition to the military and voluntary ambulances the Police made available officers and personnel carrying vehicles adapted for this emergency.

On the 14th May, 1979, the Chief Constable reported that Superintendent G.W. Jones, stationed at Cheltenham, had been invited by the Police Foundation, Washington D.C., to attend an advanced management course of 5 days' duration in the U.S.A., in September, 1979.

As attendance on the course would undoubtedly be beneficial to the officer and the Force the Chief Constable asked for permission to grant Superintendent Jones nine days' leave of absence with pay. All other expenses would be paid for by the Police Foundation.

At a Special Meeting of the Police Committee held in the Council Chamber, Shire Hall, Gloucester, on Monday, 2nd July, 1979, the Chairman congratulated Mr Brian Weigh, Chief Constable, on his appointment as Chief Constable of the Avon and Somerset Constabulary, which post he was due to take up on the 1st September, 1979. The Committee also congratulated Mr E.W. Whitmore, the Assistant Chief Constable, on his appointment as Deputy Chief Constable of Gloucestershire in succession to Mr E. Coppin, Q.P.M., who was retiring on pension on the 25th September, 1979, and authorised arrangements for the appointment of a Chief Constable and Assistant Chief Constable.

The Annual Inspection of the Combined Regular and Volunteer Cadet Corps was held at the Royal Air Force Station, Innsworth, on Saturday, 16th June, 1979, when the Inspecting Officer was Mr E. Coppin, Q.P.M., Deputy Chief Constable.

In 1978 a group of Volunteer Cadets took part in a trip to Trier, West Germany, and in July, 1979, the Western Division Unit of the Volunteer Cadets hosted a visit to Gloucester by 20 young persons from Trier, who spent an interesting and informative two weeks as their guests.

The 'Gloucestershire Constabulary Caroline Symes Memorial Bowl 1977 for Public Service', was awarded to Police Sergeant Donald Chidzoy. For about eleven years Police Sergeant Chidzoy, with his wife Alison, and daughter, Jacqueline, had given a great deal of their time in voluntary work with spastics and the disabled. As Chairman of the Gloucestershire Disabled Drivers' Association Police Sergeant Chidzoy had worked tirelessly organising trips, events and entertainment, as well as being generally involved in fund raising and social activities.

The Presentation was made by the Chief Constable, Mr Brian Weigh, on Wednesday, 25th Apri, 1979 when Don's many friends and colleagues enjoyed the excellent hospitality of Northern Division Club organised by Chief Superintendent C.J. Davis.

CHAPTER 11

Leonard A.G. Soper, Q.P.M.
1.9.1979 –

Mr Leonard A.G. Soper, Q.P.M., Deputy Chief Constable of the Thames Valley Constabulary was appointed Chief Constable of Gloucestershire to succeed Mr Brian Weigh, Q.P.M. and took up his duties at Police Headquarters, Cheltenham on the 1st September, 1979.

Mr E. Coppin, Q.P.M., retired as Deputy Chief Constable of Gloucestershire on the 25th September, 1979, after 41 years service. Mr Coppin transferred to the Gloucestershire Constabulary, from the Essex Constabulary, on his appointment as Assistant Chief Constable on the 3rd January, 1966.

At the Police Committee Meeting held at Gloucester on the 18th September, 1979, the Chairman, Councillor Wilson paid tribute on behalf of the Police Authority to Mr Coppin's many qualities and to his outstanding services to Gloucestershire. The Chairman of the County Council spoke on behalf of the Council and referred especially to Mr Coppin's involvement with young people, Social Services and the St. John Ambulance Brigade. Mr Brian Weigh, Q.P.M., former Chief Constable of Gloucestershire, who had attended the meeting especially for the purpose, paid his own personal tribute to Mr Coppin.

The Committee was also informed that Chief Superintendent L.H. Whitton of the Devon and Cornwall Constabulary had been appointed Assistant Chief Constable of Gloucestershire in succession to Mr E.W. Whitmore who would take up his appointment as Deputy Chief Constable on the 26th September, 1979.

The Police Service, and with it the Gloucestershire Constabulary, continued to benefit from the implementation of the Edmund-Davies pay award. Recruits of good quality continued to come forward and at the end of the year 1979 the actual strength of the Force stood at 1,099, just 17 short of the authorised strength of 1,116.

On the 4th October, 1979, Police Constable John Williams, Police Headquarters, Cheltenham, was admitted as a Serving Brother in the Order of St. John of Jerusalem.

1979 saw the retirement of three Senior Officers, namely: Chief Superintendent William J. Howkins, Divisional Commander at Stroud, Superintendent Kenneth W.F. Barker, Police Headquarters, Cheltenham and Chief Superintendent R. Dale, Divisional Commander at Gloucester.

The 1980 New Year's Honours List saw the award of the Queen's Police Medal for Distinguished Service, to Mr E.W. Whitmore, Deputy Chief Constable of Gloucestershire. He was presented with the Medal by the Lord Lieutenant, Colonel M. St. J.V. Gibbs, C.B., D.S.O., T.D., at the Shire Hall, Gloucester on the 13th May, 1980.

At their meeting on the 25th February, 1980, the Police Committee were informed that four Gloucestershire Police Officers, Police Sergeant Baud and Police Constables Titley, Shere-Massey and Gisborne had, earlier that month, flown to Rhodesia as part of a contingent of 587 British Police Officers who had been called by the then British Governor, Lord Soames, to act as observers and supervisors in the independence elections. The four officers performed duty at Umvukwes, some 60 miles north of Salisbury, where they were billeted with local farmers and professional people.

Police Constable Shere-Massey was responsible for a static polling station in Umvukwes while the other three officers travelled in a heavily armed mobile column between outlying farms where temporary polling had been established in tobacco drying sheds. The officers observed the black population of the new nation of Zimbabwe casting votes for the first time and their role was to reassure the world that the voting was fair and free from intimidation.

The Chief Constable, L.A.G. Soper, Q.P.M., also reported that recruitment remained at a satisfactory level and that in response to the Authority's request to increase the Establishment of the Force by 36 officers, the Home Office had approved a supernumerary increase of 15 constables.

The Police Committee, at this meeting on the 25th February, 1980, congratulated the Chief Constable and his staff on the preparation of the Annual Report which was a very readable and informative document. The Chairman referred to the desirability of giving the Report as wide a publication circulation as possible.

The Chairman of the Police Committee at a meeting held on Tuesday, 13th May, 1980, welcomed Mrs Soper, Mrs Whitmore and

Mrs Whitton, Senior Police Officers and representatives of the Police Federation.

The Gloucestershire Constabulary First Police Reserve, by 1980, was comprised of two Constables who served only in the Park area of Gloucester as Park Constables. The Gloucester City Council notified the Chief Constable that they were unable to justify the continued service of the two Park Constables and requested their services be terminated from 31st December, 1980.

The First Police Reserve dated back to 1909 but the national policy at 1980 was to allow it to die a natural death and not to enroll further members. The decision to disband the First Police Reserve was a matter for the Chief Constable and on the 24th November, 1980 he informed the Police Committee that it was his intention to formally disband the Reserve on the 31st December, 1980.[1]

At its meeting on the 6th September, 1976, the Police Committee approved an annual review of an Allowance, then being paid to members of the Force, to carry out certain internal decorations of county-owned houses which they occupied.

After consulation with the County Architect the Chief Constable asked the Police Committee at their meeting on the 8th September, 1980, that the following figures should apply as from 1st April, 1980.

(a)	Bedrooms and living rooms	£34.15
(b)	Larger than normal size rooms	£39.82
(c)	Combined lounge/dining rooms	£56.51
(d)	Kitchens and bathrooms	£22.76

The increased cost in a full year was £3,060 gross, £1,530 net.

The Queen's Birthday Honours for 1980 included the award of the British Empire Medal to Police Sergeant Clive Jefferies of Stroud – officer in charge of the Underwater Recovery Unit. At the commencement of the meeting of the Police Committee at Gloucester on the 24th November, 1980, the Vice Lord Lieutenant of Gloucestershire, Colonel Sir Geoffrey Shakerley, C.B.E., M.C., T.D., D.L., presented the Medal to Ex. Sergeant Jefferies who had recently retired from the Force on pension.

The year also saw the retirement of three of the most senior officers in the Force, Chief Superintendents C.J. Davis and L.R. Starnes and Superintendent E.J. Bradbeer. All three officers had served with distinction. Their combined service to the community in Gloucestershire totalled 99 years and 88 days.

On 31st December, 1980, the authorised and actual strengths of the Gloucestershire Constabulary were as shown below:–[2]

	AUTHORISED	ACTUAL
Chief Constable	1	1
Deputy Chief Constable	–	1
Assistant Chief Constable	2	1
Chief Superintendents	6	6
Superintendents	14	14 (1 Woman)
Chief Inspectors	19	20
Inspectors	57	57
Sergeants	170	170 (2 Women)
Constables	847	*849 (89 Women)
	1116	1119

* This included 18 men and 11 women in training as recruits.

The above figures do not include the following 16 officers who were on secondment as shown on 31st December, 1980.

SECONDMENT	INSPECTOR	SERGEANT	CONSTABLE
Regional Crime Squad	1	5	3
District Training Centre, Chatmarle	1	2	–
Home Office Forensic Laboratory, Chepstow	–	1 (Temporary)	–
Regional Police Driving School,	–	–	2
Devizes	–	–	1
Technical Support Unit, Almondsbury	–	–	–

On December 31st, 1980 a total of 117 male constables and 6 females constables had passed the examination for promotion to sergeant. Thirty eight of the male constables had also passed the qualifying examination for promotion to Inspector. Seventy one male Sergeants and one female Sergeant had passed the examination for promotion to Inspector.

During the year 21 officers qualified for the Police Long Service and Good Conduct Medal awarded to all Police Officers on completion of 22 years' exemplary service.

Her Majesty's Inspector of Constabulary, Mr R.H. Anning, Q.P.M., carried out his Annual Inspection of the Force between the 9th and 12th September, 1980.

The Annual Inspection of the Combined Regular and Volunteer Cadet Corps was held at the Royal Air Force Station, Innsworth on Saturday, 14th June, 1980, when the Inspecting Officer was Air Commodore Grennan, C.B.E., M.B.C.S., Air Officer Commanding R.A.F. Personnel Management, Innsworth.

Volunteer Cadet activities during the year 1980 included two units taking part in visits to Germany through the town exchange schemes. In June 13 members plus staff of the Eastern Division Unit visited Duderstadt and in August 16 members plus staff of the Western Division Unit visited Trier in both cases being regally entertained by German families and town dignitaries. The visits proved of immense value to the understanding of human behaviour between the youth of both countries.

Northern Division introduced Life Saving instruction for the first time and 8 cadets obtained Royal Life Saving Society awards whilst Eastern Division held a weekend camp in North Wales which included a pleasant day climbing Mount Snowdon.

The Western Division had successfully built up a relationship with local disabled groups and regularly competed with them at wheel-chair sporting events.

The strength of the Volunteer Cadet Corps at 31st December, 1980, was as follows:–

	MALE	FEMALE	TOTAL
Northern Division	8	11	19
Eastern Division	16	8	24
Western Division	14	7	21
	38	26	64

Members of the Special Constabulary continued to give valuable assistance to the Regular Force throughout the year at holiday times and at the various functions held in the County at which a Police presence was necessary in connection with Traffic Patrols, Public Order, etc.
Details of the establishment at 31st December, 1980 are as follows:

	ACTUAL STRENGTH
Northern Division	79
Eastern Division	79
Western Division	75
	233

The Annual Inter-Divisional Competition was held for the first time in the form of a quiz for a Challenge Cup, presented by the Chief Constable, which was won by Eastern Division. The Competition was well received by teams and spectators alike and revealed a high standard of knowledge on the part of the competitors.

On the 31st December, 1980, 3111 firearm certificates relating to 5807 weapons were in force in the County. The steady increase in recent years of the fees for firearm certificates had reduced the number of individual certificates, whereas clubs in particular had increased their weaponry on renewal to avoid expensive additional applications. During the year 187 new certificates were issued and 955 renewed. Of the 187 new certificates, 58 related to pistols and 46 of these were authorised ammunition. Three applicants were refused certificates during the year. Two firearm certificates were revoked.

By the end of 1980 there were 14235 shotgun certificates in force in the County. During the year 1023 new certificates were granted and 4805 renewed. Six applicants were refused and 5 certificates were revoked.[3]

Officers forming Tewkesbury Sub-Division were awarded the Caroline Symes Memorial Bowl in 1980 for their work, particularly in relation to a 'Wheelchair Association' which provided specially adapted mini-buses for the conveyance of the elderly and infirm who would otherwise remain house-bound. This work was often performed during the day, on a rota before or after shift work and on weekly Rest Days.

1980 saw the 10th anniversary of the formation of the Gloucestershire Police Choir and to celebrate the event a concert was given at the Town Hall, Cheltenham, on the 17th October, in aid of Police Charities. The Choir was supported by the Thames Valley Police Band, by kind permission of the Chief Constable of the Thames Valley Police, and a local soloist, Morfedd Burgess. The concert was compered by Shaw Taylor, actor and T.V. personality, who presents the "Police Five" programme for Independent Television Network in the Midlands and London area. The concert was a sell-out and proved to be a great success. A sum of £2100 was raised for Police Charities.

There were a number of incidents affecting Public Order during the year 1980, in and around the City of Gloucester. Unruly and inconsiderate behaviour by some groups of young people, offended and frightened shoppers and shopkeepers. As a result it was necessary to deploy additional officers at weekends, mainly Saturdays, in the Central Shopping Areas. Firm Police action was necessary to demonstrate that this form of behaviour was unacceptable and could not be tolerated. On one occasion 18 youths were arrested, charged with offences and subsequently appeared at Courts.

During the week of 5/11 July 1980, a Police presence at Sharpness Docks prevented anti-nuclear demonstrators from entering the dock area and disrupting the loading of the waste from railway wagons to the MV. 'Gem'.

The only serious incident of the week occurred on Tuesday, 8th July, 1980, at 0630 hours when it was found that demonstrators had erected 20' high scaffolding across the single track railway line near Berkeley, thus preventing the train carrying waste to proceed to Sharpness. Five demonstrators were on the scaffolding platform and they refused to be talked down. Police reinforcements were called in under the direction of the Assistant Chief Constable, Mr Whitton. After approximately 3½ hours the demonstrators were told that Police intended to lower the structure with ropes. The demonstrators climbed down and a total of 7 persons were arrested and taken to Dursley. They were all subsequently fined £300 plus £20 costs each, after pleading guilty to obstructing the railway line.[4]

At 0830 hours on the 17th October, 1980, following a breakdown in negotiations between the Home Office and the National Executive Committee of the Prison Officers' Association who subsequently refused to accept any prisoners from Magistrates' Courts, Stroud Central Police Station was opened as a temporary prison. From that day until the end of the year, the temporary prison was in use, with facilities at Cheltenham Central Police Station in use when Stroud was 'full'. To the end of the year, a total of 76 prisoners – including one female and four juveniles – had been lodged at Stroud and Cheltenham. Two adult males completed their sentences at Stroud and were released.

Additional staff on 12 hour shifts were used at the Stations involved and Task Force, Traffic and U.B.P. officers were all used on escort/transfer duties, with expenditure on manpower, food and facilities and certain additional security measures reaching £40,000 by the end of the year.

Whilst the added responsibilities of these temporary prisons brought about a shortage of staff in respect of normal policing, the efficiency and professionalism was maintained, and there was no lowering of standards, or departure from the normal service which the public had come to expect.

The following details relate to the work performed by the Scenes of Crime, Photographic and Fingerprint Departments during 1980.

Scenes of Crime Officers visited or examined items from 5,574 scenes, Officers from Scenes of Crime submitted items from 159 scenes for examination by the Home Office Forensic Science Laboratory, Chepstow.

The training of uniform officers to act as relief or reserve Scenes of Crime Officers continued during the year with the result that one officer at Gloucester was fully trained and one officer at each of the other Divisions, partly trained.

In 3,991 cases, fingerprint examinations were carried out at scenes of crimes as a result of which 1,222 submissions were made to Headquarters Fingerprint Department. Detailed examination there revealed 528 instances when the submissions were found to be those of persons with legitimate access or of insufficient detail for practical use. However, 214 positive identifications were made.

The Photographic Department, during 1980, was kept busy and produced:–

(a)	Prisoners photographs, including re-prints	18343
(b)	Road accident photographs	1182
(c)	Fingerprints	4682
(d)	Contact prints	152
(e)	Others	9604
	Total photographs produced	33963

The only type of photographs produced which showed an increase over the previous year was prisoner's portrait photographs. A total of 2372 new prisoner's portrait photographs were received at Headquarters for processing; an increase of 476 over the previous year and a corresponding increase in the production of this type of photograph was therefore inevitable.

By 1980 the Task Force was divided into three units based at Cheltenham, Gloucester and Stroud. From 1st April, 1980 operational control was centralised at Headquarters under the Detective Chief Superintendent.

This resulted in improved co-ordination, greater flexibility and increased effectiveness.

The officers attended, often at short notice, to provide valuable assistance to Divisions when emergencies arose requiring additional manpower or to provide planned tactical support. They assisted at Race Meetings, Royal visits and on occasions where their presence was effective in restoring public order. In the latter part of the year they provided prisoner escorts during an industrial dispute. Lengthy plain clothes observations were also undertaken with officers from the Drug

Squad and Criminal Investigation Department, including an operation which resulted in the arrest of a number of persons who were part of a national drugs ring and they were also involved in investigating a particularly troublesome series of burglaries in the Gloucester area.

In April 1980, assistance was given to the Chief Constable of the Avon and Somerset Constabulary at the scene of the disturbances in the St. Paul's area of Bristol, whilst in June a six day operation was mounted in conjunction with local officers to ensure the safe loading of nuclear waste on to a vessel in Sharpness Docks. During the year a total of 201 persons were arrested by Task Force officers for offences of public disorders and for crime.

During 1980 the Dog Section was increased in establishment by 1 Constable Dog Handler bringing the strength of the Section to 1 Sergeant and 9 Constables.

There was an increase in the number of calls for assistance received during the year, 1002 compared with 931 in 1979. A total of 111 arrests were made, 68 being for criminal offences, and dog handlers also assisted in the arrest of a further 78 persons and recovered a total of 71 items as a result of search. One person reported missing from home was located and 50 successful tracks were confirmed. The recovery of property included 4 drug finds by specially trained dogs.

The Underwater Search Unit functions on a 'part-time' demand and training basis with personnel who are members of various Sub-Divisions. The Unit consists of eight members who train on one day per week which enables them to keep fit and familiar with methods recommended by the Home Office and National Diving Schools. During 1980 their services were requested on 25 occasions, 5 of which were on behalf of the Wiltshire Constabulary.

In order to improve conditions generally, the team were allowed to have use of a Ford Transit box van in which to convey equipment and to provide a dry and warm area in which members could change during inclement weather. In addition, an inflatable boat and motor were purchased to afford the unit greater safety and flexibility during diving operations.

The increase in crime generally throughout the country during the period 1975/1980, led to greater activity in Force Intelligence Offices and Gloucestershire was no exception.

Divisional and Force Intelligence Officers were continually engaged in meeting the demands upon their systems and service, evaluating and disseminating information and intelligence about criminals, their activities and keeping abreast of crime patterns.

There is no doubt that intelligence officers have an important role in the fight against crime and of necessity they must maintain a good liaison with both detectives and uniform officers at all levels. The facilities of the Police National Computer was used to great advantage and proved to be of immense value.

It has long been established that in modern policing it is essential to create and maintain a good relationship between the Police and the public. This was done during the year by members of the Public Relations and Crime Prevention Department and Divisional Press Liaison Officers informing the public via the press, radio and T.V., of events reported to the Police. Many informative and advisory subjects of concern to the public were initiated by written press releases and special press conferences held as the occasion demanded.

During October 1980 Severn Sound, a new independent radio station commenced broadcasting in the county which brought the opportunity for members of the Force to give radio traffic advice on a daily basis. In addition nine officers were interviewed during the year concerning items of news affecting the Force.

Each year an opportunity has been taken to invite members of the news media to visit Police Headquarters and discuss with Police Press Officers matters of common interest. This has proved most beneficial and done much to ensure an accurate account was published of Police involvement in the community.

The service provided in this way has effectively publicized matters affecting the Force but in addition many people, during the year, visited Police Headquarteres to learn more about the service. To the many people who were unable to visit, a talks service was provided on such things as Road Safety, Crime Prevention, Police Service and Police Dogs. The requests for these talks continued to increase and during 1980 a total of 810 were given.

Visits to Police Stations and talks are a means by which the public is given an opportunity to understand Police affairs and do much to encourage individuals to act responsibly on the roads and prevent crime. The value of the '999' system was emphasized and although at times was abused, 24295 calls were received during 1980 and acted upon.

The Public Relations and Crime Prevention Department was and still is responsible for the publication of a Force newspaper called 'Grapevine' which provides a means of communication for members of the Force and for Police Pensioners in particular a newsheet of happenings within the County.

Another responsibility is the maintenance of a small museum and during the year the interest in this had continued with new items being obtained.

Crime Prevention Officers throughout the Force regularly provided advice free of any charge and during the year 1980 visited 839 premises for this purpose.

In many cases groups of people were visited and talks on security were given with every opportunity being taken to take the purpose-built display caravan to exhibitions etc. Some 49 days were devoted to displaying the caravan and 282 talks on crime prevention were given during the year.

Within the Force there are two Crime Prevention Panels consisting of civilian members of the community from all walks of life, ably supported by Police Officers. These panels based on Cheltenham and Gloucester, meet regularly and discuss methods of preventing crime.

The Cheltenham Panel put forward an idea of a 'Teaching Pack' for children at junior Schools to a national competition organised by the Home Office and were successful in winning a prize of £300 to finance their scheme. In more practical terms their efforts to prevent bicycle thefts saw the second Cheltenham Cycle Week with an increased number of children participating in a poster competition. A film aimed at preventing the elderly from being the victims of crime, being made by and for Age Concern and financed by the National Westminster Bank, came about as the result of an idea from the Cheltenham Crime Prevention Panel.

In Gloucester the Crime Prevention Panel made an impressive start to its activities by holding a 'Never Go With Strangers' campaign for children attending primary schools and junior schools. Some 10000 children were spoken to by Police Officers during the summer term – 1980 – and films shown covering the subject. A poster competition on the theme of the campaign gave the children an opportunity to test how much they had remembered with the winners receiving prizes from the Mayor of Gloucester and an interesting visit to a T.V. Studio to take part in a children's programme.

The year saw a pronounced increase in the number of offenders appearing before the Courts for various offences contrary to the Misuse of Drugs Act 1971. This increase was consistent with national figures produced by the Home Office and indicated that drug abuse remained a cause for concern.

During 1980, 206 persons appeared before local Courts for 310 offences, contrary to the Misuse of Drugs Act 1971, and 2 were officially cautioned. In those offences dealt with by the Courts the following table indicates the type of drug misused:–

DRUG	OFFENCES
Opiates and Cocaine	38
LSD	2
Amphetamines	12
Cannabis	208

The cultivation of cannabis continued to be detected and a number of large seizures were made. Seventeen cases were dealt with by the Courts, but following a Home Office recommendation proceedings for this specific offence was no longer being brought. Offenders would, in future, be dealt with for illegal production or possession of a controlled drug.

Thirty one persons were convicted for offences of deception or forgery involving prescriptions, and there were 8 burglaries of chemists' or doctors' surgeries in pursuit of controlled drugs. Six of these burglaries were detected.

During the year 224 stop searches under the Misuse of Drugs Act 1971 were carried out and on 107 occasions drugs were found. There were two formal complaints made against members of the Constabulary in relation to stop searches.

During the year 45 warrants taken out under the Misuse of Drugs Act 1971 were executed and on 28 occasions drugs were found.

Five persons died during 1980 in Gloucestershire following their misuse of controlled drugs.

The Force Drug Liaison Officer, a Detective Sergeant at Headquarters has, since April 1980, carried out county wide inspections of chemists' registers thereby ensuring uniformity and following the recommendations contained in Home Office Circular N25/1980. The Force Drug Liaison Officer also lectures on the Misuse of Drugs to all courses held at Headquarters. In addition, 57 lectures on drug abuse were given by the department to various organisations, including H.M. Forces, doctors, nurses, health visitors, youth leaders, teachers and parent/teachers associations.[5]

During the year 1980, an operation was carried out in Eastern Division, combining the resource of Task Force, Regional Crime Squad and Drug Squad. This operation successfully curtailed the illegal activities of a small group of people who, for a number of years had been involved in the supply of controlled drugs both locally and nationally. There appears little doubt that if these people had been allowed to carry on their illegal activities, the supply, not only of cannabis, but cocaine, would have been prevalent locally. Mention should be made of the computer sited at the Central Drugs and Illegal Immigration Unit, New Scotland Yard, which was used as a reference source in this operation. This was the first time the computer had been used as an "index" in this type of operation.

On the 31st December, 1980 there were 452 aliens reported as living in Gloucestershire, a decrease of 17 on the number for 1979. It is the responsibility of the Special Branch to collate the records of registration and movements of these resident aliens. During 1980 enquiries were made in respect of 49 applications for naturalisation and 45 reports were sent to the Home Office about visa applications and various other matters concerning aliens. A number of aliens appeared before the Courts during the year for infringements of the Regulations concerning their registration with the Police.

The Fraud Squad, a specialist department, continued to deal with the more complex fraud enquiries. Apart from finalising cases which came to light in 1979 and earlier, 22 new cases consisting of 18 complaints of fraud and 4 of corruption were dealt with in 1980. These new cases involved about £650,000. Criminal offences were discovered in 10 of the enquiries and 6 matters were in the early stages of investigation. Offences of theft, deception, forgery, corruption, falsification of accounts, fraudulent inducements and fraudulent trading were revealed, together with incitements to defraud and infringements of the Companies Acts 1948 and 1967 and the Bankruptcy Act 1914. Four of the matters were referred to the Squad by the Department of Trade and 2 by the Director of Public Prosecutions. A substantial number of enquiries were conducted on behalf of other Forces.

During the year 1980 the services of the Forensic Science Laboratories were used as follows:–

OCCURENCE	NUMBER OF CASES
Offences against the person	31
Burglaries	25
Thefts, etc	30
Road accidents	75
Drunken driving (breathalyser)	731
Sudden deaths	15
Drugs	227
Criminal damage and Arson	32
Counterfeit coins and forgeries	4

Firearms examinations	5
Handwriting comparison	52
Forgery – examination of documents	2
Others	12
Total	1241

Nine hundred and ninety two sudden deaths were reported to H.M. Coroners in 1980. Inquests were held in 175 cases. A summary of the verdicts is given below:–

VERDICT	NUMBER
Accidental	93
Misadventure	19
Natural causes	3
Suicide	35
Self-neglect	1
Industrial disease	4
Open	12
Cot death	4
Alcoholism	1
Pending	3
Total	175

After consultations with the Clerk to the Gloucester Justices and the Home Office Prison Department, the Gloucester Junior Attendance Centre opened in April 1980. The Centre, which provided Juvenile Courts with an additional option for dealing with youths between the ages of 10 and 17 years who had been guilty of an offence punishable with imprisonment, was financed by the Home Office, but staffed by regular Police Officers working in their own time.

Sessions were held on alternative Saturday afternoons and Courts were empowered to direct attendance by boys for not less than 10 and not more than 24 hours in all. A total of 81 orders directing attendance were made in 1980, most of which were satisfactorily completed, but 9 youths were subsequently sentenced to other punishment after their orders had been revoked for non-attendance.

Boys from most parts of the County were ordered to attend, travelling in their own time, other than from the North Cotswolds, which was outside the scheme. The programme of activities was varied but included first aid, physical training, social skills, pottery, house maintenance and advice on creative spare time activities.

A motor patrol centre is based at Bamfurlong (Junction of M5 and A40 at Golden Valley) from which all traffic patrols operate, covering the County. Vehicle examiners and Accident Prevention Officers are also based at the Centre.

Divisional Headquarters and the Communications Department are based at Police Headquarters, Cheltenham.

The authorised establishment and actual strength of personnel and vehicles of the Traffic Division at 31st December, 1980, is shown in the following tables:–

	ESTABLISHMENT	ACTUAL STRENGTH
Chief Superintendents	1	1
Superintendents	3	3
Chief Inspectors	2	2
Inspectors	12	12
Police Sergeants	18	18
Police Constables	150	146
Totals	186	182

VEHICLES

TRAFFIC DIVISION	CARS	LAND ROVERS	VANS	MOTOR CYCLES
	42	3	3	15

DIVISIONAL VEHICLES	CARS	VANS	MOTOR CYCLES	DOG VANS	SOC VANS	UBP
Headquarters	11	6	10	1	–	–
Northern	11	14	10	2	2	11
Eastern	13	13	21	1	1	–
Western	14	8	17	2	2	12

The Motor Patrol Centre provides round the clock cover for the County, especially the more remote areas. Traffic patrol cars and motor cycles are manned by experienced officers who have undergone driver/rider training at the Regional Driving School at Devizes. They patrol the main trunk routes and 'A' Class roads within the County and the M5 motorway from Strensham to Falfield. Motor cyclists, in addition to normal patrol duties, assist at traffic situations and events where they are able to operate more easily than a four-wheeled vehicle. A number of specially trained crews are also used for the detection of speeding offences using Truvelo and Vascar apparatus. This is in addition to other methods employed to detect offences of this nature.

A communications caravan is available at Bamfurlong at short notice, this vehicle can be despatched to any major incident and set up as a mobile Police Station and communications centre.

A second caravan is used by the Accident Prevention Department for display purposed but this is also available as a second mobile Police Station should the need arise.

Senior traffic officers are in constant consultation with the County Surveyor's staff, and the Regional Controller, Roads and Transportation, on all matters affecting traffic movement and traffic management in the County.

Vehicle maintenance is the responsibility of the Traffic Division which has workshops situated at Gloucester, Stroud and Cheltenham. Motor cycles only are repaired at Cheltenham. All repairs, except body damage to four-wheeled vehicles, are carried out by Police staff. A Land Rover and recovery trailer is available for removing broken down vehicles.

Motor patrol mileage in 1980 was 1643653 compared with 1725540 in 1979. The total mileage covered by all vehicles in 1980 was 4353627 compared with 4364680 in 1979.

During 1980 there were 741 arrests made by the crews of patrol cars. There were 918 arrests made by all vehicles in consequence of information transmitted from the Information Room.

The following tables give the accident and casualty figures for 1980:–

Number of fatal accidents	54
Number of injury accidents	2427
Total number of accidents	2481

Number of persons killed	61
Number of persons seriously injured	1213
Number of persons slightly injured	1919
Total number of killed or injured	3193

Accident figures are continually monitored by Shire Hall Road Safety Department. If accidents occur with any degree of frequency at a particular spot then a meeting between the Police and all other interested parties takes place to discuss remedy or measures.

Breath test figures show that during 1980, 1822 tests were administered showing an increase of 474 tests over the 1979 figure.

Whereas the authorised establishment of Traffic Wardens remained at 50, the financial restraints of 1980 made deep inroads into the resources available for this work. On 31st December, 1980, the distribution was as follows, with actual strength shown alongside:–

NORTHERN DIVISION	Cheltenham	19	8
	Tewkesbury	2	1
EASTERN DIVISION	Stroud	3	2
	Dursley	2	2
	Cirencester	2	2
WESTERN DIVISION	Gloucester	22	16
		50	31

Improvements to Police houses by the provision of full gas or solid fuel central heating or modifications to existing schemes continued but the programme did not commence until late 1980 due to delays in obtaining financial approval from the County Council. The 1980 programme was devised to give priority to police houses in exposed areas of the County.

Two houses at Winchcombe, 1 at Berkeley, 2 at Andoversford, 2 at Cirencester, 3 at Tetbury, 1 at Sharpness, 1 at Windrush, 2 at Whiteshill, Stroud, 1 at Ruspidge, 1 at Leckhampton, 2 at Cheltenham Road East, Gloucester, and 1 at Mitcheldean were due to receive the benefit of central heating.

At the end of the year 703 officers owned and occupied their own houses compared with 677 on 31st December, 1979. As was the case in 1979, some Police Authority houses were empty at the end of 1980. Unoccupied houses were regularly examined with a view to disposal, by way of sale or lease, consistent with the needs of the Force.

Twenty four houses were declared surplus during 1980, at the end of the year and Acting Valuer had sold or agreed terms for sale of 16 houses.

On 31st December, 1980, 268 officers occupied police houses. This compared with 304 in 1979.

The current maximum limit rent allowance as at 31st December, 1980, was as follows:–

Constables, Sergeants and Inspectors	£25.49p per week
Superintendents	£29.56p per week

On promotion to the rank of Superintendent, all members of the Police Service automatically became members of the Superintendents' Association of England and Wales which was set up in 1919. The Association which represents the ranks of Chief Superintendent and Superintendent produces within its frame-work an organisation which permits a proper exchange of views. Each Branch elects its own Chairman and Secretary who, in Gloucestershire, are also the representatives to district conference from which delegates are selected to serve on the National Executive.

The Police Federation established by the Police Act, 1919, represents ranks up to and including Chief Inspector together with regular Cadets. Membership is automatic on appointment and is represented in each rank on a Joint Branch Board at Force level from which delegates are sent to National Conference.

The Federation puts forward the views of its members at local level with regard to matters of efficiency, discipline and welfare and at National level in matters of pay and conditions of service.

The National Association of Retired Police Officers, also founded in 1919, has in Gloucestershire about 500 members including 170 police widows. The association is dedicated to safeguard the welfare of its members and promotes their interests with regard to pensions. A number of its social functions are held throughout the year in each of the Divisional Police Clubs, and Regular Officers willingly provide transport to these events as required. Since 1962, news and items of interest to Police Pensioners have been formulated into a newsletter by Mr H. Thomas, Q.P.M. and this is now a regular feature of the Force magazine 'Grapevine'.

The Force Welfare Officer, Mr R.E. Spencer, G.M., MIWO, ably supported by Divisional Welfare Officers, has ensured that the welfare interests of Regular Officers, civilian employees, pensioners and widows, together with their families, have been given the closest attention. Officers unfortunate enough to have been on sick leave have received visits and encouragement either at home or in hospital. Where necessary, arrangements have been made for admission to the Police Convalescent Home at Hove, Sussex. During 1980, 1 Inspector, 2 Sergeants and 6 Constables attended for periods of convalescence at the home which is financed mainly by voluntary contributions from officers of Police Forces in the southern half of the country. At 31st December, 1980, 1103 members of the Gloucestershire Constabulary were regularly contributing 18p per month from their salaries towards the maintenance of the home.

Following the success of the pensioners' and widows' holiday in the Isle of Wight in 1979, a similar venture was undertaken in 1980 at Llandudno. A total of 42 pensioners and widows under the care of the Force Welfare Officer had an enjoyable and refreshing holiday.

A pre-retirement course for 14 officers from Constable to Chief Superintendent was held for a week at Police Headquarters in April.

Lectures to refresher classes and recruits were given by the Force Welfare Officer. He also made enquiries on behalf of this Force and many other Forces concerning benevolent grants to pensioners and widows.

One hundred and sixty widows and 2 children of ex-members of this Force were visited to establish whether any financial or other need was required. This annual review is a necessary feature of maintenance plus keeping contact with those who were once associated with the Service.

In The Queen's Birthday Honours for 1985, Her Majesty the Queen was graciously pleased to award the British Empire Medal to Mr R.E. Spencer, G.M., MIWO, the Force Welfare Officer, in respect of the service he had rendered to the Gloucestershire Constabulary.

The Force Benevolent Fund which provides financial assistance where it is needed is supported by voluntary contributions of 30p per month made by 1008 serving members and 105 pensioners. In addition donations are received from the public, and annual grant is made by the National Police Fund and social functions are arranged which raise money towards this fund. A regular gift to all widows is made at Christmas, and the fund is available to provide financial relief for Regular and Retired members of the Force who for reasons beyond their control are suddenly put to additional expense.

In January 1980, Gloucestershire joined the Gurney Fund which was established 32 years ago to provide for the relief of the fatherless children of Police Officers. Weekly payments for each eligible child are made together with benevolent or educational grants where necessary, from a fund supported by voluntary contributions of 13p a month from serving officers.

The Police Dependants' Trust, which was established in 1966 after the murder of 3 Police Officers in Shepherds Bush, London, provides financial assistance to the dependants of police officers who have died or been incapacitated as a result of injury in the execution of their duty. One thousand one hundred and eleven voluntary monthly contributions of 5p from serving members of the Gloucestershire Constabulary assist in the provision of finances for the trust and during 1980 four enquiries were conducted in respect of applications by dependants resident in Gloucestershire. Grants totalling £1434 were made in these 4 cases.

Once again, in 1980, following the tragic death of a serving officer, the contents of the Force Death Levy Fund, at that time £1201, was paid to his next of kin. The fund was again reconstituted and presents an immediate means whereby members can provide some measure of practical assistance to the family of a colleague.

An overall total of 10449 days were lost due to the sickness of members of the Regular Force during 1980. Of this figures, 7403 days were certified sick leave and 500 days were attributable to the consequences of assault or other injury on duty.

Forty one officers reported sick for periods in excess of 6 weeks, their sickness alone causing the loss of 3366 days.

The average number of days lost per head of the Force – yearly strength averaging 1110 – was 9.86.

The Records of the Force over the past 140 years have shown that to be a member of the Gloucestershire Constabulary is something of which to be proud. As for the future, we can perhaps be best guided by a quotation which was included in a Christmas message from a Chief Constable, some 50 years ago:–

> On the strength of one link in the cable
> Dependeth the might of the chain
> Who knows when thou mayest be tested?
> So live, that thou bearest the strain.[6]

It is now left to Time to add its own pages of History to those already written.

> The past is our heritage
> The future our responsibility.

Presentation of B.E.M. to Ex. P.S. Clive JEFFERIES. 1980

OPEN DAY with Chief Constable, Deputy Chief and Assistant Chief Constable.

Chief Constable with Princess Diana and Prince Charles.

Princess Diana and the Deputy Chief Constable.

Prince Charles talking to Cadets.

Presentation of Long Service Medals – 20th November 1981.

Chief Constable inspecting Special Constables and Volunteer Cadets outside Gloucester Cathedral 1982.

Detective Inspector RICHINGS being presented with the Caroline SYMES Memorial Bowl.

Author and Mrs THOMAS outside Shire Hall, Gloucester after presentation of Queens Police Medal. 1970.

APPENDIX 'A'
Women Police in Gloucestershire

Although precise details cannot be determined there is evidence in records to show that, from time to time, prior to 1917, Women Patrols were sent to Cheltenham and Gloucester, both of which places were at that time receiving a great number of soldiers – mainly patients in the Hospitals. Perhaps it could be that, as and when circumstances required, requests were made to the Auxiliary Police Service which had been formed in London and Bristol under the respective commands of Miss Damer Dawson and Miss Peto, for the services of women police to patrol the streets.

During 1917, the Acting Chief Constable, through the Deputy Chief Constable, received many requests from various Women's Organisations and Societies advocating for Women Police to be attached to the County Force, as a result of which application was made to the Home Office for permission to appoint a certain number of women as Special Constables. After much consideration, the Home Office decided that women could not do duty as Special Constables, and suggested that the Standing Joint Committee might agree to Women Constables being appointed to the Force.[1]

On the 1st January, 1918, the Chief Constable, Major Stanley-Clarke who had been appointed and commenced duty that day, was requested by the Standing Joint Committee to make enquiries of other Police Authorities on the subject of the employment of Women Police. At the next meeting of the Standing Joint Committee on the 11th April, 1918, the Chief Constable reported the result of his enquiries and he was instructed to appoint two women as members of the County Force, to be employed in the Borough of Cheltenham, subject to the approval of the Cheltenham Town Council, and at the cost of the Council.

The following May and June saw the first appointment of women to the Force. Because of a recent drafting of eleven men into the Army, the Chief Constable received approval of the Chairman of the Standing Joint Committee to appoint women as Reserve Constables to be employed as clerks and, in one case, as a groom to the Deputy Chief Constable, so as to enable men employed indoors to be used for outside duties. On the 6th May, 1918, the following eight women were appointed – see General Order No. 786, dated 15th May, 1918.

Elizabeth A. Brookes Jessie M. Hagley Catherine Kelly
Jennie L. Hopkins Elizabeth Fowler Laura Mavor
Marion E. Sandover Elizabeth Tonra

Laura Mavor was appointed groom at Gloucester whilst the remainder were employed on office duties at Police Headquarters, Cheltenham and Gloucester Central Police Station.

On the 10th June, 1918, Marion E.E. Redfern was appointed and posted to 'F' Division for clerical duties, and on the 24th June two women were appointed for duties in Cheltenham, at the cost of the Borough. They were Ethel E. Gale and Gertrude M. Rowe. See General Order No. 1841 dated 13th July, 1918. Miss Gale transferred from Bath City Police to Gloucestershire and was immediately appointed to the rank of Sergeant on taking up her duties. The first Woman Police Sergeant to be appointed in the Force.[2]

It is not known for certain if the two women appointed on the 24th June were employed solely for patrol duties in Cheltenham. In the meantime Jennie L. Hopkins resigned her appointment on the 30th September, 1918. On the 12th November, 1918, Evelyn M. Soppett was appointed and posted to Gloucester for clerical duties. On the 27th November, she resigned from the Force.

Edith Mary Blair was appointed on the 7th December, 1918, and posted to Gloucester.

The scale of pay for the eleven women was the same as that paid to the First Police Reserve, i.e. 35/–d. plus 5/–d. War Bonus, making a total of 40/–d. per week. In addition they received £10 per year in lieu of uniform and £4 per year in lieu of boots. Each of the women had brought with them their necessary uniform.

It had been the Chief Constable's intention to recruit the first Women Police through the Auxiliary Police Service Training Establishments in London and Bristol, which he no doubt did, because the women appointed had previous experience. Ten came to the Force from local ammunition factories and Miss Gale of course had previous experience in the Bath City Police.

General Order No. 2105, date 14th May, 1919, refers to the appointment of the following women for patrol duties in 'G' Gloucester Division, 'J' Stroud Division and 'L' Cheltenham Division.

Edith Annie Cooper	joined 17.4.1919
Edith Jane Smith	joined 19.4.1919
Winifred E. Vincent	joined 19.4.1919
Florence Jolin	joined 22.4.1919
Eva Blanch Bloodworth	joined 24.4.1919

On the 1st July, 1919, the women police were transferred from the First Police Reserve to the Regular Force as Auxiliaries, receiving the same basic pay as the men, with a modified War Bonus. Taking into account a deduction for the pension fund, the nett increase was 6d. per week. However, within a few months it was decided that as women police could not be regarded as members of a Police Force within the meaning of the Police Act of 1890, or any Acts effecting the Regular Police, they were not eligible to qualify for a pension. As a result, deductions to the pension fund were discontinued and contributions already made were refunded. They continued to receive pay on a separate Gloucestershire Constabulary Reserve Pay Sheet and National Health deductions were made.

From the 1st July, 1919, when the women police were transferred to the First Police Reserve, up to the 1st October, 1921, the following police women left the Force:–

Marion E.E. Redfern	Resigned voluntarily	27.10.1919
Eva Blanch Bloodworth	Resigned voluntarily	22.12.1919
Catherine Kelly	Resigned voluntarily	9. 1.1920
Elizabeth Fowler	Resigned ill-health	7. 3.1920
Jessie M. Hagley	Resigned voluntarily	8. 4.1920
Florence Jolin	Resigned voluntarily	31. 1.1921

W.P.C. Hagley resigned after her marriage to Police Constable Patrick Bird, who was also serving in the Gloucestershire Constabulary. Mrs Bird died at Hucclecote, Gloucester on the 3rd January, 1975, her husband having pre-deceased her.

On the 28th February, 1919, W.P.C. Laura Mavor was discharged as injuries received in the execution of her duties rendered her unfit for further police service. She had poisoned her finger whilst grooming the Deputy Chief Constable's horse, with the result that the finger had to be amputated.

W.P.C. Edith Mary Blair had broken her ankle whilst cycling on duty and was permanently lame with the result that she was discharged medically unfit on the 20th December, 1919.

After enquiring of the Home Office as to the eligibility of these women for a pension, a reply was received by telegram recommending a pension of 10/50ths. of their pay, which was the maximum amount authorised by the Police, Factories (Miscellaneous Provisions) Act, 1916. A pension of 1/–d.

per day was granted in each case. By 1966 these pensions had been increased to £64.4.10d. annually.

W.P.C. Mavor, who sustained the finger injury, lived to receive her pension until her death on the 18th February, 1966. The other police woman, Miss Blair, went to reside in Tarporley, Cheshire and lived to a great age.

On the 28th June, 1921, it was Resolved by the Standing Joint Committee that, in future, women police would be supplied with uniform and that the cash allowance hitherto granted in lieu of uniform and boots would be discontinued.

In consequence of the Home Secretary asking the Standing Joint Committee to consider what economies could be made in the administration of the Police Service, it was decided on the 18th October, 1921, amongst other things, that the employment of women police would be discontinued except that women would be retained in Gloucester and Cheltenham, provided the Corporation of these Boroughs desired, and were prepared to pay the whole of the cost which was not borne by the State.

At this time there were two women police in each of these Boroughs. On the 29th November, 1921, three of the seven remaining police women employed were given three months' notice of dismissal and on the 28th February, 1922, W.P.C.'s Elizabeth A. Brookes, Gertrude M. Rowe and Edith Jane Smith were discharged.

This left W.P. Sergeant Ethel E. Gale and W.P.C. Edith Ann Cooper for duty in Cheltenham and W.P.C.'s Marion E. Sandover and Elizabeth Tonra for duty in the City of Gloucester.

Although the Standing Joint Committee discussed the question of employing additional women police at their meeting held in June and again in October of 1925, when reference was made to a letter received from the Gloucestershire Women's Magistrates' Society asking for more women to be employed in the County, in addition to those already employed in Gloucester and Cheltenham, it was not until the 5th April, 1927, after a circular letter had been received from the Secretary of State requesting Police Authorities to consider the employment of women police, that a decision was made to obtain the Home Secretary's approval for the appointment of four additional police women for the Force.

W.P.C. Edith Annie Cooper, stationed at Cheltenham, resigned voluntarily on the 31st July, 1927.

On the 12th December, 1927, the following five women were appointed:–

W.P.C. Janet Paton Gray
W.P.C. Rosa Mary Rouse
W.P.C. Edith Mabel Caroline Lodge
W.P.C. Annie Josephine Fay
W.P.C. Katherine Beryl Gardner
See General Order No. 3931 dated 15th December, 1927.

W.P.C. Fay resigned voluntarily from the Force on the 20th September, 1929, and W.P.C. Gardner resigned on the 31st December, 1929.

W.P.C. Rouse started her Police career in the Bristol City Constabulary which she joined on the 7th January, 1926, transferring to Gloucestershire on the 12th December, 1927. On the 4th July, 1941, Miss Rouse retired from the Force, unfortunately, because of ill-health. During her service with the Gloucestershire Constabulary Miss Rouse was Commended, by the Chief Constable, on eleven occasions. Since retiring from the Force Miss Rouse married and is now known as Mrs Rosa M. Ashby. Since the death of her husband Mrs Ashby, now in her 83rd year, went to reside at the Lilian Faithfull Home for Elderly Persons in Suffolk Square Cheltenham.[3]

W.P.C. Janet P. Gray served with the Gloucestershire Constabulary for nearly four years during which time she was twice Commended by the Chief Constable. On the 30th October, 1931, Miss Gray transferred to the Glasgow City Police and by 1959 had risen to the rank of Superintendent. In 1961, Miss Gray was appointed Assistant H.M. Inspector of Constabulary for Scotland. In the 1968 Birthday Honours Miss Gray, already the holder of the British Empire Medal, was awarded the M.B.E. Due to illness Miss Gray retired in 1970 and died in Glasgow during 1977.

W.P.C. Lodge served with the Gloucestershire Constabulary until her retirement on the 12th November, 1958. She married in 1950 and for the remainder of her service was known as W.P.C. Yeoman. After her retirement Mrs Yeoman – whose husband was not a member of the Force – became the Postmistress of Woodmancote near Cirencester. The Post Office also being the village store. On leaving the Post Office at Woodmancote Mrs Yeoman, with her husband, went to reside at Rendcombe near Cirencester. She was interested in most local affairs and was a committee member of the Gloucestershire Branch of the National Association of Retired Police Officers (N.A.R.P.O.) a post she held at the time of her death in hospital, at Cirencester, on the 1st September, 1985, at the age of 82 years.

Due to ill-health W.P.S. Gale was required to resign, on an ill-health pension, on the 12th July, 1929. She was aged 44 years, had served for eleven years and received a pension of £42.18.0d. per annum. After her retirement she married Ex. Inspector M. Millard of the Gloucestershire Constabulary and died at Cheltenham on the 30th August, 1959, aged 74 years.

At least one of the women appointed on the 6th May, 1918, completed 30 years service in the Force. She was W.P.C. Marion E. Sandover who retired on pension on the 28th May, 1948. During her service with the Force, Miss Sandover was Commended on seven occasions and was also awarded a Silver Braid, a Silver Jubilee Medal and Defence Medal.

When she retired Miss Sandover was residing at 46 St. Pauls Road, Gloucester, with Ex. W.P.C. Tonra who also joined the Force on the 6th May, 1918. Miss Tonra completed 27 years service before her retirement on the 30th September, 1945. She died on the 18th November, 1959 and was interred at Prinknash Abbey near Gloucester, aged 73 years.

Miss Sandover died in Gloucester, at 46 St. Pauls Road, the same house which she and Ex. W.P.C. Tonra first occupied in 1927.

It was during 1929, that the Chief Constable, Major Stanley-Clarke, was instructed to appear before a 'Commission of Enquiry into Police Powers and Procedure', to be held at the Caxton Hall, London, and chaired by Lord Leigh of Fareham. The Commission followed questions in Parliament about the treatment of a Miss Irene Savage, by a policewoman, when she was at Bow Street Police Station, after being arrested with Sir Leo Money, for indecency in a London Park.

A senior London Police Officer and a London Policewoman gave evidence, followed by Major Stanley-Clarke and one of his Policewomen from Gloucestershire. W.P.C. Rosa M. Rouse. Major Stanley-Clarke was the only Provincial Chief Constable called, as he was one of the few Chief Constables to employ eight policewomen in this County Force. A 'White Paper' issued afterwards recommended that more policewomen be employed on the lines of Gloucestershire.[4]

General Order No. 4325, dated 15.1.30, shows W.P.C. Phyllis L. Bennett joining the Force. She served for three or four years and then resigned and married P.C. Arthur Russell.

W.P.C. Elizabeth M. Millichip joined the Force on the 30th January, 1930. On the 14th October, 1950, Miss Millichip was promoted Sergeant, retiring on pension on the 31st August, 1958, and later married Inspector Ted Herbert who was still serving in the Gloucestershire Constabulary.

At the Standing Joint Committee meeting held on the 20th October, 1931, the Chief Constable reported that he had received a copy of the Police (Women) Regulations made by the Secretary of State on the 7th

October, 1931. These Regulations applied only to policewomen who had been attested and, as such, were applicable to the members of the Gloucestershire Constabulary.

Regulation 1 (ii) referred to the strength of women police to be employed. The number of policewomen authorised by the Standing Joint Committee, for employment in the Force, was eight but for some time past the number actually employed had been seven.

Regulation 1 (viii) dealt with the hours of duty. In Gloucestershire, ever since women police had been employed on patrol duty, their normal daily period of duty had been fixed at 7 hours and the Chief Constable recommended that the Police Authority prescribe 7 hours as the normal duty period.

Pay and Allowances were also dealt with in the Regulations and the Chief Constable reported that it would be necessary, before the 1st January, 1932, to obtain the approval of the Secretary of State to the payment of Rent Allowance on the scale as under:–

Amount actually paid, up to 10/–d. per week.

The other allowances paid to women police in Gloucestershire were:–

Boot Allowance
Subsistence, refreshment and lodging allowance when absent from home on the same scale as that fixed by the Police Regulations for men holding the rank of constable.

However these were covered by the new Police (Women) Regulations.

As the police women in Gloucestershire were paid a scale starting at 50/–d. per week, they were not liable to supplemental deductions from pay.

Under the new Regulations, collars and ties were included amongst the articles of uniform to be supplied by the Police Authority. The expense involved would be very small, so the Chief Constable said, only about 7/6d. per woman per annum.

The Standing Joint Committee approved the Chief Constable's recommendations referred to above and instructed that application be made to the Home Secretary for the approval of the employment of seven women police.

At the Standing Joint Committee Meeting held at Gloucester on the 6th January, 1931, the Chief Constable asked that, 'where officers of the rank of Inspector or women police own motor cars and use them for duty, that they be allowed to claim the County scale of mileage allowance for their use, i.e. 4d. or 5d. a mile according to horse power'. Approval was given subject to the Chief Constable satisfying the Chairman in cases where he considered motor cars over 8.h.p. were necessary.

On the 18th January, 1932, W.P.C. Betsy M.T. Cameron joined the Force. Miss Cameron resigned voluntarily on the 28th December, 1933, and married Police Constable, later Sergeant, Len Robinson.

W.P.C. Mary D. Gould transferred to Gloucestershire from Nottingham on the 1st January 1934. Miss Gould was promoted Sergeant on the 26th July, 1948, and transferred to Bristol City Police, on promotion to Inspector, on the 25th July, 1950. On her retirement from Bristol City Police Miss Gould returned to Gloucestershire to live and died at Chipping Sodbury on the 12th July, 1972.

On the 1st January, 1935, the Standing Joint Committee approved the Chief Constable's recommendation that he be authorised to obtain from Messrs Booy & Son, Portland Street, Cheltenham, tunics, skirts and greatcoats required for the women police, at the following rates:–

Tunics and Skirts	£4. 6.9d.
Greatcoats	£3.18.8d.

On the 9th April, 1935, the Chief Constable submitted a statement, for the information of the Standing Joint Committee, showing the duties carried out under certain headings by the seven Police Women, in addition to their ordinary patrols, from the 14th February to 31st December, 1934. The Statement was as follows:–

Duties of Women Police from the 14th February to 31st December, 1934

(1)	Persons arrested by Police Women alone	9
(2)	Persons arrested by Police Woman and male member of the Force together	17
(3)	Female Prisoners,	
	(a) Searched	39
	(b) Attended	67
	(c) Escorted to Prisons	21
(4)	Women and girls escorted to Homes, etc, on probation or remand	20
(5)	Statements taken re	
	(a) Indecent Assaults	95
	(b) Indecent Exposures	72
	(c) Other Offences	40
(6)	Cases of child neglect brought to the notice of N.S.P.C.C.	12
(7)	Conduct of school girls brought to the notice of Education Authorities	3
(8)	Turns of duty performed,	
	(a) In plain clothes keeping observation in connection with offences or complaints	85
	(b) In watching attempted suicides at Hospitals, etc.	1
	(c) In office doing clerical work	101

(9)	Attendances at	
	(a) Inquests	12
	(b) Children's Courts	22
	(c) Petty Sessions	261
	(d) Assizes	6
(10)	Assistance rendered in cases of accidents	7
(11)	Statements taken in connection with accidents	36
(12)	Girls and women taken to Hostels, etc.	7
(13)	Girls and women found employment	2
(14)	Visits made to homes of girls, and girls interviewed following complaints from parents, etc.	73
(15)	Girls reported missing, found and restored to their homes	10
(16)	Lost children found in streets by Police and taken care of by Police Women until claimed	12
(17)	Women and girls assisted with food, clothing etc.	2
(18)	Homes visited, wives and husbands interviewed following complaints, etc.	50
(19)	Persons interviewed and advised on various matters, at the Police Office, in streets, at their homes, or at the homes of W.P.C.'s (not included above)	276

Similar statements were submitted for the information of the Standing Joint Committee, each year, up to 1960 when Mr Gaskain, Chief Constable, decided to leave it out of his Report.

At the Standing Joint Committee Meeting on the 18th October, 1938, the Chief Constable reported that he had received an application, signed by the seven Police Women in the Force, to be placed on the scale of pay laid down in the Police (Women) Regulations, 1933. The scale for which they were asking was introduced as an economy measure and was compulsorily payable to those who joined on or after 1st October, 1931. Most of the women serving on that date were being paid on a higher scale, and were allowed to retain it. The Chief Constable stated that he had made enquiries and found that out of 187 duly attested Police Women serving in various parts of the country only 5, apart from those in Gloucestershire, were then being paid on a lower scale than that in the Police (Women) Regulations, 1933.

The Police Women's scale of pay in Gloucestershire was 50/–d. per week on appointment, rising by 2/–d. per week, per annum, to 70/–d. per week, after ten years service, with further increments of 2/6d. each after 17 and 22 years service, making a maximum of 75/–d. per week, all of which was pensionable. The scale for which the Police Women were asking started at 56/–d. per week, rising by 2/–d. per week, per annum, to 80/–d. per week after 12 years service, this amount being pensionable. There were further non-pensionable increments of 2/6d. per week each after 17 and 22 years service.

The Chief Constable further reported that men who joined the Force before 1st October, 1931, were paid on a higher scale than those who joined after that date, but the Police Women, all of whom joined before the date in question, were on a lower scale than that which must be paid to all joining after that date. He considered that the request was reasonable and recommended that it be granted. It was Resolved by the Committee that the new scale of pay for Police Women, referred to by the Chief Constable, be approved and to operate from the 18th October, 1938.

At this same meeting the Chief Constable reported that he had received a letter from the Clerk to the Justices at Cirencester, in which he stated that in the opinion of the Magistrates it was very necessary for a Police Woman to be employed in that district. Cirencester was the only Police Division to which no Police Woman was attached. The Committee considered the representations of the Cirencester Justices, and having heard the views of local members they approved a suggestion by the Chief Constable that a Police Woman from another district should, from time to time, during the ensuing three months, patrol the streets of Cirencester and report the result of the arrangement to the Committee at their next meeting.

On the 3rd January, 1939, Colonel Henn reported that he had arranged for the Police Woman at Stroud to pay periodical visits to Cirencester and patrol the town and neighbourhood. He had forwarded copies of reports by her and Superintendent Jotcham of Cirencester to the Clerk of the Standing Joint Committee. He was satisfied that there was not enough work to justify the enrolment of an extra Police Woman for full time work at Cirencester, but would arrange for the town to be periodically patrolled by a Police Woman during the Winter and would, if necessary, increase the frequency of her visits during the Summer. The Report was adopted.

The Chief Constable, Colonel Henn, reported to the Police Authority on the 2nd January, 1940, that for some years past each of the Women Police in the County had been supplied biennially with a greatcoat and mackintosh coat.

He recommended that in future these garments be issued every third year, and that a gabardine coat be issued, in addition, at similar intervals. These gabardine coats would prove most useful when some protection was needed but was not cold enough to wear a heavy greatcoat and not wet enough for a mackintosh.

He said his proposal would reduce the expenditure as a gabardine coat cost but little more than a mackintosh and less than half the price of a greatcoat.

As prices were rising very rapidly the Chairman gave the Chief Constable authority to purchase the seven gabardine coats required for the 1940 issue.

On the 15th October, 1940, the Chief Constable reported to the Standing Joint Committee that in view of the need for economy, enquiries had been made and it was ascertained that on this occasion the seven Police Women could manage without the issue of a Tunic, but each would require a Skirt. A quotation had been obtained for these garments from the tailor who had made the Police Women's uniform for a number of years, and with the Chairman's approval he had accepted it and placed the order.

A Special Sub-Committee of the Standing Joint Committee appointed at their meeting on the 31st December, 1940, reported on the 8th April, 1941, that they had met on the 24th March, 1941, when all the members were present. They were:–

Major Sir Frederick W.B. Cripps, D.S.O.
Miss E.M. Hartland
Miss C.L. Ratcliffe, O.B.E.
Mr R.E. Westaway, O.B.E.
Captain Foyle Fawcett
Sir John Percival, K.B.E.
Mr J.O.M. Skelton
Mr H.F. Wren

They had before them:

(1) Resolution passed by the Gloucester Women Magistrates' Society asking the Standing Joint Committee to consider the appointment of some additional Police Women adequately trained and equiped for the work.
(2) Resolution passed by the Cheltenham Branch of the National Council of Women recommending the appointment of one more Policewoman in Cheltenham.
(3) Report by the Chief Constable on the employment of Police Women.

At that time seven Police Women were employed in the force and they were stationed at the following places:–

Gloucester 2 Cheltenham 2 Staple Hill 1
Lydney 1 Stroud 1

Those stationed in the Boroughs of Gloucester and Cheltenham worked mainly therein but occasionally did duty in the County. They were paid for by the Boroughs.

The Sub-Committee considered the duties carried out by the Police Women, the adequacy of the number of periodical visits paid by them to the outlying parts of the County and particularly as to whether they were able, in view of the large area assigned to them, to know all the girls and children who required supervision and guidance.

After giving the matter careful consideration and hearing the views of the Chief Constable, who expressed the opinion that the strength of seven was adequate to meet all requirements of a police nature which might arise, the Sub-Committee, on the casting vote of the Chairman, decided to recommend the Standing Joint Committee, 'that no additional Police Women be appointed'. After considerable discussion, it was Resolved by the Standing Joint Committee, 'that the Report be received and adopted'.

Women Police Constable Gwendoline R. Walker, who joined the Force on the 5th February, 1940, was certified to be physically unfit for further Police service and discharged on the 30th October, 1942.

A copy of a Resolution passed by the Executive Committee of the Gloucestershire Federation of Women's Institutes in July, 1942, asking for the number of Police Women in Gloucestershire to be substantially increased, was forwarded to the Chief Constable. On the 20th October, 1942, Colonel Henn referred this Resolution to the Standing Joint Committee and stated that in view of his Special Report on this subject, considered by the Committee in April 1941, he did not wish to say more on the subject except that the views which he then expressed remained unchanged. It was Resolved, by the Committee, that no additional Police Women be appointed, at that time.

On the 5th January, 1943, the Standing Joint Committee received a deputation consisting of Mrs I. Picton-Tubervill, Mrs L.G.A. Vernon, Miss J. Estcourt, Miss A. Harris, and the Rev. Canon J.B. Goodliffe, representing the Gloucestershire Federation of Women's Institutes and other voluntary organisations. The deputation urged the immediate appointment of additional Police Women.

At the suggestion of the Chairman it was resolved:–

(1) That the matter be referred to the Finance Sub-Committee for early consideration.

(2) That, if considered desirable by the Sub-Committee, a special meeting of the Committee be called to consider the Report.

The Sub-Committee met on the 25th January, 1943, and recommended:–

(1) That the Committee do not increase the number of Regular Police Women.
(2) That the Committee do approve the steps already taken by the Chief Constable and his proposal to attest a limited number of members of the Women's Auxiliary Police Corps to deal with the problem outlined by the Conference's representatives.

The Sub-Committee, in view of the steps taken did not consider it necessary to call a Special Meeting of the Committee to consider the Report, which was adopted by the Standing Joint Committee.

Home Office Circular No. 96/1944, dated 30/3/44, regarding the need for appointing Police Women or increasing the number already appointed, was received by the Chief Constable who consulted His Majesty's Inspector of Constabulary on this matter. The Inspector was satisfied that the number of Police Women employed in Gloucestershire was sufficient. In view of this ruling the Chief Constable reported to the Police Authority that no increase would be necessary. However, he was endeavouring to fill the vacancy which existed, for one Regular Police Woman, but so far no suitable candidate had been found.

On the 14th March, 1950, the Chief Constable recommended to the Standing Joint Committee that the establishment of Police Women should be increased by two Women Police Constables, one to be stationed at Gloucester and one at Cirencester.

At that time the establishment was one Sergeant and seven Constables, the Sergeant and one Constable being stationed at Gloucester, two Constables each at Cheltenham and Staple Hill and one Constable each at Stroud and Lydney.

The Chief Constable recommended that the Sergeant should undertake supervisory duties over the Police Women in the whole County, a Constable being recruited to take her place at Gloucester, and that an additional Constable be recruited for duty in the Cirencester Division. Up to that time, Cirencester had to call on one of the other Divisions when the services of a Police Woman was required, and the position was not at all satisfactory.

As a result of the above report Colonel Henn was able to report to the Standing Joint Committee, on the 20th June, 1950, that the Secretary of State had approved the augmentation of the authorised establishment of the Force by an increase of two Women Police Constables, with effect from 19th March, 1950.

In paragraph 3 of Appendix ii of Home Office Circular No. 118/1950, dated 9th June, 1950, the Secretary of State referred to the provisions of Regulation 59 (b) of the Police (Women) (Consolidation) Regulations, with regard to the payment of a proportionate plain clothes allowance to Women Police, where they performed plain clothes duty intermittently over a protracted period, and where the minimum period exceeding 48 hours duty was performed in any period of three months.

In all cases where a period of 48 hours total duty was performed in any period of three months, the Secretary of State approved the payment of a proportionate plain clothes allowance.

At their meeting held at Gloucester on the 12th December, 1950, the Chief Constable reported details of the above Circular to the Standing Joint Committee and asked them to approve the expenditure with effect from 1st October, 1950. He stated that the payments involved would only be small amounts. His request was approved.

Woman Police Constable Evelyn E.K. Brimble, who joined the Gloucestershire Constabulary as a member of the Women's Auxiliary Police Corps on the 27th March, 1943, and transferred to the Regular Force on the 8th November, 1947, attained the age of 55 years on the 2nd December, 1955 and retired on the 31st December, 1955.

At the Standing Joint Committee Meeting held at Gloucester on the 23rd September, 1958, the Chief Constable applied for the Establishment of the Women Police to be increased by two Sergeants.

He reported that, at that time, there was one Sergeant and nine Constables stationed as under:–

Cheltenham	1 Sergeant, 2 Constables	*Gloucester*	2 Constables
Staple Hill	2 Constables	*Cirencester*	1 Constable
Lydney	1 Constable	*Stroud*	1 Constable

The Sergeant supervised the Constables as far as possible, but it would be realised that this could only be a general supervision owing to the distance they were apart.

If his application was approved, the Chief Constable said that it would enable better supervision to be excerised, in as much that each Sergeant would then have three Constables under her, viz, – Cheltenham and Cirencester, Gloucester and Lydney, Staple Hill and Stroud.

The strength of the Women Police Section had remained at 10 since 1950, not-withstanding the large increase in the juvenile population especially in Gloucester, Cheltenham and on the outskirts of Bristol. The Chief Constable felt therefore, that the time had arrived when an increase in the strength of the Women police was necessary.

On the 20th March, 1962, The Chief Constable, Mr J.S.H. Gaskain, reported to the Standing Joint Committee, details of his proposed upgradings and increase in Establishment, showing an overall increase of 122 Constables and 14 Women Police Constables.

The increase in respect of the Women Police allowed for one Woman Police Inspector at Police Headquarters, Cheltenham, a Woman Police Sergeant at Stroud and twelve Women Police Constables throughout the County.

He stated that, as a result of experience gained, it was found that Women Police Officers could be more usefully employed at the Town or Urban Divisions rather than full time in the Rural Divisions. Consequently the Establishment would be grouped in 'B'; 'D'; 'E'; and 'G' Divisions.

Their work in the field of women and children had increased, emphasized in the crime field of offences against the person.

The Force was clearly understaffed so far as Women Police were concerned, and the proposed Establishment would be:–

	Inspector	W.P.S.	W.P.C.	
'A' Division	1	—	—	
'B' Division	—	1	7	(2 W.P.C's at Filton & Kingswood) (respectively)
'D' Division	—	1	4	Stationed at Divisional H.Q.
'E' Division	—	1	5	Stationed at Divisional H.Q.
'G' Division	—	1	5	Stationed at Divisional H.Q.
Total	1	4	21	

The Chief Constable was able to report to the Standing Joint Committee on the 4th December, 1962, that the augmentation, as outlined above, had been approved by the Secretary of State.

The Chief Constable, Mr E.P.B. White, reported to the Standing Joint Committee on the 22nd September, 1964, that he wanted to increase the Establishmennt of the Women Police in Gloucestershire by 12 Women Police Constables, recruiting to commence on the 1st April, 1965.

If approved the increase would bring the Establishment to:–

1 Woman Police Inspector
4 Women Police Sergeants
33 Women Police Constables

On the 5th September, 1966 approval was given, by the Police Authority, for an additional Woman Police Officer with the rank of Chief Inspector. On the 4th November, 1966, the Chief Constable was able to report that the upgrading for a Woman Chief Insptector had been approved by the Secretary of State with effect from 1st April, 1967.

During 1967 the Home Office urged Chief Constable's to give consideration to women police officers returning to duty after marriage. The Chief Constable informed the Police Authority that, in his opinion, this would not be feasible in cases where very young children were concerned.

The following details are entered as a point of interest[5]:–

On the 5th September, 1942, W.P.C. Laura E. Ball joined the Force and resigned voluntarily on the 30th June, 1944. Miss Ball re-joined on the 10th January, 1946, and resigned again on the 28th August, 1951.

W.P.C. Hart joined on the 7th October, 1944 and resigned voluntarily on the 24th October, 1944.

W.P.C. Mary Cummings joined on the 21st August, 1944, married P.C. Richard Ford of the Gloucestershire Constabulary and, with her husband, transferred to Bournemouth Borough Force on the 31st October, 1948.

Iris M. Martin, who was a member of the Gloucestershire Women's Auxiliary Police Corps, enrolled into the Regular Force on the 8th May, 1945 and, later, on the 1st January, 1946, transferred to Plymouth Police.

W.A.P.C. Edith J. Hart transferred to the Regular Force on the 1st December, 1945, and because of ill-health, was discharged on the 31st January, 1947.

W.P.C. Beryl M. Cambridge was appointed on the 8th February, 1947 and, as Mrs Gullan, resigned voluntarily on the 31st July, 1949.

Below are details of women police officers who joined the Gloucestershire Constabulary on promotion or were promoted whilst serving with the Force during the years 1950–1979.

W.P.C. Olive S. Hinton transferred from Bath City Police on the 12th Octover, 1951, and was promoted Sergeant on the 1st September, 1958. Miss Hinton retired on the 31st March, 1974, and died at Longhope, Glos., on the 2nd August, 1974.

W.P.C Doreen Draper transferred from Gloucestershire to Rotherham Borough Force, on promotion to Sergeant, on the 31st August, 1955.

W.P.C. Rosemary J. Reed was promoted Sergeant on the 1st November, 1958. Miss Reed married 4.4.1961 and resigned, as Mrs Yeend, on the 30th June, 1962.

W.P.S. Mary Rodwell transferred from the Metropolitan Police to Gloucestershire on the 1st January, 1959, and transferred to Bristol City Police on the 31st March, 1960.

W.P.C. Veronica Morgan joined Gloucestershire on transfer from Gwent Police on the 1st December, 1960. Miss Morgan was promoted Sergeant on the 8th July, 1963, and went over to the Avon and Somerset Constabulary when that Force took over the old 'B' (Staple Hill) Division. She retired on pension in 1984.

Elizabeth B. Hughes transferred to Gloucestershire from Birkenhead Borough Police on the 1st January, 1963, and was appointed Inspector – the first woman police Inspector in the County. On the 1st April, 1967, Miss Hughes was promoted Chief Inspector and Superintendent on the 1st September, 1972 again, the first Woman Superintendent in Gloucestershire. She retired on pension on the 20th October, 1976, continuing to reside in Cheltenham.

W.P.S. Dulcie M. Blowen transferred from the Metropolitan Police on the 22nd April, 1963, and was promoted Inspector on the 1st June, 1971. Miss Blowen retired on pension on the 26th August, 1979, and continued to live in the Cheltenham area.

W.P.S Jennifer E. Bassett transferred from Coventry City Police on the 1st June, 1965, was married on the 25th November, 1967, and resigned voluntarily, as Mrs McCormick, on the 30th April, 1969.

Mary L. Pincombe transferred from Berkshire Constabulary to Gloucestershire on the 14th June, 1967, and was appointed Inspector, which rank she held until her voluntary resignation, as Mrs Gibson, on the 31st December, 1970.

W.P.C. Margaret Hall was promoted Sergeant on the 19th May, 1969, and was later, attached to the C.I.D.

W.P.C. Beryl Ainscough was promoted Sergeant on the 1st June, 1971, and posted to the Regional Crime Squad on the 1st April, 1972, as Detective Woman Sergeant.

W.P.C. Monica J. Juggins transferred to West Mercia Police on promotion to Sergeant.

W.P.C. Jill Digweed, promoted Sergeant on the 1st April, 1972, was married on the 31st March, 1973, and resigned voluntarily, as Mrs Price, on the 30th July, 1974.

W.P.C. Elizabeth A. Timms was promoted Sergeant on the 21st August, 1972.

Marion E. Chandler transferred to Gloucestershire, from Kent Constabulary, on the 1st November, 1976, and appointed Superintendent to replace Miss Hughes. Miss Chandler retired on pension on the 31st December, 1985.

W.P.C. Margaret A. Morgan was promoted Sergeant on the 1st June, 1975, and resigned voluntarily on the 31st March, 1978.

W.P.C. Caroll P. Seville was promoted Sergeant on the 1st March, 1979.

From February 1976, the Home Office decreed that, from that date, the prefix 'Woman' would be dispensed with and officers would be referred to according to their rank.

Now an accepted part of the police set-up the police woman, today, is trained and has the same powers as her male counterpart. She undertakes exactly the same duties and many of the women are capable of handling grown men and indeed are frequently required to arrest male persons.

The days when women police were regarded as a novelty by members of the public and an unknown quantity by their male colleagues are a thing of the past. The usefulness of the work they do in matters relating to women and children in the various Courts, as well as in the general duties of a police officer, are now accepted as part of the service.

APPENDIX 'B'

Chief Constables
Who's Who

Anthony Thomas Lefroy[1]

Anthony Thomas Lefroy, son of Captain Anthony Thomas Lefroy who served as a Captain at Gibraltar and the Cape of Good Hope, was born in the year 1802 and baptised at Warkworth Parish Church, Morpeth, Northumberland, on the 26th April, 1802.

Mr Lefroy joined the Irish Police in 1823 at the age of 21 and by 1839 was Chief Constable for County Wicklow.

On the 18th November, 1839 he was appointed Chief Constable of Gloucestershire.

On the 12th May, 1851, Mr Lefroy married Amelia Jane Elliot, the 25 year old daughter of a retired Bombay Civil Serveant, at St. Mary's Church, Cheltenham.

Mrs Lefroy never enjoyed good health and she died in July, 1865 aged 40 years, within weeks of Mr Lefroy's retirement on the 1st July, 1865.

Whilst Chief Constable of Gloucestershire Mr Lefroy was quite often referred to, in the local press, as Captain Lefroy. This must have been a misnomer as there is no record of him having served in H.M. Forces and bearing in mind that he was only 21 years of age when he joined the Irish Police. It could well have been a mix up with his father who held the rank of Captain and bore the same christian names.

Anthony Thomas Lefroy died on the 23rd March, 1980, at 2 Segrave Place, Pittville, Cheltenham, aged 88 years, after nearly 25 years on pension.

Admiral Henry Christian, M.V.O., K.P.M.[2]

Henry Christian, son of Samuel Christian, was born in Malta in the year 1828.

In 1865 he married Emily Margaret, daughter of James Moore of Liverpool.

He entered the Navy in 1841. In 1849 he was promoted Lieutenant, Commander in 1858, Captain in 1863, retired Captain 1870, retired Rear Admiral 1878, Vice Admiral 1884 and Admiral in 1889.

Much of his early service in the Navy was taken up with the suppression of the Slave Trade. From 1858/61 he was in command of H.M.S. Evryalus and was Commander of the Royal Yacht, Victoria and Albert, from 1861 to 1863.

As Captain Henry Christian he was appointed Chief Constable of Gloucestershire on the 1st July, 1865, and took up residence, with his wife, at 'Heighthorne', The Park, Cheltenham. At that time he was a member of the Army and Navy Club.

The M.V.O. was conferred upon Admiral Christian, by His Majesty King Edward the Seventh, in June 1909, and the King's Police Medal was awarded to him in the New Year Honours for 1911.

Mrs Emily Margaret Christian was President of the Soldiers and Sailors' Families Association for many years.

After nearly 45 years service Admiral Christian retired as Chief Constable of Gloucestershire on the 2nd May, 1910, aged 81 years and died on the 10th June, 1916, aged 88 years.

Lieut. Col. Richard Chester Chester-Master, D.S.O.[3]

Richard Chester Chester-Master was the eldest son of Colonel T.W. Chester-Master, of Knole Park, Almondsbury, Glos. He was born at Stratton, Near Cirencester on the 29th August, 1870, and was educated at Harrow and Christchurch, Oxford.

Joining the King's Royal Rifle Corps, from the Gloucester Militia in 1893, he served with the Regiment at Gibraltar, Malta, Cape Colony, etc.

He was appointed Aide-de-camp to the High Commissioner for South Africa in 1898 and served in the South African War, 1899 – 1902, when he was mentioned in despatches and granted Brevet rank of Major in 1901. The Queen's South African Medal with Six Clasps and the King's South African Medal with Two Clasps was awarded to Major Chester–Master. In 1901 he was appointed Commandant General in Southern Rhodesia in 1905.

On the 3rd May, 1910 he was appointed Chief Constable of Gloucestershire.

In 1901 he married Geraldine, eldest daughter of John H. Arkwright, Hampton Court, Herefordshire. There were two sons of the marriage, William Alfred born 1903 and John Robert born 1904. The family residing at 'St. Clair', The Park, Cheltenham.

Colonel Chester-Master was Killed in Action, during the First World War, on the 30th August, 1917

Major F.L. Stanley-Clarke, O.B.E.[4]

Major F.L. Stanley-Clarke, son of Major General W. Stanley-Clarke was born in 1876 and died at his home at 'Lanesborough', College Lawn, Cheltenham, on the 6th April, 1946, aged 70 years.

He served 18 years in the Army, two of these years in M.I.5 Department at the War Office as a Staff Captain in Intelligence. He was fluent in French and also acted as an interpreter in Russian.

During the 1914–18 Great War he was wounded and invalided out of the Army in 1915. He later joined the Kent Constabulary and took over the duties of Deputy Chief Constable, to allow that officer to join the Colours for Military Service.

With the post of Deputy Chief Constable he combined the duties of Chief Weights and Measures Officer for Kent and held these posts until 31st October, 1917.

On the 1st January, 1918, Major Stanley-Clarke was appointed Chief Constable of Gloucestershire and held this post until the 30th April, 1937 when, due to ill-health he had to retire.

He was married to Muriel Bentley Carr and there was one daughter of the marriage.

During 1926 Major Stanley-Clarke was awarded the O.B.E. in recognition of his duties during the General Strike of that year.

He was greatly interested in the British Legion and was Chairman of the Cheltenham Branch in 1933, later becoming President, a post which he held until 1937 when, because of ill-health he had to retire.

In 1942 he was appointed Cheltenham Representative of the Association of Friends of the French Volunteers and, when this definition was changed to the Fighting French Association, he became Chairman.

As an artist Major Stanley-Clarke was associated with the Cotswold Art Club and exhibited three works in 1940.

Major Stanley-Clarke was made an Officer Brother of the Order of St. John in 1932.

Colonel Walter Francis Henn, C.B.E., M.V.O., K.P.M.[5]

Walter Francis Henn was born in 1892, the son of Francis Blackbourne Henn, R.M., J.P., Paradise, Ennis, Co. Clare, Ireland.

In 1915 he married Geraldine Frances, youngest daughter of T.G. Stackpoole Mahon, D.L. Corbally, Quin, Co. Clare, Ireland. There were two sons and one daughter of the marriage.

Educated at Aldenham School and Magdalene College, Cambridge, Colonel Henn served throughout the European War of 1914–1918, with the Royal Munster Fusiliers, was wounded and mentioned in despatches.

From 1920 – 1937, he served with the Egyptian Civil Service and Police and was commandant of Alexandria City Police from 1930 – 1937.

Colonel Henn was appointed Chief Constable of Gloucestershire on the 1st May, 1937, was awarded the M.V.O. in 1946, the C.B.E. in 1955 and the King's Police Medal.

He was a keen fisherman and always interested in motoring.

Colonel Henn died on the 27th April, 1964 and Mrs Geraldine F. Henn died on the 21st January, 1981.

John Stuart Hinton Gaskain, C.B.E., M.B.E., Q.P.M.[6]

John Stuart Hinton Gaskain, son of William Francis Gaskain and Gladys Therese Gaskain, was born on the 11th May, 1910, and was educated at Haileybury College.

He married Nancy Evelyn Swan and there was one son and one daughter of the marriage.

Mr Gaskain joined the Metropolitan Police in 1936 and attended the Hendon Police College 1936 – 1937. In 1942 he was appointed Assistant Chief Constable of Norfolk, and became a Barrister at Law in 1944.

Whilst serving with the Norfolk Constabulary Mr Gaskain was seconded as Commandant of the Police Training Centre at Eynsham Hall, Witney, Oxon., from 1946 – 1950.

In 1952 he was appointed Chief Constable of Cumberland and Westmorland and remained head of that Force until 1959, when he was appointed Chief Constable of Gloucestershire.

He stayed with the Gloucestershire Constabulary until 1962 when he was appointed one of H.M. Inspectors of Constabulary. In 1966 Mr Gaskain was selected as Commandant of the National Police College at Bramshill, near Reading and remained there until ill-health caused his retirement in 1968.

On leaving the Police College Mr & Mrs Gaskain took up residence in Brighton, where Mr Gaskain died in 1971.

He was awarded the M.B.E. in 1950, the Q.P.M. in 1960, the Order of St. John in 1962 and the C.B.E. in 1968.

Herbert D.J. Smith, M.B.E., Q.P.M.[7]

Herbert D.J. Smith, whose father was a serving officer in the Gloucestershire Constabulary, was born at Staple Hill on the 27th December, 1908, and was educated at various schools throughout the country, due to his father's various postings.

On leaving school Mr Smith found employment in a Solicitor's Office at Cirencester and later transferred to the Justices' Clerk's Office.

Joining the Gloucestershire Constabulary on the 13th February 1928, Mr Smith served in various Stations throughout the county and passed through all ranks to Chief superintendent until 30th July, 1962, when he was appointed Assistant Chief Constable of Gloucestershire.

When Chief Constable J.S.H. Gaskain left the Force on his appointment as H.M.I., Mr Smith was established as Acting Chief Constable on the 19th December 1962, and remained in that post until the 7th April, 1963, when Mr E.P.B. White took over his duties as Chief Constable of Gloucestershire.

Mr Smith reverted to his old rank of Assistant Chief Constable when, on the 3rd January, 1966, he was appointed Deputy Chief constable of the County. He held this post until his retirement on the 30th June 1973, after 45 years service in the Gloucestershire Constabulary.

On the 12th December 1934, he married Clarice and there was one daughter of the marriage.

Mr Smith was awarded the Queen's Police Medal in the 1965 Birthday Honours and the M.B.E. in the 1974 New Year Honours.

He is a keen gardener and golfer and, since his retirement, has always taken an interest in the work of the Gloucestershire Branch of the National Association of Retired Police Officers and is a Vice President of the Branch.

Edwin Peter Blake White, O.B.E., Q.P.M.[8]

Born Cowes, Isle of Wight, 1914, son of Alfred Sydney and Florence Isabella. Educated at Brighton College where he was School Captain.

Joined Metropolitan Police 1935 and passed through all ranks to

Superintendent until 1953, when he was appointed Assistant Chief Constable of Buckinghamshire Constabulary.

In 1957 Mr White was appointed Chief Constable of East Suffolk and Chief Constable of Gloucestershire in 1963, which post he held until his retirement from the Police Service on the 30th June, 1975.

Married Marjorie 1939 and there is one daughter, Penelope, born 1944.

During the Second World War Mr White served with the Royal Navy 1943/1945 and was Commissioned in Light Coastal Forces.

He was President of the Association of Chief Police Officers, 1971 and Direcetor of Home Office Unit C.S.S.B. from 1972 – 1975.

Awarded the Queen's Police Medal 1964, the O.B.E. 1969 and the Order of St. John, 1970.

Interest, all sports as participant and was no mean golfer, music and selection procedures.

Brian Weigh, C.B.E., Q.P.M.[9]

Brian Weigh, son of the late Edwin Walter Weigh and Ellen Weigh, was born on the 22nd September, 1926 and educated at St. Joseph's College, Blackpool and Queen's University, Belfast.

During 1952 he married Audrey and there is one daughter of the marriage.

Joining the Metropolitan Police in 1948, Mr Weigh passed through all ranks to Superintendent, until 1967, when he was appointed Assistant Chief Constable to the Somerset and Bath Constabulary.

In 1969 he was appointed Deputy Chief Constable to the same Force and when the Avon and Somerset Constabulary was formed in 1974, he was appointed Deputy Chief Constable and remained as such until 1975 when he took over Command of the Gloucestershire Constabulary, as Chief Constable.

During 1979 Mr Weigh was appointed Chief Constable of the Avon and Somerset Constabulary and remained with that Force until 1983, when he retired.

He was immediately appointed one of Her Majesty's Inspectors of Constabulary with responsibility for South West England and part of East Anglia.

He is a member of the Royal Life Saving Society and Deputy President of the United Kingdom Branch.

Mr Weigh was awarded the C.B.E. in 1982 and the Queen's Police Medal in 1976.

The 1985 Who's Who quotes Mr Weigh as enjoying walking, gardening, golf and badminton.

Leonard A.G. Soper, Q.P.M.

Leonard A.G. Soper, son of Leonard Charles and Winifred Soper, was born at Aldershot, Hampshire on 3rd September, 1928 and educated at Peter Symonds School, Winchester.

After service in the Fleet Air Arm from 1945 – 1948, he joined the Hampshire Constabulary in 1949. The same year he married his wife Margaret and there are two children of the marriage, a daughter Jane and a son, Richard.

Following service in the Hampshire Constabulary and at the Police College, Bramshill, as a member of the Directing Staff, Mr Soper joined the Thames Valley Police as Assistant Chief Constable (Operations) in 1973. In 1977 he was appointed Assistant (Crime) to H.M. Chief Inspector of Constabulary, but returned to Thames Valley Police later the same year to take up appointment there as Deputy Chief Constable. Whilst Deputy Chief Constable he also served as Acting Chief Constable of Thames Valley Police.

Mr Soper was awarded the Queen's Police Medal in 1979 and appointed Chief Constable of the Gloucestershire Constabulary on 1 September, 1979.

APPENDIX 'C'

Deputy Chief Constables and Assistant Chief Constables of the Gloucestershire Constabulary

Charles Reilly or Keilly Original reports refer to Charles Reilly. Later reports refer to Charles Keilly. As all original reports were hand-written it is quite possible that an error has occurred with the formation of the letter R and letter K.

Charles Reilly or Keilly was appointed Superintendent and Deputy Chief Constable on the 7th July, 1840, after Mr Lefroy had reported to Quarter Sessions on the 30th June, 1840, that he was making the appointment.

On the 21st June, 1853, Reilly or Keilly, after cashing a cheque for £445.10.2d., which money should have been used to pay Police Officers in Cheltenham and Tewkesbury, absconded and was never brought to book. Further discrepanies were found making a total of £485.9.4d. and as a result the Deputy Chief Constable was formally Discharged the Force on the 24th June, 1853. (As reported in the Gloucester Journal on the 2nd July, 1853.)

Edmund Wilkinson was appointed Superintendent and Deputy Chief Constable on the 21st April 1854. During July 1855 he was Dismissed the Force 'for taking improper liberties with a policeman's wife'.[1]

John Nicholls was appointed Superintendent and Deputy Chief Constable on the 1st September, 1855. He died in office on the 8th March, 1867, leaving a widow and six children.

Up to the death of John Nicholls all the Deputy Chief Constables were stationed at Cheltenham.[2]

Charles Griffin, the Superintendent in charge of the Gloucester Division was appointed Deputy Chief Constable on the 1st April, 1867 and remained at Gloucester. He retired on pension on the 30th June, 1877.[3]

E.T. Chipp was appointed Superintendent and Deputy Chief Constable on the 1st July 1877 and took up duties at Gloucester. He died suddenly, after attending a Civic Dinner at Gloucester Guildhall on the 12th July, 1892.[4]

Nehemiah Philpott was appointed Superintendent and Deputy Chief Constable at Gloucester, as from the 13th July, 1892. He retired on the 31st January, 1902, after 45 years service and later became an Alderman of the City of Gloucester.[5]

William Harrison was appointed Superintendent and Deputy Chief Constable and took up duties at Gloucester on the 1st February, 1902, retiring on the 13th April, 1919 and, for many years, served on Gloucester City Council.[6]

Arther Wm. Hopkins was appointed Deputy Chief Constable at Gloucester, with the rank of Chief Superintendent, on the 14th April, 1919 and retired on pension on the 15th August, 1931.[7]

Robert Henry Hopkins was appointed Chief Superintendent and Deputy Chief Constable at Gloucester on the 16th August, 1931, retiring on the 30th November, 1935. He was the last Deputy Chief Constable to be stationed in the City of Gloucester.[8]

Joseph Wm. Parry Goulder was appointed Chief Superintendent and Deputy Chief Constable on the 1st December, 1935 and took up his duties at Police Headquarters, Holland House, Cheltenham, that day. He retired on the 31st December, 1945, the last of the Superintendents to hold the rank of Deputy Chief Constable.[9]

Albert H. Carter was appointed Assistant Chief Constable of Gloucestershire on the 1st January, 1946 and took up his duties at Police Headquarters, Cheltenham on that date. He retired on pension on the 31st August, 1960.[10]

Robert G. Fenwick was appointed Assistant Chief Constable on the 10th October, 1960 and came to Police Headquarters, Cheltenham from the Metropolitan Police. On the 30th June, 1962 he was appointed Chief Constable of Shropshire and resigned from the Gloucestershire Constabulary on that date.[11]

Herbert D.J. Smith, a Gloucestershire Police Officer, was appointed Assistant Chief Constable on the 30th July, 1962.

From the 19th December, 1962 to the 7th April, 1963 Mr Smith was Acting Chief Constable during the period when Mr J.S.H. Gaskain was appointed one of Her Majesty's Inspectors of Constabulary and the appointment of Mr E.P.B. White as Chief Constable of Gloucestershire.

Mr Smith continued his duties as Assistant Chief Constable until the 31st January 1966, on which date he was appointed Deputy Chief Constable of Gloucestershire, a post he held until his retirement from the Force on the 30th June, 1973.[12]

Edward Coppin of the Essex Constabulary was appointed Assistant Chief Constable of Gloucestershire on the 3rd January, 1966, which post he held until the 30th June, 1973, when he was appointed Deputy Chief Constable. Mr Coppin retired on pension on the 25th September, 1979.[13]
Edward W. Whitmore of the Somerset and Bath Constabulary was appointed Assistant Chief Constable of Gloucestershire on the 1st July, 1973 and Deputy Chief Constable on the 26th September, 1979. He retired on pension on the 31st October, 1982.[14]
Louis H. Whitton of the Devon and Cornwall Constabulary was appointed Assistant Chief Constable of Gloucestershire on the 27th September, 1979, which post he held until his appointment as Deputy Chief Constable on the 1st November, 1982. In the New Years honours list for 1984, Mr Whitton was awarded the Queens' Police Medal for distinguished Police Service. The medal was presented to him on Monday, 21st May, 1984, at Shire Hall, Gloucester by the Lord Lieutenant of Gloucestershire M. St. J.V. Gibbs.[15]

H.F.G. Reynolds of the Norfolk Constabulary was appointed Assistant Chief Constable of Gloucestershire on the 22nd November, 1982.[16]

Acknowledgements

Leonard A.G. Soper, Q.P.M. Chief Constable of Gloucestershire

Edwin Peter Blake White, O.B.E., Q.P.M.

Herbert D.J. Smith, M.B.E., Q.P.M.

J.A. Cratchley, Superintendent, Gloucestershire Constabulary.

Ian P. Clark, Police Sergeant, Gloucestershire Constabulary.

Ronald E. Spencer, M.B.E., G.M. Force Welfare Officer.

Leslie G. Wheeler, Gloucestershire Constabulary Central Registry

Elizabeth E. Hughes W/Superintendent, Gloucestershire Constabulary (Retired)

Mrs Rosa M. Ashby, nee Rouse, W.P.C. Gloucestershire Constabulary (Retired)

Reginald A. Hale, P.C. Gloucestershire Constabulary (Retired)

Miss Barbara D. Stanley-Clarke. Daughter of Major F.L. Stanley-Clarke

County Records Office, Gloucester

Reference Library, Cheltenham

Reference Library, Gloucester

Notes and Sources

Chapter 1

1. Gloucestershire Quarter Sessions Archives 1958.
2. County Records Office.
3. Ibid.
4. Ibid.
5. Gloucestershire Quarter Sessions Archives 1958.

Chapter 2

1. County Records Office.
2. Gloucestershire Quarter Sessions Archives 1958.
3. Chief Constables Letter Book 1840–1884.
4. Ibid.
5. Ibid.
6. County Records Office.
7. Police Accounts 1840–1888.
8. Chief Constables Letter Book 1840–1884.
9. Ibid.
10. County Records Office.
11. Chief Constables Letter Book 1840–1884.
12. Gloucester City Reference Library.
13. Cheltenham Reference Library.

Chapter 3

1. Gloucester City Reference Library.
2. Chief Constables Report.
3. Chief Constables Letter Book 1840–1884.
4. Standing Joint Committee Report.
5. Ibid.

6. Gloucester City Reference Library.
7. Standing Joint Committee Report.
8. Police and Constabulary Almanac 1902 supplied by Ex. P.C. Reginald A. Hale.

Chapter 4

1. General Orders.
2. Standing Joint Committee Report.
3. Ibid.
4. Ibid.
5. Ibid.
6. Ibid.
7. General Orders.

Chapter 5

1. Standing Joint Committee Report.
2. Ibid.
3. Ibid.
4. General Orders.
5. Gloucester City Reference Library.
6. Standing Joint Committee Report.
7. Ibid.
8. Gloucester City Reference Library.

Chapter 6

1. General Orders.
2. Gloucester City Reference Library.
3. Standing Joint Committee Report.
4. Ibid.
5. Ibid.
6. Ibid.
7. Ibid.
8. Ibid.
9. Ibid.
10. Ibid.
11. Gloucester City Reference Library.
12. General Orders.
13. Standing Joint Committee Report.

Chapter 7

1. Standing Joint Committee Report.
2. Ibid.
3. Ibid.
4. Ibid.
5. General Orders.
6. Ibid.

Chapter 8

1. Standing Joint Committee Report.

Chapter 9

1. Standing Joint Committee Report.
2. Ibid.
3. Ibid.
4. Ibid.
5. Police Committee Report.
6. General Orders.
7. Police Committee Report.
8. General Orders.
9. Police and Constabulary Almanac 1969.
10. General Orders.
11. Police Committee Report.
12. General Orders.
13. Provident Fund Minutes.

Chapter 10

1. Annual Police Report.
2. Ibid.
3. Force Orders.
4. Annual Police Report.
5. Ibid.

Chapter 11

1. Police Committee Report.
2. Police Annual Report.

3. Ibid.
4. Gloucester City Reference Library.
5. Police Annual Report.
6. Chief Constable of Berkshire – 1936 Christmas Message.

Appendix 'A'

1. Elizabeth E. Hughes (Superintendent – Retired).
2. General Orders.
3. Mrs R.M. Ashby – née Rouse.
4. Ibid.
5. General Orders.

Appendix 'B'

1. Cheltenham Reference Library.
2. Gloucester City Reference Library.
3. Cheltenham Reference Library.
4. Miss Barbara D. Stanley–Clarke (Daughter).
5. Gloucester City Reference Library.
6. Cheltenham Reference Library.
7. Herbert D.J. Smith. Esq., M.B.E., Q.P.M.
8. E.P.B. White, Esq., O.B.E., Q.P.M.
9. Cheltenham Reference Library.

Appendix 'C'

1. Gloucester Records Office.
2. Ibid.
3. Ibid.
4. Gloucester City Reference Library.
5. Ibid.
6. Ibid.
7. Ibid.
8. Ibid.
9. General Orders.
10. Ibid.
11. Standing Joint Committee Report
12. Ibid.
13. Ibid.
14. Ibid.
15. Ibid.
16. Ibid.

INDEX

Index to Personal Names

General Index